Politics and Social Change in Latin America
The Distinct Tradition

Second Revised Edition

Edited by Howard J. Wiarda

The University of Massachusetts Press   1982

Library of Congress Cataloging in Publication Data

Main entry under title:
Politics and social change in Latin America.
Bibliography: p.
1. Latin America—Politics and government—
Addresses, essays, lectures. 2. Latin America—
Social conditions—Addresses, essays, lectures.
I. Wiarda, Howard J., 1939–
JL966.P635   1982   320.98   81-16022
ISBN 0-87023-333-5 (pbk.)   AACR2

Contents

Preface

This volume is different from the usual texts and collections dealing with Latin America: it has a central theme and focus. It is aimed at challenging our easy, often biased and ethnocentric ideas about Latin America, at stimulating our thinking, and at forcing us to reconsider our usual—and usually misconceived—interpretations of social change and political development in the Latin American context. No claim is made in these pages to having discovered that elusive, evolving concept called final truth; instead the book will have served its purpose if it stimulates, provokes, sometimes angers, and raises important questions and controversy for serious consideration.

The chapters in this book explore the distinct tradition of social change and political development in Latin America. Their unifying, integrating theme is the distinctive socio-political framework within which Latin American development takes place. The Latin American experience of development (and in parallel fashion that of Spain, Portugal, perhaps Italy, and some other countries as well) is subject to special imperatives of analysis and interpretation that the general, "Western" (that is, Northwest European and North American) literature on development and social change fails to provide. The main thrust of the book is toward an explanation of how and why Latin America fails to conform very well to our commonly known models of socio-economic and political change; why, hence, policies and development strategies based on such Eurocentric models so often fail or produce unanticipated consequences; what it is that makes the Latin American development experience so different.

Essentially the book wrestles with the issue of whether there is a distinct Latin America/Southern European sociology and politics of development, one that serves as an Iberic-Latin counterpart to the great sociological paradigms formulated by Marx, Durkheim, or Weber; and, if there is such a unique Latin American model, what its precise dimensions and components might be. For the fact is that Latin America fails to conform very well to the processes of historical change outlined in mainstream sociology and political science, which is one key reason why the policies and developmental strategies based on the "Western" formulations have so often missed the mark. The distinctive features of Latin America provide one important set of reasons why, in Chilean sociologist Claudio Véliz's words, the efforts to "reform," "modernize," "democratize," or "revolutionize" Latin America have so often produced failure, disillusionment, and perplexity.[1]

The interpretations included here examine what the special requirements of Latin American development are, provide the historical and background materials for a better comprehension of the area, and explore the political theory, sociological processes, and institutional structures by which development in Latin America takes place (or fails to take place). The book both criticizes the oft-times inappropriate models of development and modernization based on the United States or Northwest European experiences, and begins to formulate a framework for understanding that is more attuned to the distinct traditions and processes of Latin American development. These traditions of Latin American political theory, sociology, and political change have been almost entirely ignored in our general studies, our liberal arts education, and our understandings of modern, Western development; but they are critical for a proper comprehension of Latin America. We ignore them at the cost not only of continuing to misunderstand the region, but also of missing an important comparative perspective on our own contemporary malaise as well.

For it is clear that as the faults and crises in our own and other industrial societies become more apparent, as we prove unable to resolve pressing social problems, as society-wide conflict and divisiveness increase, and as we also have become something of a "banana republic," we must call into question the happy, facile assumption that we are more "developed" than other nations. Economically we are (though a dozen other nations have by now equaled or surpassed the United States in per-capita income), but it is hard to make the argument that we are sociologically, politically, or morally, somehow superior. Hence, rather than viewing them as "less-developed countries" or "LDCs," this book suggests the heretical notion that the Latin American nations are following an *alternative* route to modernization, quite distinct from our liberal-pluralist one but perhaps—on *their* terms—no less functional or viable. Furthermore, as the tendencies toward bureaucracy, statism, and centralization grow in the United States and other industrialized nations, it may be that we can profit from studying a group of nations—those of Latin America—that have always been organized on that basis. The question must therefore be seriously raised: Could it be that we can learn from the way Latin America has sought to cope with the great socio-political crises of the modern world—industrialization, rapid urbanization, accelerated social change, the rise of mass society and a conflict-prone polity—instead of assuming that they must always "learn" from us?

These are meaty, important questions, and their implications go

1. Veliz, *The Centralist Tradition in Latin America* (Princeton, 1980).

beyond the immediate subject matter of Latin America. They deal also with the presumed universality of the social sciences, with the feasibility or desirability of a distinct Latin American (or Islamic? or sub-Saharan African?) sociology and politics of development, and with the quest of many Third World nations to fashion an indigenous model of national development rather than one derived exclusively and ethnocentrically from the Western experience. The essays included in this volume deal with these themes in a serious and scholarly way, exploring different and not always exactly complementary facets of the issues, but united in their quest for explanations of Latin America's development and its distinctiveness, addressing themselves to contemporary and universal questions regarding the human condition, with clear relevance to our own time and place.

There are many other suggestive interpretations of the Latin American tradition that, space permitting, could have been included in this book; many of these are listed in the notes and Suggested Readings. Nor should it be thought that the interpretations offered here are the final word on the subject; they offer a beginning point for analysis, not an end point, and their use should be supplemented through such interpretations as class analysis, dependency analysis, political economy, and others. The argument needs to be further fleshed out through detailed country case studies and comparative analysis, and with an appreciation of where the comments offered apply to a greater or lesser extent.

The essays, collected here are all of a general kind that in broad terms outline the socio-cultural and political-institutional bases of the Latin American systems. It is hoped that they will help stimulate the more rigorous comparative and theoretical examinations that are clearly still needed, and the gathering of greater country-specific information on which such interpretations can alone be based. Most of the selections in this book have been published previously, though often in a form or place where they are difficult to read; others are published here for the first time. The chief criterion of selection, however, has been to bring together a set of intriguing, stimulating, provocative essays by some of the foremost scholars in the field emphasizing the distinctiveness of the Latin American tradition but in a way that relates that experience to more universal themes of development, modernization, and social change.

The book may be read with profit by both general readers and specialists in the field. It could appropriately serve as a text or as required supplemental reading in undergraduate and graduate courses and seminars dealing with Latin America, or with the more general topics of comparative history, social change, and Third World development studies. The Introduction was written to *introduce* the nonspecialist to the area, to bring up some of the basic issues, and to encourage consideration of them. The chapters that follow raise some more complex themes and ideas, but they too are highly readable and readily comprehensible. The book thus reaches toward a number of audiences in the hope of providing a perspective that has been ignored too often in the past and serving to correct the bias and ethnocentrism that previously have pervaded our thinking, teaching, and policy. There can be no doubt that we only weakly and often mistakenly understand the Latin American tradition and its socio-political processes; yet it is equally clear that the processes and crises of development in these and other modernizing nations, as well as our response to them, are among the most critical issues with which we shall have to cope in the final decades of the twentieth century.

The appearance of the first edition of this book provoked a vigorous, on-going controversy, a major debate within the field, and varied efforts on the part of some to distort its contents and misrepresent the arguments presented. Even those who disagreed with some of the points of view, however, recognized the important arguments involved, the need to deal with the issues raised, and the challenging nature of the theses presented for all students of the area. That perspective, the sense of controversy, the provocative nature of the arguments have been retained in this new edition. At the same time, the Introduction and Conclusion have been entirely rewritten both to refine the analysis and to deal with the objections raised. Part Three, the weakest section in the first edition, has been strengthened and entirely recast; and with an explosion of new literature the Suggested Readings has been thoroughly updated. But the main arguments remain; and, if anything, I would now express them even more forcefully than I did eight years ago. For the concepts advanced here of corporatism, organic-statism, and bureaucratic-authoritarianism, of critical importance in understanding the Iberic-Latin tradition, have by now become widely used in the literature; we are today even more cognizant than we were then of the ethnocentrism of our major social-science models of development; and events such as the Iranian Revolution (whatever we may think of it or of subsequent Iranian-American relations) have taught us that there are alternative models of national socio-political organization "out there" besides our own preferred liberal-pluralist one.

This volume is dedicated to the students with whom I have worked in precisely those courses mentioned above. Though the fact is often doubted, education *is* a two-way process; and though it does not always show immediately, teachers *do* learn from the questions, perspectives, and viewpoints of their students. That has certainly been true in my case and in terms of the differences between the first and second editions of this book. It is no more than fair, therefore, that this volume, which represents a part of my own learning process, should be dedicated to those who assisted in that education.

Many others have stimulated me with their ideas and research findings; that debt is acknowledged here and in the notes and Suggested Readings. Leone Stein, director of the University of Massachusetts Press, has been exceedingly generous in her encouragement and sound advice. Jorge Domínguez at Harvard, where the book is used as a text, has provided some valuable suggestions for revision; and Iêda Siqueira Wiarda continues always to give to this and an immense variety of other efforts, both scholarly and familial, immense amounts of time, patience, sympathy, and helpful encouragement.

Cambridge, Massachusetts   Howard J. Wiarda
Spring 1981

Part One

Introduction

Social Change,
Political Development,
and the Latin American
Tradition

Howard J. Wiarda

Appreciating Latin America

Before the dramatic onset of revolution in the Caribbean and Central
America, Latin America was generally ignored in the United States and
worldwide, in the books people read and the courses they took, because
of a widespread sense of the area's unimportance. Latin America was
viewed as something of an aberration, an area where democracy failed
to work, constant coups and military takeovers occurred, and "underdevelopment" (social, moral, and political, as well as economic) persisted. Our popular image of the nations to our south was (and in some
quarters still is) shaped by stereotypes, magazine cartoons, and old
movies: peasants with big sombreros either taking siestas or dancing
gaily in the streets, and mustachioed, comic-opera men-on-horseback
galloping in and out of presidential palaces with frequent regularity.

Scholarship and teaching often reflected both this ignorance and the
bias and ethnocentrism of the popular stereotypes. Latin America was
thought to have little to contribute materially or from a social-science
point of view. It had "no history" according to Hegel, "no political culture" according to many sociologists and political scientists. The few
books on Latin America that appeared were preoccupied with lamenting
the weakness of legislatures, the strength of various dictators, and the
absence of elections and United States style democracy. Reflecting this
North American ethnocentrism, the focus of most studies was on explaining why Latin America failed to measure up to United States or Western
European standards of the "good" democratic society and polity. On the
international front, meanwhile, despite some occasional flare-ups, Latin
America remained marginal to the major balances of power, an "American backyard" protected by the Monroe Doctrine and "safe" from
communism.

Castro's revolution in Cuba began to change all this. Students, scholars, and government officials were suddenly confronted with a new
situation that thrust Latin American affairs to the forefront. A great deal
of scare literature was produced on Latin America, books with the titles
of *The Eleventh Hour* or *One Minute to Midnight*. Suddenly the Congress was concerned, new "task forces" to study "the problem" were set

up, and a host of fellowships materialized to help channel our best young minds into Latin American studies. A new image, that of the guerrilla revolutionary, replaced the older stereotype of the sleepy peasant. New aid programs and cooperative endeavors were suddenly announced by the United States government and various private agencies. Stemming initially from the Cuban revolution and then reinforced by upheaval in Nicaragua and El Salvador, the concern was widespread that unless *we* did something, the fire would spread up and down the Andes, and the entire Hemisphere would fall prey to Castro-Communist takeovers.

The potential for revolution spreading throughout the Hemisphere tomorrow is surely greatly exaggerated, but one cannot fall back into the older habits of neglect and indifference either. Indeed, there is a whole body of literature that argues that Latin America is a profoundly "unrevolutionary society," perhaps inherently and permanently so, that genuine social revolution is unlikely to occur in any but two or three spots in the Hemisphere. Neither the peasants, the workers, nor the students in the major countries are really very revolutionary; their guerrilla movements have not achieved widespread popular support or great success; the local communist parties are generally old and tired; revolutionary strategies have not proved successful. Moreover, the area's traditional structures and institutions—the extended family pattern, the assumptions of hierarchy and authority, the Church and the Army, traditional beliefs and culturally conditioned habits—have proved to be remarkably flexible and persistent, bending and adapting to change instead of giving way or necessarily being crushed under the onslaught of modernization. Midnight has not tolled—or if it did, nothing very dramatic happened. The choices of reform or revolution, or of dictatorship versus democracy, have proved to be false, or at least did not take into account all the varied Latin American possibilities. In Washington this perception of the essentially conservative nature of Latin America, particularly during those periods when no "threatening" Castro-like revolutions loomed, was reflected in a renewal period of official neglect and indifference.

Neither of these scenarios or models, the revolutionary or the conservative, necessarily describes or delineates accurately and completely the nature of the Latin American development process. The apocalyptic "eleventh-hour" theme is probably useful for prying aid funds from a reluctant United States Congress, for getting students interested and involved in the area, and for raising the level of public consciousness about Latin America. But the idea that all Latin America is about to explode in violent upheaval has proved to be a myth, a phantom notion that has greatly obscured our understanding of how the Latin American systems do, in fact, change and modernize. The social and economic transformations occurring in Latin America are considerable, but these

5

**Howard J.
Wiarda**

have not always or uniformly produced fundamental alterations in the class structure or political behavior. Nor have they given rise, except in a handful of countries and for some quite special circumstances, to a noticeable strengthening of revolutionary sentiment and movements. The fundamental assumptions on which the scare literature and the dramatic, hyped-up television specials were based have proved to be inaccurate or at best only half-truths, a reflection once again of the inappropriateness of trying to interpret Latin America through the lenses of United States political understandings. Not only have we persisted in viewing Latin America through our own rose-colored glasses and our own preferred political perceptions but—through our aid, our Peace Corps, our human rights policy and other initiatives—we have often sought to impose United States or Western European solutions and political formulae on societies where they simply do not fit.

The scare tactics and verbal overkill employed in much of the literature have not only produced wrong and misleading interpretations but they have also produced the inevitable reactions in the form of renewed public and official indifference and in the production of a new body of literature that, in seeking to correct past misconceptions, overcompensates by focusing solely on Latin America's conservative aspects. But the image of Latin America as a wholly static and reactionary area is not very accurate either. In fact, the changes occurring throughout the area have been many and profound—class changes, social and economic changes, and political transformations as well. But these changes have not often been in the direction or the precise form envisioned in most of the "development" literature written by North Americans or Northwest Europeans. For example, the Latin American middle class does not behave as this literature leads us to expect, political parties seldom play the same role as in the United States, the military continues to intervene, and so on. Our biases and ethnocentrism have helped both to perpetrate some fundamental misunderstandings of Latin America, as well as to render a positive disservice to a more accurate comprehension of how the Latin American systems do in fact function, change, and modernize.

These criticisms of some of the conventional "wisdom" regarding Latin America—a wisdom derived from divergent poles on the political spectrum and from different assumptions about development, but none of it very useful for comprehending Latin America—serve as the point of departure for the main theme of the book, namely, that there are some distinctive aspects to the process of social and political change in Latin America that do not correspond to the development models usually employed. Latin America has its own social and political institutions and its own ways of achieving change, and it is both presumptuous of us and detrimental to a proper understanding of the area to look at it exclusively through the prism of the United States or the Western European developmental experience. If we wish to appreciate and come to grips realistically with Latin America and its change processes, we must do so on Latin America's own terms and in its historical context, not through some model of society derived from outside the Hemisphere and rooted in circumstances having little to do with the present conditions of Latin America itself. We cannot seek to impose some narrow, preconceived general theory on a set of societies to which it does not correspond, nor seek to understand Latin America's often times unique developmental pattern exclusively in the light of the Northwest European–North American experiences. Instead we must look at Latin America through its own eyes and institutions and seek to come to grips with the processes of change there using a framework for analysis and understanding that grows out of Latin America's own history, tradition, and special circumstances. That is precisely what the present book seeks to provide: an understanding of the historical and cultural conditions and determinants of Latin American social and political behavior that shows also the implications of these factors for understanding concrete contemporary issues of political change and social and economic development.

Let us be more specific in our criticisms of the Western model of development and why it has but limited relevance to Latin America. *First,* the timing and context are entirely different. The United States and Western Europe began their drive to accelerated development in the nineteenth century, and it seems obvious that for countries like those of Latin America that began a full century later, the conditions and circumstances are quite dissimilar. *Second,* the sequences of development are distinct. In the European context economic development and the rise of capitalism served as the motor force of modernization, stimulating social change that in turn triggered political reform. But in Latin America the social, economic, and political transformations are occurring all at once, and a good case could be made for its being political requirements that stimulated economic growth rather than the other way around. *Third,* the international settings are wholly changed. Countries like the United States, Britain, and Japan were able to develop relatively autonomously and on their own; Latin America, in contrast, cannot do so and is caught up in a web of international dependency and interdependency over which it has no control. One need only look at market and trade patterns, the dependence on foreign, OPEC-produced oil, the Cold War and the alliance systems and rivalries to which it gave rise, and the important role of the international lending agencies (the World Bank and others) to see how different the conditions are for Latin America.

Fourth and most important for our purposes here, we have learned that "traditional institutions," in Latin America and elsewhere, have remarkable persistence and staying power. Whether it is African tribalism, Indian caste associations, Islamic theocracy, or Latin American personalism, Catholicism, and familism, we now know that these institutions are

not fated inevitably to disappear or be submerged as modernization
advances. Rather, traditional institutions have proved to be adaptable
and accommodative, absorbing some elements of Western modernization, transforming others to fit local circumstances, and often rejecting
the rest. There has been no one-way, automatic, or unilinear process by
which traditional institutions have been *replaced* by modern ones.
Rather, the process has been much more complex, involving blends and
fusions of traditional and modern. Instead of being replaced by modern
(read Western) institutions, traditional institutions have overlapped with
them. Traditional institutions have also served as filters and brokers
of the modernization process, absorbing that which was useful from the
outside world and keeping out the rest. In this way the historic institutions of Latin America have not only survived but thrived. Moreover,
as nationalism has intensified throughout Latin America and as the institutions imported from the West have proved unworkable and dysfunctional, a new pride has developed in indigenous institutions. An effort
has been made to adapt them to modern circumstances, to fashion an
indigenous model of development instead of seeking to preserve the
rather pale and artificial institutions imported earlier from the outside.

The Latin American systems have their roots in the ancient Greek
notion of organic solidarity; in the Roman system of a hierarchy of laws
and institutions; in historic Catholic concepts of the corporate, sectoral,
and compartmentalized organization of society based on each person's
acceptance of his or her station in life; in the similarly corporate
organization (Army, Church, towns, nobility) of Iberian society during
the late medieval era; in the warrior mentality and the walled enclave
cities of the period of the Reconquest of the Iberian Peninsula from the
Moors; in the centralized bureaucratic systems of the early modern
Spanish and Portuguese states; and in the absolutist, scholastic,
Catholic, political culture and institutions of Spain of the Inquisition
and the Counter Reformation. Of course, in the vast empty and "uncivilized" Western Hemisphere, which was under the constant threat that
the thin veneer of Spanish and Portuguese culture and institutions
would be submerged, and which had huge Indian (ten times larger in
Latin America than in North America) and later African populations,
the institutions transplanted from Iberia underwent various changes and
permutations. The amazing thing is their capacity to survive, persist,
and adopt even into the contemporary period.

Latin America is essentially Western, but it represents a particular
tradition in the West and one with which we are not very familiar. Latin
America is a fragment of Europe circa 1492–1570 (the era of the Conquest), and a fragment of a quite special part of Europe, the Iberian
Peninsula. As a fragment of Catholic, corporate, Roman, semifeudal
Europe at that time, and as a reflection of the main institutions of Spain
and Portugal and not of France, Germany, Great Britain, or other of the

Northwest European countries, Latin America has some special characteristics. Its economy was mercantilist and state-directed rather than capitalist and individually directed; its social structure was two-class rather than multi-class and pluralist; its political institutions were hierarchical and authoritarian rather than democratic; its culture and religion were orthodox, absolutist, and infused with Catholic precepts as contrasted with the religious nonconformity and Protestant precepts of the North American colonies. Latin America was condemned eventually to lag behind the United States in terms of its economic growth, but that should not lead us to assume its political, moral, or social institutions were also "retarded" or "underdeveloped." If nothing else, this book conveys the idea that Latin America socially, politically, and culturally represents an *alternative* to the Northwest Europe and United States model, not an "undeveloped" version of it.

Latin American development, therefore, was bound to take on some special features that reflected the area's historic past. Moreover, as the change process began to accelerate in the late nineteenth and early twentieth centuries, Latin American development acquired some special dynamics and went forward in ways that were consonant with its own traditions and institutions but that often bore only superficial resemblance (its constitutions and formal structures) to the North American or Northwest European examples. The exploration and analysis of what these distinct features and special dynamics are lie at the heart of this book.

The change process throughout Latin America has gained increased momentum in recent decades and some far-reaching socio-political transformations have occurred. The middle class has grown greatly in size and influence, peasants and workers are being mobilized and organized, new ideological currents are being felt, the level of popular demands is rising, and new institutional paraphernalia and policy programs have appeared. Despite these changes, however, the traditionalist, elitist, clientelistic, authoritarian, corporatist, and paternalistic structures of Latin America have proved amazingly adaptive and durable. Some sweeping changes are underway throughout Latin America (thus demonstrating that its institutions are not nearly so rigid, unyielding, and reactionary as we had thought), and yet this has seldom resulted in very many fundamental alterations in Latin America's basic structures (thus confounding the classic theories of revolution). Latin America has modernized and developed, but it has done so in its own way and without sacrificing those elements considered valuable from its past. In Latin America, to use the old saw, the more things change, the more they remain the same. It is toward the illumination of how these processes work, the dynamic blending (and sometimes crazy-quilt arrangements) of both traditional and modern currents in Latin America, that the present collection is dedicated.

9

**Howard J.
Wiarda**

The Latin American nations have proved remarkably adept at accommodating their traditional institutions to modernity and at reorienting their modernizing forces in traditional or system-conforming directions. In the process they have evolved quite a distinctive way of assimilating and absorbing the newer social forces and of managing the entire development process without destroying or sweeping away the traditional institutions themselves. One must guard against romanticizing this process, however, for the inequities and injustices existing in Latin America are great and plain for all to see. Nor can one have great sympathy for those Latin American systems where the legitimate demands of the people have been consistently smothered, or for those Latin American leaders who, in the name of "tradition," have exercised brutal and repressive power. And yet, our attention must be commanded by the ability of many of the Latin American nations to manage the change process in a relatively peaceful and orderly fashion, to provide for economic growth and considerable social justice even in contexts of dependency and limited natural resources, and to preserve, albeit unevenly, those institutions and societal norms considered valuable from the past (the extended family, personalism and humanism, a sense of community, individual dignity and worth, social solidarity and mutual interdependence, moral and ethical values) even in the face of the immense pressures toward impersonality, mass society, and alienation imposed by the impact of modern, twentieth-century life. Surely as confidence wanes in the capacity of the United States and other "advanced" industrial societies to cope with their social ills, as we lament the passing of our own sense of community, family, individual worth, and mutual respect and tolerance, it is worth examining closely a society and cultural tradition seeking—with some success—to preserve the heritage deemed valuable from its history while at the same time adapting it to the currents of modernization.

No claim is here made that this is the one and exclusive explanation of Latin America. Other major explanations—class analysis, international economic dependency relations—must also be employed. Nor should it be thought that the explanation offered here applies to all the Latin American countries uniformly. It applies to some more than others and in varying degrees within the several countries. But although not a complete explanation, the interpretation offered here is an essential one and one that is often ignored in the literature; furthermore, it represents a model or "ideal type" that should be tested comparatively in the different national contexts. But with these qualifications, the main point should not be lost: because of their distinct backgrounds and the pattern of their socio-cultural evolution, the Latin American nations merit separate treatment and interpretation. Their development patterns are unique and poorly understood. Because of the biases within the social sciences that focus on the Northwest European and United States experiences, the Latin American system and model seldom find expression in our studies of political theory, sociology, or political development. Indeed in Latin America it is likely we are looking at a "Fourth World of Development," one that corresponds neither to the "First World" of liberal-capitalist countries, nor to the "Second World" of Soviet-type socialism, nor to the "Third World" either, which is such a big category and spans so many diverse continents as to be almost worthless as a descriptive or analytical term. Latin America has evolved its own ways of seeking to manage the major challenges of modern times, one that borrows from the models of the first and second worlds but is not identical to either, one which increasingly builds on indigenous, *Latin American* institutions. That model, which is quite distinct from the United States and the dominant Northwest European systems, has not received the attention it deserves, nor have its implications been adequately explored. This book seeks to analyze the special nature of the Latin American development process and to suggest some of these broader implications.

The Place of Latin America in the Literature on Development

In recent years the fields of economic development studies and social and political modernization and development have mushroomed. This corresponds both with the sudden entrance of a host of new nations in Africa, Asia, and the Middle East onto the world stage, and with a dawning realization in the West that such developing or emerging nations can no longer be safely ignored. The study of development has itself become a growth industry, and there can be no doubt that the analysis and understanding of how societies change, modernize, and reorient their institutional life correspondingly are and will remain among the most exciting, challenging, and important subject areas with which we and the world, both those in the so-called developed world and those in the developing one (even the phrases used illustrated the paternalism and ethnocentrism involved in much of the literature), must be concerned.

Unfortunately, in the rush to study such development, two major problems have emerged. The first has to do with the pervasive ethnocentrism with which we view Latin America. Almost everything said and written about the developing nations has been from a Western, white, Northern European and United States perspective. The assumption is widespread that to be developed is to be "just like us"—presumably that means liberal, democratic, moderate in our politics, pluralist, middle class, and so on. The second problem is that in all the new, grand, and universal theories of development, Latin America is largely left out of consideration. This is a curious omission because with their common cultural background, histories, colonial past and parallel development

11
Howard J.
Wiarda

experiences, the Latin American nations provide a particularly fertile area—almost a living laboratory of sociological and political development—for comparative analysis and the testing of distinct theoretical models of the change-modernization process. The trouble is that Latin America doesn't fit very well into the great designs that sociologists, economists, and political scientists have erected. But rather than revising the theory to deal with these distinct realities, social scientists have often preferred to ignore the entire area. Obviously that is unacceptable from any point of view that presumes to social-science accuracy.

The ethnocentrism of our familiar approaches to studying development has already been noted, but a further point needs to be made here. Most of us are students of what we call the liberal arts, but it must be remembered that liberal-arts education is concerned almost entirely with the Western tradition. Sociology, political science, and economics all have their roots in the Western experience of Europe and North America, and that is where their major concepts and understandings derive from. That is not bad, of course, so long as we recognize the narrowness and particularism of that approach and its limited relevance in the rest of the globe. The trouble is that in our models of development we have generalized from the Western experience to the entire world, and the same categories do not fit very well. We have made the mistake of assuming that development necessarily means Westernization. That is not only wrong and inappropriate, contributing to a perpetuation of our lack of comprehension regarding other culture areas, but it represents some of the worse forms of what we might call cultural imperialism. Liberal-arts education, by which we mean the Western European tradition, is really the first area study; but it is erroneous and presumptuous to assume that the concepts and categories derived from that area have universal validity.

As to why Latin America is not included in the major general books on development, several reasons may be offered. First, there exists a series of prejudices about Latin America. The area is based upon hierarchical, elitist, Catholic, corporatist, and authoritarian assumptions, and the fact is that social scientists, like most Americans, do not like societies based on such assumptions. A second reason is that those most prominent in the field of development studies—Gabriel A. Almond, W. W. Rostow, S. M. Lipset, Lucian Pye, Bert Hoselitz, David Apter, Karl Deutsch—have all been European, African, or Asian experts and therefore have concentrated in their writings on erecting models based on the areas they know best. Third, the knowledge (and appreciation) of Latin America in the general social-science disciplines remains limited, and in the general studies of development written by social scientists, Latin America is usually ignored or glossed over quickly. The comments about Latin America in the general development literature are often limited to a few unenlightening (and often dead wrong) paragraphs or, in some cases, a meager footnote. This omission has resulted in a large body of literature propounding a supposedly universal model of development that, in fact, ignores a major area of the globe, one that has much to tell us concerning the processes of development particularly of nations in the intermediary and transitional stages. If one remembers, moreover, that a number of these leading development theorists were also among the new mandarins (those foreign policy advisers helping design the often misconceived, misapplied, and ruinous United States programs directed toward Latin America in the 1960s and 1970s), then this indictment becomes even stronger.

But the problem is not simply ethnocentrism, a lack of empathy, and a lack of knowledge concerning Latin America. The difficulty also lies in the fact that Latin America does not fit very well the models and metaphors that scholars and government officials (for the most part, from the United States) have concocted. With more than a century and a half of independent life behind them, the Latin American countries could hardly be called "new nations." With its Catholic, Iberian, and Southern European heritage, Latin America is certainly not "non-Western"—though, as we shall emphasize, it represents a quite distinct set of threads and socio-political currents within that Western tradition which is quite at variance with the better known (and usually more admired) northern example. Nor has Latin America followed the sequential "stages of growth" that these same Northwestern European nations and the United States went through. And the classical Marxian categories—in a continent where capitalism in its laissez-faire form hardly exists, where the workers and peasants are not always revolutionary, and where class and economic variables may be part of the superstructure and largely determined by socio-political factors instead of the other way around—provide only a partial and often incomplete explanation. In short, Latin American development resembles only in limited ways the African, Asian, or Middle Eastern patterns, fits uncomfortably in any pancontinental or Third World category, and corresponds only partially to the major theories and frameworks of "modernization" growing out of the Northwest European and United States experiences. Any effort toward grand theory construction on a global basis that seeks to stuff Latin America into some narrow and ill-fitting intellectual straight jacket is bound to be misleading and inaccurate.

The community of Latin America scholars, however, must also shoulder part of the blame. Long apart and isolated from the most recent theoretical thinking in their respective disciplines, they have tended to reject out of hand the newer analytical tools and models or to use them only half-heartedly. Rather than update their own thinking and research, the older school of Latin Americanists has often sought refuge in arguments for the discreteness of all historical events and the noncomparability of times and nations. In contrast, the younger generation of Latin Americanists have often accepted the universalist models learned in graduate school uncritically and indiscriminantly, applying them to an area where they may not fit or may fit only partially. Little effort has been made to sort out, with empathy and rigor, in what precise areas Latin America is in fact unique and where it conforms to more universal—i.e., Western—modes of development.

That is what this book is all about. Clearly Latin America can and must be included within the broader, global context of change, development, and modernization. To ignore the Latin American experience because it does not exactly fit our preconceived, generally Western and hence ethnocentric notions of how the development process unfolds is both bad scholarship and disastrous for our understanding of the area. It is clear also that the Latin America area specialist must have a firm grasp of the general development and theoretical literature and must be able to conceptualize the area's change processes within this larger historical and comparative perspective. At the same time he must be sensitive to the area's distinctiveness and recognize that the major development models fashioned for Northwest Europe and the United States must be modified, reshaped, supplemented, and sometimes rejected and reformulated altogether in order to have relevance for Latin America. Only by bridging our broad and theoretical understanding of the overall development process (adjusting, amending, and recasting that understanding to account for major national and cultural area-specific variations) with a thorough mastery of the functioning of particular institutions, processes, and countries in Latin America—only then can significant and useful advances occur in our learning of how development generally proceeds and of the alternative forms development may take.

This volume attempts to provide just such a perspective and interpretation, a way of looking at and seeking to understand Latin America that not only advances our comprehension of the area but also better enables us to compare and contrast Latin America's development experience with that of other areas. The attempt is both ambitious and modest: ambitious in terms of its broad sweep and the long time period covered, and modest in terms of the realization that a great deal of work yet remains if we are to comprehend fully the distinct flavor of Latin American development and its comparison to other areas. Yet there can be little doubt that we must come to grips with these issues if we are to avoid the bias and ethnocentrism that so frequently conditions our view of the rest of the world, if we are to develop the empathy required for a proper understanding of foreign areas, if we are to build sound theory for the comparative study and analysis of the development process, and if our policies at the international level toward this critically important area are to be enlightened and wise.

The Pattern of Latin American Development: An Overview

Latin America's roots lie deep in the past.* History hangs heavily over the area. Its historical traditions are both strong and persistent.

The major historical influences on the Iberian mother countries of Spain and Portugal were the Roman system of law and governance, Christianity and the Thomistic tradition, the centuries long Reconquest of the peninsula from the Moors, and the special character of Iberian feudalism, the guild system, and corporatism. Roman law helped provide Spain and Portugal with both unity and a hierarchical, structured, integral, and imperial political foundation; Christianity provided not only a religious and moral base but also a strong scholastic and natural law tradition and a pervasive Catholic political culture that still undergirds behavior and institutions. The Reconquest of Iberia from the Moorish "infidels" helped give religion a more militant, crusading, and intolerant attitude and also shaped the Iberian pattern of walled enclave cities, military orders and special privileges, and the class *and* caste stratification system that persists even today. Spanish feudalism and the guild system also emerged from the Reconquest period and thus became especially rigid and hardened in place. At the same time, the early forms of Iberian corporatism were forged in the relations between such institutions as the Church, the towns, the military orders, the universities, and the privileged castes with each other and with an emerging central state. These traditions and institutions came together and were becoming firmly established in Iberia at precisely the time Spain and Portugal launched their great overseas ventures.

Latin America may thus be viewed as a fragment of Southern European and Iberian culture and civilization of approximately 1500. The time period and the Iberian heritage were especially important in shaping Latin America's future. In terms of the history of Western civilization, Latin America was founded on a basis that was precapitalistic, preenlightenment, pre-Protestant Reformation, prescientific revolution, and prerepresentative government. These features not only helped retard Latin America's later development but also gave it some of its most distinctive characteristics. An understanding of this also enables us to see why Latin American development should be both slower and quite different from the pattern in the North American colonies. These features are explored in greater depth in the following chapter by Richard M. Morse.

---

* No attempt in these few pages is made to present a complete picture and history of Latin American development. This discussion is purposely brief and interpretive, designed to provide only a skeletal outline and overview of the Latin American development pattern as a way of introducing the area.

It goes a long way toward understanding Latin America if we comprehend the time frame in which the area was settled, colonized, and its major institutions established, *and* the special character of these institutions as offshoots not of Elizabethan and Stuart England but of the Spain of Ferdinand and Isabella, Charles I, and Philip II. The major institutions transferred to the New World were "feudal," not "modern." In the Spain and Portugal of that time, and now in their colonies, the dominant institutions were a feudal-patrimonial system of land ownership and of lord-peasant relations; an authoritarian, absolutist, hierarchical, and organic structure of political authority; a similarly authoritarian and absolutist Church that buttressed and reinforced the state concept and provided little room for pluralism; a social order divided vertically in terms of segmented corporate units (Church, Army, bureaucracy, university) and horizontally according to a rigid system of classes, estates, rank orders, castes, and purportedly God-given inequalities; an exploitive, centralized, monopolistic, statist, and mercantilist economic system; and an educational system and intellectual tradition based on scholastic learning, rote memorization, absolute truth, and deductive reasoning. Forged and crystallized during and in the aftermath of the centuries long crusade against the Moors, these traditions and institutions had been firmly established in Spain and Portugal by the end of the fifteenth century. Beginning in 1492 they were transferred to the Americas where they not only were strongly institutionalized but also received a new lease on life—either as established forms or as goals and aspirations for Latin American society to achieve. The theme does not get much attention in this book, but it should be noted that one reason for the durability of the institutions carried over from Iberia is that they closely paralleled and reinforced the similarly authoritarian, absolutist, and theocratic institutions of the indigenous, pre-Columbian Indian civilizations in the Americas. The main threads of these arguments concerning the distinctiveness of Latin America are explored in more detail in the second Morse and the Newton essays that follow.

The isolation of Latin America from the outside world during the next three centuries of colonial rule, buttressed both by Iberian colonial policy and by immense distances and premodern communications, combined with the fact that it was largely unaffected by the powerful modernizing forces stirring elsewhere in the West—the rise of capitalism and accelerated social change, religious nonconformity and pluralism, the scientific revolution and the Enlightenment, the thrusts toward representative government and participation—served to lock Latin America into the fifteenth- and early sixteenth-century pattern and to prevent its evolution along other lines. In contrast to the North American colonies, settled more than a century later when the hold of feudal institutions had been considerably weakened in England, the Latin American colonies remained essentially authoritarian, absolutist, feudal (in the peculiarly Iberian sense), patrimonialist, elitist, and organic-corporatist.

Right from the start, therefore, the Latin American colonies were destined both to lag behind their North American counterparts and to evolve in some quite distinct directions. If we recall, for instance, that in our usual history texts the modern era is thought to commence in roughly 1500, then we may begin to comprehend the fundamental differences between the colonies in the two parts of the Americas. Latin America was settled and colonized on the basis of a set of essentially feudal and medieval institutions still reigning at that fundamental breakpoint, and it took on a special character because of its bases in the Iberian tradition; North America, on the other hand, was colonized a full century later when the thrusts of capitalism, religious and political pluralism, modern science, concepts of limited and representative government, and a new enterprising middle class had all begun to have a powerful impact.

Given the time period and the Iberian background it should not be surprising that Latin America was established on this authoritarian, feudal, Catholic, scholastic, mercantilist, patrimonialist, and corporatist basis. What is remarkable is that these institutions proved so long lasting. They survived not only three centuries of colonial rule but also, with some modifications and restructuring, the transition of the colonies to independent nations early in the nineteenth century and even the immense pressures that began to be thrust upon them in the twentieth century by the newer forces of modernization. It is in this sense of having been cut off from and only marginally affected by the great transformations that molded the modern world, while keeping its traditional institutions largely intact, that Latin America may be referred to as a profoundly, historically conservative and nonrevolutionary area. Glen Dealy's first essay deals with this theme of Latin American monism in detail.

This of course is not to say there were no significant changes at all or that Latin America remained wholly static. New laws and changes were continually promulgated by the Crown, considerable reorganization of the institutional mechanisms took place, foreign interlopers seeking to break the Spanish monopoly system had to be dealt with, Spanish power waxed and waned, there were depressions and population shifts, a new merchant class eventually began to grow up, some Enlightenment ideas filtered in, the Spanish Bourbon kings of the eighteenth century sought to streamline and modernize colonial rule, and the revolutions in North America and France eventually had an impact. Nevertheless, the basic structures and pillars of the system remained intact. The social and political institutions developed by Spain and Portugal proved flexible enough to accommodate themselves to the changes while also persisting without any revolutionary challenges and with only minor modifications in the fundamental character of the system.

It is not our intention here to review the chronology of events and battles that led to independence. Suffice it to say that by the end of the eighteenth century independence sentiment had grown and that between 1807 and 1824 all Latin America (except Cuba and Puerto Rico) became independent—in some areas as the result of vigorous fighting and in others peacefully, as the result of administrative fiat or the withdrawal of the Spanish military forces and the Crown's authority. It does need emphasizing, however, that these were wars of separation rather than genuine social revolutions and, hence, that the essential structure of top-down authority and society continued, for the most part, as it had been. In many respects the independence movements in Latin America should be seen as conservative movements rather than liberalizing ones, designed to secure and enhance the status of traditional institutions and of the native-born oligarchies. The local elites wanted not to destroy the ancient system but to make it their own, unfettered by the inconveniences of Spanish decrees and officialdom.

Royal authority, the apex of the Spanish-Portuguese pyramidal system, had been lopped off by independence, but the role and power of the Church, the system of patrimonialism and of lord-serf relations, the hierarchical and rigidly stratified system of power and society, and the norms and values of traditional Catholic political culture all continued. Some of the ancient guilds were abolished and there was a reordering of Church-state relations, but these were more in the nature of adjustments within the system than they were fundamental alterations to it, and soon new corporate units were created as replacements for those abolished. Into the power vacuum created by the Crown's withdrawal stepped the indigenous oligarchies and the armies created during the independence struggles and their *caudillo,* men-on-horseback leaders, seeking to take over the mantle of authority previously centered in the king and to reestablish the time-honored system of authority and power, but now with themselves in charge.

In keeping with the preferences then current, the constitutions adopted in Latin America for these "new nations" provided for civil, republican, representative rule. But the Iberic-Latin social structures underneath were hardly conducive to or supportive of liberal or democratic government. Latin America adopted the forms of democracy but not its substance. Indeed when one examines these constitutions closely, as Professor Dealy does in Part 3 of this book, one sees that the principles of democratic government were largely concessions to a foreign (United States and European) fad and had little basis in Latin American reality. Rather than instituting democratic rule, the founding fathers of Latin America were chiefly concerned with preserving existing hierarchies and the authoritarian and nondemocratic institutions of the past (which they would of course dominate), while paying only lip service (and occasionally somewhat more than that) to democratic principles. The elitist, absolutist, authoritarian, and patrimonialist structure of Latin America thus demonstrated remarkable staying power, both before independence and after it.

The legitimacy vacuum ushered in by the Crown's withdrawal, however, coupled with the lack of nationally organized institutions and the typical discontinuities attendant upon new nationhood, resulted in a period of considerable instability in the immediate postindependence period. Neither the creole oligarchies nor the new armies were able to fill the void entirely. In a number of countries periods of anarchy alternated with periods of dictatorship. Rival *caudillos* and their retinues vied for control of the presidential palace, which in the absence of the Crown was now the center from which power, patronage, and spoils flowed. From the 1820s to the 1850s the efforts to create viable nation-states out of the fragmented elements that made up society resulted in discord and instability. Only Brazil, which solved its legitimacy problem by continuing as an independent monarchy, and Chile, which quickly reestablished conservative oligarchic rule, were able to avoid the disruptions experienced by the other nations.

From roughly the 1850s, varying somewhat from nation to nation, the situation began to stabilize. The first postindependence generation of men-on-horseback had passed from the scene. The Church-state issues were largely settled. Agriculture and commerce began to expand and a new merchant and artisan class began to grow up in the cities. The first national banks and industries were established. The romantic political notions of the French Revolution—liberty, equality, and fraternity— gave way to more realistic assessments of the area's realities and possibilities. The early rejection of Spain and what it had stood for was now replaced by an effort to come to grips practically with Latin America's own past and historic traditions.

By the last quarter of the nineteenth century, in virtually all the Latin American nations, a considerable degree of order had been achieved. This was a period of national consolidation; of the growth, enlargement, and increasing centralization of national armies and bureaucracies; of immigration and population increase; of rising nationalism; of increased foreign investment and national infrastructure building (railroads, highways, port facilities); of gradually rising affluence and economic expansion. In some countries (Argentina, Brazil, Chile) power was firmly consolidated in the hands of landed oligarchies; in others (Mexico, Venezuela, the Dominican Republic) a new breed of stable, nation-building "order-and-progress" *caudillos* arose to replace the unstable men-on-horseback of the past. A third pattern occurring a decade or two later in a number of the Caribbean and Central American countries involved direct United States military occupation, which, in alliance with the indigenous oligarchies, helped produce some of the same consolidating and infrastructure-building trends.

Although this was a period of increasing change and development in Latin America, it implied few fundamental breaks with the past. The growing stability and progress of the late nineteenth century came not through any revolutionary transformations but essentially through a reconsolidation of the old colonial system of hierarchy and elites—albeit now without the Crown and often dressed up in republican garb—with some new elements added to the prevailing systems. Whether *caudillo* or oligarchic dominated (or even under United States hegemony) the Latin American nations sought to achieve growth within the structural framework of the past, which thus included authoritarianism, monopoly, hierarchy, elitism, and patrimonialism. Considerable development occurred in terms of economic growth and greater institutionalization, but very little democraticization resulted. For instance, a new commercial, import-export merchant class rose up but it was quickly absorbed within the elitist and oligarchic structure (now expanded somewhat) and came to share the values and assumptions of the older elites. In many instances the older elites either intermarried with the children of the rising entrepreneurial class or themselves went into business, thus both diversifying and modernizing their economic activities while also maintaining an elite-dominated monopoly on wealth and power. Concurrently, a new and fledging middle class emerged, but it lacked coherence and consciousness as a class. Its members, once they had "made it" economically and politically, also aped upper-class ways and the traditional elitist disdain both for manual labor and for the lower classes. Elections even in the "liberal" regimes remained controlled so as to perpetuate rule by a small minority. The beginning of the economic "take-off" in Latin America thus produced some new social and political forces but implied no fundamental realignment of the socio-political order, nor did it give rise to the political pluralism and greater egalitarianism that these transformations sparked elsewhere in the West. These trends are discussed in Part 3, especially in the essays by Fredrick Pike.

The period from roughly 1890 to 1930 was the heyday of oligarchic rule in Latin America. The terms of trade were advantageous and, by exporting their mineral wealth and agricultural products, many nations of the area prospered. A new era of order, stability, and progress ensued; it was hardly democratic but represented chiefly the reinstitutionalization and further elaboration of the older pattern of autocracy and special privilege. In some countries "revolutions" continued, but these were not social upheavals and implied usually the changing of only the names and faces of those in the presidential palace, a rotation of the ruling elites rather than any fundamental restructuring. Seldom in any of these revolts were there many people killed or much property destroyed for that was costly and not in accord with the accepted rules of the game.

In this way the Latin American nations began to adjust and accommodate themselves to modernization, but it did not result in any genuinely revolutionary changes in the structure of elite and oligarchic rule or even in much alteration in the prevailing political culture. Authoritarianism, patrimonialism, hierarchy, elitism, monism as distinct from pluralism (see again Professor Dealy's first essay), these remained the dominant institutional norms. Development in Latin America thus went forward within the framework, which was still only slightly altered, of an older historic pattern that stretched back to colonial and precolonial eras; it was a framework that was more conservative and "feudal" than liberal. Only in Mexico from 1910 to 1920 did a full-fledged social revolution occur, and even that was a limited and essentially middle-class revolution not out of harmony with the historic Latin American pattern and eventually evolving a similar authoritarian and corporatist structure. Argentina in 1916 and Chile in 1920 also experienced middle-class take-overs that served to incorporate these rising elements into the system but did not change the system very much itself.

A major break came in 1930. The world-market crash of 1929-30 and the ensuing Depression eroded the demand abroad for Latin America's primary products and helped undermine the older system of oligarchic rule. In 1930 and the years following, a rash of revolts occurred throughout the area, reflecting the dissatisfaction of the rising middle classes with the traditional elitist system and their demand for a restructuring of it—chiefly to include themselves. Hence, even the accelerated changes and search for new solutions in the post-1930 period have generally had as their goals the remodeling of the traditional system of authority and privilege, now updated to include some of the newer social groups and political "power contenders" (see Charles W. Anderson's essay "Toward a Theory of Latin American Politics" in this book) but not repudiating the older historic system. In some countries there ensued a period of alternation between traditional and more forward-looking regimes; in others what we think of as right-wing dictators (Trujillo in the Dominican Republic, the elder Somoza in Nicaragua) reestablished order—often with a vengeance—but also brought the new middle classes into power and accomplished a variety of changes necessary for adaptation to the new circumstances of greater (albeit still severely limited) pluralism; in still others, civilian and military populist leaders (Vargas in Brazil or Perón in Argentina), backed usually by middle sector and often some emerging labor elements, redirected and restructured the prevailing systems. Nineteen thirty marked a significant turning point in Latin America, but in the classic fashion the changes did not often produce a very sharp or revolutionary break. It signified the grafting on of a number of new social elements to a system that had been absorbing such new elites in this manner for centuries. Some new pillars were added but Latin America's historic pyramidal structure was maintained. Chilean author Claudio Véliz has some provocative things to say in Part 3 concerning these continuities.

As the development process began in Latin America in the nineteenth century, the new merchant and entrepreneurial elements had been quickly absorbed within the dominant elitist system. The continued growth of the middle classes throughout Latin America has implied since the 1930s the increased participation (and, now, often dominance) of these elements in politics, government, the Church, and the armed forces officer corps. Significantly, however, though the class composition of these institutions has been altered, there have been few changes in the cultural norms and elitist-authoritarian behavioral patterns that predominate in them. The middle sectors have absorbed the elitist ways and often have been stronger defenders of the traditional order than even the traditional elites themselves. There are a number of new elites but the patterns of elite rule and circulation in power persist. Since the 1930s also, as Latin America has increasingly industrialized, the urban (and sometimes rural) trade-union movement has also emerged as an influential force in all the Latin America nations. But as with other groups, organized labor led by middle-class spokesmen has generally also been assimilated into the prevailing system through the creation of government-sponsored and controlled labor movements, paternalistically directed from above rather than reflecting much mass or grassroots challenge from below. A manifestly *corporatist* system of controls on trade-union activity and incorporation of cooperative labor elements into the prevailing system represents the historic elites' response to the rise of this new social force; this process forms the focus of my essay in Part 4 and in the Conclusion of the book.

More recently, as a result of the transistor radio and the extension of other communications and transportation grids that have brought new demands and expectations to the previously isolated countryside, it has become the peasants' turn to be assimilated in a partial fashion. The laws governing the "rights" (in Latin America still more a feudal than a modern concept, implying group obligations and privileges rather than individual rights) of organized labor have now been extended to rural workers; similarly "agrarian reform" became more an instrument to structure and control peasant participation in the national life than to liberate or bring revolutionary transformation to the countryside. These same laws in many of the countries of the area have also been extended recently to women workers and domestics. In a few countries (Cuba, Nicaragua, El Salvador) such changes came too slowly or were perverted under brutal dictatorship and revolutionary upheavals resulted. But in the majority of countries the pattern has been one of continued "civilization" of new social groups into the prevailing political culture and the incorporation of such groups into the system under elite tutelage and direction, rather than one of revolutionary overthrow.

All this has given the development process in Latin America a distinctive flavor and structure that help distinguish it from the Western European and United States pattern. Not only are the times and circumstances obviously different in Latin America today from what they were for the Western nations in the nineteenth century; but the process by which modern institutions are filtered in and out, the timing and sequences of development, and the social and political concomitants of economic growth are quite different as well. In Latin America the traditional structures have, for the most part, proved remarkably malleable and adjustable. With some exceptions, they have accommodated the forces of change instead of being overthrown by them. In contrast to our more familiar models of development, which picture traditional institutions as hardened shells that must either crack and disintegrate under the onslaught of modernization or else be overthrown, the Latin American systems have proved both remarkably tenacious and surprisingly adjustable, absorbing what is useful in modernity, rejecting most of the rest, and in the process largely retaining their historic tradition, essence, and distinctiveness. In these ways Latin America has sought to adapt to the main currents of the modern industrial world while also maintaining what it considers valuable and characteristic of its own civilization.

Latin America should thus be looked on as having opted for and chosen because of historical circumstances a developmental path that is *alternative* to the United States model, not some pale, retarded, "unsuccessful" version of it. Moreover, as the United States cracks and creaks; as we realize this nation had no monopoly on virtue or efficient political institutions; as hierarchy, corporatism, and centralized state-directed control and direction grow in the United States and other advanced industrial nations; *and* as we long for the sense of community, moral values, and unity that we seem somehow to have lost, the Latin American experience may offer some valuable instruction from which we can learn. The question cannot be finally answered in this book but it is too important to be ignored: Can it be, heretical though it seems in the United States, that the Latin American nations with their organic, unitary, and patrimonialist conception of the proper ordering of state and society will in the long run prove to have coped better with the wrenching crises of modernization than the United States with its secular, divisive, fragmented interest group pluralism? That is a question that transcends the study of Latin America, but it is one whose implications we must begin to consider.

The focus in this book is on the historic and prevailing political culture of Latin America, the institutional and socio-political context in which development takes place and which shapes it in various ways. That is an important, often neglected, and necessary explanation, but no claim is put forward that it is the only explanation. We must also, as indicated in the preceding discussion, examine the great motor forces of economic development and class change, and also the patterns of Latin American dependency. But religion, culture, values, language, law, and history are also crucially important in understanding the institutional framework through which development is fashioned and filtered, and even in shaping the processes of economic development and class change themselves. Although the particular form that development has taken in Latin America has both multiple causes and has produced multiple effects, anyone with even a nodding acquaintance with the area cannot help but be impressed by the continuing importance of the historical, sociological, and political-cultural variables stressed here as fundamental in molding and determining development's direction.

Latin America, we shall see, remains hierarchical, authoritarian, paternalistic, Catholic (in the broad political-cultural sense as used here), elitist, corporatist, and patrimonialist to its core. These ingredients have been *and remain* at the heart of its development tradition and are what help make it distinctive. At present, however, new ideologies and movements have begun increasingly (and in several countries successfully) to challenge the traditional ones, the bases of order and legitimacy of the old system are being progressively undermined, the outside world has had more and more of an impact, and a new framework of class and issue-oriented politics has appeared. The clash between traditional and modern has intensified throughout the Hemisphere, raising strong doubts as to whether Latin America's traditional structures are any longer capable of managing and controlling the rising tide of popular demands, and whether its historic patterns and institutions can survive. Yet even in the face of these newer and in some cases revolutionary pressures for change, the traditional Latin American ways of adapting and accommodating to the pressures of modernization are often dominant—and they may well remain so. Thus the model and explanation of Latin American development presented here may not only help us understand the more traditional regimes in Latin America but also the revolutionary ones, where hierarchy, top-down authority, and institutionalized corporatism also prevail. As Claudio Véliz reminds us, Cuba is highly centralized and authoritarian not just because it is socialist but also because it is Latin America. The examination and analysis of this unique tradition, both in its historic forms and in its fusion and overlap with other, more modern, even revolutionary forms, make up the heart of this book.

A Distinct Latin American Political Sociology of Development?

With this general background concerning the Latin American development tradition and the place of Latin America in historical and comparative perspective, we are now in a position to look at this tradition more closely, to trace its historical evolution, and to assess its contemporary implications. That is what the following selections provide.

But the collection does something more than that. Charles W. Anderson, Richard M. Morse, Fredrick Pike, and Claudio Véliz are all senior scholars well known for their significant and extensive writings on Latin America; their work is so sound and full of provocative ideas that interested readers should pursue it further. Glen Dealy, Lawrence S. Graham, and Ronald C. Newton are younger scholars who have already published extensively on Latin American politics and sociology.

One of the contributions included here is by a major Latin American scholar; the rest are by United States scholars who have come to have an especially close understanding of Latin America *on its terms,* and who are able to bridge and compare the two main cultures and civilizations implanted in the Western Hemisphere. One of the chief advantages of this collection, therefore, is that it brings together a number of fascinating interpretations of Latin America, rich in ideas and provocative insights and organized around the common unifying theme of the distinctiveness of the Latin American development tradition. That theme is treated in varying contexts and approached from different perspectives. Sometimes our authors even arrive at different conclusions! But that is as it should be, for our aim here—unlike that of many texts—is to raise some fascinating and ultimately exceedingly important issues with which students of Latin America must grapple rather than to present any pat formulas or ideological orthodoxies.

One final issue merits our close attention. The emphasis here has been on the in many ways unique tradition of Latin American development and the inappropriateness of the usually biased and ethnocentric Western models in seeking to understand it. That implies that we require a separate political sociology of Latin American development, as distinct from the major models with which we are familiar. That is also what the readings here present. They explore whether there is or ought to be a separate Latin American political sociology of development; if so, what its precise ingredients might be; where Latin America is in fact distinctive and where it conforms more or less to familiar and universal patterns of development. The editor tries to formulate an initial statement of such a distinctive Latin American political sociology of development in the Conclusion.

One suspects that what is said here for Latin America may also have implications for our understanding of South and East Asia, the Middle East, sub-Saharan Africa, and perhaps other areas. That is, first, that the Western and Northwest European model of development may have only limited utility in helping us understand these areas; and second, that within these other areas there are also strong, indigenous institutions (African tribalism, Indian caste associations, Islamic fundamentalism), comparable to those in Latin America, that have proved more persistent than expected and through which our understanding of development in these areas must be seen. That implies that alongside the familiar Western models and social science paradigms we shall also need an Islamic social science of development, a sub-Saharan African social science of development, a Latin American social science of development, and so on. For if the West and more specifically the United States is no longer to be the world's policeman, it seems unlikely that it will any longer serve as its philosopher-king either, in terms of the claim and assertion of its *particular* development model as the one and universal. Hence these others, as well as the distinct Latin American model of development, command our attention. Not only are they critical for a nonethnocentric understanding of non-Western areas and their change processes, but one suspects that the fashioning, exploration, and analysis of such indigenous models represents the next great frontier in the social sciences.

Part Two

Historical Interpretations

In this section we shall be concerned chiefly with describing and analyzing the historical context and setting in which Latin American development takes place. The essays included here are eclectic and interpretive; they provide a narrative of the unfolding of history in Latin America, but even more important for our purposes they seek to assess and draw meaning out of that history for our present understanding of the area. Wide ranging in scope, drawing upon both historical and contemporary literature, closely complementing each other, these chapters explore the social, political, philosophical, religious, and legal origins and antecedents of the Latin American nations, trace their later evolution and development, and analyze the implications of these historic foundations for our contemporary understanding of the area.

These historical perspectives amplify and provide greater depth to a number of themes presented in the Introduction. In his seminal essay "The Heritage of Latin America" Richard M. Morse, a historian formerly at Yale and now at Stanford, traces and analyzes the pattern and unfolding of the Latin American tradition. After discussing the background and peoples of Latin America, Morse focuses on the special nature of the institutional and political order, analyzes the socioeconomic and philosophical foundations and later development of these norms and institutions from the colonial to the independence period, and concludes with a series of political premises helping to explain why contemporary Latin America differs so greatly from the United States. Students interested in comparative political development may also want to consult the other essays in The Founding of New Societies, *from which the Morse essay is reprinted, for it includes not only summaries of the United States, Canada, Australia, and South Africa—all parallel but dissimilar stepchildren or fragments of a common Western and European civilization—but also a stimulating essay by general editor Louis Hartz in which he sets forth a theory of the development of new societies.*

Once we have the background provided by the Morse essay we are ready to tackle the complex and controversial essay by Glen Dealy entitled "The Tradition of Monistic Democracy in Latin America." Dealy, a political scientist at Oregon State University, delves deeply into the classic political theory (Saint Augustine, Saint Thomas, Machiavelli,

Bolívar) that undergirds the Latin American tradition, and he explores its implications for our understanding of contemporary politics and society. In contrast to the more laissez-faire and pluralistic traditions of the United States, Dealy sees the Latin American tradition as essentially monolithic, with all the various groups and corporate units centralized, coordinated and controlled from above in a "monistic" or unitary arrangement. A parallel note is struck in the third essay in this section, "Toward a Theory of Spanish American Government," also by Richard Morse, in which he contrasts the liberal-Lockean tradition of the United States (separation of powers, individual rights, checks and balances, limited government) with the Spanish and Spanish American tradition whose dominant influences have been Thomism (an organic theory of the state, natural inequalities among men, authoritative if not authoritarian rule, hierarchy, scholasticism, a corporate or sectoral ordering of society) and Machiavellianism (personalism, princeship, imperial rule, and centralized state-building royal authority).

Ronald C. Newton's essay overlaps and complements nicely the contributions previously discussed. Newton shows how in Suárez, Spain's great sixteenth-century political thinker, the Thomistic-Catholic conception was updated to meet the requirements of modern statecraft and national development and how the model fashioned by Spain and carried to America proved so stable and protective of the status quo. As the title of his essay indicates, Newton's main concerns are the ideas of pluralism and interest group balance that undergird the United States political system and how problematical these concepts are when applied to Latin America. The quotation marks around the main terms in his title are used to indicate that the same terms may have quite different meanings and carry distinct implications in the two different parts of the Americas, and in his discussion of the traditional political-legal culture of Latin America he builds upon the Morse and Dealy essays in showing how and why the Latin American tradition is different. Along with Morse, he also sees the crisis of the traditional order, analyzes the possibilities for change, and shows why development in Latin America often results in fragmentation and breakdown.

The Heritage of
Latin America

Richard M. Morse

1. The People

For the past twenty-seven thousand years the sprawling, geographically variegated continent-and-a-half now occupied by the twenty nations of Latin America has been a melting pot for tribes and nations of the world. The prehistoric migrations from Asia, which lasted for millennia and brought to the Western Hemisphere the peoples known to history as Indians, were followed after 1492 by tens of millions of migrants from Southern Europe, from Africa and, in lesser but significant numbers, from all other parts of the world.

The term melting pot, however, is most often associated with the society of the United States. Here it characteristically refers to the later phases of immigration from Europe, when newcomers from north, central, south, and east Europe were added in large numbers to the original nucleus from the British Isles. It also tends to suggest more strongly the diversity of the immigrants' national origin than a diversity of class and occupational background. Applied to Latin America, "melting pot" has similar connotations only for the southern countries, notably Argentina and southern Brazil. For here the Indian and Negro fractions of the population are small, and since the late nineteenth century there has occurred heavy non-Iberian immigration. Persons of Italian and German descent number in the millions. There are important contingents of Slavs and Near Easterners, while contemporary Brazil has nearly half a million inhabitants of Japanese descent.

Even this southern "sub-melting pot," however, exhibits typically Latin-American patterns of acculturation. A Brazilian sociologist contrasts race and ethnic relations in the São Paulo region with those prevailing in the United States. In Brazil color prejudice occurs in a relatively mild (if complex) form, and the public ideology is "assimi-

From *The Founding of New Societies,* © 1964 by Louis Hartz. Reprinted by permission of Harcourt Brace Jovanovich, Inc.

lationist and miscegenationist." In such a society the immigrant is accepted "to the degree that he offers the probability of ceasing to be foreign." According to the study, which modifies certain stereotypes, Brazilians tolerate less patiently than do Americans the perpetuation of cultural enclaves, and they are more resentful of the public and private use of foreign languages. This attitude hastens the assimilation of immigrants. In Brazil the identification of a descendant of immigrants with his original ethnic group rarely lasts beyond the second generation, while in the United States it may last much longer.[1]

In contemporary Latin America this assimilative "ideology" may be linked to the newly kindled nationalism of a people of "mixed-race" provenience. More significant, perhaps, are its affinities with certain enduring premises of a Catholic society to be examined later in this essay. For what is demanded of the immigrant to Latin America is not so much outward conformity as the inner acceptance of a hierarchical, diversified, and functionally compartmented social order which permits of much eccentricity and affective release.

The drama that is central to the forging of Latin-American society, or societies, is not a narrowly construed history of interethnic or inter-"racial" accommodation. When we survey the whole land area of Latin America—the South American continent, Middle America, and the Caribbean archipelago—we perceive it as the theater for a massive confrontation of three peoples, each at the start playing a broadly different functional role: the Europeans (predominantly the Spanish and Portuguese), the African Negroes, and the aboriginal Indians. The first came as conquerors and settlers. The second came in slavery. The third occupied an ambivalent status as servants and burden bearers for the settler and as his special ward to be Christianized and "civilized."

Gradually the initial categories of "race" and function ceased to coincide. Some Negro slaves became free. Some Indians were uprooted and Europeanized. Occasional whites became peons. Miscegenation produced a host of mixed types. As the schema of this Catholic, hierarchical society continued to proliferate, social and economic function—in an almost Aristotelian sense—took priority over biological origin in determining social status. This is reflected in the term *castas,* which was applied to persons of mixed race and lower social standing.

Of the three main peoples, the Indians and the Africans each contributed greatly more ethnic and cultural diversity to Latin-American society than did the Europeans. The Indians of the Americas spoke hundreds of tongues and were ranged on a cultural scale from technological simplicity and bare subsistence production to the great

Maya, Inca, and Aztec civilizations that the missionary Las Casas compared favorably (if somewhat misleadingly) to those of Greece and Rome. The enslaved Negroes came from a congeries of African tribes and kingdoms that were perhaps as culturally diverse as the Indian societies.

Apart from the latter-day immigration to southern South America, the European migration to Latin America has been mostly Iberian. With limited exceptions non-Iberians were denied admittance to the Spanish Indies and colonial Brazil. Incursions of other European nations in the Western Hemisphere were warded off, as happened in the case of the French and Dutch in Brazil, or else they caused the removal of territory from Iberian sovereignty, as in the case of the Guianas, British Honduras, Saint Domingue, Jamaica, the lesser Antilles—and the vast tracts of British and French North America. In the nineteenth century the migration of United States settlers to northern Mexico led to similar territorial amputation.

The Iberian migration to the New World has been of exceptional duration. And although the early waves of conquerors and colonizers were selective, the subsequent flow came to represent a relatively full class, occupational, and regional spectrum of Spanish and Portuguese society. In our own century forty per cent of the nearly one million immigrants to Brazil since the Second World War have been from the mother country, while one of the most important cultural influences upon modern Mexico has been the arrival of large numbers of exiled Spanish intellectuals.

Spanish and Portuguese colonization was fed by a highly orthodox migration, rather than one by which the mother country spun off unmanageable dissident sects. In 1501 Governor Ovando, of Hispaniola, was instructed to admit to the colony no Jews, Moors, or even reconciled heretics and recent converts from Islam. Later, sons and grandsons of such persons were excluded, as well as gypsies and, of course, Protestants. The exclusion was not wholly effective, particularly in the case of converted Jews, or New Christians, who possessed commercial aptitude. There were always clandestine means of reaching America, which Portuguese Jews especially found ways to utilize. During the colonial period, however, there existed no openly practicing heterodox communities of European or Mediterranean origin. To preserve the purity of the faith the Inquisition was established in Peru (1570), New Spain (1571), and New Granada (1610); but the prevalent religious solidarity caused its attention to be directed, with notable exceptions, largely to censorship and petty discipline.[2] The Indians were not even subject to its jurisdiction.

Although from a political point of view the church in Spanish America was practically a national one, its members shared in a spiritual community that was age-old and universal, the "true" Church. The realm of faith, therefore, worked against the factors making for the separatism of America from the mother country and from the medieval Christian heritage. Religious exclusivism was imposed on the Indies by the crown, and by the agents of state and church, to unify the empire. It did not, as in the Puritan colonies, emanate from the settlers as a point of self-definition vis-à-vis the old continent. Crystallizations of religious practice and doctrine that are characteristically Spanish American must therefore be viewed as occurring within a Catholic realm of faith deemed timeless and boundless. Among these mutations one might list: (1) The tension between fundamentalist or millennialist missionary programs and the bureaucratic conservatism of the ecclesiastical hierarchy and the urban clergy. (2) The emergence of syncretic Indo-Catholic and Afro-Catholic forms of worship. (3) The pragmatic, utilitarian, and pedagogical emphasis given to scholastic thought when it was transplanted to the colonial universities.

With regard to social origins the settlement of Spanish America has been called "a work of eminently popular character." Spanish aristocrats of the highest stratum maintained "an attitude of reserve and inhibition" toward the conquest. They took part in it neither as *caudillos* nor as entrepreneurs. They opposed the recruitment of rural workers from their estates for overseas colonization. "It was the *segundones hijosdalgo* [younger sons of the lesser nobility] who in large part fed the expeditions of new discovery and settlement that left for the Indies."[3] These were marginal persons, claimants of social prestige to whom the primogeniture system denied economic security and for whom only bureaucratic, military, or ecclesiastical careers were socially acceptable. The spectrum of emigration during the sixteenth century has been identified as follows:

Friars and priests were numerous, especially after the third decade of the century; members of the upper nobility, almost none; segundones *of noble houses,* caballeros, and hijosdalgo, *doubtless many, and . . . they gave the general tone to the emigration, beyond what their numerical proportion would suggest. The warrior group, more or less veterans in the service of arms, predominates at the start and falls off after the big conquests. Lawyers and intellectuals were relatively few, but here also their prestige and influence are disproportionate to their number. There are many merchants and even more farmers and artisans of many crafts, whose emigration the Crown encouraged with perhaps more tenacity than result. Under the equivocal label "servants and retinue" given to some emigrants there traveled many who are today impossible to identify and were of very diverse social condition. Adventurers and persons of the lowest social status emigrated in great number but without setting the general tone of the nascent society overseas.*

Foreigners were few in the emigration, which was legally prohibited to them save for partial and temporary authorizations, above all during 1526-1538. But at the margin of the law they were quite numerous, especially Portuguese, and some Italians, French, Germans, English, etc. . . . But in any case they are soon assimilated by the Spanish population.[4]

Royal decrees of 1492 and 1497 authorized recruitment of criminals for overseas expeditions, but these were rescinded in 1505. The criminal element among the settlers was probably not significant, although as late as 1680 the Laws of the Indies approved the participation of delinquent persons in colonizing expeditions providing they were not under accusation by a private party.

The royal instructions of 1513 to Pedrarias Dávila, Governor of Tierra Firme, ordered that he minimize quarrels among his settlers by including no lawyers among them, and that instead he take "farmers so that there they may attempt to plant the soil." Charles V, who had supported Las Casas' ill-fated scheme for colonizing Tierra Firme in 1520, ordered in 1523 that "as many farmers and working people as possible" be sent to New Spain. In 1565 Philip II authorized passage to Hispaniola for a hundred and fifty Portuguese farmers, at least a third to be married and accompanied by their families.

By and large, however, a society of small farmers failed to take shape. Spain could not export many, and in America the lure of the mines, the possibilities for large-scale, pre-emptive acquisition of land, and the opportunities for exploiting Indian and African labor militated against such a design. Yet two points are well to remember. First, an interstitial class of small, independent, often mestizo landowners did arise, descended from conquerors who had not "struck it rich"—such as the rancheros of northern Mexico. It has been pointed out that in the seventeenth century the vigorous growth of small holdings in Cuba contrasted sharply with the rapid centralization of sugar plantations in British-held Barbados.[5] Second, the ideal of a society of modest but prosperous communities of landholders has always been present in Latin America. It has roots in the Iberian municipal tradition of the Middle Ages and to some degree in pre-Columbian Indian tradition. It was kept alive in the colonial period by latecoming immigrants, who made the towns their battleground for rights to farm in peace. It reappeared, cast in Lockean rhetoric, in the often misconceived or misapplied agrarian laws of the nineteenth century. And the image of a prosperous, independent peasantry still hovers in land-reform proposals of our own time.

The ratio of men to women is another important aspect of the early Spanish migration. Columbus took no women on his first voyage, and probably none on the second. Of the twenty-five hundred persons who accompanied Ovando in 1502, about seventy-five were women with their husbands. Laws were soon passed prohibiting the emigration of single women or of married ones without their husbands. Then in 1511 the House of Trade was ordered to let single women sail as deemed necessary, and a year later Morisco women were authorized to take passage as "white slaves" so as to reduce intermarriage with the Indians. Although not opposed in principle to miscegenation, the crown increasingly opposed the Spaniards' informal domestic arrangements with Indian women. Laws were repeatedly passed to forbid married men to emigrate without special license and to repatriate emigrants whose wives remained in Spain. Sometimes a governor's wife would bring to America an entourage of well-born ladies, who were easily married off. To many expeditions of conquest the wife or mistress of a leader added a special dash of romance. Yet by and large the female emigrants were few. Between 1509 and 1533 they numbered only four hundred and seventy of the forty-six hundred recorded passengers to the Indies. Three centuries later, at the close of the colonial period, Humboldt found only two hundred and seventeen European women in Mexico City as against two thousand one hundred and eighteen European men.

The universality with which Indian and Negro women served as wives or concubines for the white men leads one to suspect the transmission of lasting psychological tonalities to the New World society. To be sure, many stable and legal interracial unions occurred from the earliest years, especially between the Spaniards and Indian women. Such marriages were even of social benefit to the lowborn European if his wife was of Indian nobility. The offspring in these cases tended to become thoroughly Hispanized in their upbringing. More frequently the interracial conjugal liaison was unstable, sexually exploitative, and scarcely conducive to the psychological composure of the offspring. Possibly this type of union between the conquering and the subject races permanently affected the tone of male-female relations throughout Latin America. On the sugar plantations of Brazil and the Antilles, for example, the Iberian woman came to represent for the white man a chivalric ideal of purity bordering on frigidity, quite divorced from the sensuality of the slave girl.

In the formative years of the new societies mixed offspring tended either to be absorbed into the class and culture of the mother or, if recognized by the father, to become Europeanized, that is, to become creoles. By the seventeenth century separate categories of the social schema were developing to accommodate mixed-blood types. At the same time the diversification of economic life created marginal or intermediate avenues of release from servile status. A cultural consequence of miscegenation was that in the long run the mother, the principal transmitter of culture during childhood, could impart her Indian or African heritage only fragmentarily to her mestizo or mulatto children. This contributed to strip down the cultural legacy, to make the mixed-blood generation creatures more of environment than of tradition.

Historically the mestizo or mulatto has been viewed as having a wandering, unreliable spirit with no fixed allegiance. His ambivalent station at the threshold between two culture groups, whatever its penalties, evoked a sharp talent for pragmatic accommodation. This was acknowledged in the saying that northern Brazil was "a hell for blacks, a purgatory for whites, and a paradise for mulattoes." Eric Wolf calls the mestizo the ancestor of that "multitude of scribes, lawyers, go-betweens, influence peddlers, and undercover agents" who are the *coyotes* of modern Middle America, a term once applied to the mixed-blood, now designating the whole tribe of the socially and culturally disinherited who spend their days blinding the eyes of the law. Wolf goes on to posit an antithesis between Indian and mestizo. The Indian was community-rooted, the mestizo rootless. The Indian clung to group norms, the mestizo could change his behavior like a mask. One was saturnine, introverted, closed in a local universe, the other outgoing, adroit, and worldly. One valued land and manual work, the other valued personal power and the talent for manipulating people and situations. The Indian was bound to routine and reality, the mestizo was estranged from society, caught up in fantasies of personal domination and plagued at the same time by fears of his own worthlessness.[6]

In the nineteenth century, when Latin-American intellectuals felt called upon to apologize for the economic and political backwardness of their countries, many had recourse to newly fashionable theories of social evolution which deplored the deleterious effects of race mixing. The mestizo image just presented lent credence to such views. Yet this same image has positive components which under the pressures of insurgent nationalism serve self-congratulatory ends. Our own century has heard militant declarations about an emergent "cosmic race" in Latin America. Revolutionary movements, notably the Mexican, have accorded the mestizo a central cultural identification. For public purposes stress may now be given to the creative cultural composite which the mestizo is alleged to represent rather than to his psychological ambivalences and roguish talents for accommodation. Whatever the new mythology may lack in sociological accuracy is compensated by the vigor of its political appeal.*

*Octavio Paz, however, notes the ultimate irrelevance of any racial propaganda in modern Mexico: "The Mexican does not want to be either an Indian or a Spaniard. Nor does he want to be descended from them. He denies them. And he does not affirm himself as a mixture, but rather as an abstraction: he is a man. He becomes the son of Nothingness. His beginnings are in his own self." *The Labyrinth of Solitude* (New York, 1961), p. 87.

Given the extent of miscegenation, and the extent to which the
successive Spanish and republican regimes have weighed upon the
Indian burden bearers, it may well be wondered how the Indian peoples themselves and their culture traits have been preserved over large
areas of the Middle American and Andean highlands. If the proportion of Indian-speaking citizens has decreased to fifteen per cent in
Mexico, it is still over fifty per cent in Guatemala and Bolivia. Aspects
of the Indian labor system under the Spaniards will be treated later.
Suffice it for now to observe that it depends wholly on one's point
of view whether Spanish colonizing policies be deemed a success or
a failure for the extreme gradualism with which large groups of Indians are still being assimilated into Western culture. Similarly, how
do we evaluate the fact that the monuments in modern Mexico are to
Cuauhtémoc and not Cortés, or that Indian prayermakers of Guatemala still chant to their own gods in their own tongue in the Catholic cathedral of Chichicastenango?

By most criteria the Indians were exploited under Spain. Indeed,
they were virtually exterminated in the Antilles, while in Middle
America the aboriginal population dropped within a century from a
preconquest total of twelve to fifteen million to perhaps two million—
a decline attributable, however, more to the white man's diseases
than to out-and-out maltreatment. Only in our own time has the population of central Mexico recovered its pre-Cortesian density. Yet
throughout this long and traumatic confrontation of cultures, the
plight of the Indian and the remnants of his civilization were always
present to the Spanish state and to the church. Even when the Indian
became a "forgotten man" under the ostensibly egalitarian constitutions of the nineteenth-century republics, members of his "race"—a
Carrera in Guatemala, a Júarez in Mexico—might become national
chief executives. It is in fact a truism that "race" has socioeconomic,
not biological, meaning in Latin America, and an adage that an Indian who puts on shoes ceases being an Indian.

In our century the presence of the Indian is once again deeply felt.
The symbols of his culture are invoked in nationalistic or demagogic
appeals, both with and independently of the mestizo composite.
They are reimbodied, militantly or nostalgically, by the artist. Social
scientists lavish more analysis on the process of the Indian's acculturation, or Westernization, than on the pivotally important role of the
emerging middle classes. All this may have only meager benefits for
the Indian in equivalent social justice. If so, it is partly because the
current stage of economic development and capital accumulation
implies upheaval and sacrifice for the whole of the proletariat. The
image of the Indian is still a cultural force to be conjured with. So
lastingly did Spain identify this force that J. C. Mariátegui, a Peruvian Marxist of the nineteen-twenties, expressed guarded admira-

tion for the "socialistic" Jesuit missions of colonial Paraguay, and some agrarian reformers of our own day are known to take Spanish colonial legislation as a model for their proposals.

If the mountain backbone of Latin America from Mexico south to Bolivia and Paraguay can be thought of as Indo- or Mestizo America, it is justifiable to think of the Antilles (especially Haiti and the non-Hispanic islands) and the Caribbean-Atlantic coastal zone from Mexico south to northern Brazil as Afro-, Negro, or Mulatto America. In this area, and also in the coastal valleys of Peru and the hot lands of Mexico, the Europeans organized afresh a system of intensive tropical or semitropical agriculture rather than, as in the highlands, taking over and adapting an existing regime of production. As the early missionaries witnessed the rapid disintegration of Indian society in the Antilles they recommended, as a solution *faute de mieux,* the importation of African slaves. Later some, like Las Casas, had second thoughts about the advice. But by 1520 the African slave trade was well under way.

The characteristic rural employment for the Negro was on the sugar plantation, a more clearly "modern" or capitalistic agricultural system than the Indian encomienda to be described later. The Negro was imported as a capital investment and was bought and sold as chattel. Within the Iberian tradition, however—notably in the *Siete Partidas,* the thirteenth-century Spanish law code—the slave was still accorded a position in society which assured him certain minimum guarantees. He was not considered infrahuman. Spanish laws for the Indies contained no such comprehensive protective code for the Negro as for the Indian. Yet there existed stipulations for his treatment and education which were tardily brought together in 1789.

It is generally from a contemporary vantage point and in contrast to situations in the United States or South Africa that the history of Negro-white relations in Latin America is termed "mild." It does seem true that manumission, both by masters and through co-operative efforts of the slaves themselves, was a fairly general practice in Latin America. It also seems true that Negro freedmen enjoyed reliable assurances of their status as free Christian subjects, even though they may have been denied many perquisites of personal dignity (ostentatious dress, firearms, et cetera) or had difficult access to education. The case can perhaps be made that the elaborate nomenclature applied in the colonial period to scores of the possible biological combinations of Negro, Indian, and white reflected less a morbid preoccupation with racial "purity" ("purity" could in fact be legally purchased, even by the slightly "impure") than a classificatory, Catholic habit of mind representing acceptance of a diverse and unwieldy order of the world.

Two contrasting interpretations of the antecedents of Negro-white relations in the New World are those of Frank Tannenbaum and Eric Williams. Tannenbaum holds that the Negro in Latin America, as slave and freedman, has always been recognized to have a legal and moral personality. This he attributes to the long, precapitalist experience of the Iberian peoples with the institution of slavery, to safeguards embedded in their law and custom, to the tolerant and humane ethos of the Catholic church. That is, their inherited experience and wisdom place the Latin Americans *ahead of* North Americans.[7] Williams argues from a Marxist viewpoint that an ostensibly milder slave regime in a Latin country simply meant that it was *behind* in its institutional development. If, for example, slaves were less oppressed in Cuba than in Jamaica in the eighteenth century, this signified that the sugar industry did not reach its exploitative, fully capitalistic phase in Cuba till a later period.[8] A more recent analysis, pitched on psychosocial rather than historico-institutional grounds, suggests that racial attitudes are partly governed by differing "somatic norm-images" of the dominant groups. The Iberian norm-image, it is held, is "darker" than the northwest European one, thus allowing the mulatto, but not necessarily the Negro, greater mobility in an Iberian society.[9] This argument has at least the merit of addressing the question of race relations without detouring to establish a comparative index of slaveowners' malevolence.

Perhaps as important to the tone of contemporary race relations as the nature of the institution of slavery is the process of emancipation. Much of Jim Crowism in the United States originated in the fears, resentments, and trauma consequent upon a bloody fratricidal war. Abolition in mainland Spanish America was declared as part of the movement of national independence (Mexico, Central America, Chile, Argentina) or peacefully a generation later as an expression of liberal nationalism (Andean countries). For Puerto Rico (1873) and Cuba (1880) it came through domestic and international political pressures upon the mother country. In Brazil emancipation did not come until 1888, when it was enacted with a stroke of the pen, by which time alternative sources of immigrant labor had been found in Europe and the coffee planters themselves were forming abolition societies. The most dramatic case was that of Haiti, whose independence (1804) was the result of a mass revolt against a slave-owning oligarchy. With the expulsion of the French, a new "mulatto" elite of those who had previously been freedmen faced the Negro masses. Haitian society and politics today still gravitate around this polarity, which has aspects too complex for explication by conventional paradigms for "race relations."

In the panorama of colonial Spanish American society it was the Indians, Negroes, and a growing class of half-caste laborers and artisans who accomplished the toil of economic production. Here and there existed groups of white farmers, grazers, or artisans, but they were uncharacteristic. At the same time the creole, or American-born white, was practically excluded from high civil and ecclesiastical offices and from important commercial enterprises. This was despite the fact that both creoles and mestizos from legitimate unions enjoyed theoretical parity with Spaniards under the law. It has been calculated that only four of all the viceroys were creoles (all sons of Spanish officials), fourteen of the six hundred and two captains-general, governors, and presidents, and one hundred and five of the seven hundred and six bishops and archbishops. Paradoxically, the breed of conquerors and colonizers became a marginal group with respect to economic production and administrative responsibility except on a local and subordinate scale.

In the sixteenth century all whites, whether American- or Spanish-born, were called "Spaniards." Inevitably the career expectancies, life styles, and even personalities of these groups began to diverge. As a way of asserting self-identity the "Americans" appropriated the term "creole," hitherto applied, somewhat disparagingly, only to Africans born in America. The early creole elite were the conquerors who secured encomiendas of Indians and their direct descendants who enjoyed them. Most of the conquerors were of humble origin, and the crown, fearing creole autonomy and separatism, never bestowed titles of nobility on Americans. By the late seventeenth century this informal aristocracy was broken up because of the unproductiveness or the revocation of many early encomienda grants. There consequently occurred a circulation of the creole elite as new landed oligarchies arose and those once privileged drifted into lesser bureaucratic, commercial, or openly parasitic occupations. The creole group therefore ranged widely on the social scale, yet internally it was fluid and demarcated neither by formal titles of nobility nor by gradations of fiscal privilege. The Indians paid tribute, whites did not. As the creole element grew in size and in self-awareness, their disparate composition failed to prevent them from sharing, by and large, feelings of resentment toward the peninsular Spaniard and of hauteur toward the Indians and *castas*. Their pride of origin and status, their inclinations toward leisure, indolence, and luxury, their mannered elegance and verbalism engaged the notice of more than a few travelers from the mother continent.

After independence it was the creoles who took over the organization and leadership of the new republics. Although habituated to the attitude of command, they had been accorded no generously defined functions and responsibilities in the colonial world. They had been born into a vast, tradition-bound, seemingly permanent Hispano-Catholic society, highly layered and compartmented, in which status, after the conquest years, was a matter more of definition than of achievement. Yet in the anarchic fragments of that society there was suddenly thrust upon them the role of forging new nations. It is largely the ideals, attitudes, ambitions, confusions, and compulsions manifested by this group which, in constellation, have become the cultural determinants for society and personality in Latin America: their medieval, Catholic concern with hierarchy, with honor and personal loyalty, with rhetoric, with casuistry, with expressiveness, with the wholeness of things; their creole ambivalences, sensitivities, self-denigration and braggadocio, habits of command and of deference; and their stock of half-absorbed ideas from the arsenals of Anglo-French "enlightened" thought.

The intricate structure of the mixed-blood *castas* which interposed between the creoles and the servile races reached its apogee in the eighteenth century. By the end of that century it was in dissolution, and the functional boundaries between creole and mixed-blood, particularly between creole and mestizo, became more and more permeable. The mestizo became creolized socially and culturally; the creole was increasingly absorbed into the racial mix. In our own century it has become clear that the homogenizing process will not be stayed even at the threshold of the "exotic" enclaves of Indian and African culture which still remain. These remnants will in the long run leave coloration rather than structure in the creole patterns of life and society. Those who plan the social and economic "development" of modern Latin America must therefore reckon primarily with the creole cultural fix which it long ago took.

Population of Latin America c. 1570

	Whites (or so considered)	Negroes, mestizos, mulattoes	Indians (Tribute-paying)	Total Indians	Total population
Mexico, Central America, Antilles	52,500	91,000	(893,370)	4,072,150	4,215,650
Spanish South America	65,500	139,000	(980,000)	4,955,000	5,159,500
Brazil	20,000	30,000	—	800,000	850,000
Totals	138,000	260,000	(1,873,370)	9,827,150	10,225,150
Per cent	1.4%	2.5%		96.1%	100%

41
Richard M.
Morse

Population of Latin America c. 1825
(Era of independence)

	Whites (or so considered)	*Negroes, mestizos, mulattoes*	*Indians*	*Total population*
Mexico, Central America, Antilles	1,992,000	4,641,000	4,580,000	11,213,000
Spanish South America	1,426,000	2,913,000	3,250,600	7,589,600
Brazil	920,000	2,660,000	360,000	3,940,000
Totals	4,338,000	10,214,000	8,190,600	22,742,600
Per cent	19.1%	44.9%	36.0%	100%

Source: Angel Rosenblat, *La población indígena y el mestizaje en América*
(2 vols., Buenos Aires, 1954), I, 36, 88.

2. The Institutional Order

The impression which many may have of the Spanish colonization
of America is that it was the work of relatively free-acting conquistadors and their followers, avid for products of soil and subsoil, in particular gold and silver, and for the servile labor to be used in extract-
ing them. Others, who applaud the "individualism" of the self-reliant
settlements of British North America, criticize the Spanish regime
in America for having stifled colonial development with statism, bureaucracy, and discrimination against creoles. It is therefore important to distinguish the roles played by private and public initiative
and to appreciate the connotations of each in the Spanish American
context.

The early institutional history of Spanish America is conventionally divided into a preliminary period of exploration and conquest,
when individual enterprise loomed large; a period of institutional
organization, lasting for a generation or more after the arrival of the
first viceroy of New Spain in 1535; and a long period of institutional
stability lasting until the eighteenth-century Bourbon reforms.

This periodization has been challenged by Mario Góngora, who
argues that exploration, conquest, and colonization were intermingled
and alternating processes. He therefore posits a combined phase of
settlement lasting from 1492 to 1570. Although the state's resources
were insufficient to underwrite and manage the vast colonizing oper-

ation: "Neither the conquests nor the colonization are private enterprises, undertaken at the margin of the Castilian state."[10] Apart from a
few important voyages subsidized by the crown (Columbus, Pedrarias
Dávila, Magellan), the recruitment and financing of most expeditions were left to private initiative. Permission was given for such
undertakings, however, only if they conformed to the broad policies
of the state.

Góngora reminds us that although the Spanish state had acquired
a strong administrative nucleus by the sixteenth century, it was not
yet, as it later became, "a unitary and rationalized whole, dominated
by the 'monism of sovereignty.'" Political jurisdiction and other
rights brought together in the king were exercised through the bureaucracy. But they might be delegated or conceded as privileges that
could be defended juridically against the king himself.[11] The categories
of the public and private spheres, established under revived Roman
law, were still in process of elaboration. Thus the conquistador was
not a "free" entrepreneur under a private contract. He was under
continuing obligation to ask the crown for privileges, such as grants
of Indian labor. His contract (*capitulación*) linked "freely assembled
[social] forces with the power of the state" and "converted them into
political elements."

The state, then, is a colonizing state (*Estado Poblador*), operating
through laws, customs, and judicial and administrative decisions.
Grants of soil (farm and ranch) and subsoil (mines) are founded in
royal concession, not in private law. Colonization implies the organizing of a congeries of civil and ecclesiastical jurisdictions and hierarchies; a regime of defense, taxation, and tribute; systems of schools
and universities. Not only do economic life and claims to the land
have their origin in the state, but also the whole colonizing process is
conceived as having the "politico-civilizing" function of transmitting
Western Christian culture. Some political and philosophical implications of the foregoing will be examined later. For now, the critical
point is that the sixteenth-century Spanish conception of the state was
in many respects still medieval. The state was an "institutional equivalent of temporal human life in all its fullness."[12] It contained only in
embryo such possibilities as the rationalistic "statist" state of seventeenth-century mercantilism, the bourgeois free-enterprise state, or
the nineteenth-century "imperialist" state.

From Columbus onward the discoverers and conquistadors took
possession of new lands and new oceans in the name of the crown.
The Indians were considered crown vassals to be protected and Christianized—and to be taxed. An expeditionary leader might be given a
liberal contract for life (or for two or more lives, i.e., generations) to
distribute and settle land, found towns, engage in commerce, use
Indian labor, and so forth. But his expedition was accompanied by

royal officials and ecclesiastics, representing the broad political, fiscal, and spiritual interests of the crown.

Gradually there emerged as an embedding context for the *capitulaciones:* (1) an elaborate casuistry distilled from the polemics of jurists and theologians which justified the Spanish title to the Indies and set down principles for treatment of the native Indians, and (2) a multiform series of hierarchies, civil and ecclesiastical, that exhibited both functional overlap among agencies and coalescence of function (especially administrative and judicial) within given agencies. These hierarchies culminated in the arbitrating crown, which delegated its power hesitantly and erratically. The legal apparatus for empire betrayed its medieval origins. It was *informed by* the broad Christian principles of the theologians and jurists, and it frequently *took the form* of trifling adminstrative detail. The various legal codifications such as the 1573 colonizing ordinances and the 1680 Laws of the Indies were essentially compilations, rather than systematizations that might have brought natural-law principles and administrative decrees into a single rationalized frame.

That this form of government signified deprivation of autonomy for Spanish America and meager preparation for independent nationhood is often pointed out. Nevertheless, the theoretical premise for royal centralization was not colonial subjection of the Indies, but the assumption that the New World viceroyalties were realms coequal with those of Spain, having equal claims to redress from the crown. The Council of the Indies was not a mere colonial office, but had ministerial status. The viceroy of New Spain or Peru was the king's proxy. He and the lesser crown-appointed officials were under elaborate regulations not to acquire local interests, economic or personal, in their jurisdictions, and they underwent judicial review at the end of their terms. In the case of both Spanish America and Brazil one can argue that it was only under the "enlightened" peninsular monarchies of the eighteenth century and the "liberal" revolutionary regimes of the Napoleonic era that a status, "colonial" in the modern sense, was adumbrated. The differences between Hapsburg rule, under which Spanish American institutions were established, and Bourbon rule, which tried somewhat ineffectually to reform them, has been called the difference between absolutism and despotism.

The insistence upon the neo-medievalism of Spanish American colonial institutions reflects no intent to romanticize them. It looks toward identifying an institutional model which the first eighty years of Spanish rule left implanted in the Indies. This model, which has sociopsychological as well as sociostructural implications, was to conflict with many adminstrative directives of the Bourbon period. It was to conflict even more sharply with the ideas and ideals, constitutions and reforms, which swept in on the independent Spanish American nations after 1830. It continues to conflict at many points with twentieth-century programs of "development"—political, social, and economic.

There was, of course, a practical motivation for the Spanish monarchs' concern with the Christian treatment of the Indian and for the sixteenth-century debates as to his rationality and the propriety of enslaving him. This was the threat to the crown's income and political control posed by the conquistadors once they were established in their new domains. The centrifugal movement of settlers out into farm, ranch, and mining lands, far removed from seaports and administrative centers (with these in turn distant from Spain by a long and arduous sea voyage), created the danger of virtually sovereign satrapies, each enjoying absolute control of Indian workers who, in the Mexican and Andean highlands and in Paraguay, offered relatively slight resistance to their new masters. As a result, and:

... in the face of the excessive privileges granted by the monarchs themselves to the first discoverers and their descendants, the officials of the Court and the Audiencias *reacted by retrieving all the grants of the Crown in the discovered lands, through long suits, tenaciously sustained.*[13]

Since Tocqueville the growth of the centralized state in Western Europe has been described as a process which undermines local autonomy and initiative and which, by equalizing all citizens before the law and the state bureaucracy, weakens the protection afforded them by community ties and customs. In Spanish America under the Hapsburgs the role of the state was in some respects precisely the opposite. Central to its function was the preservation or creation of Indian communities which would maintain their own way of life, be protected against excessive exploitation, and have independent access to royal justice and to spiritual guidance and consolation. The Laws of the Indies contained extensive tutelary legislation which respected the Indians' cultural identity. Indian tongues were taught in the universities. Indians were not subject to the Inquisition. Spaniards, Negroes, and mulattoes were not permitted to live in Indian villages, nor were mestizos who had not been born there. Even the Spanish encomenderos were not to live among the Indians from whom they received work. A traveling Spaniard could stay in an Indian community only "the day he arrived and one other"; merchants could stay only three days.

In short, the cultural assimilation of the Indian, as distinct from his formal religious conversion, was conceived as a long-term process during the course of which he was to be protected from exploitation, degradation, and slavery at the hands of encomenderos, merchants, and bureaucrats. Some have called the Laws of the Indies the most comprehensive and humanitarian code ever devised by an important colonizing power. Few would deny, however, that their enforcement was greatly wanting. As the occasion demanded and circumstances permitted, ways were found in which to exact grueling forced labor of Indians, notably in the mines and in the *obrajes* (textile factories). The corregidors of Indian towns, who exercised political and juridical authority, regularly exploited their wards for personal gain, often in conspiracy with the priests and Indian caciques.

It serves little purpose, however, to assess out of context the degree of the Spaniards' cruelty toward or exploitation of the conquered Indians. In an age which saw the predatory forces of commercial capitalism unleashed, and the face of Europe ravaged by religious persecution and the havoc of the Thirty Years' War, it would be fatuous to expect the conquest of a new continent and its millions of pagans to have lacked ferocity and trauma. What concerns us are the implications which the particular premises and patterns of colonization held for the long-run "set" of New World institutions. Before specifying some of these implications, we should examine more closely the actual assault upon the land and resources of America, from which local interests and social structures flowed as an undertow to the wave of formal colonizing policy and missionary purpose.

We have suggested that there was much which was medieval to the apparatus, operation, and rationale of the Spanish state. Such traditional characteristics, however, as the Christian, tutelary purposes of the state, the multiform hierarchy culminating in a mediatorial monarch, and the scholastic intellectual orientations served as an armature to a core of relations between man and land and between privileged and underprivileged groups that was largely defined by place and circumstance. Mario Góngora has said that the system of estates, in the strict sense of social orders having rights of representation, did not exist in the Indies because no Cortes (i.e., parliamentary body) was established.

> *In a period when the granting of subsidies or pecuniary assistance to the King and the accompanying request for privileges was at the heart of the internal life of the State, the Indies—relatively free of tribute and paying the King the royal fifths and other perquisites which did not require consent—did not exhibit the political density and the pronounced King-Kingdom dualism characteristic of Europe in this era.*[14]

Only in the broader sense of groups "having common jurisdictional privileges" can estates be said to have existed in Spanish America. The state was of a corporate character. Within it, there were independently defined privileges and jurisdictions for broad groups (Indians, Europeans, ecclesiastics, Negroes) as well as for smaller component groups, such as: Indians in missions, *pueblos de indios,* Indians on encomiendas; merchants, university students, artisans; regular clergy, secular clergy, inquisitorial officials; Negro slaves, colored freedmen, and so forth. The medieval imprint which the system as a whole bore was not that of parliamentary representation, but that of pluralistic, compartmented privilege and of administrative paternalism.

Sánchez-Albornoz argues persuasively that the institutions of classical feudalism had never fully developed in Spain itself.[15] In summary his argument runs as follows. During the reconquest of the central tableland from the Moors, roughly A.D. 850 to 1200, cities and castles served as the advance points of resettlement. From these nuclei the work of colonization was undertaken only with maximum guarantees of personal liberty and freedom of movement. Few colonists were tied permanently to the soil or to a lord. Society had, relatively speaking, a fluidity which worked against the solidifying of a complex net of vassalic relations or the emergence of a stable, conservative bourgeoisie. The commoner who could equip himself with arms and a steed was valuable to the crown and could become a lesser knight or, in the almost contradictory phrase, a *caballero villano.* He might even owe fealty directly to the king rather than to a blood noble.

The importance of the central authority to the reconquest meant that the strength of the crown and the organization of the state never faded out, as in the Carolingian realm. Even when the centralizing process was temporarily checked in the tenth century, the crown never recognized the usurpations of nobles. The flood of feudal ideas and practices which entered Spain in the eleventh century with warrior or pilgrim knights from Northern Europe, and with royal marriages to French princesses, was not accompanied by the juridical formulae of feudalism. Thus in Castile-León lay lords had not the privilege to coin money; a vassal could not acquire contractual relations with two or more lords; the ties between all subjects and the state were never displaced by personal ties between vassals and lords.

The advancing frontier periodically renewed the spoils and prebends which the crown could distribute, thus renewing its economic and military potential. The towns were strong and numerous, and not merely islands dispersed in a feudal sea. They were an active counterweight to the church and the nobility; to keep pace with them the nobles were forced to beg additional lands, honors, and prebends from the crown. When in the thirteenth century a struggle developed between crown and nobles, it was not one by which the crown strove to break feudal power (as in France) or by which the knights strove to retrict royal power (as in Germany), but a contest by both to control an extant state apparatus.

With respect to organization for economic production, as distinct from sociopolitical organization, the following factors should be borne in mind as militating against the emergence of a manorial regime in the Spanish Indies:

(1) Spain itself never witnessed a flowering of the classic manorial pattern of other parts of Europe because of the seven centuries of strife between Christians and Moors, and because of the privileges, prejudicial to agricultural development, acquired by the medieval sheep raisers' guild.

(2) A manorial system implies that lord and worker share a common culture and a traditional legal regime of mutual obligation. Clearly, such a context was lacking for Spaniard and Indian, to say nothing of Spaniard and African. As suggested above, the tutelary state or the "universal" church (usually through its regular orders) was the ultimate protector of the Indian worker, not the local agrarian unit.

(3) The manorial system takes form in vegetative, decentralized fashion in a nonurban economy, generating and perpetuated by local tradition, reflecting stability and balance both social and ecological. The initial settlement of America was accomplished by a mere handful of men, not simply avid for gold as is sometimes said, but certainly in quest of status and fame as these might be embodied in specie (however fleetingly retained), land, and a situation of authority free of manual toil. In vast land areas with immeasurable natural resources and native labor potential, it was inevitable that honor, status, and possession should be factored out of the medieval social complex. Henceforth, for example, status might be acquired by control of land rather than the relation to land being a function of status. Or, honor and status might be achieved through heroism, rather than heroism being assumed as an attribute of status.

The role of the city must be seen as pivotal to the Spaniards' assault upon the land. The preliminary institution of settlement was customarily the chessboard town or city with its spacious central plaza surrounded by substantial buildings for municipal, imperial, and ecclesiastical administration and for worship. When a town was laid out, the founders each received an urban lot, a grant of outlying farm or ranch land, and rights to lands set aside for common use. Possession of land was contingent upon occupation and cultivation of it, often for five years. In effect, vast tracts of the royal domain were alienated with no operative restriction.[16]

Before the end of the sixteenth century the usurpation of public lands and Indian community lands had become general. As land values rose, the crown became interested in putting unclaimed lands up for sale, and it began to wage intermittent warfare against improper land titles. Finally in 1754 the *audiencias* were empowered to make land grants and were given jurisdiction over questions of title. But all lands that had been occupied since before 1700 were adjudged held by prescription and, if they were under cultivation, their titles were unchallengeable. It was by then too late to arrest the formation of a landed elite whose holdings surrounded the towns and had often made large inroads upon the commons and upon Indian lands. This elite, often of humble or socially marginal origin, was the colonial creole aristocracy. It had extensive social power, especially in the regions distant from the viceregal capitals of New Spain and Peru, although its political participation was generally limited to town government. After Spanish American independence this elite became free to assert its political, economic, and social hegemony on a national scale.

The distribution of land was a process distinct from the distribution of Indian labor. It was a principle early established, though not conscientiously adhered to, that the only enslaveable Indians were cannibals or Indians who refused to acknowledge the Spaniards' sovereignty and were therefore taken in a "just war." In the early years of the occupation of the Greater Antilles, however, the natives, many of them quite submissive, were in effect parceled out for labor. Their culture offered no resistance to the conquering one, and they were soon virtually extinguished. Although the encomienda was used in name in the Antilles, it received institutional definition and development only with the settlement of the mainland.

An encomienda was a distribution and entrusting of a community of Indians to a Spanish colonist who collected from them various forms of tribute and was obliged to protect them and assist their assimilation into Christian civilization. After 1542 the exaction of personal services was expressly, if not effectively, forbidden. The encomienda took its classic form among the more advanced, sedentary Indian societies of the Mexican and Andean highlands, although it gave new and enduring organization to less advanced Indian communities, such as those of Paraguay. The purposes of the encomienda were several: (1) as recompense to deserving conquistadors and their descendants, (2) as a source of tribute to colonist and crown, (3) as a means of utilizing and safeguarding a vast and ready-to-hand labor supply, and (4) as an agency for bringing the aborigines into Spanish Christendom.

The encomienda was not a grant of land. An encomendero had only limited rights to acquire holdings within his encomienda, and these were not to encroach upon Indian community lands. The encomienda further differed from a land grant in that: (1) it was a grant for a limited number of lives and not a permanent alienation, (2) it was a grant conferred by the crown and not locally (although governors and viceroys of Peru enjoyed more delegation of authority in this respect than those of New Spain). Because the encomienda bore only limited resemblance to the medieval manor Góngora prefers the term "patrimonialism" to "feudalism" or "manorialism" for describing the system it represented. His reason is that the conquistadors in their urgency to acquire land and sources of wealth were at the same time bearers of royal authority. They conceived of the state as a mass of lands, tributes, offices, benefices, grants, and honors, belonging to the royal patrimony but legitimately claimed by those who had made them available to the crown.

The specifically vassalic relation of loyalty evaporates before general loyalty of subjects to King; the link between conquistadors and King assumes a new aspect, not through a personal bond distinct from what they have as subjects, but through the relation which they have with the lands, won for the royal domain. [17]

Having distinguished between the medieval manor and the encomienda, we must also differentiate the encomienda from the subsequent hacienda and plantation of Spanish America. By the early eighteenth century encomiendas were becoming less desirable for their holders because of the crown's heavier tributary exactions. Then, in 1718 to 1721, royal decrees ordered the reversion of encomiendas to the crown upon the death of the holders. The institution lingered on for a century more, but only in certain outlying areas.

There may have been regions where encomiendas became converted into haciendas through the years, as the holders asserted claim to Indian lands and virtual authority over Indian workers. There may have been other regions where control of both land and workers was asserted from the start, perhaps in the form of the *estancia*. But more typically, the hacienda seems to have grown out of the municipal land grant and not the encomienda. By offering them manufactures, liquor rations, and prepayment of tribute, landowners could attract Indian communities into bondage through debt. The process began as early as the mid-sixteenth century in Mexico, although it was in the nineteenth century that the hacienda achieved its classic form. In these main respects the hacienda differed from the encomienda: (1) The proprietor held title to the land. (2) The Indian workers had little or no land and were bound to the hacienda through debt peonage. (3) The Indians enjoyed no tutelage from the state and in effect were under the jurisdiction, and at the mercy, of the *hacendado*. Although the Spanish crown was largely ineffectual in controlling the abuses of the hacienda system, it was only when the Indian workers became nominal citizens of independent republics that they suffered the full impact of the predatory social and economic forces unleashed by the conquest, three centuries earlier.

Even in the nineteenth century, however, the hacienda was not a depersonalized, cash-nexus unit of production. The Indians lived community lives in their own cultural ethos, preserving personality traits quite different from the whites and Westernized mestizos. Although victims of the arbitrariness and enforced submissiveness of an overbearing paternalism, they had access to land for their own use and were not subjected to capitalistic demands for maximizing production.

Organized for commercial ends, the hacienda proved strangely hybrid in its characteristics. . . . Geared to sell products in a market, it yet aimed at having little to sell. Voracious for land, it deliberately made inefficient use of it. Operating with large numbers of workers, it nevertheless personalized the relation between worker and owner. Created to produce a profit, it consumed a large part of its substance in conspicuous and unproductive displays of wealth.[18]

It is permissible to think of the hacienda (which occurs mainly in livestock and cereal zones) as a form of agrarian organization intermediate between the encomienda and the plantation. (The term *latifundio* is applied to both haciendas and plantations.) Of the three, the last is most nearly a "capitalistic" institution. The plantation specializes in intensive single-crop production for a world market; it tends to be heavily capitalized and to rely on slave or immigrant labor, utilized more or less efficiently to minimize labor costs. Mechanization, as it becomes available and economical, tends to be introduced on plantations, not on haciendas.

The classic plantation systems were those of the Caribbean sugar islands—the French and British ones in the seventeenth and eighteenth centuries, the Spanish-speaking ones in the nineteenth and twentieth. In Brazil the colonial sugar fazendas, although slave-based, had some features in common with the hacienda. The Brazilian coffee plantations of the past hundred years or so—at first slave-based but soon immigrant-labor-based—more closely follow the plantation model.

In contemporary Latin America the ideal of land reform receives wide support and well-nigh universal lip service. The program of an actual agrarian revolution, however, is importantly determined by whether it affects an hacienda or a plantation economy. In the former case, a revolution such as the Mexican or the Bolivian encounters the problems of expropriating inefficiently used land and redistributing it to peasant communities. At this stage the education of the peasantry to more productive methods—a difficult task in itself—may merely increase production for local consumption and

for betterment of the subsistence level. The next step may have to
be the encouragement of industrialized or plantation agriculture,
for suitable crops in suitable regions, as a means of improving the
national export balance.

When revolution comes to a plantation economy, as it has to Cuba,
the agrarian phase is also difficult to accomplish. For if production
of the leading crop is already rationalized, reasonably efficient, and
best served by large landholdings, loss of efficiency is almost inevitable when control of the plantations passes to the state or to cooperatives. If lands planted to a single cash crop are replanted to
other crops, the nation's foreign trade position probably suffers. If
unused lands are programmed for diversified agriculture, it will be
difficult to recruit labor for them from an already "industrialized"
rural proletariat, and even more difficult to recruit from the cities.

In these ways the agrarian heritage of four centuries weighs heavily upon contemporary Latin America, and the contagious slogan
of "land reform" gives little clue to the diversity and complexity
of the situations where it is to be effected.

3. Political Foundations

Having stressed the adaptation and mutation of Spanish culture
and institutions in the New World, it is important that we examine
more closely the premises and structure that are common to the
parent society and to its New World offshoots. Just as there are
political and psychological assumptions which characterize Protestant societies and transcend, or underlie, the circumstances of time
and place, so may we expect there to exist a common ethos within
which Catholic societies find their historical development.

For conveying the spirit of Protestant colonization there is no
more revealing statement than that made by Martin Luther in his
Open Letter to the Christian Nobility:

*If a little group of pious Christian laymen were taken captive and
set down in a wilderness, and had among them no priest consecrated
by a bishop, and if there in the wilderness they were to agree in
choosing one of themselves, married or unmarried, and were to
charge him with the office of baptizing, saying mass, absolving and
preaching, such a man would be as truly a priest as though all
bishops and popes had consecrated him.*

This passage contains two suggestions important for our purposes.
The first is that a land uninhabited, or inhabited by heathen, is a

"wilderness," a no man's land outside the pale of society, civilization, and church. The second is that the world is composed not of
one highly differentiated society for which certain common forms,
acts, and ceremonies are a needed binding force, but of a *multitude
of unrelated societies,* each of them a congregation of similar persons which is finite in time and place and ordered by the declara-
tive terms of a compact rather than by common symbolic observ-
ances. As Kenneth Burke puts it:

> [*In*] *contrast with the church's "organic" theory, whereby one put a
> going social concern together by the toleration of* differences, *the
> Protestant sects stressed the value of* complete uniformity. *Each
> time this uniformity was impaired, the sect itself tended to split,
> with a new "uncompromising" offshoot reaffirming the need for a
> homogeneous community, all members alike in status.*[19]

If, then, Christendom was for the Spaniard "universal," this
meant that his overseas settlements were not truly "colonies,"
whether orthodox or heterodox, that had been spun off from the
mother country into a "wilderness."[20] Nor was Spanish expansion
properly a "conquest" insofar as this means the acquisition of alien
lands and peoples. In fact the word itself, which Las Casas called
"tyrannical, Mohammedan, abusive, improper, and infernal," was
banned from official use in favor of *pacificación* or *población.*[21]
The term frequently used to designate the extension of Spanish
political rule to America is "incorporation," as for example "the
incorporation of the Indies to the crown of Castile." What is implied is not the annexation of terra incognita but the bringing together of what should rightfully be joined.[22]

To say this much is not to idealize the motives of those who
erected the Spanish empire in America. Fortune-seeking, aggrandizement, fanaticism, escapism were all in evidence. Economically
and otherwise the Spanish Indies were exploited. The point is that
they were incorporated into Christendom, directly under the Spanish crown, by a specially designed and carefully legitimized patrimonial state apparatus. Oppression certainly occurs within such a
realm. But subjects tend to attribute it to bad information, misunderstanding, incompetence, and selfishness originating at lower
administrative levels. The system itself is not seriously challenged,
nor is the authority of the symbolic and irreplaceable crown.[23]

These principles of society and government help us not only to
understand Spanish rule in America, but also to assess the impact
of the Enlightenment on Spanish America, to analyze the process
by which the Spanish American nations became independent, and
to interpret their subsequent political careers. There are scholars
who emphasize the relevance of the ideas of such postmedieval

Spanish thinkers as Vitoria, Molina, and Suárez to the later institutional development of Spain and Spanish America.[24] Others, however, are impatient with any suggestion that the mists of the medieval, Catholic heritage of Spanish America cannot be, or are not being, evaporated by the rays of the Enlightenment. As we see it, the critical question is not the rather empty one as to whether the neo-Thomist Suárez or the Jacobin Rousseau was the intellectual lodestar for the sovereign Spanish American juntas of 1809 to 1810 at the dawn of the independence era.[25] If we accept seriously the notion that Spanish America had taken a cultural and institutional fix long before this time, we are interested in identifying a deep-lying matrix of thought and attitude, not the rhetoric by which it may for the moment have been veiled.

Francisco Suárez (1548-1617) is generally recognized as the thinker who most fully recapitulated Thomist political thought in Spain's age of *Barockscholastik*. This recapitulation was far from being a mere disinterment of Thomism. It reformulated the philosophic dilemmas of the past in a very modern search for a metaphysics that would be epistemologically autonomous. The significance of Suárez for Spanish American political history therefore does not depend upon whether or not he provided a Spanish, pre-Enlightenment precedent for contract theory and popular sovereignty. It lies, rather, in the fact that his fresh marshaling of scholastic doctrines, under powerful influences of time and place, encapsulated certain assumptions about political man and certain political dilemmas that pervade Hispanic political life to this day. Some of the points of Suarezian philosophy relevant to this consideration are the following:

(1) *Natural law is clearly distinguished from conscience.* Natural law is a general rule; conscience is a practical application of it to specific cases. Natural law is never mistaken; conscience may be. Society and the body politic are therefore seen as properly ordered by objective and external natural-law precepts rather than by consensus sprung from the promptings of private consciences. (In societies where such an assumption prevails it is unlikely that the free election and the ballot box will ever attain the mystique which is theirs in Protestant countries.)

(2) *Sovereign power originates with the collectivity of men.* God is the author of civil power, but He created it as a property emanating from nature so that no society would lack the power necessary for its preservation. A proposition of this sort allowed the view that most of the pre-Columbian Indians were not savages but lived in societies ordered by natural law. A second implication, important for the period of independence, was that in the event of a collapse of central authority, power would revert to the sovereign people.

(3) *The people do not* delegate *but* alienate *sovereignty to their prince.* Although the people are in principle superior to the prince, they vest power in him without condition *(simpliciter)* that he may use it as he deems fitting. By contract, then, the prince is superior to the people.

(4) *In certain cases the law of the prince loses its force,* namely: (a) if it is unjust, for an unjust law is not a law; (b) if it is too harsh; (c) if the majority has already ceased to obey it (even though the first to cease obeying would have sinned).

(5) *The prince is bound by his own law.* He cannot, however, be punished by himself or by his people, and is responsible only to God or His representative.

In modern times the difficulties that Spanish American peoples experience in erecting constitutional regimes based on wide popular participation are commonly attributed to: (1) inadequate suffusion with Anglo-French democratic principles; (2) disorderly or unwholesome social conditions characterized by ignorance, poverty, disease, and malnutrition; (3) "Spanish" or "Latin" personalistic psychology. Anchored in the scholastic propositions of Suárez, however, we discern precisely those seeming inconsistencies of political attitude which many would attribute to modern Spanish Americans. Paul Janet summarized them as follows:

> *Such are the Scholastic doctrines of the 16th century, incoherent doctrines in which are united . . . democratic and absolutist ideas, without the author seeing very clearly where the former or the latter lead him. He adopts in all its force the principle of popular sovereignty: he excludes the doctrine of divine law . . . and he causes not simply government but even society to rest upon unanimous consent. But these principles serve only to allow him immediately to effect the absolute and unconditional alienation of popular sovereignty into the hands of one person. He denies the need for consent of the people in the formulation of law; and as guarantee against an unjust law he offers only a disobedience both seditious and disloyal. Finally, he shelters the prince under the power of the laws and sees over him only the judgment of the Church.*[26]

We need not say that Suárez himself was a decisive intellectual influence upon Spanish America's institutional development (although the University of Mexico did have a Suarezian chair, and his doctrines won increasing attention in New Spain during the seventeenth century). The evidence does suggest, however, that his writings are symptomatic of a postmedieval Hispano-Catholic view of man, society, and government which is by no means superseded in modern Spanish America.

It is important to grasp that Spanish neo-Thomism was not a blind, obstinate reaction to the Protestant Reformation any more than it was a romantic revival of ethereal religious aspirations. What it did was to offer sophisticated theoretical formulation of the ideals and many sociological realities of the Spanish patrimonial state. In some ways the political philosophy of Saint Thomas was more relevant to sixteenth-century Spain and her overseas empire than to feudal, thirteenth-century Europe, in which it was conceived—just as the ideas of John Locke, some say, were better keyed to Jeffersonian America than they were to seventeenth-century England.

The two central principles of Thomist sociopolitical thought, as Ernst Troeltsch states them, are organicism and patriarchalism.[27] First, society is a hierarchical system in which each person or group serves a purpose larger than any one of them can encompass. Social unity is architectonic, deriving from faith in the larger *corpus mysticum* and not from rationalistic definitions of purpose and strategy at critical moments of history. To the social hierarchy corresponds a scale of inequalities and imperfections that should be corrected only when Christian justice is in jeopardy. Thus casuistry becomes more important than human law, because to adjudicate is to determine whether a given case affects all of society or whether it can be dispatched by an *ad hoc* decision.

Second, the inequalities inherent in society imply the acquiescence of each person in his station with its attendant obligations. Such acquiescence is naturally contingent upon public acceptance of the supreme power—king, prince, or pope—who must enjoy full legitimacy to serve as the ultimate, paternalistic source of the casuistical decisions that resolve the constant conflicts of function and jurisdiction throughout the system.

Troeltsch suggests why this majestic philosophic edifice was partly inconsonant with the thirteenth century. He points out that the image of the Aristotelian city-state influenced Saint Thomas more strongly than did the constitutional life of his own day. "Catholic theory is, largely, comparatively independent of feudal tenure and the feudal system; the relation between the public authority and subjective public rights is treated in a highly abstract manner." Moreover, Saint Thomas displays an urban bias: "[In] contrast to the inclination of modern Catholicism towards the rural population and its specific Ethos, it is solely the city that St. Thomas takes into account. In his view man is naturally a town-dweller, and he regards rural life only as the result of misfortune or of want."[28]

Previously we stressed the weakness of the feudal tradition in Spain and the important role of the medieval Spanish city. We are now in a position to appreciate that it was for sociological rather than mere doctrinal reasons that Thomist theory struck such resonances throughout the Spanish empire in the sixteenth and seventeenth centuries.

It remains to cast the model of the patrimonial state in terms that allow us to trace its persistence unequivocally in modern Spanish America. This task was accomplished by Max Weber when he distinguished "patrimonialism" as one of the forms of "traditional domination."[29] The patrimonial ruler is ever alert to forestall the growth of an independent landed aristocracy enjoying inherited privileges. He awards benefices, or prebends, as a remuneration for services; income accruing from benefices is an attribute of the office, not of the incumbent as a person. Characteristic ways for maintaining the ruler's authority intact are: limiting the tenure of royal officials; forbidding officials to acquire family and economic ties in their jurisdictions; using inspectors and spies to supervise all levels of administration; defining only loosely the territorial and functional divisions of administration so that jurisdictions will be competitive and mutually supervisory. The authority of the ruler is oriented to tradition but allows him claim to full personal power.[30] As he is reluctant to bind himself by "law," his rule takes the form of a series of directives, each subject to supersession. Thus problems of adjudication tend to become problems of administration, and the administrative and judicial functions are united in many different offices throughout the bureaucracy. Legal remedies are frequently regarded not as applications of "law," but as a gift of grace or a privilege awarded on the merits of a case and not binding as precedent.

This typology of the patrimonial state describes with surprising accuracy the structure and logic of the Spanish empire in America. It also assists us to understand why chaos ensued when the ultimate authority for the system, the Spanish crown, was suddenly removed.

Until the moment that Napoleon's troops took Ferdinand VII of Spain into custody in 1808, there had existed throughout the Spanish empire a relative lack of concern with the remoter framework of society and general acquiescence in the ultimate authority. A study of those dispersed and sporadic uprisings against authority which did occur in Spanish America before independence classifies them as: revolts by the original conquistadors, uprisings of the subject races, and creole movements of protest. If we except seditious revolts caused by a single leader's personal ambitions for power, we find all the three kinds of uprising to have common characteristics. They are precisely the characteristics one could define as "legitimate" for revolt within the framework of the Thomist, patrimonial state.

*Those movements were spontaneous, in the double sense of in-
digenous (that is, not determined by any foreign influence, although
subsequently certain foreign elements might be employed for their
development and legitimation) and accidental (that is, they did
not respond to an organic plan or to a doctrine elaborated ex
professo).*

*They were in embryo energetically local, produced by a crisis
affecting the region or zone and directed to regional needs. When
various movements broke out simultaneously at various points, this
was a sociological and chronological coincidence, not a planned
prior agreement.*

*Lastly, in the cases when abstract principles are invoked to en-
courage revolutionary activity, the latter never occurs as a mere
ideological outburst; it tends always toward the immediate resolution of a severe and urgent crisis.*[31]

In the second half of the eighteenth century Enlightenment ideas
and writings circulated freely in Spanish America among intellectual, professional, and clerical groups, within the universities, in
the new economic societies, and, with restrictions, in the public
press. Yet their effect was to stimulate reformist criticism, not to
engender programmatic opposition to the regime or revolutionary
Jacobinism. The traditions of the Spanish system itself in fact allowed possibilities for greater autonomy for the colonies and parity
for the creoles. It has been argued that the main shortcoming of the
"enlightened" reforms of the most notable Bourbon king, Charles
III (1759-1788),[32] was that they were alien to tradition in being too
rationalistic and technocratic, that they failed to develop initiative,
self-rule, and human resources *in loco.* His expulsion of the Jesuits
in 1767 (accompanied by a ban on the teachings of Suárez!), to the
dismay of many creoles and Indians, deprived the Indies of important intellectual, pedagogical, and even economic leadership. It is an
example, not without relevance to modern Latin America, of how
"progressive" administration can stifle internal sources of potential
progress.

4. Independence

The best historical analogue to the Spanish American wars for
independence is the Protestant Reformation. Both movements
occurred within a far-flung, venerable Catholic institutional order
which was exhibiting decadence at its upper levels. Both movements
developed as unco-ordinated patterns of dispersed and disparate

revolt. Neither was heralded by a coherent body of revolutionary doctrine, and each improvised its multiple "ideologies" under pressure of events. Indeed, each movement at its inception betrayed a strong conservative or fundamentalist character. Each was the final cluster of a centuries-old series of random and localized heresies, uprisings, or seditions; and, in the case of each, world events were finally propitious to transform the impromptu outbreak into a world-historical revolution.

On the South American continent it was not until a number of years after Napoleon's deposition of the Spanish king that the goal of independence became defined and was pursued in the military campaigns conducted separately by Simón Bolívar and José de San Martín. Even then the mass of the people played no role in the movement. The independence of the Spanish South American countries was achieved under the auspices of the creole elites in the more outlying regions. The impetus for the two main campaigns was imparted from Venezuela in the north and Buenos Aires in the south. Both of these regions were offering fresh promise for agricultural and commercial development. After independence, both Venezuela and Argentina fell under strongman rule. This served to entrench the somewhat reconstituted creole oligarchies, which were now unhampered by the presence of Spanish bureaucracy.

If we except the special case of Saint Domingue, where a massive slave revolt produced Haiti's independence from France, Mexico is the only Latin-American country where there occurred substantial popular uprisings. Under Hidalgo an inchoate crowd of humble Indians and mestizos in central Mexico was led to fight for land, for Mexican autonomy, and for an end to the caste system (1810-1811). Under Morelos they were led to fight for independence (1813-1815). Both leaders were liberal parish priests. Both were captured and executed. Well-to-do creoles resisted identification with the rebellion or with a French revolutionary spirit. Some creoles even suspected the Spaniards themselves of being tainted with freemasonry and Illuminism. The army, church, and landowners remained loyal to the crown during the Napoleonic interregnum and after the establishment of reaction and despotism under the restored Ferdinand VII (1814). The Mexican insurgent movement was flickering out when suddenly, in 1820, liberal, constitutional reforms were forced upon the Spanish monarchy. At this point, fearing for their privileges, the Spaniards in Mexico and the upper creoles joined to embrace the separatist cause, setting up the short-lived emperorship of Agustín de Iturbide. Mexican independence was an act of counterrevolution.

It cannot be said, therefore, that "nationalism" was an ingredient of the Latin-American independence movement. Simón Bolívar,

the *líder máximo* of independence, was torn between the generous
vision of a transnational amphictyony of the Hispanic American
peoples and a keen perception of the feuding local oligarchies and
earthbound peasantries from which only phantom nations could be
formed. One surmises that Bolívar's use of the term "amphictyony,"
dictated by the Enlightenment fashion of neoclassicism, was a sur-
rogate for his instinctive sense of a Hispanic unity rooted in a political and religious heritage having medieval coloration.[33] A modern
Colombian writes, "Had Bolívar not feared to be Napoleon and had
he abandoned the paradigm of George Washington, perhaps our
national destiny would have been saved." The independence of the
United States caused a bonding through compact of autonomous
colonies. The independence of Spanish America caused the decapi-
tation of a realm that had ever been, if not unified, at least unitary.
In one case *e pluribus unum,* in the other *ex uno plures.* The Panama
Congress of 1826, while it served as a first utterance of the Pan
American ideal, symbolized the abandonment of attempts to regulate the internal affairs of the Spanish American peoples on a continental scale.[34]

The extent of the politico-administrative crisis faced by the independent Spanish American nations of 1830 can be appreciated
when we recall our model of the Thomist-patrimonial state. The
lower echelons of administration had operated by the grace of an
interventionist, paternal monarch, thoroughly sanctioned by tradition and faith. His collapse straightway withdrew legitimacy from
the remnants of the royal bureaucracy. It was impossible to identify
a substitute authority that would command general assent. Decapi-
tated, the government could not function, for the patrimonial regime had developed neither: (1) the underpinning of contractual
vassalic relationships that capacitate the component parts of a feudal regime for autonomous life; nor (2) a rationalized *legal* order
not dependent for its operation and claims to assent upon personalistic intervention by the highest authority.

Although legitimacy was withdrawn from the hierarchies of
government and society by independence, no revolutionary change
occurred. "Thus the social and spiritual structure of the past is preserved under new forms; its class hierarchy, the privileges of special
bodies . . . the values of the Catholic religion and Hispanic tradition
are maintained. At the same time its political and legislative forms
and its international status change."[35] To state the case more fully,
political or social revolution was neither cause nor concomitant
of the independence wars. Once independence was achieved, however, the bureaucracy found a new role thrust upon it. Whereas the
mission of the colonial bureaucracy had been to protect and uphold
a traditional order, the republican one took on just the contrary
function. As Villoro puts it:

[*The new bureaucracy*] *has arisen from the destruction of the old*
political order, and it has raison d'être *only as a force to transform*
society. Far from finding itself, like the colonial functionaries, at
the summit of the established power, it must for its preservation
oppose the economically privileged classes. The decrees it applies,
the institutions it creates, do not repeat old models but are fated to
deny those that exist and provoke the transformation of society.
From the moment this task is over, its bureaucratic function also
ceases. The colonial bureaucracy, tied to preserving the past, was
necessarily antirevolutionary. The creole bureaucracy, sprung from
a negation of the past, is condemned to be revolutionary for its own
preservation.[36]

The collapse of the supreme authority activated the latent forces
of local oligarchies, municipalities, and extended-family systems in
a struggle for power and prestige in the new, arbitrarily defined
republics. These telluric creole social structures were direct heirs of
social arrangements proliferated in the conquest period but held in
check by the patrimonial state. Now again they seized the stage.
The *caudillo* of the independence period, controlling a clanlike or an
improvised retinue through charismatic appeal, was the latter-day
version of the conquistador. In the absence of developed and interacting economic interest groups having a stake in constitutional
process, the new countries were plunged into alternating regimes of
anarchy and personalist tyranny. The contest to seize a patrimonial
state apparatus, fragmented from the original imperial one, became
the driving force of public life in each new country.

There is abundant testimony that Spanish America universally
suffered a collapse of the moral order during the early decades of
independence. The face of anarchy was somewhat masked, however,
by that ancient habit of legalizing and legitimizing every public act
which had been so important a cement to the former empire. Each
new country duly produced its constitutional convention and one or
more Anglo-French-type constitutions. The political mechanism which
emerged was generally a biparty system. Party programs faithfully
reflected the rhetoric of Western parliamentary politics, though not
without occasional shrewd adaptation to local situations. Although
only an elite was politically active (as was the case in the England of
1830, for that matter), party adherence frequently reflected an alignment of "conservative" landed and monied interests, high clergy,
and former monarchists against the "liberal" professionals, intellectuals, merchants, and those with a creole, anticlerical, and anti-
caste outlook. Given a static rather than a dynamic social system,
however, the game of politics became a naked contest for power.

Chile was an example perhaps unparalleled of a Spanish American country which managed, after a twelve-year transitional period,

to avoid the extremes of tyranny and anarchy with a political system unencumbered by the mechanisms and party rhetoric of an exotic liberalism. Despite its outlandish contour the country had a certain ecological cohesion around its central agricultural zone. Because the landholding class had been infiltrated by mercantile groups partly composed of recent immigrants from northern Spain, the elite represented a spectrum of moderately diverse economic interests. A Valparaiso businessman, Diego Portales, was shrewd enough to identify and co-ordinate those interests within a constitutional system having an aura of native legitimacy. The centralizing 1833 Constitution which bore his influence created a strong executive without stripping the congress and courts of countervailing powers. The first president had the aristocratic bearing which Portales himself lacked; a staunch Catholic and brave general who stood above party factionalism, he helped to legitimize the office itself. The first several presidents each served double five-year terms. The official candidate was generally victorious and handpicked by his predecessor. Thus the structure of the Spanish patrimonial state was recreated, with only those minimum concessions to Anglo-French constitutionalism that were necessary for a nineteenth-century republic which had just rejected monarchical rule.*

From our broad premises and from the specific case of Chile we may infer that for a newly erected Spanish American political system to achieve stability and continuity it had to reproduce the structure, the logic, and the vague, pragmatic safeguards against tyranny of the Spanish *patrimonial state*. The collapse of monarchical authority meant that this step required the intervention of strong *personalist* leadership. The energies of such leadership had to flow toward investing the state with suprapersonal *legitimacy*. The ingredients of legitimacy, in turn, were native psychocultural *traditions*, leavened or perhaps merely adorned by the *nationalism* and *constitutionalism* which had become watchwords of the age.

The usual political trajectory of a Spanish American nation can be plotted as one or another form of breakdown or short circuit in this model. The most notorious form is personalist leadership that constitutes its own untransferable legitimacy. In a telluric setting of moral and institutional collapse, the instances of personalism ranged from the superb, intellectually informed, yet tragically frustrated

*Brazil, which gave refuge to the Portuguese ruling family when Napoleon invaded the mother country, is another example of nineteenth-century political stability. If space allowed the coequal treatment which Portuguese America deserves, the Brazilian case could be used to confirm and refine the arguments here presented. Some of the relevant points are dealt with in my essay "Some Themes of Brazilian History," *The South Atlantic Quarterly,* LXI, 2 (Spring 1962), 159-182.

political genius of a Bolívar all the way to careers dominated by
sheer enactment of impulse, such as those of the Argentine *caudillo*
Facundo described by Sarmiento; or the Bolivian president who
commanded his aides to play dead like poodles, and who had his
ministers and generals troop solemnly around the table on which
his mistress stood naked.

It is beyond our purposes to present even a perfunctory account
of the careers of the twenty Latin-American nations during the past
century and a half. At this point we will merely suggest a way of
periodizing Spanish American history that allows us to explore
the political dilemmas of the modern countries in the light of their
Thomist, patrimonial heritage. The historical divisions conventionally used are the following:

Indigenous Period	To 1492
Colonial Period	1492 to 1824
National Period	Since 1824.

Here is our radically revised schema (offered chiefly for heuristic
purposes):

Indigenous Period	To 1520
Spanish Period	1520 to 1760
"Colonial" Period	1760 to 1920
National Period	Since 1920.

We extend the Indigenous Period to 1520 because for a generation
after Columbus's discovery Spanish colonization was restricted to the
islands and shores of the Caribbean Sea and conducted on a trial-
and-error basis, with commercial exploitation rather than effective
colonization usually in the ascendant. Hernando Cortés, who conquered the Aztec empire in 1519 to 1521, was the first of the explorers
and conquistadors to make clear to the crown the full scope of the
colonizing and civilizing venture upon which Spain had embarked.[37]

The rationale for the Spanish Period was set forth above in sections
2 and 3. It was the time of "incorporation" of the Indies into Hispano-
Christian civilization.

The term "Colonial" (used hitherto in this essay in the conventional
meaning) serves in the new schema to characterize the period when
the creole, Catholic culture and institutions of Spanish America lay
open to influences and pressures of the Western world which were
on the whole ineffectually mediated to the ethos of the formative
Spanish Period.

The National Period is still today in its inception. It is a time
when political arrangements are being devised, erratically and
painfully, which directly accommodate the traditions, structures, and
psychology of the patrimonial state to the imperatives of a modern

industrial world. It is a time when Spanish Americans are beginning to contemplate their countries' first sustained involvement with each other and with the world as autonomous nation states.

The start of the "Colonial" Period we set at 1760, the eve of the most important Bourbon reforms. As Octavio Paz sums up the case for it:

The reforms undertaken by the Bourbon dynasty, particularly Charles III, improved the economy and made business operations more efficient, but they accentuated the centralization of administrative functions and changed New Spain into a true colony, that is, into a territory subject to systematic exploitation and strictly controlled by the center of power.[38]

As Paz goes on to make clear, the critical matter is not quantitative exploitation. It would be hard to make the case that the financial enrichment of Spain at the expense of the Indies, or the cruelty to Indians and Negro slaves, was greater in 1780 than it had been in 1680 or 1580. The primary sense of "colonial" as here used designates not a unilaterally exploitative relationship, but a discontinuity of structure and purpose between two systems. The fact was that the "enlightened," rationalistic, technocratic Bourbon policies were an overlay upon and not a radical reform of Spanish American institutions.

Bourbon economic reforms aroused antagonism from creole merchants in Mexico City, Caracas, and Buenos Aires who were thriving under the old monopolistic system. It can even be concluded that "while Spain evolved toward [economic] liberalism, there were interests in America which obstructed those new currents."[39] Administrative reform, and specifically the creation of the intendant system, "revealed a fatal lack of integration in Spanish policy." New officials were underpaid without being allowed the traditional extralegal fees and exactions. The division of authority between the intendants and the viceroys was unwisely or vaguely stipulated. The activities of the intendants aroused the town governments to greater activity without their receiving a commensurate increase of authority. "[The] reforms of Charles III, both in their administrative and in their commercial aspects, helped to precipitate the collapse of the imperial regime they were intended to prolong."[40]

The assumptions and programs of Western liberalism continued to be a bone in the throat of Spanish America, whether their guise was enlightened despotism, Manchester economics, or Anglo-French constitutional democracy. The tendency of doctrinally liberal reforms was to withdraw legitimacy from the patrimonial state, to dismantle its apparatus, and to cancel the shadowy, paternalistic safeguards of status for the inarticulate masses. Since, however, the stimuli to economic change came from without—from the Western world—and not from within, there did not occur even among the new oligarchies that competitive differentiation of economic function which gives liberalism its *raison d'être*. Mexico's liberal Constitution of 1857 was informed by the vision of a prosperous independent peasantry. But its enactment merely hastened the delivery of traditional Indian communities to systems of debt peonage that were beyond the tutelage of church and state. A similar process occurred in the other Indian countries south to Bolivia. It gave to the landowning oligarchies a measure of absolute local power that would have exceeded even the dreams of the conquistadors.

The anti-Spanish rallying cries of Democracy! Liberalism! and Civilization! provoked by the Spanish American independence wars contained hopes which were persistently undermined by the drift of the nineteenth century. This trend is implied by the "two stages" into which Leopoldo Zea divides the period's intellectual history.[41] The first was a romantic, eclectic phase when such diverse and often contradictory currents as Cartesianism, sensationalist psychology, physiocratic economics, Saint-Simonianism, utilitarianism, Scotch realism, and French traditionalism were all commingled in a multiple attack on the Hispanic, scholastic legacy. The second phase saw many of these streams of thought, and some new ones, merge to form a unified intellectual position, that of positivism.

Positivism occurred in many versions throughout Latin America, sometimes with an Anglo-Spencerian rather than a Franco-Comtean emphasis. Whatever its guise, it appeared to offer a unitary, constructive, systematic, scientific approach to the problems of stratified societies, stagnant economies, and archaic school systems. In practice, however, the watchwords of positivism could be used to justify systems of vested interest and entrenched privilege. Frock-coated bourgeois *caudillos* had replaced the soldier *caudillos* of the postindependence era. Their regimes were secured less by charismatic leadership and military prowess than by creation of orderly conditions for attracting foreign trade and investment in this heyday of European capitalism. Liberalism tinctured by social evolution could justify limiting economic freedom to those who already possessed it. Tinctured by nineteenth-century anthropology it acquiesced in the continued exploitation of Indians, Negroes, and those of "mixed race."

It might be imagined that Latin America's intellectual drift from romanticism to scientism, from eclecticism to determinism, merely reflected the general European movement. Zea offers us two caveats to correct this impression. One is that the acceptance of positivism in Latin America represented a search for the inclusive doctrine and instrument of order which might replace scholasticism. Seen thus, positivism appears to serve familiar casuistical purposes more importantly than those of speculative scientific inquiry.

Secondly, at the same time that the Latin-American, especially the Spanish American, mind groped unconsciously to recover a habitual mold of thought, it was explicitly attacking the civilization within which that mold had been shaped. Spanish Americans were condemned to the impossible task of denying and amputating their past. Yet Spain was always with them. Unable to deal with their past by a *dialectic logic* which would allow them to assimilate it, they rejected it by a *formal logic* which kept it present and impeded their evolution. The Conquest, Colonialism, and Independence were problems never resolved, never placed *behind*. They are still alive in our own century.

The Hispanic American continued as if no change had taken place. And in truth none had. Nothing real or conclusive seemed to have been gained. The political freedom which had been attained was only a formality. . . . Every Hispanic American sought only to take the place left by the conquistador. From the dominated man which he was, he aspired to be the dominator of the weakest. . . . Meanwhile the rest of the world marched forward, progressed, and made history. Hispanic America continued to be a continent without history, without a past, because the past was always present.[42]

Not only did ideas from nineteenth-century Europe assume new coloration and use in the Latin-American setting, but some were screened out before reaching it. Marxism, for example, made virtually no impact whatsoever. A philosophy which identifies an engine of political demolition in society will scarcely win general acceptance among a people groping to recover and legitimize an overarching patrimonial state. The clarion call to a single solidary and militant class echoes weakly in a society where all groups look separately to a patrimonial structure for accommodation, tutelage, and salvation. The model toward which the Thomistic society tends must be formulated in statics, not dynamics. Its ultimate law is natural and moral, not scientific and sociological. These strictures were for the most part overlooked in nineteenth-century Latin America. But they continued in clandestine operation.

5. Contemporary Latin America: Five Political Premises

The date 1920 was suggested as the start of Latin America's truly "National" Period. Some nations have not yet entered it, and none has fully emerged from "colonial" status and outlook. But within the decade or so preceding and following 1920 one can say that certain key countries produced political regimes, social programs, and cultural statements which evinced a new fealty to historical realities. Mexico's was the classic Latin-American national revolution because of the decadence and corruption of the bourgeois-*caudillo* regime which it overthrew and because of the outright theatricality with which it was conducted and perpetuated. Its many facets and phases, however disconnected in actuality, are bonded in a rhetorical and emotive mystique.

The fact that the Mexican Revolution was, among other things, fiercely anticlerical does not mean that it was not deeply consonant with Hispanic tradition. Traditions which are matrices of social action and not mere ceremony retain vitality precisely because they accommodate to many guises and purposes. This same anticlerical revolution had as its martyr-hero the spiritualistic (and literally a practitioner of spiritualism), "Christ-like" Madero. Revolutionary teachers sent among the poor and the Indians went as "missionaries," sometimes too as martyrs. Revolutionary painters revived the tradition of monumental public art, spreading the walls of government buildings with murals depicting the Indian's exploitation through the centuries like so many stations of Calvary leading toward chiliastic redemption.

After the long Porfirio Díaz interregnum, the subsoil was declared to be the patrimony of the state, as it had once been of the Spanish crown. The *ejido* system, by which the soil itself was redistributed to rural workers on a quasi-communalist basis, took its name from the town commons of the old Spanish municipality. Reawakened interest in the Indian, his problems and his culture, restored him to his former position of special tutelage. Groups hitherto neglected politically, the rural and urban workers, were brought into national prominence through paternalistic institutions established or heavily influenced by the new patrimonial state. Laborers, capitalists, managerial and commercial groups, syndicates of professionals and teachers, tend to relate primarily to the strong politico-administrative core of the central government, only secondarily to each other. State and regional conflicts are often referred to the central government for resolution, except where a local *caudillo* manages to establish a temporary satrapy.

The Mexican Revolution is customarily described as a dynamic, protean movement that is not yet ended. As evidence one can point to the shifting emphasis over the decades upon successive programs of education reform, trade unionism, anticlericalism, land reform, oil expropriation, industrialization, and public works. This apparent dynamism conflicts with our static model for the patrimonial state.

67
Richard M.
Morse

On closer inspection, however, it turns out that the Mexican Revolution differs from the "permanent revolution" of a capitalist society. Mexico's official and, in practice, single political party changed its name in 1946 to the Party of Revolutionary Institutions. Revolutionary institutions, above all the institutions of a particular revolution, are hardly the same as a revolutionary process or a dynamic interplay among institutions.

The Magna Carta of the revolution, its Constitution of 1917, does not primarily serve as a social compact or set of ground rules for the conduct of public life. This lengthy codification, which like the old Laws of the Indies mixes general precepts and regulative specifics, is characteristically viewed as a document to be put into effect. No one was concerned that many provisions of the Constitution were in abeyance for years after its promulgation. In the Hispano-Thomist tradition there is no urgency to enforce law if enforcement is for good reasons unfeasible and if the community at large shows no great concern. Once having attained legitimacy, the Revolution was regarded as something to be permanently institutionalized, not as point of departure for open-ended process.

This view of the Mexican Revolution is highly schematic. It takes no account, for example, of Bourbon survivals (such as, perhaps, overcentralization and technocratic tendencies) or positivist tendencies (such as, perhaps, the "socialist education" of the nineteen-thirties). It suggests little of rapid socioeconomic change (much of which, however, appears to be triggered by the external industrial world, not generated internally). What it does attempt is to identify a historical matrix of social action and attitude, now recovered sufficiently to endow the eclectic solutions of the moment with legitimacy and partial coherence.

Earlier we said that the first political problem of a Latin-American country is the routinization of charisma. We now suggest that the ideal form toward which this routinization gravitates is the patrimonial state. Once a version of this state is achieved, however imperfectly, the second great political problem is how, in the twentieth century, to reconcile the static, vegetative features of the patrimonial state with the imperatives of a dynamic industrial world. This problem is one of accommodation and not, as many liberal Western minds would have it, one of transcendence—not even perhaps, in its ultimate terms, a problem of "development."

At this point we may summarize some of the presuppositions, limiting conditions, and possibilities for political change in the Latin-American countries as they advance into the genuinely "national" phase of their history. However heavily the Western, industrial world—or, for that matter, the Communist, industrial one—may impinge upon these countries, quickening their pace of life, engendering new hopes, wants, and fears, introducing new programs, equipment, technology, and wares, it seems probable that any changes wrought will in some way eventually accommodate to a number of enduring premises that underlie Latin-American political life.

The first point is that *now as in the past the sense that man makes and is responsible for his own world is less deep or prevalent than in many other lands.* The Latin American may be more sensitive to his world, or more eloquently critical of it, or more attached to it. But he seems less concerned with shaping it. The natural order looms larger than the human community. The old tradition of "natural law" has not atrophied as it did in the United States. The individual conscience is presumed more fallible, the process of voting less consequential than in the northern democracies. The regime of voluntary, rationalized political association, of seesaw bi-party systems, of quasi-rational legislative procedure has a fitful existence after almost a century and a half of "republican" life.

These characteristics, some will argue, are generic to all "underdeveloped" countries. Scales of political maturity have been devised for ranking the emergent nations of Latin America, Africa, and Asia. Granted that Latin America has much in common with other "developing areas," the point stressed in this essay is that Latin America is subject to special imperatives as an offshoot of postmedieval, Catholic, Iberian Europe which never underwent the Protestant Reformation. In its shaping of the present, such a past differs substantially from a Confucian or a Mohammedan or an African tribal past.

To Spanish American society Talcott Parsons applies the rubric "particularistic-ascriptive pattern" and in so doing differentiates it explicitly from, for example, Chinese society. In Spanish America, he observes, the larger social structures, beyond kinship and local community, tend "to be accepted as part of the given situation of life, and to have positive functions when order is threatened, but otherwise to be taken for granted."

Such societies tend to be individualistic rather than collectivistic and non- if not anti-authoritarian. . . . The individualism is primarily concerned with expressive interests, and hence much less so with opportunity to shape the situation through achievement. There tends to be a certain lack of concern with the remoter framework of the society, unless it is threatened. Similarly, there is no inherent objection to authority so long as it does not interfere too much with expressive freedom, indeed it may be welcomed as a factor of stability. But there is also not the positive incentive to recognize authority as inherent that exists in the cases of positive authoritarianism. The tendency to indifference to larger social issues creates a situation in which authority can become established with relatively little opposition.[43]

The second point, implied in the quotation just given, is that the Latin-American peoples still appear willing to alienate, rather than delegate, power to their chosen or accepted leaders, in the spirit long ago condoned by sixteenth-century Hispano-Thomist thought. Yet the people retain also a keen sense of equity, of natural justice, and their sensitivity to abuses of alienated power. It may be that the classic image of the Latin-American "revolution" is the barracks coup by an insurgent *caudillo* against an incumbent whose authority lacks legitimacy. But the more significant if more infrequent uprising is that having a broad popular base and no clearly elaborated program beyond reclamation of sovereignty that has been tyrannically abused. Socioeconomic change of a truly revolutionary character which may occur in the wake of such movements tends to be improvised under leadership that desperately seeks to legitimize its authority.

The third point, therefore, is that *the present "National" Period is marked by a renewed quest for legitimate government.* The regimes of the last century did not, by and large, attain legitimacy. Most have not yet done so. A "legitimate" revolution in Latin America needs no sharp-edged ideology; it need not polarize the classes; it need not produce an immediate and effective redistribution of wealth and goods. The regime it produces need not be conscientiously sanctioned at the polls by a majority vote. (The difference between popular political support in Latin America and in the United States recalls Rousseau's mystical distinction between the general will and the will of all.)

On the other hand, a legitimate revolution probably necessitates generalized violence and popular participation, even though under improvised leadership and with unprogrammed goals. It needs to be informed by a deep even though unarticulated sense of moral urgency. It needs to be an indigenous movement, unencumbered by foreign support. It needs charismatic leadership of special psychocultural appeal. Even with all their bluster and blunder, Perón and Fidel Castro have such appeal. So may gentler, saintly types, especially if martyred at an early stage as were Martí and Madero. Mere tyrants are not acceptable revolutionaries.

Liberal North Americans are congenitally unable to deal with charismatic Latin Americans—precisely because they project upon the latter their own criteria for leadership. One might almost venture that the shape and feel of politics in the southern United States equips the Southern conservative better than it does the Northern liberal to understand the political life of Latin America. However much a Lleras Camargo may have been respected by Latin Americans as a reforming, law-abiding, conscientious democrat, his sort does not inspire revolution. And it is a revolutionary as well as a national era which Latin America now enters.

Why is a somewhat vague legitimacy so important in modern Latin America? It is because the lawmaking and law-applying processes in Latin America do not in the last instance receive their sanction from popular referendum, from laws and constitutions, from the bureaucratic ideal of "service," from tyrannically exercised power, from custom, or from scientific or dialectical laws. As Gierke said of the Middle Ages: "Far rather every duty of obedience was conditioned by the rightfulness of command."[44] That is, in a patrimonial state, to which command and decree are so fundamental, the legitimacy of the command is determined by the legitimacy of the authority which issues it. Hence the importance of sheer legalism in Latin-American administration as constant certification for the legitimacy, not of the act, but of him who executes it. Hence too the unsatisfactoriness of the personalist regime which fails to take the extraordinarily difficult step of institutionalizing leadership.

Fourthly, *the innate sense of the Latin-American people for natural law is matched by a more casual attitude toward man-made law.*[45] Human laws are frequently seen as too harsh or impracticable or inequitable or simply as inapplicable to the specific case. Hence the difficulty of collecting income taxes; the prevalent obligation to pay fees or bribes to officials for special or even routine services; the apathy of metropolitan police toward theft and delinquency; the thriving contraband trade at border towns; the leniency toward those who commit crimes of passion—all the way down to the non-observance of "no smoking" signs on buses and in theaters.

One of the impediments to nation-building in Latin America appears to be precisely the fact that natural law most effectively guides judgment either at the international level or at the level of the family and the smallest communities and villages, not at the national level. It is no accident that Latin Americans are so often prominent as international jurists, or that "community development" figures so importantly in modern plans for reform in Latin America. In confrontation with the complexities, abstractions, and compromises of policy-making for the nation-state, instinctive moral sentiments tend to be weakened or suppressed. Understandably therefore, North Americans with their strong and viable nation structure show moral ambivalence in international affairs and in domestic family relations.

From the point being made flow two conclusions. First, as Latin-American countries in the new National Period shrug off the long-standing tutelage of the United States, they may be expected to develop relations—economic, political, cultural—with all nations of the world, particularly the non-Western. Informed by traditions of Catholic universalism, they will do so with greater ease and understanding than characterize United States overtures in such directions. Second, it appears essential that the architects of social and economic reconstruction in Latin America challenge those models which overstress the organizational and depersonalizing aspects of "development." Plans for the largest factories, the largest bureaucracies, even the largest metropolises must somehow build in the small, revitalized face-to-face group as the nodal element.

Finally, it seems scarcely less true now than in the sixteenth century that *the larger society is perceived in Latin America as composed of parts which relate through a patrimonial and symbolic center rather than directly to one another.* A national government operates not as a referee among dynamic pressure groups, but as a source of energy, co-ordination, and leadership for occupational groups and syndicates, corporate units, institutions, social "estates," and geographic regions. In the absence of powerful internal pressures generated by competitive institutional life, and lacking strident ideological imperatives or world power aspirations, there is a tendency for political regimes to vegetate after the enthusiastic seizure of power. Many Mexicans say this today of their "revolutionary" government. Vegetative political regimes, however, are intolerable in the twentieth century. Thus the patrimonial state model, in some ways so viable under the Hapsburgs, becomes revolution-prone in twentieth-century Latin America.

If a last reckless prophecy may be permitted, it is this: that the salvation and energizing of the Latin-American patrimonial state cannot be expected to occur merely in rational response to the demands of a fast-moving technological world. They may not even be significantly advanced by massive education programs, industrialization, higher economic production, better living standards, and free elections—though all these, with their ambivalent effects, are bound to come. What may more significantly change the tendencies of the Latin-American state are the thrusts of nationalism from within and the impingement of world politics from without. These will disrupt the hemisphere's somewhat unhealthy Pax Monroviana and bring the Latin-American nations increasingly into intense, sustained involvement with the nations of the world, and with each other. The first steps will be erratic, sometimes timid, sometimes melodramatic. But eventually they may lead to greater maturity and to national self-images of deeper coherence. A Protestant civilization can develop its energies endlessly in a wilderness, as did the United States. A Catholic civilization stagnates when it is not in vital contact with the diverse tribes and cultures of mankind.

Notes

1. O. Nogueira, "Preconceito racial de marca e preconceito racial de origem" in R. Bastide and F. Fernandes, *Relacoes raciais entre negros e brancos em São Paulo* (São Paulo, 1955), p. 552.

2. The inquisitors in Cartagena complained in 1619 that Negro slaves about to be flogged by their masters would cry out, "I renounce God!" On the spot they became subject to inquisitorial trial and the flogging had to stop. After a juridical formality they would be scolded and released, a process which might be indefinitely repeated. H. C. Lea, *The Inquisition in the Spanish Dependencies* (New York, 1922), pp. 465-466.

3. J. M. Ots Capdequí, *Manual de historia del derecho español en las Indias* (Buenos Aires, 1945), p. 191.

4. G. Céspedes del Castillo, "La sociedad colonial americana en los siglos XVI y XVII" in J. Vicens Vives, ed., *Historia social y económica de España y América* (4 vols., Barcelona, 1957-59), III, 395-396.

5. R. Guerra y Sánchez, *Sugar and Society in the Caribbean* (New Haven, 1964), pp. 9-57.

6. E. R. Wolf, *Sons of the Shaking Earth* (Chicago, 1959), pp. 235-242.

7. F. Tannenbaum, *Slave and Citizen: The Negro in the Americas* (New York, 1947).

8. E. Williams, *Capitalism and Slavery* (Chapel Hill, 1944); see also his "Race Relations in Caribbean Society" with "Discussion" by Tannenbaum in V. Rubin, ed., *Caribbean Studies: A Symposium* (Kingston, 1957), pp. 54-66. A review article by S. W. Mintz in *American Anthropologist*, 63,3 (June 1961), 579-587, is a good conspectus of the problem.

9. H. Hoetink, "'Colonial Psychology' and Race," *The Journal of Economic History*, XXI, 4 (Dec. 1961), 629-640.

10. M. Góngora, *El estado en el derecho indiano, época de fundación (1492-1570)* (Santiago, 1951), p. 300.

11. *Ibid.*, p. 301.

12. *Ibid.*, p. 303.

13. J. M. Ots Capdequí, *Instituciones* (Barcelona, 1959), p. 8.

14. Góngora, *op. cit.*, pp. 178-179, 183.

15. G. Sánchez-Albornoz, *España, un enigma histórico* (2 vols., Buenos Aires, 1956), II, 7-103. Also, M. Bloch, *Feudal Society* (London, 1961), pp. 186-187.

16. See R. M. Morse, "Some Characteristics of Latin American Urban History," *The American Historical Review*, LXVII, 2 (Jan. 1962), 317-338.

17. Góngora, *op. cit.*, pp. 184-185.

18. Wolf, *op. cit.*, p. 204.

19. K. Burke, *Attitudes toward History* (2 vols., New York, 1937), I, 176-177.

20. The Argentine historian Ricardo Levene even proposed that the preindependence era of his country no longer be called the "colonial period" and that, instead, the phrase "period of Spanish domination and civilization" be employed. *Las Indias no eran colonias* (Buenos Aires, 1951), pp. 161-165.

21. F. Morales Padrón, *Fisionomía de la conquista indiana* (Seville, 1955), pp. 43-47.

22. Interestingly enough, the word "conquest," or the Spanish *conquista*, derives from the Latin *con-quaerere*, which means to "seek out" or "bring together" without the intimation of aggrandizement.

23. See R. M. Morse, "Toward a Theory of Spanish American Government," *Journal of the History of Ideas*, XV, 1 (Jan. 1954), 71-77; reprinted in this volume.

24. Notably M. Giménez Fernández, *Las doctrinas populistas*

en la independencia de Hispano-América (Seville, 1947).

25. For an off-target exchange on this subject see C. W. Arnade and B. W. Diffie in "Causes of Spanish-American Wars of Independence," *Journal of Inter-American Studies,* II, 2 (April 1960), 130-131, 141-144; also C. C. Griffin, "The Enlightenment and Latin American Independence" in A. P. Whitaker, ed., *Latin America and the Enlightenment* (2nd ed.; Ithaca, 1961), pp. 124-125.

26. P. Janet, *Histoire de la science politique dans ses rapports avec la morale* (3rd ed.; 2 vols., Paris, 1887), II, 76.

27. E. Troeltsch, *The Social Teachings of the Christian Churches* (2 vols., New York, 1960), I, 280-328.

28. *Ibid.,* I, 314-318.

29. M. Weber, *The Theory of Social and Economic Organization* (New York, 1947), pp. 341-358, 373-381. Also R. Bendix, *Max Weber: An Intellectual Portrait* (New York, 1962), pp. 334-369.

30. The exercise of arbitrary free will at the expense of limiting traditions gives rise to what Weber calls "sultanism."

31. L. Machado Ribas, *Movimientos revolucionarios en las colonias españolas de América* (Montevideo, 1940), p. 23.

32. Sometimes called the Diocletian of the Spanish empire.

33. The thesis that Bolívar's political thought was cast along Thomist lines is advanced in J. Estrada Monsalve, "El sistema político de Bolívar en la doctrina tomista," *Bolívar* 13 (Sept. 1952), 463-474.

34. J. Sanín Echeverri, "Los Estados Unidos y los estados desunidos de América Latina," *Revista de la Universidad de Antioquia,* 149 (April-June 1962), 393-411.

35. L. Villoro, *La revolución de independencia* (Mexico City, 1953), p. 194.

36. *Ibid.,* p. 207.

37. This argument is developed in M. Giménez Fernández, *Hernán Cortés y su revolución comunera en la Nueva España* (Seville, 1948).

38. O. Paz, *op. cit.,* p. 117.

39. E. Arcila Farías, *El siglo ilustrado en América* (Caracas, 1955), pp. 255 ff.

40. J. Lynch, *Spanish Colonial Administration, 1782-1810* (London, 1958), pp. 279-289.

41. L. Zea, *The Latin-American Mind* (Norman, 1963), pp. xv-xvi and *passim.*

42. *Ibid.,* pp. 9-10.

43. T. Parsons, *The Social System* (Glencoe, 1951), pp. 198-199.

44. O. Gierke, *Political Theories of the Middle Age* (Boston, 1958), p. 35.

45. For the natural-law revival in modern Latin-American legal philosophy see J. L. Kunz, *La filosofía del derecho latinoamericana en el siglo XX* (Buenos Aires, 1951), pp. 49-71.

The Tradition of Monistic Democracy in Latin America

Glen Dealy

The *geist* of the Western world has proclaimed an inevitable movement of the nation-state towards the development and perfection of pluralistic democracy. The pervasive influence of this *geist* can be seen in such divergent academic conclusions as who governs New Haven and who governs (or will govern) the Kremlin. In terms of Latin American scholarship, we see this assumption in works such as Robert Scott's *Mexican Government in Transition*.[1] And within the world of politics the position was typified by John F. Kennedy, who said at Berkeley, California, in 1962, "No one who examines the modern world can doubt that the great currents of history are carrying the world away from the monolithic idea towards the pluralistic idea."[2]

This teleological proposition derives from a near universal agreement that a middle class is the father of pluralistic democracy. Westerners are nurtured upon the idea that the French and North American revolutions gained their impetus from the rising bourgeoisie. Liberal pluralistic democracy, we are told, is the theory by which these middle sectors held on to power once control was achieved. An absence of pluralistic democracy in Latin America was in turn explained by the lack of a rising middle class in that area at the beginning of the nineteenth century. Wars of independence in Latin America were seen as essentially conservative movements in which the position of the creole aristocracy was enhanced at the expense of the Spanish aristocracy, but in which no middle class initially emerged.

This paper was originally prepared for delivery before the Annual Meeting of the American Political Science Association, Chicago, September 1971. To be published almost simultaneously with this volume in *Journal of the History of Ideas* (July 1974). Printed here by permission of the Journal of the History of Ideas, Inc.

The assumed relationship of the middle class to pluralistic democracy can now be called into question by the rise of the middle sectors in Latin America. For despite the significant increase of that class in this century, no perceptible movement toward liberal pluralistic democracy is in sight. Since 1945 Latin American governments, both civilian and military, appear to have been almost exclusively in the hands of the middle sectors. Yet instead of seeing an advancement of pluralistic democracy, we observe that if anything, there appears to be a parallel between the *rise* of the middle class and a *decline* of liberal pluralistic democratic tendencies in Latin America. It appears that the rising middle class wishes to sweep away the existing superficial institutional overlay of liberal pluralistic democracy that has belonged to their governments since independence. It is not just the leftist revolutionaries who agree with Francisco Julião when he says:

I confess to you, brother, friend, and fellow, that I would pray, and with me millions of Brazilians, a Lord's prayer for the eternal rest of this democracy that fattens the shark and starves the people, grants tax-exemptions to the landlords and denies the land to the campesino, allows a corporation to make a 9,000 percent profit but orders a machine gun pointed at the chest of the worker who strikes for a wage raise, gives foreign investment a free hand to monopolize the country's resources and moreover lets it freely transfer its earnings abroad, manufactures field marshals, five-star generals and admirals, but denies stability to the sergeant and the vote to the soldier and the sailor. The law is enforced only when it favors the powerful.[3]

The Cuban and Bolivian revolutions of the 1950s and 1960s, as well as the earlier major social readjustments carried out by Perón in Argentina, were middle class sponsored movements. At the time of the Argentine "revolution" under Perón, that country had one of the largest middle classes in Latin America. Cuba was allegedly third in per capita income when the Castro revolution occurred. Yet these revolutions embraced either Marxist or fascist premises with relative ease. None of the social revolutions of this century in Latin America have been inspired or carried out under the premises of pluralistic democracy. [Nicaragua may be the exception—Ed.]

Whatever historical conclusions we may entertain about twentieth-century Latin American social revolution, two things seem clear: the middle class today is in power throughout Latin America, and this middle class is not inclined toward liberal pluralistic democracy.

The conventional wisdom of the Western world is wrong in assuming that Latin America today constitutes part of an inevitable, historical development towards pluralistic democracy. A most cursory glance at recent political history in Latin America clearly shows, as exemplified in purest form in the history of Cuba and Mexico in the twentieth century, that the movement is in the opposite direction. That is to say, Latin Americans appear to be moving from halfhearted imitations of pluralistic democracy toward the structuring of more monistic institutional arrangements.

This turn toward monism indicates an attempt to recapture their authentic tradition. Latin America finds itself in a revolutionary state. But revolutions are inherently conservative.[4] It is the weakness of our perspective that often causes us to miss the similarity between more contemporary national revolutionary movements and their historical antecedents. Latin America today eludes us, I believe, because we fail to take account of those constants of her past.

The issue in Latin America is not, as most would have one believe, whether their protest movements are labeled Marxist or capitalistic, or even whether their revolutions are peaceful or violent. In the long run, the question is, What part of their past will Latin Americans try to conserve? We laugh at the Churchillism that Stalin was Genghis Khan with a telephone. Yet the saying is funny precisely because we suspect that Stalin did indeed tap in the Russian people and exhibit himself some facet of their (tsarist) past. Should it, then, be any more preposterous to say that Castro is Bolívar with a beard? I think not.

If one looks into the Latin American past one fact emerges: Latin Americans have consistently favored some form of political monism.[5] The resurgence of monistic political arrangements and the failure of the pluralist's dream for Latin America call for a reexamination of the basic premises of Latin culture.

Latin Americans, whether speaking about their tradition of democracy, *statism,* or of communism, are thinking about political monism or *monistic* democracy: that is, the centralization and control of potentially competing interests. In the broadest sense this implies support for the unification of groups at all levels of society: an attempt to eliminate competition among groups in their pursuit of wealth, power, prestige, or whatever men may aspire to within a country. It also means that power may be traded among a number of groups, but only with difficulty may power be shared.

To a North American liberal, political pluralism is the opposite of the monolithic society endemic to Latin America since colonial times. North Americans feel that the basis of true democracy is political pluralism: that is, the representation and propagation of a plurality of interests. In the broadest sense this implies support for a diversity of groups at all levels of society: support for the concept of competition among groups in their pursuit of wealth, power, prestige, or whatever men may aspire to within a country. It also means that power is shared among a number of groups.

Latin America lives within a monistic tradition as surely as the United States lives within a liberal tradition. Louis Hartz, in *The Liberal Tradition in America* (New York, Harcourt Brace Jovanovich, 1964), maintains that we are all basically Lockean in our outlook. One can with equal justification, I think, conclude that Spanish Americans are all essentially Thomists in outlook. Both world views imply a basic value agreement. But this fundamental agreement must be kept separate from the content of the two world views: most fundamental being the liberal democrat's rationale for diversity or plurality, and the monistic democrat's defense of unity.

A consensus model informs the *modus operandi* of political behavior with monistic democracies. Basic to this pervasive drive for consensus is the Latin American continual emphasis upon unity as both an ideal end state and a necessary means. Not through plurality comes union, not *e pluribus unum,* but through unity comes union, argues the Latin American. The founders of these countries were agreed that only by means of a basically unified socio-economic-political order could nations be created. Latin America was eminently suited for such an assumption.[6] Consider, for example, the preface to the translation of the United States Constitution written by a Colombian, Miguel Pombo, in 1809.

Such are the features that characterize in general the American of the North and the American of the South. But if the uniformity of ideas and of sentiments most readily unite individuals, if the similarity of hearts [almas] *form the base of friendship, as Cicero says, the more uniform character and customs of the Provinces of Nueva Granada must form among them a more durable and close union than that established among the different provinces of North America. The climate of these, the original formation of the Colonies, the different epochs in which they were founded by peoples that had diverse origin, diverse languages, different religion, different laws and customs, has formed of all according to the judgment of Masson, a heterogeneous body that with diverse necessities and diverse interests could not have that harmony, that is so badly needed for the perfection of the general union. But if the observation of this political philosopher is correct, if the notable differences that are observed between the provinces of the North weaken the principal bonds of their federation, paralyze the means of the Government, and enervate the movements of the social body; the uniformity of origin, language, religion, government, laws, and customs of the Provinces of Nueva Granada must, on the contrary, tighten more easily the bonds of its reciprocal union, and establish on a more solid basis a more perfect federation.*[7] [my translation]

Latin American countries at their inception did have a great deal in common: one king, one system of law and administration, one religion (Judaism and Protestantism were not treated as religions, but as heresies), one military system, one language among their effective governing population, and one general approach toward education. The historical contrast with the United States is obvious, with the latter's diversity in these matters well articulated above by Pombo.

The fact that modern Latin America was born out of such a remarkable unity in these things and still feels it must create more unity should give pause. One must consider the possibility that the very consensus and commonality that existed in Latin America at her independence could be the basis for her contemporary political arrangements. With so much in common in the realm of religion, language, and traditions, it may be that these nations did not recognize the necessity for a theory and a formal mechanism whereby political differences might be resolved.

Political arrangements in Latin America were derivative of a fundamental cultural-religious-economic consensus.[8] Given a wide range of agreement in these areas, it seemed natural to the founding fathers of these nations to set up a political framework whereby such consensus could be continued. Spanish Americans hypothesized that strong political foundations could best be established by creating an organic system of government whereby the general consensus might be carried over into politics, just as had been the case in colonial times. This outlook was embraced by Simon Bolívar, political theorist to Latin America. In his famous speech at Angostura in 1819, he said:

Unity, unity, unity must be our motto in all things. The blood of our citizens is varied: let it be mixed for the sake of unity. Our Constitution has divided the powers of government: let them be bound together to secure unity.[9]

In relation to such a world view, a separation of powers was nonsensical. Legislatures saw themselves as spokesmen for the general will, and courts became appendages of that national interest, prepared not to deal out an impersonal justice, but to defend the general welfare.

Thus, while the North American founding fathers had busied themselves with protecting the dispersion of power, the Latin American founding fathers sought to unify power. Disagreement over a wide range of religious, cultural, and economic issues led the original thirteen colonies here to seek a mechanism for resolving inevitable conflict, whereas Spanish American original unity kept them from seeing a need for such a mechanism. Fidel Castro is no less representative of Spanish America than Bolívar, in continuing this traditional emphasis upon unity. In a 1965 interview with Lee Lockwood he explained his party:

First, it is the revolutionary vanguard, the political organization of the workers who, manifesting the power of the state, mobilize the masses to the accomplishment of the tasks and functions of the revolution. It educates them, it organizes them, it directs and controls the administration, it draws up the plans of work and controls the carrying out of those plans. It is, in short, the political power. There is no duality, neither of powers nor of functions.[10]

Either legally or extralegally, Spanish Americans have sought unity to eliminate competing centers of power. The nonlegal coups and countercoups are familiar to all. But it is often overlooked that such phenomena as the Mexican one-party system or the Colombian elimination of conflict through periodic trading of power between Liberals and Conservatives also constitute part of a drive for consensus through the elimination or channeling of competition. Viewed in this light, present-day Cuba presents only the most obvious of a long line of unitary governments.

It may well be that the general inability of Spanish American nations to adopt either Marxism or pluralistic democracy follows from the fact that both of these are conflict theories. Madison and Marx both saw man as a somewhat self-interested creature within a capitalistic social order. When this view of man was interpreted in political terms, in the one case the solution emerged as a continued clash of factions representing group interests; and in the other, a struggle between two great classes made up of the bourgeoisie and the proletariat. Both theories revolved around property and both accepted conflict as a natural (if not everlasting in the case of Marx) state of man.

In looking for an explanation of this monistic world view (other than the obvious existence of a great deal of agreement at the moment of independence) one cannot but be struck by the importance of a common Catholic culture. Both late medieval and modern Catholicism embrace certain propositions which support consensual politics.

The monistic character of Spanish American social and political action is based upon medieval assumptions regarding the correct governing of men, the basic proposition of which is the belief in a telos. Monistic democracy finds its definition, its *raison d'être*, in a worldly teleology. The salient feature of this type of government is an earthly *summum bonum*. Participants in the ethic of the Earthly City have consistently found their *summum bonum* in the concept of the *common good*. The common good is the highest goal of Saint

Augustine's City of Man. It is the referent point of Catholic politics. While recognizing that man's ultimate goal is in the hereafter of the Heavenly City, the common good is seen as a *realistic* goal for fallen man while participating in the life of the Earthly City. It is this end which unites and makes possible monistic government.

The common good serves as the standard for worldly activity. The nature of man's activity within the *civitas terrena* is derived from the end which Catholicism embodies in the common good. Because the end is common, man is not seen as alone and afraid in a world he never made pursuing his own good.[11] Thus, unlike liberal democracy which focuses upon the pluralistic goals of its members, monistic democracy demands a secular teleology. And whereas liberal pluralistic democracy centers around the otherworldly goal of individual salvation (self-interest), monistic democracy stresses the importance of the worldly goal of the communal good. From Saint Thomas Aquinas who stressed that "in human affairs there is the common good, the well-being of the state or nation,"[12] to Machiavelli's contention that "it is not individual prosperity, but the general good that makes cities great,"[13] this had been a consistent belief of Catholic theorists.[14]

It is a teaching of the Catholic religion that the common good has an intrinsic worth and character of its own which is apart from the sum of many private interests.[15] Participants within this world view are convinced that to the extent one pursues his private interest to that degree the public interest is being sacrificed; "for private and common pull different ways," as Saint Thomas phrased it.[16] The two are incompatible: one makes selfish demands, the other moves one toward commonality. "The particular interest and the common good are not identical. We differ in our particular interests and it is the common good that unites the community."[17]

Monistic democrats argue, perforce, that as particular interests differ they are invariably divisive. This world view was brought into the modern Latin American nation-state during her independence period, 1810 to 1830. Bolívar's bitterness over the early loss of Venezuela to the Spaniards in the Wars of Independence should be read in this light: "Party spirit determined everything and, consequently, caused us more disorganization than the circumstances themselves. Our division, not Spanish arms, returned us to slavery." He summed up the situation by concluding that it was "the internal factions which in reality were the fatal poison that laid the country in its tomb."[18] He reasoned that if the polity has a common goal, then obviously it could not be balanced, negotiated, or bartered; it could not be divided up. His solution to the problem of internal diversity was to seek unity by whatever means were available. Thus was born the famous War to the Death which he initiated in 1813.

Few monistic democrats would disagree with Bolívar's historical diagnosis of the problem or his tough-minded solution. Most believe that factional diversity of any kind is the single greatest threat to monistic democracy and must be eliminated.[19] Latin America as a civilization is convinced that true political, social, and economic unity cannot be born out of diversity. In their minds the words *diversity* and *anarchy* have become synonymous. To the extent that diversity exists, therefore, it is assumed that unity is precluded. One or the other must give way. Competing factions have been successfully controlled or eliminated for a century and a half in Latin America. It is this fact that runs like a thread through the life of such apparently different polities as, for example, Paraguay, Mexico, and the Cuba of both Batista and Castro. Today it is continued through ECLA- and AID-sponsored projects for the *planificación* of development at the expense of any potentially faction-ridden *improvisación*.

Catholicism as a theory of governance has continually advocated the primacy of the common (or public) good over private interest. But such a worldly teleology demands unity. It can only be successfully effected when the population has much in common. That is, the people must have ties that bind. According to Catholic theorists, unity is the prerequisite for arriving at the common good.[20] Saint Thomas argued therefore that "the most important task for the ruler of any community is the establishment of peaceful unity."[21] And once such an entity is established "the welfare and safety of a multitude formed into a society lies in the preservation of its unity, which is called peace."[22]

This common good teleology demands a degree of unanimity far in excess of that "consensus" to which liberal democratic countries are accustomed. For while liberal democracy's consensus has been built around an agreement upon private morality extended into the public sphere, monistic Catholicism's worldly teleology requires public religious (ideological) unity as well. This dualistic ethic is most workable when basic legal, structural, and political forms are agreed upon. "It is clear," said Saint Thomas, "that that which is itself a unity can more easily produce unity than that which is a plurality."[23] Or, as Bolívar said at Angostura, "All our moral powers will not suffice to save our infant republic from this chaos unless we fuse the mass of the people, the government, the legislation, and the national spirit into a single united body."[24] Aquinas, in believing there exists a conflict between private and public interests, saw that the less diversity within the society the better. Monistic society should prevail over pluralistic society. Drawing upon history he concluded that "nearly every pluralistic regime has ended in tyranny."[25] Common acceptance of this basic world outlook of Catholicism is as necessary to monistic man as a common acceptance of a pluralistic world view appears essential to liberalism.

It is this tradition that has had a singular effect upon Latin Americans until the present day. Diversity of all types is actively opposed by governments. Monolithic education, monolithic political parties, monolithic local government, and monolithic planning are all fostered in the name of unity and the common good. The political opposition is almost without exception in agreement with this premise.[26] Usually they are only waiting for the day when they may achieve power and impose their concept of the common good upon their old adversaries. This is as true of the political Right as it is of the political Left.[27]

Thus, the definitional qualities of the common good have remained constant ever since Saint Augustine first set forth the limited goal of the Earthly City as an "ordered concord of its members in rule and obedience." Peace, order, concord, unity are almost synonymous terms when used by Catholic theorists and practitioners of the ethic.[28] The vision of an earthly *summum bonum* is possible in monistic democracies because these lands are, as we noted above, primarily ones of concord, of order, and of harmony. It is hardly puzzling but certainly ironic that the United States traditionally has been considered the land of unity and consensus, while Latin America has been seen as the continent of unmanageable diversity.[29] Social commentators on the area have seen only hopeless diversity rather than the basic social monism because they have been looking through cultural, i.e., liberal, blinders.

Monistic democrats in Latin America have been remarkably successful in maintaining their secular teleology. While contemporary commentators sometimes bemoan this social stability and chastize them for their inertia, the fact remains that the ethic has been extremely durable and resilient when judged by its own standards. That is, these polities have maintained a considerable amount of peace and order during the past two centuries. Hence, while republican Latin America was born and reared upon enormous cultural unity, the area has also, during the era of monistic democracy, lived up to ethical injunctions to increase or maintain the unitary vision of the common good and preserve order, peace, and unity.

Monistic democracy becomes more intelligible once one considers the coincidence between liberalism and Protestantism. In contrast to the Catholic politicization of the City of Man, Protestantism politicized the City of God. Economic, political, and social self-interest became an extension of religious self-interest. This was possible because Protestantism sees a coincidence between private and public goods. The coterminous relationship arose out of the Protestant's rejection of the idea of a secular common good. All life, he maintains, should be directed toward one religious end, that of the Heavenly City. As Calvin said, "Where the glory of God is not made the end of the government, it is not a legitimate sovereignty, but a usurpation."[30] Worldly ascetics sought to introduce monasticism into everyday life. But in the politics of the monastery there could be no friction between the particular and the common.

Reformation thinkers turned the modern world to Saint Augustine's premise that the state is an extension of the desires of individuals aggregated: it was Calvin who held that "from the private vices of multitudes . . . has arisen public error."[31] Liberalism stood the proposition on its head. Mandeville with his *Fable of the Bees* concluded that one could have "private vice, public good." He was mercilessly attacked for calling private interest "vice" when it contributed to the public welfare. Classical liberalism rephrased the philosophy to state, "private interest equals the public good."[32] Utilitarians sought, in contrast to Saint Thomas, to place "the interest of every individual as nearly as possible in harmony with the interest of the whole."[33] Economic theorists joined the chorus. Consequently, from Adam Smith's natural identity of interests to Madison's *Federalist* no. 10, pluralistic democrats have assumed that no fundamental contradiction exists between private and public interests.[34]

At Geneva Calvin had endeavored to erect a society in which the private virtues would be uplifted, and from private good would flow the public good. Thus, he would partially achieve in the Earthly City what Saint Augustine had relegated to the City of God: the kingdom of Heaven on earth.[35] The two spheres would be united.[36] As Cromwell in England planned "a moral and a spiritual kingdom of God, perhaps superior to the one at Geneva,"[37] so our Pilgrim Fathers, tutored in the Protestant tradition, sought to construct societies in North America where public morality and private morality would coincide. The blue laws epitomize this endeavor, and that tradition of moral coincidence has continued in a secularized form.

While we are accustomed to think of the uniting of church and state in Catholic countries, I am suggesting that this is only a leftover from medieval times in which these were the two power centers, the "two swords," of Western Europe. Catholicism since Saint Augustine never seriously entertained the notion that politics could be effectively Christianized. Even under the closest church-state relationship such as exists in modern-day Colombia, there is no suggestion that the ethical morality of the Earthly and the Heavenly Cities can be joined. Yet this was the position of early Protestantism, of puritan life, and this was carried over into twentieth-century United States. Here is the premise that moral man leads to moral society.[38] The paradox is that in the Protestant-based unity of the private and the public, the religious and the political, pluralistic life became possible. A unity of public and private interests could only end in either theocracy or in interest politics. If one were to insist upon the beatific vision of the Heavenly City, then the theocracy of Calvinistic Geneva was the logical solution.

But the natural alternative to the theocratic implications of Calvin's *Institutes* was Madison's *Federalist* no. 10. In the latter, one accepted the fact that Protestant man was unable to advance any goal which did not include personal salvation; one accepted that Protestant man was unprepared to embrace any theory whereby his private goals ("appearance" of salvation) conflicted with those of the Earthly City. Having but a single otherworldly teleology and lacking the means to define this end, goals either had to be eliminated as a political factor, or life had to be lived with all of the ordered hierarchy of the monastery which we see in Calvin's Geneva. As Daniel J. Boorstin has pointed out, the United States "started from the necessity of not allowing sectarian diversity to interfere with national unity. And this partly because of the fact that for a long time we had established religions in our separate states."[39] Protestantism, in making the conscience the ultimate authority in matters of salvation, meant that to have republican civil government at all one had to cease discussing the heavenly goals and concentrate exclusively upon individual self-interest. Communal, i.e., political, goals were not possible.

Before interest politics could become a possibility, moderns had to be persuaded of the compatibility of mankind through Lockean visions of a benign state of nature and the Protestant emphasis upon the equality of souls. Even if understandable, it seems the height of irony that simultaneously as liberalism eased up on man's sinful nature it appears to have lost, perhaps forever, the vision of a common worldly goal. Monistic democrats, by contrast, have consistently maintained a simultaneous belief in the evilness of man and the politics of a common earthly *summum bonum.*

Anyone who should align the argument of this paper with the behavioral reality of Latin America is bound to ask, How is it that if monistic democracies rest upon a premise of the public good, there appears to be so much self-interest practiced within that area of the world? One has the feeling that monistic democracies exhibit nothing so much as personalistic struggles in which private good prevails over considerations of public welfare; that agreements between political candidates, political parties, and factions in general are every bit as common, constant, and perhaps sordid as those ententes arranged within pluralistic democracies.[40] How can this apparent contradiction be explained? Self-interest *is* an important ingredient of monistic politics. To be noticed, however, is that self-interest is not seen as legitimate within the public sphere.[41] It therefore cannot be used as an organizing concept for government as long as the Catholic world view is maintained. To adhere to the *bien comun* is to deny status and respectability to interest. Monistic democrats, for example, cannot understand liberal political, social, and economic processes because they do not comprehend the notion of private interest, public good. In fact, they see all around them the obvious: private interest leads to public disregard—a fact which North Americans are only recently suspecting as our tradition rests upon the harmony of interest thesis. The unity hypothesis of Latin America is premised upon the assumption that private interest must be given up in order to secure the common interest. The two are in conflict. As Bolívar said, "It is necessary to sacrifice selfish ambitions for the sake of order and strength in our administration."[42]

But if private interest is not legitimate within a public setting, then it can be restrained only with difficulty. The United States, in recognizing the utility of interest, set up procedures for the neutralization of interest: competing political parties, competing branches of government, competing religions, competing school systems, et cetera. Monistic democracies, by contrast, in looking for teleological unity cannot build a political system upon the competition of interest. It is consistent with their philosophy, then, that political parties should be monolithic, government should be centralized, school systems centrally controlled, religious diversity discouraged. This does not suggest, however, that monistic democracies have no means of checking interest. Obviously, a system which celebrates the common over the particular must have built some checks upon the exercise of the particular. What these are will become more evident as we turn to an examination of monistic man's response to the common good standard.

Implied within the common good philosophy of monistic democracy is an appreciation of goals. Whenever hereditary monarchical government has ended in Catholic countries, some formal enumeration of these goals has been felt to be needed. Machiavelli with his call for a civil religion finds a counterpart in Latin American constitutionalism. Constitutions are written to provide a basis for unity through the statement of common socio-economic-political goals.

Constitutionalism is embraced by monistic democrats as a theoretical outline of the common good. Believing that the public good is anything but an automatic extension of private interest, they find such definitions of public ends necessary. For republican Latin America, constitutionalism is the means toward that definition.

In both medieval kingship and Machiavellian princeship it is law which defines and delineates the common good. Law, in turn, is "nothing else than a rational ordering of things which concern the common good; promulgated by whoever is charged with the care of the community."[43] Saint Thomas said that a law which "does not serve the common good is not 'law' at all."[44] This principle was continued by Machiavelli, who spoke of the ability of great lawgivers of history "to establish laws suitable for the general good."[45]

Monistic democracy following this tradition also endeavors to give juridical definition to the *summum bonum.* It is this need for statement of the teleological goals of the *civitas terrena* that has led to the proclamation of some of the most beautiful laws the world has ever seen. Everyone "knows" that Latin American constitutions begin with the sublime and project the republic upward to the higher reaches of worldly ecstasy. A goodly proportion of the constitution is often devoted to an outline of the common good. The general welfare is perceived to exist in the right of all to work, to be educated, to have security, et cetera. In this way goals are provided that are necessary for a teleologically oriented society. As statements of the common good these constitutions reflect the medieval perception of law as being a code.[46]

Liberal constitutionalism, by contrast, focuses upon process. It says little about ends and much about the means of government. Constitutionalism seemed so self-evidently good to liberal man because it did not involve goals. Checks and balances only make sense when the *summum bonum* is in abeyance. In the United States Constitution one reads of promoting the general welfare. But traditionally Americans gave such clauses little thought. It is the process by which power is balanced, interests checked, and rights preserved that merits the pluralistic democrat's attention. As such, a statement of the general welfare or general good is unnecessary because this end is what emerges out of the struggle of private interests. In the liberal's belief that private good and public good were not at odds, we founded a republic. To have assumed otherwise would have been to challenge the Protestant belief in the pursuit of individual salvation through individualistic means.[47]

True monistic nationhood in Latin America began with the framing of the Mexican Constitution at Querétaro in 1917. This constitution marks the beginning of an explicit return to the secular teleology of the common good in Latin America. Despite the worldly teleological statements of the constitutions prior to that time, the nineteenth century had been disastrous for Latin America in that the private had prevailed over the public. The Mexican Constitution of 1917 marked a shift away from the pluralistic democratic institutional overlay back to the traditional Catholic ethical concern for the common good.[48] Private interests of every kind had been violently eliminated by the 1910 Mexican Revolution; Church, foreign, landed, and business interests were bathed in blood. Prerogatives were erased, and the common welfare was reestablished as the rightful referent of all public actions.[49]

Since 1917 we have seen in other parts of Latin America similar attempts to reestablish their ethical legacy of the common good.[50] Every country of the area has directly or indirectly borrowed the goals set forth in the Mexican Constitution. Borrowing has been widespread, because the original statement of the traditional principles so clearly reflected Latin American aspirations for this secular teleology.

The Cuban example is instructive in this regard. In 1940 the government of Cuba presented the country with a constitution which in many ways reflected the Mexican Constitution of 1917. It provided for an earthly *summum bonum* in terms of land reform, and the right to work, shelter, clothing, and education. Castro, in his famous "History Will Absolve Me" speech, asserted his intention to return Cuba to the principles of that constitution. When he arrived to power, most middle-class Cubans who had supported him soon felt betrayed by his sweeping reforms. They pointed to his earlier defense of the 1940 constitution and saw a contradiction. Yet the contradiction was not in these principles per se. Castro, just as surely as had the Mexicans forty years earlier, made a social revolution to return Cuba to a previous vision of the earthly *summum bonum* that was implicit within the 1940 constitution but of course never before implemented in Cuba. In his defense one must concede that it is doubtful whether the goals set forth in the Constitution of 1940 could have been realized through the kind of pseudo pluralist democratic institutional government envisioned by the middle class.[51] It was Castro who called the Cubans to their colonial tradition of vox populi under the tutorial rule of the enlightened prince. In slapping down the Church, foreigners, and middle-class privilege in general, he was repeating the Mexican experience. The common good of the Earthly City was and remains the referent of his political action: "There is only one interest," says Castro, "the collective interest, the interest of all."[52] How he interprets that referent is, of course, open to many sorts of opinions and judgments.

It is this attempt to recapture a past, to realign their ethical values with the political, social, and economic reality of their countries, which has provided the impetus for Latin American revolution in this century. The appeal of communism for these nations is grounded on the somewhat similar teleology which it proclaims. But one must recall that the Mexican Constitution which is so widely emulated preceded the Russian Revolution. It is from Saint Thomas and Machiavelli rather than from Marx and Lenin that Latin Americans ultimately derive their political bearings.

Since 1917 Latin American revolutionaries have had one primary goal: social justice. For them, social justice means the reestablishment of the common good over the private good. One should recall the words of Saint Thomas at the beginning of this article to the effect that the common good is not the sum of particular interest, in order to see the direction of these movements. A vision of social justice invariably consists in a teleological statement of the earthly common good.[53]

According to Catholicism, social justice cannot be based upon economic competition.[54] Competition denies the essential unity of society and is contrary to the common good. This suggests that no amount of social engineering in Latin America will likely lead to acceptance of capitalism as a legitimate economic mode. Capitalism, both foreign and local, is perceived as detracting from the communal and contributing to the private.[55] No claims as to taxes paid, schools built, or medical services provided by industry are likely to be accepted. Economically what is evident is that private investment in the area is now and probably will continue to be subject to scorn, outrage, and, given the chance, expropriation. The reason for this is that, however benevolent these corporations may be, from the Catholic ethical point of view private interests are contrary to the public good,[56] and private profit almost invariably takes away from public well-being. Consequently there exists a persistent effort within Latin America to integrate private and public economic enterprise on the one hand, or, as the radicals advocate, eliminate the private altogether.[57] Extension of this world view into legal form can be seen in article 145 of the 1961 Constitution of Bolivia: "The Executive Power shall periodically formulate a general plan for the economic and social development of the country, the execution of which shall be obligatory. Private initiative shall receive the encouragement and cooperation of the State whenever it contributes to the improvement of the national economy."

In pluralist democracies the lack of an earthly teleology leads to an emphasis upon equality rather than justice. Thomas Hobbes began this tradition by asserting that "justice is a certain equality, as consisting in this only; that since we are all equal by nature, one should not arrogate more right to himself, than he grants to another, unless he have fairly gotten it by compact."[58] Granting that justice follows upon compacting or agreement, quite naturally Hobbes could reject the idea of the common good: "For there is no such *finis ultimus,* utmost aim, nor *summum bonum,* greatest good."[59] It is only in very recent years that we have begun to debate justice, which presupposes some idea of the common good. Perhaps a major problem in both the United States and South Africa concerning the matter of racial equality is that the Calvinistic tradition of an exclusive otherworldly teleology makes it extremely difficult to discuss worldly justice. Nothing within the Protestant vision prepares one for dealing with this matter.[60] Liberal governments have only with reticence intervened in such questions of social justice. Our tradition can be seen in the words of Adam Smith, who said that "we may often fulfill all the rules of justice by sitting still and doing nothing."[61] The implementation of any social justice program presupposes a vision of the common good which pluralistic democrats would rather believe is automatic given the protection of private "civil" rights.

The monistic tradition of Latin America continually calls forth certain behavior in the present age. Monism presents us an acting model for understanding the area. In the following I have tried to articulate two major political stances of monistic democrats. One concerns rights, the other representation.

Rights

Monistic democrats argue the correctness and utility of limiting individual rights, whereas liberal or pluralist democrats contend for a much more rigidly defined and absolute statement of rights.

Where the common good of the Earthly City takes precedence over the particular interest, individuals per se can have no inalienable rights. Individual rights may conflict with the attainment of the goals of the political order and must therefore be qualified. Saint Thomas was precise in his qualification: "Laws are passed to ensure the smooth running of the common wealth. Unrestricted rights are not allowed in any civil constitution. Even in a democratic state, where the whole people exercise power, rights are not absolute but relative."[62]

Bolívar followed the tradition established by Aquinas. He held that the defeat of the first Venezuelan government by Spanish power was due to its form, which was adopted "in keeping with the exaggerated precepts of the rights of man."[63] A concept of individual rights appeared selfish if not arrogant to the founding fathers of Latin America. Absolute rights are presumptuous in that they appear to stand outside the common good. For monistic democrats the public or common good is always to be chosen over the individual good. An absolute right position denies this. It is not surprising therefore that the founding fathers of Latin America reinterpreted Enlightenment premises. The rights of Man became the common rights of men, or something comparable.[64]

Natural right theory made sense to liberal man because he believed in the coincidence between the public and the private good. As Protestant man had no defined earthly *summum bonum*, rights did not have to be qualified but could be natural, and unalienable. As the doctrine evolved, therefore, Western liberalism concluded that there was no essential conflict between the private rights of citizens and the undefined public good. Edwin S. Corwin has synthesized that historical position: "That the public good might not always be compatible with the preservation of rights, and especially with the rights of property, never once occurs to [Locke]. A century later the possibility did occur to Adam Smith, and was waived aside by his 'harmony of interests' theory."[65] In the United States one sees that the contract between citizens and their government provided for the protection of individual rights and, through the protection of groups, factional rights. In the *Federalist* papers North Americans find a lucid explanation of the attempt to found a government while protecting these individual and group rights.[66] Diversity of interests is the primary ingredient. Warring factions are accepted as inevitable.

The pluralistic tradition and perceptions of this undefined common good are best summarized by Madison in *Federalist* no. 51: "If a majority be united by a common interest, the rights of the minority will be insecure."[67] From this he derived the proposition that it is only within a pluralistic society that one's rights and interests are protected. This attitude is so strongly entrenched within our tradition that few would stop to think about it.

Yet for monistic democrats the idea that the existence of a plurality of competing interests could lead anywhere except to anarchy is almost beyond comprehension.[68] As Simón Bolívar once put the matter, "Chile will not alter her laws, ways, and practices. She will preserve her uniform political and religious views. In a word, it is possible for Chile to be free."[69] The reason for the plurality-anarchy thesis is clear: diversity is not by nature directed toward the common good, but toward the particular good.(In contrast to the United States fear of a tyranny of a unified majority, Latin America has concerned itself exclusively with the tyranny of ruling minorities.) Good government demands a defense of the earthly *summum bonum* against encroaching minorities. Consequently, the Latin American tradition has always viewed rights as limited by the will of those who govern. Relying upon Roman law concepts and rejecting the natural law premises of the liberal tradition, Latin American governments thus deny the possibility of men having rights of a constant nature. In colonial times it was the king who defined these rights. He had the power to give and to take away one's freedom. It was King Alfonso of Spain who said, "Liberty is a power that every man naturally has of doing whatever he wishes, so long as force, law, or custom do not take it away."[70] The scenario was prepared for modern times with these significant exceptions. Force, law, and custom early came to be considered as legitimate qualifications to individual liberty and rights.[71] Yet this qualification to rights occurred because Latin American founders saw in these things the only acceptable means for avoiding anarchy. "Unless there is a sacred reverence for country, laws, and authority," said Bolívar, "society becomes confused, an abyss—an endless conflict of man versus man, group versus group."[72] A monistic orthodoxy was thus attempted and continues to be the *sine qua non* of Latin American government.

Monistic democracy arose out of a theory which advocated unity, but it must be recalled it also grew out of a situation of de facto unified religious world: monolithic Catholicism. Unlike most areas of the Western world, their classic revolutionary era in no way embraced premises of religious diversity. Monolithic Catholicism survived the Latin American revolution not because of a triumph of Catholicism over Protestantism, but rather due to the lack of a true religious conflict situation. Leaders of the Independence, while widely read in classical and Enlightenment philosophies, took their bearings from their tradition and reinterpreted what they read in terms of that tradition.[73] Unlike liberal democrats, they did not embrace atomistic theories of human nature. Man was not seen as egoistic and oriented entirely toward private ends. On the contrary, the Catholic world view is premised upon public goals and a communal orientation.

Lacking a theory of religious multiplicity, political diversity was not self-evident. As Bertrand de Jouvenel has commented, "I need not 'stand on my rights' when I am in a company of like-minded people."[74] Such was the case in Latin America. The ongoing importance of religious consensus for Latin America can be seen in a 1963 conference, "Religion, Revolution, and Reform," sponsored by the University of Notre Dame. Following the presentation of papers by Latin and North Americans, a panel discussion was held. "One of the major questions considered was whether religion could be expected to serve in the foreseeable future as a cohesive force that might contribute to a political consensus."[75] Within the context of a liberal polity, such a consideration would be brushed aside. Political pluralism in the United States, for example, had been intimately linked with religious pluralism.[76] In the matter of rights this premise had been made explicit. James Madison wrote in *Federalist* no. 51, "In a free government the security for civil rights must be the same as that for religious rights. It consists in the one case in the multiplicity of interests, and in the other in the multiplicity of sects." Legislatures were forbidden to make laws prohibiting or abridging these rights.

In contemporary Latin America the constitutions subject one's civil rights to the will of legislatures. These constitutions disagree with the liberal democrat's assertion that it is the concern of law not to lay down what is right but to maintain rights.[77] They deny the pluralistic *sine qua non,* for example, by limiting the freedom of association to "purposes not prohibited by law";[78] association "in accordance with the law";[79] association "for any lawful purpose."[80] The rights of speech and press are similarly qualified.[81] In this manner, a monistic society maintains itself. Opposition political parties automatically find their rights curbed. Economic and social groups that pose a threat to the party in power similarly find restrictions upon their civil rights. This holds true whether the party in power is of the Right or of the Left.

Monistic democracy holds that the capricious exercise of free speech and free press can endanger the stability of constitutionally elected governments. A government exercising legitimate authority cannot allow its entire program for advancing the common good (for example, one of economic development) to be endangered by the careless, irresponsible, or devious words of its detractors. Nor, they believe, would a legitimate government last long which permitted its opponents to assemble in public or in private for whatever evil ends they chose.

Representation of the *Bien Comun*

Monistic democrats adhere to the belief that a nation can best be represented when congressmen represent the common good. Liberal or pluralist democrats, by contrast, tend to favor a representative government whereby congressmen stand for the interests of a defined constituency. Monistic democracy holds that the primary function of legislators is the representation of the national interests. As individuals, they insist upon the basic unity of the social order and the government's role as that of insuring that the various factious entities contribute to the general welfare of the nation as well as to their own private interests. Where these two conflict, it is the public good that in every case must be sought and defended.

In Latin America there is rather common agreement that representatives, once they are elected, do not represent their constituents, but rather the nation as a whole. An indication of this common Latin American (Roman law) way of thinking is given by the Constitution of Panama: "Deputies, once elected, represent the entire Nation, are not subject to any mandate and obey only the dictates of their conscience."[82] This Rousseauian premise fits well with the medieval Thomistic concept of unity. It tends to preclude intraparty conflict over socio-economic issues. Pluralistic critics might point out that as legislators are not asked to contemplate the necessities of a given state or department, they tend to represent essentially their own party or private interests. Reelection does not depend upon their performance within the legislature in terms of the constituents' interests. Their campaigns are waged on the basis of party affiliation and not on local issues. Legally this is often reenforced by preventing representatives from running as independents and by a system of proportional representation. Thus, the rewards of politics are sought and gained by building a base within one's political party rather than within the state, department, or municipality.

Yet monistic democrats see some positive effects to be gained. First, this theory of representation unites an otherwise divisive separation of powers. As Latin American elections tend to be party elections, the president, as head of the winning party, is also the natural leader of the parliamentary majority as in England. Legislators have little local support or base and owe their primary allegiance to the newly elected president. By this means a president commands his party and thereby tends to control the legislature which is dominated by his party members. And in all probability he can simultaneously control the judicial system, which more often than not is elected by the legislature. Consequently, most Latin American nations can maintain their monistic nature by constitutional means. A new election or a coup may bring a change in domination through the ascendency of a new party or group, but ritualized conflict is avoided.

Another positive aspect of the representation of the common good is that it creates and perpetuates ideological political parties. As representatives are legally responsible to no one in particular, their tendency is to defend nationalistic or ideological propositions. Communal goals are thus kept constantly before the eyes of both fellow politicians and constituents.

Political representation of the *bien comun* is grounded in a corporate conception of interest articulation. Monistic democrats believe that the common good most appropriately can be advanced by placing restrictions upon the number and type of interest groups. Liberal democrats, by contrast, favor a more free swinging exchange between a wide range of factions. A diversity of interest groups is the alpha and omega of pluralistic politics. As Tocqueville held, "There are no countries in which associations are more needed, to prevent the despotisms of faction . . . than those which are democratically constituted."[83] Hence, the key to pluralism, liberals maintain, is the liberty of interests to organize and seek to be heard. Wherever the right of association is arbitrarily or inconsistently restricted, there exists by definition a limitation upon the pluralistic society.

In Latin America there are a number of institutional groups such as the Catholic Church, the armed forces, and traditional liberal and conservative political parties. There are political parties of an ideological, personalistic, and pragmatic nature. There are associations of landowners, professionals, commercial interests, industrial interests, and laborers. And each country has a number of lodges and social clubs. Two general observations make clear the noncompeting nature of interest groups in Latin America in the face of this seeming plurality of groups. First is the fact that few of these interest groups have ever simultaneously existed for any length of time with their natural opposites. When the liberal party is in power, chances are that the conservatives are in exile; where the Catholic Church is dominant, the Protestants have been historically proscribed; where the landowners are organized, the *campesinos* are exploited; where rural cooperatives are functioning, the large landowners try to destroy them; where labor is strong, industry is afraid to invest; and where industry is strong, organized labor is somewhat suppressed. Thus, while Latin America evidences a certain plurality of interest groups, there are few examples of stable competing interests. In addition, as a general rule, in a field of potentially competing interests, one group tends to be aligned with the government to the exclusion of its natural opposite. With this alignment often comes official proscription or harassment of the competing interest. Unity is achieved by suppression of the opposition and the traditional quest for monolithic control continues.

A second observation is that lower-class and lower middle-class groups are seldom organized. Usually they function as passive masses rather than as positive defenders of their interests. In terms of politics, they are only slightly represented, and lack influence. The reason for this is evident, according to Tocqueville: "When some kinds of associations are prohibited and others allowed, it is difficult to distinguish the former from the latter beforehand. In this state of doubt, men abstain from them altogether, and a sort of public opinion passes current, which tends to cause any association whatsoever to be regarded as a bold, and almost an illicit enterprise."[84]

This unity of interest groups is the cornerstone of monistic politics. The Latin American recognizes and agrees with the pluralist's description of his past as characterized by a paucity of competing interest groups. They do not, however, draw the same conclusions. It is not the monolithic (corporate) character of interest groups that make the Latin American angry, but the ends for which such groups have worked. Social justice will be achieved, he maintains, when these groups begin to serve the masses and not only an elite. In countries of scarce capital resources, he argues, the luxury of strikes and strife between various labor organizations is intolerable and inefficient. Some dominant force must prevent such actions. The same basic proposition holds for the business and agrarian interests. Therefore, it seems to them wise to foster the growth of strong monolithic corporate interest groups which can advance their positions and needs within a monolithic framework. Argentine corporatism under Perón, and Mexican centralism under the PRI are two of the most obvious examples of this way of thinking. Indirectly, monistic theory has been given wide currency in Latin America through the theories of Raul Prebisch and the Economic Commission for Latin America. This stress upon the need for programming economic development has had the effect of reenforcing the traditional monistic beliefs of the area. The state has officially been empowered to deal with society's ills and competition between interest groups has not been encouraged.

Both economic and political theories of public welfare as approximating the collection of private interests run counter to the premises and practices of Latin America. These liberal theories erase the distinction of the dualistic Catholic ethos. They reduce the public good to an extension of the private good. To the mind of the liberal democrat, political-economic self-interest is valid, because religious self-interest is valid. Monistic democrats deny the politics of interest, economic self-interest and the role of religious self-interest or private morality a place in the world. Thus, what stands out in these countries is an elevated goal of the public good being pursued by essentially amoral means.

This article began with a suggestion that not pluralism, but monism is part of the Latin American tradition, and that revolutions are inherently conservative. If such is true, then one can, it would seem, expect a resurgence in the coming years of monistic democracy. Latin Americans will say increasingly with Bolívar, "Surely unity is what we need to complete our work of regeneration."

Notes

1. University of Illinois, 1961. Scott analyzes Mexican political phenomena with "the group approach to the study of the political process." He justifies his method thusly: "This generalized approach has universality in that the decision-making process and the interaction of the interest groups which participate in it are common to all political systems, no matter what the constitutional structure or the values under which the government machinery is operated."

2. Cited by W. W. Rostow in *View from the Seventh Floor* (New York: Harper, 1964), p.4. Frederick Harbison delivered a speech entitled "Human Resource Develop-

ment in Venezuela" to the IDES Conference on the Development and Promotion of Man (July 17, 1964). Commenting upon the multitude of interest groups in Venezuela he said, "The pluralistic rather than the monolithic society holds the keys to progress."

The Realist School of Politics has been particularly ethnocentric in its espousal of political pluralism. For example, Hans Morgenthau says, "This school, then, sees in a system of checks and balances a universal principle for all pluralist societies. It appeals to historic precedent rather than abstract principles, and aims at achievement of the lesser evil rather than of the absolute good" (*Politics Among Nations*, 2d ed. [New York: Knopf, 1954], p. 31).

3. "Brazil, A Christian Country," in *Whither Latin America* (Monthly Review Press, 1963), p. 110.

4. Nowhere has this fact been more clear than in the breakup of "monolithic" communism in the past fifteen years. Without the power of the Red Army, communism in Czechoslovakia, Yugoslavia, Hungary, Poland, and Rumania would in each case evolve differently. Indeed, it is now obvious that despite the Red Army, distinct national roads to communism have occurred within these countries. Communism has repeated in the twentieth century, primarily in Eastern Europe and Asia, the experience of the revolutionary age of the eighteenth century. The French and North American revolutions preceded by a few years the Latin American revolutions. Yet despite the common fund of Enlightenment ideas current at the time, each of these areas of the Western world took a very different course. Significant is that from the enigma of Cuban and Chinese communism today, backward in time to the French Revolution, nations have played out their revolu-

tions in such a way as to conserve much of their past. There is more than a little of the prerevolutionary past in Napoleon's crowning himself emperor. And one can see shades of the Mayflower Compact in the North Americans' attempt to establish themselves as a nation under law with individual rights.

5. It is perhaps relevant to add that I see no indication whatever that Latin Americans want to change this world outlook. Nor, if we truly believe in self-determination of peoples, should we want them to. The danger to our foreign policy and the social sciences is rather that we may fail to recognize this basic difference between Latin American and United States political aspirations; and, not recognizing this difference, we might unwittingly force Latin Americans to choose between a form of North American pluralism and Marxist monism. In forcing such a choice we must recognize that the latter have a monistic similarity to their past that our own system cannot match. An indication of those similarities between Jesuits and Marxists has been sketched by Gerald Brenan in *The Spanish Labyrinth* (Cambridge University Press, 1960), p. 326. Yet such a choice is, happily, not the only one available. The true choice for Latin America is among the various forms of political monism. As a nation we have the power to influence that choice: we can foul it up with visions of sugar-pluralisms dancing in our heads, or we can accept and support a monistic style of government that is in keeping both with their past and with our interests.

6. Latin America is a land of unity, of concord, of order. The travel brochures are wrong: however diverse it may look to the tourist, the people of these lands have a unity of tradition and outlook perhaps unparalleled in the

world. (The particularly Indian communities with their colorful blend of Catholicism and primitivism are not considered here for the reason that before these Indians become participants in the political process, they tend to become socialized into the Spanish Catholic ethical tradition—this despite the hopes and efforts of both Protestant missionaries and communist revolutionaries!) It is this commonality, consensus, and unity that is at the base of their contemporary political-economic problems. For some reason the idea has grown in North America that Latin America is an area of great diversity and conflict, only waiting upon the achievement of "consensus" society in order to develop. The forefathers of Latin America would have been astounded at these facile assertions of diversity. They saw themselves as part of a unified order, which hardly implies an egalitarian order.

7. Miguel Pombo, "Discurso Preliminar," *Constitución de los Estados-Unidos de América,* Traducida del Inglés al Español por el Ciudadano Miguel de Pombo (Bogotá: En la Imprenta Patriotica de D. Nicolas Calvo, 1811), p. 73. Francisco Miranda, a better-known revolutionary of the Independence Movement, wrote in a similar vein, "Since we are all sons of one father, since we all have the same language, the same customs and above all the same religion . . . let us unite in the great work of [gaining] our common liberty" [my translation] ("Proclama," *Textos sobre la independencia* [Caracas: Academia Nacional de la Historia, 1959], p.151). Modern Latin American writers, of course, take quite an opposite position. For example, Vianna Moog, in *Bandeirantes and Pioneers,* says in comparing Brazil and the United States, "From the viewpoint of orography, hydrography,

or climate, the advantages of the United States are obvious" (New York: Braziller, 1964, p. 23).

8. A Colombian, Diego Padilla, gave one of the clearest expositions of this unity: "Aqui no hay Romano, ni Barbaro, no hay Griego, ni Judio; todos somos Americanos, todos somos hermanos, y aunque hayamos nacido en diversos lugares, todos somos hijos de un mismo Reyno, todos nos amamos, no hay diferencia entre nosotros, ni espiritu de partido" (20 October 1810).

9. *Selected Writings of Bolívar,* Compiled by Vicente Lecuna, Edited by Harold A. Bierck, Jr. (New York: The Colonial Press, 1951), pp. 191-192. Francisco Miranda did not give up hope even in prison that a unity could be found whereby in the future Americans and Europeans "formasen una sociedad, una sola familia y un solo interés" (*Textos sobre la independencia,* p. 165). The premise was soon narrowed to include only nationals, but the idea remained intact. Colombia, perhaps the country that was most influenced by Bolívar, included in her 1960 Constitution the following: "Congress, the Government, and the Judges have separate functions, but they collaborate harmoniously in the realization of the ends of the State" (title 5, art. 55).

10. Lee Lockwood, *Castro's Cuba, Cuba's Fidel* (Vintage, 1969), p. 154 (the italics are mine).

11. Indicative of the communal over the private is the finding of a well-known study of political attitudes. In Mexico nearly thirteen hundred persons were presented with this statement: "The individual owes his first duty to the state and only secondarily to his personal welfare." Almost twelve hundred respondents agreed with the sentence. Actual count was as follows: 1,190 agree; 62 disagree; 43 don't know; et cetera. (Gabriel A. Almond and Sidney Verba, *The Civic Culture* [Prince-

ton University Press: 1963]).

12. *Summa Contra Gentiles,* 3. 80.

13. Niccolo Machiavelli, *The Discourses,* 2. 2.

14. Montevideo's Catholic newspaper carries the name *El bien publico.* For a glimpse of the rather overwhelming importance of the common good in the thought of Catholicism's official dogmatist, see Th. Eschmann, "A Thomistic Glossary on the Principle of the Preeminence of a Common Good," in *Mediaeval Studies* (Toronto, 1943), pp. 123-65. Machiavelli referred extensively to the idea of the common good, or the "public benefit." Indeed, according to Allen H. Gilbert, "the chief of his political ideas is to be found in the traditional political conception of the common good" (*Machiavelli, the Chief Works and Others* [Durham: Duke University, 1965], 1:15). It is this good which constitutes the highest end of life and also justifies acts of cruelty. Machiavelli says, for example, that "Romulus deserves to be excused for the death of his brother and that of his associate, and that what he had done was for the general good" (*The Discourses,* 1. 10).

15. Saint Thomas said, "The common good of the state and the singular good of the person do not differ merely as many and one, for there is a formal difference" (*Summa theologica,* 2a-2ae. 58. 7, ad 2).

16. *De regimine principum,* 1. 1. In this as in most matters, Aquinas was following Saint Augustine, who wrote, "The Scripture saith, 'They were but one heart and one soul toward God' (Acts 2: 41; 4: 4, 32, 35). But many, so as not to make a place for the Lord, seek their own things, love their own things, delight in their own power, are greedy for their private interests. Whereas he who would make a place for the Lord, should rejoice not in his private good but in the common good. They did this with their private goods; they made them common.... Let your charity consider this; that on account of those things which we individually possess there exist lawsuits, enmities, discords, wars between men, tumults, dissensions against one another, scandals, sins, iniquities, murders" (*Enarrationes in Psalmos,* 131. 5, 6).

17. Thomas Aquinas, *De regimine principum,* 1. 1. "People fall apart by their private interests and come together by their common interests" (ibid.). See also Jacques Maritain, *The Person and the Common Good* (Scribner's, 1947), p. 39.

18. *Selected Writings of Bolívar,* pp. 22-23. Elsewhere in this volume Bolívar speaks of "the shame of our own internal cleavage" (p. 123). Some patriots saw unity arising not out of factions, but out of fraternity: "La nueva república, cuyas partes se reunirán con vínculos de amor y fraternidad para formar un todo permanente e indisoluble" (from "Diario Político," Enero 29 de 1811, in Luis Martínez Delgado y Sergio Elías Ortiz, *El periodismo en la nueva Granada, 1810-1811* [Bogotá: Editorial Kelly, 1960], p. 328).

19. Pedro Molina, an influential Colombian writer, summarized this position: "Yo no he hablado en mis escritos de crímenes sino de abusos, que pueden no obstante llegar a ser perjudiciales a los intereses de la nación y por lo mismo llegar a ser delitos. Hablo de partidos, o más bien de facciones, perniciosas siempre en un estado libre" (*El editor constitucional,* 16 October 1820).

A more contemporary example can be found in the words of Raúl Ampuero, Secretary-General of the Socialist Party of Chile: "In practice, the real threat to unity is constituted by factional activities, that is, when several members unite to work together, creating a clandestine machine within the official organization. The mere fact of promoting such a group indicates contempt for normal procedures and institutions and, in essence, for the party itself" (cited in Ernst Halperin, *Nationalism and Communism in Chile* [Cambridge: MIT Press, 1965], p. 173).

According to Colombian conservatives, "... lo que Colombia necesita en estos momentos es un gobierno de genuina unión nacional, no contaminado del espiritu de partido, en que sean llamados a colaborar todos los hombres capaces, para que en completa armonia, en un haz apretado de voluntades y de esfuerzos, contribuyan a la obra comun de progreso y bienestar nacionales.... Ningun espiritu de exclusivismo o represalia podra animarlo" (*La convención nacional conservador,* 1946).

20. "Unity does not formally constitute the happy life of the multitude, but is rather a condition necessary for reaching it," points out Jaime Vélez-Sáenz, *The Doctrine of the Common Good of Civil Society in the Works of St. Thomas Aquinas* (University of Notre Dame, 1951), p. 58. Or, as Fidel Castro says, "Strength is in the unity of the people" (Fidel Castro, *Cuba's Socialist Destiny* [New York: Fair Play for Cuba Committee, 1961], p. 7). Bolívar's affinity for monarchy grew out of a similar outlook. Monarchy, he said, "has won its claim for approval by means of the hereditary principle, which renders it stable and by unity which makes it strong" (*Selected Writings of Bolívar,* p. 601).

21. *De regimine principum,* 1. 2.
22. Ibid.
23. Ibid. Compare United States conventional pluralist wisdom which says, "A society that in normal times cannot function adequately without unanimity is unfit for freedom" (Eric Hoffer, *The Ordeal of Change* [New York: Harper, 1952], p. 98).

24. *Selected Writings of Bolívar,* p. 191.
25. *De regimine principum,* 1. 5.
26. An example is that provided by the Chilean Comite Coordinador de la Unidad Popular, in *Programa básico de gobierno de la unidad popular* (no publisher, June 1970).

27. The right-wing Argentine position has been stated by Father Julio Meinveille in *Guerra contrarevolucionaria:* "Counterrevolutionary war urgently demands unity of doctrine, especially within the Armed Forces of the nation. And unity can only be achieved by a return to Catholic, Roman and Hispanic principles upon which the nation was founded and which are the same as those of Western Christianity."

"Without unity of doctrine, the military does not know what to do with the weapons they have at their disposal. Unity is first and foremost that which is most needed and the most truly practical; the rest is just so much trimming" (Cited by Arthur P. Whitaker, "Nationalism and Religion in Argentina and Uruguay," in William V. D'Antonio and Frederick B. Pike, eds., *Religion, Revolution and Reform* [New York: Praeger, 1964], p. 88).

28. "So the first object of whoever rules a multitude is unity, or peace...." (Saint Thomas Aquinas, *De gubernatione rerum in communi,* Q. 103, Art. 3). "Now the welfare and safety of a multitude formed into a society lies in the preservation of its unity, which is called peace. If this is removed, the benefit of social life is lost and, moreover, the multitude in its disagreement becomes a burden to itself. The chief concern of the ruler of a

multitude, therefore, is to procure the unity of peace. It is not even legitimate for him to deliberate whether he shall establish peace in the multitude subject to him, just as a physician does not deliberate whether he shall heal the sick man encharged to him, for no one should deliberate about an end which he is obliged to seek, but only about the means to attain that end. Wherefore the Apostle, having commended the unity of the faithful people, says: 'Be ye careful to keep the unity of the spirit in the bond of peace.' Thus, the more efficacious a government is in keeping the unity of peace, the more useful it will be" (*De regimine principum*, 1. 2).

29. I think Latin Americanists as a whole have usually assumed this position. Of the more explicit recent examples see Kalman H. Silvert, *The Conflict Society: Reaction in Latin America* (Harper, 1961); and James Petras and Maurice Zeitlin, eds., *Latin America: Reform or Revolution?* (Fawcett, 1968), p. 1.

30. John Calvin, "Dedication to Francis I" in *Institutes of the Christian Religion*, trans. from John T. McNeill, ed., *John Calvin on God and Political Duty* (New York: Liberal Arts Press, 1950), p. 6.

31. Calvin, *Institutes*, p. 16.

32. Elie Halévy, *The Growth of Philosophic Radicalism* (Boston: Beacon, 1955), p. 16.

33. John Stuart Mill, "Utilitarianism," in Mary Warnock, ed., *Utilitarianism, On Liberty, Essay on Bentham* (New York: Meridian, 1962), pp. 268-69.

34. Non-Catholic writers to whom monistic men turn for ideas have, of course, denied the existence of any natural identity of interests. Primary of these is perhaps Cicero, who said, "Each one of us . . . should make it his chief aim to identify his own interests with the common good" (*On Duties,* trans. Hubert M. Poteat [University of Chicago, 1950], p. 569).

35. Note how Augustine sees a sharp cleavage between the two cities: "There are two kinds of love, of these the one is holy, the other selfish; the one consults the common good for the sake of the supernal fellowship, the other reducing the affairs of the commonality to their own power for the sake of arrogant domination; the one subject to God, the other endeavoring to Equal Him; the one tranquil, the other turbulent; the one working for peace, the other seditious; the one preferring truth to the praise of those who are in error, the other greedy for praise however got; the one friendly, the other envious; the one wishing for the neighbor what it would wish for itself, the other wishing to subject the very neighbor to itself; the one guiding the neighbor in the interest of the neighbor's good, the other in that of its own. . . . These two kinds of love distinguish the two cities established in the human race . . . in the so to speak commingling of which the ages are passed" (*De genesi ad litteram libri duodecim,* 11, 15, 20).

36. It is precisely the presumptuousness of this undertaking that Reinhold Niebuhr has sought to demonstrate. The failure of Christianity and the problem of our age, says Niebuhr, is due to the intrusion and triumph of rational intelligibility as the key to history. It is based on "the realization that there is actual growth and development in both nature and history" (*Faith and History* [Scribner's, 1949], p. 30). Liberal Protestantism has capitulated to the relative optimistic values of liberalism, says Niebuhr. It has seen in this tradition the *summum bonum.* These Christian ideals have therefore become "possibilities of history." Liberal Protestantism has seen the

opportunity for the realization of the Kingdom of God on earth—herein lies its failure, says Niebuhr. See *An Interpretation of Christian Ethics* (New York: Harper, 1935), pp. 19-20; *Faith and History,* pp. 14-15; *Christian Realism and Political Problems* (Scribner's, 1953), pp. 9-12.

37. Franklin C. Palm, *Calvinism and the Religious Wars* (New York: Holt, 1932), p. 93.

38. Reinhold Niebuhr has effectively attacked this position in his *Moral Man and Immoral Society* (Scribner's, 1948).

39. *The Genius of American Politics* (University of Chicago, 1953), p. 139.

40. The Mexican José Mora directs himself to this matter. See Leopoldo Zea, *The Latin American Mind* (Norman: University of Oklahoma Press, 1963), pp. 52-54.

41. This position has been briefly articulated by Mauricio Guzmán, "El faccionalismo: supervivencia medieval en America Latina," *Journal of Interamerican Studies* 5, no. 4 (October 1963): 465-70. His solution to the problem of faction typifies Latin America: (1) More education to raise the "cultural level" of the masses and leaders of the nation so they hopefully will act for the common good; and (2) form some type of corporate, i.e., unified, government wherein various interests can be represented. Countries which come to mind that have quite directly followed this path are Mexico, Cuba, Argentina, Uruguay, and Colombia.

42. *Selected Writings of Bolívar,* p. 46.

43. *Summa theologica,* Prima Secundae, Q. 90, Art. 4.

44. *Summa theologica,* Prima Secundae, Q. 90, Art. 2.

45. *The Discourses,* 1.9.

46. A. D. Lindsay points out that "the modern constitutional state has reverted to the medieval view that the state rests on law, but with this difference, that its 'fundamental law' is a constitution, a method of deciding questions, not a code" (*The Modern Democratic State* [London: Oxford, 1959], p. 21). Lindsay, of course, is thinking of pluralistic constitutionalism.

47. One may suggest that it is just this traditional view of the world that is breaking down in the United States. It is only when interest fails as a harmonizer that we have need for a President's Commission on National Goals. Politicians and political scientists since the inception of our nation have dealt primarily with variations upon the theme of who gets what, when, how. Emphasis is upon the manner in which the scarce goods of the society are allocated and not upon the teleological question. This appears to be changing.

48. As Mr. Tannenbaum aptly expressed it when comparing the Mexican constitutions of 1857 and 1917: "In one the principle that dominates is that the individual must be before and more than society, in the other the principle that dominates is that society must be before and more than the individual" (Wilfred H. Callcott, *Liberalism in Mexico* [Hamden, 1959], p. 272). During the latter part of the nineteenth century Mexico and Latin America in general looked to positivism for a statement of their common good position. One author speaks of the period of the dictatorship of Porfirio Díaz as that "in which the idea of the good for the Mexican state was defined by the positivistic philosophy of the Frenchman Comte, supplemented, as Leopoldo Zea has shown under the leadership of Justo Sierra with the British positivism of Mill and Spencer" (F. S. C. Northrop, *The Meeting of East and West* [New York: Macmillan, 1946], p. 31).

49. Mexicans can be justly proud

of their constitution. Yet they, as much as North Americans, have failed to perceive the differences between the politics of private interest and the politics of the common good. See as an example of this misunderstanding based on comparison with an earlier constitution, José Antonio Murillo Reveles, *La constitución de apatzingan de Mexico es mucho mas avanzada en principios políticos y sociales que la de los Estados Unidos* (Mexico: Sociedad Mexicana de Geografía y Estadística, 1965).

50. Similar goals had repeatedly been advanced by officials of the colonial Spanish American Empire. That such worldly ends did in fact govern the ordering of Spanish America can readily be seen with the most elementary perusal of the *Siete partidas* or the *Leyes de las Indias.*

51. This realization has since occurred to revolutionaries all over Latin America. As was suggested at the beginning of this article, the middle classes in Latin America are not inclined toward liberal democracy. When this class says it was betrayed by Castro, who promised a democratic government, they are clearly arguing for a government of privilege and not of either pluralist interest politics or the common good.

52. Fidel Castro, *Cuba's Socialist Destiny,* p. 7.

53. The relationship between justice and the common good is stated in the *Summa theologica,* 2-2, Q. 58, Art. 5, conclusion and Art. 12.

54. Pope Pius XI wrote in 1931, in his restatement of Leo XII's encyclical, *Rerum novarum:* "The right ordering of economic life cannot be left to a free competition of forces" ("Quadragesimo Anno," in *The Papal Encyclicals,* ed. Anne Fremantle [New York: Mentor, 1956], p. 233).

55. Emilio Maspero, writing on

"Trade Unionism as an Instrument of the Latin American Revolution," states the feelings of probably most Latin American workers in this regard: "Latin American laborers are disconcerted when the voice of United States trade unionism preaches the advantages of free enterprise and popular capitalism. Among the majority of urban laborers and peasants, free enterprise capitalism is regarded as one of the most formidable forces opposing their betterment. . . . Democracy has many times been confused with capitalism, as if the capitalist system were essential to democracy. The fact is that the majority of the governments on our continent, wrongly called democratic, have always been in the hands of financial oligarchies that have practiced exploitation through capitalism. For us in the Christian trade union movement, democracy is the political form that the social revolution we hope to wage will introduce. This democracy has nothing to do with capitalism as it now exists in Latin America" (In Irving Louis Horowitz et al., *Latin American Radicalism* [New York: Random House, 1969], p. 220).

56. José Figueres stated Catholic conventional wisdom in 1943 in a pamphlet entitled *Palabras gastadas:* "Capitalism or laissez faire, not admitting that the production and use of goods for the consumption of all is . . . an essentially social activity, not a private one, duplicating services without need, destroying goods by speculation and in many other ways, creating an arbitrary division of classes, prejudicial to the group, between directing groups and those engaged in productive activity . . . refining the natural egoism of the human beast, and reducing the field in which the head and heart can develop. . . ." (Cited in Robert J. Alexander, *Prophets of the Revolution* [New York: Mac-

millan, 1962], p. 149). Figueres' words recall an earlier thesis set forth in matchless style by the Uruguayan José Enrique Rodó (1871-1917), "Specialization, utilitarianism, materialism, represent the mediocre life," said Rodó in *Ariel*. Fidel Castro continues the anticapitalism tradition: "We cannot encourage or even permit selfish attitudes among men if we don't want man to be guided by the instinct of selfishness, of individuality, by the wolf, the beast instinct, man as the enemy of man, the exploiter of man, the setter of snares for other men.... The concept of a higher society implies a man devoid of those feelings; a man who has overcome such instincts at any cost, placing above everything, his sense of solidarity and brotherhood among men" (Martin Kenner and James Petras, eds., *Fidel Castro Speaks* [New York: Grove Press, 1969], p. 278).

57. "Concerning Mexico, Raymond Vernon has commented that it is not always possible to distinguish the public from the private sector, as the government is involved in so many ways with industrial and commercial operations. The same may be said in some degree, of many Latin American countries. The Cuban revolution obviously did nothing to alter this generalization. The current efforts of the Chilean government under a political moderate, Eduardo Frei, are not to replace the private sector—to eliminate foreign private ownership of the great mining operations—but to enter as a partner in them so as to begin to gain control over a sector of national activity that has remained more responsive to the needs of the United States than to those of Chile" (Richard N. Adams, *The Second Sowing* [San Francisco: Chandler, 1967], pp. 119-20).

58. Thomas Hobbes, *De cive,* 3. 6.

59. Thomas Hobbes, *Leviathan,* 1. 11.

60. Perhaps this also explains why "socialism" is a bad word in the United States. It suggests a worldly teleology. Self-interest can lead us to embrace socialistic programs, but the ethic prevents us from labeling it as an earthly goal. We thus condemn all "isms" just as we are puzzled as to what to do with the concept of justice, as these suggest worldly political goals or patterns to be striven for.

61. Adam Smith, "Theory of Moral Sentiments," in *Works* (London, 1812), vol. I; 136. Compare Simon Bolívar's opinion that "Justice compels us to act" *(Selected Writings of Bolívar,* p. 82).

62. *Ethics,* 5. Commentary, lect. 2.

63. *Selected Writings of Bolívar,* p. 21.

64. *Selected Writings of Bolívar,* p. 248. In Bolívar's writings there is almost no reference to rights of any kind. Never does he defend individual rights as apart from the common good. When monistic democrats spoke of rights they usually meant collective rights. Thus, Bolívar could speak of "Colombia's rights," "the broadest of rights permitted a people," or act "contrary to social rights," but individual natural rights were not part of his thought.

This way of thinking was, no doubt, helped along by the Spanish word *derecho*. The word means both "law" and "right." The rights of Man in Spanish could be interpreted to mean the "laws" of men by those who had a disposition to do so in order to stay within their tradition. Monistic democrats had, in general, such a desire and, either consciously or unconsciously, soon turned the revolutionary doctrine of natural right into the medieval Catholic doctrine of natural law.

65. Edwin S. Corwin, *The "Higher*

Law" Background of American Constitutional Law (Cornell University Press: Great Seal Books, 1959), p. 71. It is this classical liberalism which made possible a twentieth-century North American statement that "what is good for General Motors is good for the nation." Yet it would be most naive of us to assume that this kind of liberalism is only an economic theory. It coincides with religious premises, albeit long since secularized. No one raised with the ethical tradition of Catholicism would ever have uttered Mr. Wilson's words regardless of the degree to which he embraced laissez faire economics!

66. "Madison's view on the relation between people and government has important consequences. From his conception of government as a means follows not only the primacy of the individual's protection before popular participation in government, but also that his Federalist, advocating the Union, can be a treatise on the Union only in a relative sense and must, in an absolute sense, be a treatise for the individual's rights" (Gottfried Dietze, The Federalist, a Classic on Federalism and Free Government [Baltimore: Johns Hopkins Press, 1960], p. 115).

67. "This policy of supplying, by opposite and rival interests, the defect of better motives, might be traced through the whole system of human affairs, private as well as public. We see it particularly displayed in all the subordinate distributions of power, where the constant aim is to divide and arrange the several offices in such a manner as that each may be a check on the other—that the private interest of every individual may be a sentinel over the public rights" (Federalist no. 51).

68. I personally have never encountered a Latin American who understood the basic premises of North American pluralism as outlined in the Federalist papers. The tradition of nonunderstanding goes back a long way. Miguel Pombo, a Colombian, in 1811 after writing 62 pages of explanation and praise for the North American system of government in his commentary upon our constitution says: "[The United States Constitution] has excluded from the Legislative Bodies those persons who would carry to the deliberations particular interests contrary to the general interest" (Discurso Preliminar, p. 63).

69. Selected Writings of Bolívar, p. 117.

70. Las siete partidas del rey Don Alfonso el Sabio (Paris: Lasserre, 1847), 22. 1.

71. Colombia stated the matter clearly in her fundamental law: "When the enforcement of a law passed for reasons of public utility or social interest conflicts with the rights of individuals, private interests must give way to the public or social interests" (title III, art. 26 [1936]; title III, art. 30 [1945]; title III, art. 30 [1960]).

72. Selected Writings of Bolívar, p. 191.

73. The Colombian patriot, Antonio Nariño, famed throughout South America for his liberal ideas through the 1794 translation of the Declaration of the Rights of Man and of the Citizen, is a clear example of Spanish America not surrendering her tradition and also suggests the kind of reinterpretations that were made by Latin Americans when confronted with Enlightenment ideas. Article Ten of the French Declaration reads: "No one ought to be disturbed on account of his opinions, even religious, provided their manisfestation does not derange the public order established by law." Nariño footnotes his translation of this article with the following comment: "Es decir: qe. si la ley no admite más culto qe. el verdadero, la

manifestación de las opiniones contra la religión no podrán tener efecto sin quebrantar la ley, y pr. consiguiente, no son permitidas por este artículo en donde no se permita más qe. una religión" (José María y Vergara, *Vida y escritos del Antonio Nariño* [Bogotá: Imprenta Nacional, 1946], p. 5). An ideology far removed from the belief in natural and inalienable rights of man is surely implicit in this statement! But it is hardly an isolated instance of his defense of Catholicism. In discussing the advisability of entering into an alliance with either France or England he makes his position more clear. "Esta unión por pactos, no trae los mismos inconvenientes que la subyugación; porque no es lo mismo obedecer que pactar. El primero de nuestros pactos será la Religión de nuestros Padres, y el segundo nuestra libertad, sin la qual no se puede pactar." In attempting to reassure those who worried about the decline of religion he had these words: "Aunque oigas decir que la Religión ha padecido, no lo creas. . . . Lo que sucede en el día es que hay menos hipocritas que antes, pero los hombres son los mismos, y la Religión se mantiene en toda su pureza" (*La bagatela* [Bogotá] 3 November 1811; 26 January 1812).

In the case of the important Argentine revolutionary, Mariano Moreno, one arrives at much the same conclusion. Among other actions, he is famous for the reimpression of Rousseau's *Social Contract* in Buenos Aires during the year 1810. The "Prologo" that Moreno attached to this work is of particular interest. In it he comments on Rousseau: "este hombre inmortal," "la profundidad de sus discursos," "un corazon endurecido en la libertad republicana," "una profundidad de moral" "quiza el primero, que disipando completamente las tinieblas, con que el

despotismo envolvia usurpaciones, puso en clara luz los derechos de los pueblos." However, after these eulogistic phrases Moreno adds, "Como el autor tubo la desgracia, de delirar en materias religiosas, suprimo el capitulo y principales pasages, donde ha tratado de ellas." Moreno thus showed by his action in omitting passages on religion that he disbelieved in free expression and the interplay of ideas at least in the matters of religion. On the positive side one can note his desire to preserve Catholicism from attack in an essay on the liberty of the press. Therein Moreno said, "Que los pueblos yaceran en el embrutecimiento mas vergonzoso, si no se da una absoluta franquicia y libertad para hablar en todo asunto que no se oponga en modo alguno a las verdades santas de nuestra augusta Religión, y a las determinaciones del Gobierno, siempre dignas de nuestro mayor respeto" (Mariano Moreno, *Escritos* [Buenos Aires: Estradas, 1943], vol. 2: 287 and 305).

74. *The Pure Theory of Politics* (New Haven: Yale University Press, 1963), p. 60, n. 1.

75. Frederick B. Pike, "Introduction," in D'Antonio and Pike, *Religion, Revolution and Reform,* p. 19. See also page 112.

76. Emilio Willems lists as among the basic values which North American missionaries tried to spread in Brazil and Chile after 1860 the following: "Complete freedom of conscience or 'soul liberty' enables the individual to seek the truth and to make his own choice and decisions with regard to the supernatural. This includes not only free choice among existing religious bodies and doctrines but also the right to dissent. The logical result of this principle is the acceptance of a 'pluralistic' society and mutual toleration of divergent creeds" ("Culture Change and the Rise of Protestantism in Brazil and Chile,"

in S. N. Eisenstadt, *The Protestant Ethic and Modernization* [New York: Basic Books, 1968], p. 184).

77. Sheldon Wolin, *Politics and Vision* (Boston: Little, Brown, 1960), p. 388, defines constitutionalism as "a system of legal guarantees for enforcing the rights of citizens." The socio-economic-political drifting of Latin America during the nineteenth century was partially due, I believe, to the confusion which pluralistic constitutions introduced to Latin America. A few of the more overtly "liberal" of the documents provided procedural guarantees and suggested that individuals did have rights. These documents were the "utopian" ones for Latin America in that they were not grounded in Catholicism—and did not survive!

78. Constitution of Ecuador, art. 187, par. 13.

79. Constitution of Paraguay, art. 38; Constitution of Nicaragua, art. 32; Constitution of Bolivia, art. 6.

80. Constitution of Mexico, art. 9; Constitution of Costa Rica, art. 25; Constitution of Nicaragua, art. 91. Limitations upon association may be noted in the Constitutions of Venezuela, art. 70; Panama, art. 40; Guatemala, art. 63; Paraguay, art. 32; Chile, art. 10; Colombia, art. 44; Peru, art. 27; Honduras, art. 88.

81. For references on these and other qualifications see Glen Dealy, "Prolegomena on the Spanish American Political Tradition," *Hispanic American Historical Review* 48, no. 1 (February, 1968): 52-54.

82. The same outlook was voiced by Ampuero in Chile with regard to the representative function of the Socialist Party: "The supreme authority of the National Organization Commission represents this common interest and guarantees the national unity of the party." Halperin, *Nationalism and Communism in Chile,* p. 172. The Constitution of Colombia says that "the members of the two Houses represent the entire nation and should vote in the sole interest of justice and the public good." See title 10, art. 99 (1936); title 10, art. 105 (1945); title 10, art. 105 (1960).

83. Alexis de Tocqueville, *Democracy in America,* 1, 12.

84. Ibid., 2. 2, 7.

Toward A
Theory of
Spanish American
Government

Richard M. Morse

The Viceregal Period and Its Antecedents

The purpose of this essay is neither fully to analyze the political experience of Spanish America nor to construct a mature theory which will comprehensively illuminate it. The histories of these eighteen countries are, taken singly, too fragmentary and, taken jointly, too uncorrelated to permit of so systematic a project. In this as in most areas of New World studies the elements for conclusive synthesis are still unavailable. Therefore a heuristic device will be used, which will be to examine certain formal European notions in the hope, not that they will concisely epitomize Spanish American political experience, but that they may be played off against that experience—contrapuntally, perhaps—in a way to evoke corresponding themes.

Professor Northrop has done something of this nature in collating Lockean philosophy with United States political history. As is suggested in the "Note" that concludes this essay, he perhaps oversimplifies the case; but a summary of his argument will be useful here as a point of departure. Professor Northrop asserts that Locke's atomistic conception of the sovereign individual squared neatly with British North American conditions of life. Until the twentieth century the United States was a laissez-faire state: not an active intervenor assuring distribution of limited resources among the needy many, but a passive guarantor of private claims to the new continent's ample wealth. Unlike their North American counterparts, nineteenth-century British Conservatives—with their traditions of noblesse oblige and of a state religion—inclined toward paternalistic social-mindedness and away from Lockean atomism, unbridled laissez-faire and unqualified obeisance to rights of the sovereign individual. British Liberals, who held closer to Lockean ideals, eventually yielded before a socialistic Labor Party. Locke, by this reckoning, was therefore less congenial to his homeland than to the trans-Atlantic

Reprinted from *Journal of the History of Ideas,* 15 (1964), pp. 71-93, by permission of Journal of the History of Ideas, Inc.

England which was colonized during the century into which he was born, and in 1776 the colonists' fealty to him was, for urgent cause, consummately affirmed.[1]

The question now to be raised is: Are there other European philosophies which might be comparably correlated with Spanish American political history?

Spanish American preceded British colonization by more than a century and thus belongs to an era that antedates not only the Lockean rights of man but also the Bousset-and-Hobbes-type apology for the absolutist national state. It is the Catholic kings, Ferdinand and Isabella, who symbolize Spanish America's political heritage.

Isabella in a sense prefigures the divine-right monarch. Her thwarting of the nobles and of the Cortes wherein they formed an estate; her royal agents and administrative reforms that centralized the government; her replacement of feudal levies with a modern army; her use of the faith to further political unity—all have been cited to identify her as a precursor of the Hobbesian autocrat. Yet it must be remembered that for three centuries after Isabella's death the Spanish empire retained, in comparison at least with the burgeoning capitalist countries, many hallmarks of the medieval, hierarchical state.

The "common law" of Isabella's Castile was the *Siete Partidas*, drawn up c. 1260 and promulgated in 1348. Though tinctured with Roman law, the *Partidas* were less Roman rules *for* conduct than medieval-type principles *of* conduct that approached being moral treatises. As late as the nineteenth century Dunham found that:

> ... *if all other codes* [*than the* Siete Partidas] *were banished, Spain would still have a respectable body of jurisprudence; for we have the experience of an eminent advocate in the royal tribunal of appeal for asserting, that during an extensive practice of twenty-nine years, scarcely has a case occurred which could not be virtually or expressly decided by the code in question.*[2]

The *Partidas* assumed the nuclear element of society to be not Lockean atomistic man, but religious, societal man: man with a salvable soul (*i.e.,* in relationship with God) and man in a station of life (*i.e.,* having mutual obligations with fellow humans, determinable by principles of Christian justice). The ruler, though not procedurally responsible to the people or the estates, was bound, through his conscience, to be the instrument of God's immutable, publicly ascertainable law. The *Partidas,* in fact, specifically excoriated the tyrant who strove to keep his people poor, ignorant and timorous and to forbid their fellowship and assemblies.

As mistress of the hierarchical Castilian state whose governance was largely by immanent justice and specially ceded privileges (*fueros*), Isabella found constant occasion to make inter- as well as intranational assertion of her spiritual authority. Unlike Aragón—from whose border the Moorish menace had been lifted in the thirteenth century and whose rulers were therefore indifferent to the Reconquest—Castile directly confronted Moorish Granada until 1492. Furthermore, it was Cisneros, the Queen's confessor, who largely animated the African campaigns against the infidel Turks and Moslems. And it was with the Castilian sovereign that the expeditions which claimed dominion over millions of pagan Amerinds were initially associated. In her major foreign ventures, therefore, Isabella's policy reflected not only politico-military vicissitudes of statecraft but also spiritual responsibilities in the face of non-Christian multitudes. After Columbus had assigned three hundred Indians to forced labor, it was as the imperious agent of the Church Universal that Isabella demanded: "By what authority does the Admiral give my vassals away?"

If Isabella, in her enterprises to the south and overseas to the west, symbolizes the spiritualist, medieval component of the emergent Spanish empire, then Ferdinand, whose Aragón was engaged to the east and north, represents a secular, Renaissance counterpart. His holdings (the Balearics, Sardinia, Sicily, Naples) and his Italian and Navarrese campaigns confined his problems of rule, alliance and warfare to the European, Christian community. Isabella presented the unity of spiritually intransigent Christendom to infidel and pagan. Ferdinand was committed to the shifting, amoral statecraft of competing Christian princes in maintenance and expansion of a domain which, within its Christian context, was diversely composed.

Ferdinand ruled under transitional conditions which precluded resorting for authority to Isabella's Thomistic sanction or to statist apologetics. Managing with sheer personal verve and cunning, he was, in the fullest sense, Machiavellian. Indeed the Florentine, who regarded religions as instruments for political centralization and who denied that Italian well-being depended upon the Church of Rome (*Discourses*, I, xii), called Ferdinand "a new prince" who had become "the first king in Christendom" by great and extraordinary actions, "which have kept his subjects' minds uncertain and astonished, and occupied in watching their result" (*Prince*, XXI).

Spanish conquistadors, colonizers and catechizers, then, carried with them to American shores this dual heritage: medieval and Renaissance, Thomistic and Machiavellian. Through a close study of the letters of Cortés and the *Historia de las cosas de Nueva España* of the missionary Sahagún, Luis Villoro has projected the conquest as a two-way revelation. To the Indian were revealed a triumphant "universal" Church and its militant temporal agent, the Spanish crown; to Europe were revealed civilizations, fauna, flora and geography of a vast New World, which crumbled agelong sureties and challenged the imagination. The Indian, that is, was seen bifocally: through the eyes of the self-assured knight-errant or proselytizer and through those of the freely inquiring humanist. At the unspanned hiatus between these outlooks Villoro pitches the Indian's four-century tragedy.[3]

For half a century after Isabella's death in 1504 Spanish New World administration hovered between medieval and Renaissance orientations. Were men of other races, even though their hierarchical status might be politically and socially inferior, to be accorded equality as salvable souls and safeguards against exploitation? Or was amoral expediency, perhaps reinforced by the Aristotelian concept of "natural slaves," to determine their lot?

In the case of Negroes, Isabella in 1503 revoked permission to ship Christianized slaves from Spain to the Indies; but Ferdinand condoned the traffic in 1510, and, soon after, direct levies from Africa commenced. In the case of Indians, wide-ranging polemics, dating from Isabella's reprimand to Columbus, sought to fix the extent, if any, to which forced labor could be exacted of them. For decades royal decrees on the subject were a history of statement and reversal. Finally the "New Laws" of 1542-3 (modified in 1545-6 and 1548-51) definitively declared Indians to be free persons and vassals of the crown, canceled the judicial authority of their immediate overlords (*encomenderos*) and imposed on the latter a full scale of obligations vis-à-vis the Indians. In other words, to safeguard the Indians' Thomistic status in society, the king was forced to curb exploitative *encomenderos* who, in earlier times, would have been feudal lords more concerned than he with that status.[4]

Another question was: Would medieval exclusivism be maintained in matters of trade with and emigration to the Indies? Isabella's monopolistic contract with Columbus and her denial of emigration, except with special license, to all but Castilians and Leonese was the first answer. Ferdinand, however, extended privileges to his own subjects, and Charles I (1516-56) went much further. Of the latter's vast, pluralist, polyglot empire Spanish Europe was but a segment. Charles spoke Spanish with an accent, brought a Flemish court to Spain and played the Machiavellian cosmopolite to bring a modicum of unity to the congeries that was his realm. He even went so far as to have his delegates to the Council of Trent oppose the papal party in an effort to conciliate the Protestants. In administering overseas Spain he allowed emigration of Germans, Flemings, Italians and others of his subjects. For its economic development he enlisted aid from newly risen international commercial capitalists of northern Europe—the Welsers, the Fuggers, the Ehingers.

On the accession of Philip II (1556-98), however, the realm became somewhat less heterogeneous with the dismemberment of Bohemia, Hungary and Austria, while Philip's arduous campaigns in the Netherlands were dramatic proof of his uncompromising, militant, profoundly felt Catholicism and Hispanicism—qualities sharply intensified by the great Catholic reassertion of the period. Machiavelli went on the Index (1557), and insurgent Lutheranism restored Spain to its medieval role as the universal Church's knight-in-arms against the forces of darkness. It was under Philip that the structure of the Spanish American empire assumed the cast which, for purposes of this essay, it kept until c. 1810. That cast I describe as dominantly Thomistic, with recessive Machiavellian characteristics. (I use the terms "Thomistic" and "medieval" for contrast with northern Europe's emergent capitalist societies of 1500-1800, and not to designate a residual facsimile of the thirteenth century.)

In the 1570s, by extending the Inquisition to America and by declaring Church patronage inalienable from the crown, Philip set his governance definitively within a larger framework of divine law, imbuing his own and his agents' directives with spiritual purpose. No entry was left for the atomistic tolerance that England, despite its state religion, had already begun to evince. (England seen through Spanish perspective takes on characteristics of the United States seen through the English one.)

The crown considered the political and social hierarchy to be energized at every level and in every department. As Indian peoples were absorbed, for example, they were not indiscriminately reduced to a common stratum. Certain of their leaders retained prestige in the post-conquest society, and many low-born Spaniards raised their own status by marrying caciques' daughters. Unlike prim New England meetinghouses, moreover, the Spanish baroque church showed the Indian's craftsmanship (and, by the eighteenth century, his artistry); to his people it made a lavish visual, auricular, ritual appeal, while its saints tacitly re-embodied his native gods. English colonists mobilized militarily *against* the Indian; Spaniards, apart from the actual conquest, mobilized socially, politically, economically, religiously and culturally to *assimilate* him.

To be sure, the social hierarchy had its anomalies. Creoles (American-born whites or near-whites) rarely received the prestige and the economic and political opportunities that were officially assured them. Mestizos, mulattoes, Indians and Negroes, on the contrary, occasionally found a social fluidity that they could not officially have expected. Broadly speaking, however, a man's status was defined somewhat fixedly by his occupation and by his place and condition of birth. Transferral from one status to another (*e.g.*, an Indian who passed from mission to *encomienda*, a Negro from slave to free status, or a mestizo to the creole nobility) generally entailed official sanction and registration.

The multiplicity of judicial systems underscored the static, functionally compartmented nature of society. The fact that they—like the several hierarchies of lay and clerical administrators—constantly disputed each other's spheres of influence only served to reaffirm the king's authority as ultimate reconciler. Nuclear elements—such as municipalities or even individual Indians—as well as highly placed officers could appeal directly to the king, or to his proxy, the viceroy, for redress of certain grievances. The king, even though he might be an inarticulate near-imbecile like Charles II, was symbolic throughout his realm as the guarantor of status. In Thomistic-idiom, all parts of society were ordered to the whole as the imperfect to the perfect. This ordering, inherently the responsibility of the whole multitude, devolved upon the king as a public person acting in their behalf, for the task of ordering to a given end fell to the agent best placed and fitted for the specific function.

In the economic realm, Spanish mercantilism lacked the enterprising free play of the state-guided commercial capitalism of seventeenth- and eighteenth-century England. The very anatomy of the economy showed the impress of medievalism: primary dedication to extractive pursuits; confusion between bullion and real wealth; dogged (but ineffectual) prohibition of foreign and even intercolonial trade; a multiform, burdensome tax structure; monopolistic merchant- and craft-guilds (*consulados* and *gremios*); lack of credit and banking facilities; use of the simplest forms of partnership (*commenda*, *societas*); scarcity of currency (and in outlying areas the use of pre-Columbian tokens, such as cacao beans); commercial exchange through annual fairs; municipal price control.

The Spanish empire, to be sure, could scarcely avert contagion from the post-medieval world in which it existed and for which it was in part responsible. The Jesuits, who had received extensive privileges overseas for the very purpose of bolstering the empire's moral and religious base, were outstandingly versed in modernism. An "enlightened" Bourbon regime expelled them in 1767 less for their reactionary perversity than for their shrewd, disciplined commercial activities and their faith-defying "probabilist" dialectics.

Spanish American bullion was a lodestar for foreign merchants. Introduced as contraband or else covertly within the Spanish system itself, the wares of Dutch, French and English were temptingly cheap, well-made and abundant. They, like the fiscal demands of the mother country, were a constant incentive for creoles to organize local economies from which bullion and exportable surplus might readily be

factored out. The calculating acquisitiveness of capitalism, if not its
institutions for unlimited accrual, was frequently in evidence.

Moreover, Indian and Negro burden-bearers were, unlike the
medieval serf, never fully identified with the historical and cultural
ethos of their masters. For this reason they suffered more from the
emergent exploitative psychology than, perhaps, post-medieval peasants who remained bound to the land. The African received no comprehensive protective code until 1789. And the very laws that assured
the Indian status in return for fixed services could in practice be perverted, rendering him servile to an *encomendero* or a royal agent
(*corregidor*). Indeed, the existence of Thomistic guarantees for the
common man can be confirmed only by examining Spain's New
World experience in selected eras and locales, or by comparing it en
bloc with other European ventures in the Antilles and North America.

Yet however strongly such "recessive" Machiavellian, proto-
capitalist or secularistic traits might erupt, the underpinning of the
empire—social, economic, political, intellectual—bore a rubric of the
earlier era. Eighteenth-century Bourbon reforms (the notable ones
being those of Charles III, 1759-88) did little to alter this generalization. Some reforms—like the intendant system—were superimposed
on the old structure, caused added confusion and were revoked.
Others—like the Caracas Company, a more modern and enterprising
trade monopoly—found harsh opposition because their services entailed strict enforcement of regulations which a more adaptive, personalistic regime of local control had traditionally winked at.

The hierarchical, multiform, pre-capitalist Spanish America of
1800 was ill prepared for the ways of enlightened despotism, still less
for those of Lockean constitutionalism.

The Republican Period

That the heterogeneous Spanish American realm was for three
centuries relatively free from civil strife and separatist outbreaks
must largely be explained by a steadfast loyalty to the politico-
spiritual symbol of the crown. Even the sporadic Indian revolts of
the eighteenth century were directed not against the Catholic sovereign and imperium but against malfeasance of local agents. Daniel
Valcárcel says of Túpac Amaru, the Inca scion who led an abortive
uprising in 1780:

*And when the decision to fight is made, the cacique already has in
his spirit a clear purpose to achieve: he must eliminate the evil functionaries who with their venality and greed for riches corrupt the*

*wise laws of the monarch, run against the precepts of religion and
ruin the life of the Indians,* cholos *and* mestizos. *His rebellion will be
more apparent than real. . . . Túpac Amaru is the most distinguished
champion of His Majesty; fidelity is his principal virtue. A fervent
Catholic and vigorous monarchist, his attitude is wholly normal for
a mestizo of the 18th century in indirect contact with the new ideas
of the era of the Enlightenment.*[5]

Not until 1809, during Spain's Napoleonic interregnum, did local
juntas appear overseas. Yet even then their autonomy, in expectation of a legitimist restoration, was provisional. Only when the ad
hoc "liberal" Cortés, established in unoccupied Spain, tried to reduce Spanish America from viceregal to colonial status did the independence campaign, championed by a few firebrands, gather momentum.

Ferdinand VII was restored in 1814. But in the face of the independence movement, his character and policy discredited both himself and the Church, whose support he retained. For Spanish America
the Thomistic keystone had been withdrawn. Efforts to supplant it,
on a continental basis or even within regional blocs, were vain. No
creole caudillo and no prince of European or Inca lineage could
command universal fealty or age-old spiritual sanction. A Thomistic
sovereign could not be created *ex nihilo,* and Spanish America's centrifugal separatism was for the first time unleashed.

Another idiom than the Thomistic is therefore needed to be played
off against the republican experience. Hitherto the most satisfying
analyses have been those that attribute Spanish American instability
to the imposition of French-, British- and American-type constitutions upon peoples whose illiteracy, poverty, provincialism, political
inexperience and social inequalities rendered ineffectual the mechanisms of constitutional democracy. This somewhat negative view,
however, does not fully draw one into the fabric of Spanish American
politics. If postulates of the Enlightenment were not relevant to that
milieu, how, in a positive sense, may we comprehend it?

The answer this essay proposes is that at the moment when the
Thomistic component became "recessive," the Machiavellian component, latent since the sixteenth century, became "dominant."

This circumstance was sensed by Keyserling, the perceptive (if
unnecessarily occult) philosopher-voyageur: " . . . in the undisciplin-
able revolutionary and the unscrupulous *caudillo* of all South American States survives the son of Machiavelli's age."[6] A Venezuelan
cosmopolite in a novel by Manuel Diaz Rodríguez (1902) remarked on a similarity between his country and fifteenth- and
sixteenth-century Italy:

Are not our continual wars and our corruption of customs . . . the

*same continual wars and depraved customs of the Italy of those
times, with its multiple small republics and principalities? There
were then in Italy, as among us, brutal condottieri and rough cap-
tains, exalted overnight, like the first Sforzas, from the soil to the
royal purple.*[7]

Machiavelli was born into an "Age of Despots." Italian city states
had lost their moral base; they no longer shared a common Christian
ethos. The pope had become one of many competing temporal
rulers. Machiavelli perceived that the mercenary "companies of ad-
venture" of his time, unlike national militias, were undependable
since they lacked any larger loyalty. They could be used to further
intrigues of statecraft, but not to wage open and steady warfare. The
Italian was effective only in duelling and individual combat.

Like Machiavelli, the Spanish American nation-builder of c. 1825
had to contend with nucleated "city states," the rural masses being
passive and inarticulate. The absence of any communities intermediate between such nuclei and the erstwhile imperium had been revealed by the autonomous urban juntas of 1809-10. Only the somewhat arbitrary boundaries of colonial administration defined the
new nations territorially. Only virulent sectionalism could define
them operatively. The Church, once coterminous with the State, had
become the intruding handmaiden of a hostile sovereign power
(Spain). For lack of a politico-spiritual commonalty, sources and
directions of leadership were wholly fortuitous. The consequent
emergence of opportunist caudillos—as of Italy's city tyrants—de-
ranged the predictable interplay of hierarchical class interests.

The Spanish American who held to constitutionalism and avowed
the existence in fact of a state-community was swept away before
winds of personalism. Mexico's Gómez Farías, vice-president under
Santa Anna, was a statesman who, despite his energy and dedication,
would not infract "the principles of public and private morality,"
before which, wrote his contemporary Mora, vanished "his indomitable force of character." Why did he not cast out the treacherous
Santa Anna? "Because the step was unconstitutional[:] . . . a famous
reason which has kept the reputation of Señor Farías in a very secondary place at best and caused the nation to retrogress half a century."[8]

A similar case was Rivadavia, Argentina's first president and pro-
ponent of bourgeois democracy and economic liberalism. His plans
and principles had been no match for provincial *caudillismo.* The
exiled statesman wrote sadly from Paris in 1830 (shortly before the
personalist tyranny of Rosas):

*In my opinion what retards regular and stable advance in those
republics stems from the vacillations and doubts that deprive all
institutions of that moral force which is indispensable to them and*

can be given only by conviction and decision. It is evident to me, and would be easy to demonstrate, that the upheavals of our country spring much more immediately from lack of public spirit and of cooperation among responsible men in sustaining order and laws than from attacks of ungovernable, ambitious persons without merit or fitness and of indolent coveters.[9]

Machiavelli's writings are the handbook *par excellence* for the leader who could cope with "lack of public spirit and of cooperation among responsible men." Just as Lockean precepts were more congenial to the British-American than to the European scene, so the Florentine seemed to write for the New World. For the latter's detailed counsels regarding personalistic rule were of secondary importance to Eurpean monarchs who would soon find sanction in the traditions, panoply and universal acceptance of a Divine Right.

The embryonic nature of New World political forms, the lack of state traditions and state mysticism, were observed by Hegel (c. 1830):

In South America . . . the republics depend only on military force; their whole history is a continued revolution; federated states become disunited; others previously separated become united; and all these changes originate in military revolutions. . . .

. . . As to the political condition of North America, the general object of the existence of this State is not yet fixed and determined, and the necessity for a firm combination does not yet exist; for a real State and a real Government arise only after a distinction of classes has arisen, when wealth and poverty become extreme, and when such a condition of things presents itself that a large portion of the people can no longer satisfy its necessities in the way in which it has been accustomed so to do. . . . North America will be comparable with Europe only after the immeasurable space which that country presents to its inhabitants shall have been occupied, and the members of the political body shall have begun to be pressed back on each other.[10]

Another European, Carlyle, in an essay on Paraguay's Francia (1843) described with certain envy the free-acting caudillo, unfettered by traditions of the national community: "Such an institution of society, adapted to our European ways, seems pressingly desirable. O Gauchos, South-American and European, what a business is it, casting out your Seven Devils!"[11]

Locke and Machiavelli both wrote for peoples who were without an organic, pre-existing state. The former, however, addressed an articulate, relatively homogeneous bourgeoisie that was free to ascertain and pursue private interests, economic and otherwise; the latter addressed the leader who with craft and foresight was to unite an inchoate, inarticulate populace whose only claim was that it be not too heavily oppressed.

On nearly every page of Machiavelli appears practical advice
which almost seems distilled from the careers of scores of Spanish
American caudillos. Of crucial importance is the leader's command-
ing physical presence. In time of sedition he should:

> ...*present himself before the multitude with all possible grace and
> dignity, and attired with all the insignia of his rank, so as to inspire
> more respect....[For] there is no better or safer way of appeasing an
> excited mob than the presence of some man of imposing appearance
> and highly respected.* [Discourses, *I, liv*]

Among countless leaders and incidents one recalls the moment
when Bolivia's ruthless Melgarejo, with six men, entered the palace
where his rival, Belzu, was celebrating a coup d'état. The intruder,
icily calm, shot the President, then with imperious presence faced
and overawed the mob in whose throats the shouts of victory for
Belzu had scarcely died away.

The personalist leader must be physically disciplined, skilled in
warfare, and "learn the nature of the land, how steep the mountains
are, how the valleys debouch, where the plains lie, and understand
the nature of rivers and swamps" (*Prince,* XIV; see also *Discourses,*
III, xxxix). This is almost a page from the autobiography of Páez,
who knew Venezuela's vast *llanos* ("inland plains") like the palm
of his hand, a knowledge that confounded the royalists in 1817
and later earned respect for him as caudillo of the new republic.
Writing of an assault against the Spaniards, Páez recalled:

> *Necessity obliged us not only to fight men but to challenge the
> obstacles opposed by nature. Counting on these, we proposed to
> turn to our advantage the impediments that gave the enemy surety
> and trust in his position, for to no one would it occur that in that
> season cavalry troops could sortie from the lower Apure to cross so
> much inundated terrain and especially the many streams and five
> rivers, all at the period of overflow.*[12]

This telluric, earthbound quality so vital to Spanish American leaders
was matched in Argentina's Quiroga and San Martín, Uruguay's
Artigas, Mexico's Pancho Villa, Venezuela's Bolívar, Peru's Santa
Cruz and innumerable others. Their guerrilla warfare was a far cry
from the chessboard strategy and diplomatic power alignments of
Europe.

Space does not permit analysis of the host of Machiavelli's dicta
empirically confirmed by caudillos. It remains, however, to emphasize that he was concerned not merely with leadership per se but with
state-building. His ideal was a republic with "laws so regulated that,
without the necessity of correcting them, they afford security to those

who live under them" (*Discourses,* I, ii). Significantly, the most difficult time to preserve republican liberties is when a people, accustomed to living under a prince who binds himself "by a number of laws that provide for the security of all his people" (cf. Spanish colonial experience), recovers "by some accident" its freedom. Such a people

> . . . *ignorant of all public affairs, of all means of defense or offense, neither knowing the princes nor being known by them, . . . soon relapses under a yoke, oftentimes much heavier than the one which it had but just shaken off.* [Discourses, *I, xvi*]

Government, to be created in such cases *ex nihilo,* is most expediently organized by a single leader of strength and sagacity. Yet "it will not endure long if the administration of it remains on the shoulders of a single individual; it is well, then, to confide this to the charge of the many, for thus it will be sustained by the many" (*Discourses,* I, ix).

If at length a republic is established, that very fact certifies a fundamental "goodness" and certain "original principles" conducing to its "first growth and reputation." To maintain republican vigor and repress "the insolence and ambition of men" those principles must find periodic reassertion through "extrinsic accident" or, preferably, "intrinsic prudence" (*Discourses,* III, i). The Machiavellian leader, therefore, is to be bound by *original principles* (environmental, human and customary components) generic to the nascent nation-community.

Writing in about 1840 the Argentine socialist Echeverría diagnosed and prescribed for his country's political chaos in identical terms. He found it impossible to organize a people without a constitution rooted in "its customs, sentiments, understandings, traditions." If the sole credentials of a nation-building legislator are those bestowed by electoral victory, his official acts will be no more in the public interest than the activities of a private businessman. The indwelling fact of commonalty is not externalized in a manner that automatically informs such a legislator. Eschewing solutions of other nations, he must himself actively sound out the "instincts, necessities, interests" of the citizens and, through laws, reveal to them their own will and communal identity. Only on this preliminary basis of wise and public-minded paternalism may one hope for an eventual "faculty of perpetual communication between man and man, generation and generation—the continuous embodiment of the spirit of one generation in the next."[13]

The general cast of Spanish America's "original principles"—its "instincts, necessities, interests"—is inherent in Keyserling's perception of a ubiquitous *gana*—or loosely, "urge." By this he meant a raw, telluric spirit: formless, unchanneled, diffuse, self-sustaining; lacking past traditions or future hope. Sarmiento had expressed himself similarly almost a century earlier in describing the nomadic yet earthbound life of the pampas, having a morality unto itself and calling Asiatic comparisons frequently to mind. And in 1821 Bolívar, criticizing Colombia's lawmakers, wrote:

These gentlemen believe that Colombia is filled with dullards who sit around the firesides of Bogotá, Tunja, and Pamplona. They have not troubled to notice the Caribs of the Orinoco, the herdsmen of the Apure, the seamen of Maracaibo, the boatmen of the Mag-dalena, the bandits of Patia, the indomitable citizens of Pasto, the Guajibos of Casanare, and all the savage hordes from Africa and America who, like deer, run untamed in the solitudes of Colombia.[14]

Not only the peons and gauchos, but the bourgeoisie has shared in this New World atomism, as evidenced in Thoreau's *Civil Disobedi-ence* (1849):

Thus the State never intentionally confronts a man's sense, intel-lectual or moral, but only his body, his senses. It is not armed with superior wit or honesty, but with superior physical strength. I was not born to be forced. I will breathe after my own fashion. Let us see who is the strongest.[15]

The meaning of *gana* in relation to the pampas, the Chaco, the *llanos* or Mexico's arid northland—or to jungle-dwellers of Panama and the Amazon—is perhaps clear. But is there a counterpart among the nucleated, tradition-bound communities descended from highly organized Aztec, Maya and Inca civilizations?

Some writers assert that these areas are still distinguished for elaborate functionalism, for concentrated and well integrated com-munalism; whereas it is in Portuguese (and British) America that one finds "gangliated" rural settlement and, until recent times, a locality group structure remaining in the "neighborhood" stage.[16]

That Brazilian settlements, rural and urban, were not by and large as cohesive as those of Spanish America is true. Yet the compactness of, say, the Andean *ayllu* (rural Indian community) is misleading. Once the conquerors removed the ruling Inca, the tribes and nations of his empire

... dispersed like the beads of a necklace whose thread has been broken. Each community returned, politically and economically, to the pre-Incaic stage. Thousands of communities, isolated, strangers each to the other, could thus be conquered one at a time.[17]

The Indian was turned earthward by the Spaniard, made an instru-ment of production for a vast imperial community which, despite its proselytizers and Indianist legislation, the Indian could not feel himself purposefully a part of. When in the 1920s Mariátegui applied Marxian analysis to the Peruvian scene, he reformulated it to make allowance for this "earth-consciousness" of the Indian.[18]

How is it, then, that Spanish American caudillos or governments have in certain countries and eras achieved political stability in the face of this New World brand of social and moral centrifugalism? I define three essential modes of stability, which are categorized here merely for schematic purposes and with the understanding that the "pure" type never occurs. By way of further analogy I suggest a correspondence between these types and the three "legitimations of domination" which Max Weber distinguishes in his essay, "Politics as a Vocation."[19]

The first mode of stability is furnished by the Machiavellian leader who asserts himself by dynamic personalism and shrewd self-identification with local "original principles," though without ever relinquishing government, as Machiavelli would have wished, "to the charge of many." The system remains subordinate to the man and unless a suitable "heir" is available, which happens infrequently, it falls with him. Here we perhaps have Weber's charismatic leader with the personal gift of grace, who flouts patriarchal traditionalism and the stable economy, whose justice is Solomonic rather than statutory, who maintains authority "solely by providing his strength in life." One recent writer, Blanksten, holds that the caudillo and charismatic types correspond.[20] George S. Wise, on the other hand, claims that the "stratagem and chicanery" of at least one caudillo (Venezuela's Guzmán Blanco) revealed an insecurity and lack of purpose precluding the oracular, prophetic qualities that he attributes to charismatic legitimacy.[21] Weber's specific consideration of the condottiere type leads me to feel, however, that charisma need not invariably imply "anointment."

The charismatic leader may be dedicated to molding the self-perpetuating traditions of a state-community—for example, Bolívar's vision of federated Andean republics, Morazán's Central American union, the constitutionalism of Mexico's Juárez and perhaps the quasi-theocracy of Ecuador's García Moreno. Or, which is more usual, he may set about exploiting the country as his private fief. In the decades after independence such a caudillo would win the army's allegiance (or create his own plebeian militia), then assert control over the several classes by blandishment, personal magnetism or threat of force—the method depending, in the case of each segment of society, on "original principles" and the leader's own antecedents. Examples are Argentina's Rosas, Mexico's Santa Anna, Guatemala's Carrera, Paraguay's Francia. (Venezuela's Páez seems to fall between the two sub-types.)

Toward the end of the century the exploitation of new sources of mineral and agricultural wealth, together with a strong influx of foreign investments, gave caudillos more dependable leverage for control. Though force and personalism did not go in the discard, financial resources and the protective favor of foreigners allowed the leader to govern by "remote control." He adopted bourgeois bon ton and even paid lip service to constitutionalism. Such men were Venezuela's Guzmán Blanco, Mexico's Porfirio Díaz, Guatemala's Barrios.

Intensified economic activity might also give rise to a second type of state: a modified version of laissez-faire democracy. This development, which Weber calls legitimation through bureaucratic competence and public respect for rational legal statutes, has been rare in Latin America, even in hybrid form. Argentina affords an example. In that country after 1860, and especially after 1880, the pampas experienced a torrential land rush, occasioned by a world demand for meat and grains and by improved methods of husbandry, transportation and refrigeration. Though the lion's share of the benefits accrued to an oligarchy of large proprietors, many immigrants took small homesteads in the northern provinces; moreover, the expanding economy created niches for articulate, middle-class city dwellers. Argentines were, relative to Latin America, homogeneous and white. A growing nucleus identified its interests with the stability and prosperity of the nation-community, even though the positions of highest socio-economic authority were already pre-empted.

Given Argentina's economic direction and momentum, it remained for a series of statesmen-presidents merely to encourage and guide its development, in tolerable conformance with the Lockean Constitution of 1853. Eventual malfeasance in high office led not back to tyranny, but to the emergence in 1890 of the Radical (liberal, middle-class) Party, to free suffrage and the secret ballot, and finally to Radical control of the presidency (1916-30). Twentieth-century Radical leaders, however, reined back certain socio-economic forces from a natural course by acquiescing in the continued entrenchment of the landowning oligarchy. Only then did thwarted urban classes fall prey to demagoguery of an ominous breed—and to Juan Domingo Perón.

A third solution for anarchy has been a full-scale implementing of the Machiavellian blueprint. A personalist leader emerges (as in the first case), but goes on successfully to create a system, larger than himself, that is faithful to "original principles." In Spanish America such a system is larger than the leader, to frame a paradox, only when it *recognizes* the leader to be larger than itself. This statement has Thomistic implications, and the more successful Spanish American constitutions have translated into modern idiom certain principles under which the viceroyalties enjoyed three centuries of relative stability.

This solution, insofar as it reinvigorates the body social by setting its classes, or "estates," into centrally stabilized equilibrium, is a neotraditionalism reminiscent of Weber's third category: "the authority of the eternal yesterday." Of Mexico's present Constitution—brought into being in 1917 by Carranza, a shrewd, opportunist caudillo—Frank Tannenbaum has written:

> *By implication, the Constitution recognizes that contemporary Mexican society is divided into classes, and that it is the function of the State to protect one class against another. The Constitution is therefore not merely a body of rules equally applicable to all citizens, but also a body of rules specially designed to benefit and protect given groups. The community is not made up of citizens only; it is also made up of classes with special rights within the law. What has in fact happened is that the old idea of the "estates" has been re-created in Mexican law. The pattern of the older Spanish State, divided into clergy, nobility, and commons, has been re-created in modern dress, with peasants, workers, and capitalists replacing the ancient model. This is not done formally, but it is done sufficiently well to make it evident that a very different kind of social structure is envisioned in the law, even if only by implicit commitment, than that in a liberal democracy....*
>
> *The Revolution has certainly increased effective democracy in Mexico. It has also increased, both legally and economically, the dependence of the people and of the communities upon the federal government and the President. The older tradition that the king rules has survived in modern dress: the President rules. He rules rather than governs, and must do so if he is to survive in office and keep the country at peace.*[22]

I have reserved any mention of Chile until now because its history usefully illustrates our three political types as well as a twentieth-century variant which has yet to be considered. Like its sister nations, Chile fell after independence into anarchic factionalism. A revolution of 1829-30, however, brought the conservatives into power; at their head was Diego Portales who, as a business man, was atypical among Spanish American nation-builders. Portales appreciated more keenly than most the need for disciplined, predictable conditions of life and was more empirical in perceiving that liberal slogans and mechanisms were meaningless within an aristocratic, agrarian society. His views were reflected in the centralized, quasi-monarchic Constitution of 1833 which, by recognizing Chile's hierarchic social anatomy and at the same time guaranteeing status and justice for the component members, lent the government a supra-personalist sanction.

Portales himself did not become president, but wisely designated a military hero, General Prieto, whose prestige, aristocratic bearing and benevolence, traditionalism and religiosity further enhanced the office with an aura of legitimacy.[23] None of Chile's presidents was overthrown for sixty years, while the Constitution lasted nearly a century.

Portales, alone among his Spanish American contemporaries, brought to fulfillment the policy of "the compleat Machiavellian." As the century advanced, however, a leavening took place within the system he had fathered. A law of 1852 abolished primogeniture, infusing new blood and interests into the landed oligarchy. Mineral exploitation in the north and the activities of German immigrants in the south posted new directions for economic change and opportunity. The consequent desire for more effective economic competition provided a rallying cry for enthused liberals emerging from the new (1843) University. So too did growing dissatisfaction with the constitutional ban on public exercise of non-Catholic religions.

At length the Chilean élite, larger and more diversely composed than in 1833, revolted against centralized, one-man rule by ejecting President Balmaceda from office in 1891. This élite then governed through its congressional representatives, and the fitfulness of public policy for the next thirty years reflected the jostling of private economic interests.

As in Argentina, however, the modified laissez-faire state could not indefinitely subsist if it was to victimize the increasingly self-aware lower classes, such as, in Chile's case, the copper and nitrate workers. The little man eventually found his champion in President Arturo Alessandri (1920-25, 1932-38).[24]

Alessandri's and subsequent administrations represent an attitude toward government that has in this century become universal throughout Spanish America. It has in varying degrees infiltrated the three earlier systems, or combinations thereof, wherever they exist. Essentially, it is a recognition of the need to build into public policies a dynamics for socio-economic change. This need stems from two interrelated phenomena: first, the urbanization and industrialization of hitherto extractive economies; second, the growing self-awareness and articulateness of the citizenry at large.

The Spanish American leader, whether dictator or democrat, is fast adopting a broader, more sophisticated view of how modern political power must be won, maintained and exercised. He also knows that, regardless of any nationalistic rhetoric to which he may be committed, he must import more and more blueprints and technical solutions from abroad. Such solutions, however—whether socialism, fascism, exchange control or river valley authorities—take on a new complexion as they flash into amalgam with conditions of life wholly different from those by which they were engendered. Not only is the receiving ethos broadly speaking *sui generis*, but in a strictly techno-logical sense the particular juxtapositions of ancient and modern in Spanish America are quite beyond the experience of any of the capi-talist countries. Therefore slogans of foreign systems ring far differ-ently upon Spanish American ears than their originators imagine.

In fact, Peru's *Aprista* movement and Mexico's forty-year-long "Revolution" attest that Spanish America is starting to generate its own credos. Sometimes, as with Perón's *justicialismo,* they are heartlessly cynical rhetoric. At best they designate, as did our own New Deal, a piecemeal pragmatism, uncommitted to the mysticism or fixed morality prescribed for the New World by Hegel. Yet the fact that Spanish America is by tradition accustomed and by economic necessity forced to rely heavily on official planning, intervention and protection has on occasion led its statesmen to a "total view" (to be distinguished carefully in nature and intent from a totalitarian view). From such views flow social, economic and cultural agenda which, however imperfect of execution, uniquely contribute to an under-standing of man-in-community.

Co-existent, indeed, with Spanish America's atomism, or *gana,* is a sense of commonalty, however latent, deriving in large part from its Catholicity (in the ingrained, cultural sense) and from its agrarian, Negro and Indian heritage. Native to this commonalty is an ethic upon which the hyper-rationalist logos of the industrial world seems able to make only limited and conditional encroach-ments. The prediction is sometimes heard among Spanish Americans that this logos will in the long run exhaust itself; that their descend-ants will be freer to weave certain principles of a pre-Machiavellian age into the new patterns of an entering one; that the promise which erratically flashes in the travail of twentieth-century Mexican democ-racy is yet to be realized.

A Note on Portuguese and British America

The theme that has emerged from our analysis of Spanish American government is that the sense of moral community imparted by Spain to its New World colonies lost its staying power in the early nine-teenth century and could no longer yoke the amoral, anti-traditional atomism of the American hemisphere. It is logical to ask whether a similar process occurred in other American areas. The following remarks on Brazil and the United States, while suggesting this to be the case, are too sketchy to be conclusive and will chiefly serve to place the Spanish American experience in broader perspective.

The course of Portuguese colonization differed from that of the Spanish in many respects. The mother country was more restricted in resources and population, politically more centralized, more strongly commercial and agricultural, less militantly religious. Brazil itself lacked the densely settled, highly civilized Indian peoples of Spanish America and, for the first two centuries, its abundant supply of precious gems and metals. These factors inhibited the growth of a multiform politico-ecclesiastical hierarchy with sophisticated urban centers of radiation. Political control and initiative were more fully diffused among slave-owning seigneurs of the sugarfields and among hardy municipalities of the poorer backlands. Even so, Portugal's empire bore enough similarities to Spain's to make the two comparable for present purposes. Both participated in a quasi-feudal, precapitalist, Catholic ethos.

The transition to independence, however, was another matter, for the Portuguese king João VI fled overseas to Brazil upon Napoleon's invasion of his country. When summoned home in 1821 by the Portuguese Cortés, he left his son, Pedro, in Rio de Janeiro as Brazilian Regent. The following year the latter declared Brazil's independence, and the transition was relatively peaceful; for since he was of the royal line accredited by the creoles, Pedro's accession to the new Brazilian emperorship went unchallenged.

The benevolent, paternalistic reign of João's grandson, Pedro II (1840-89), convincingly demonstrated the stabilizing effect of the transferral of the ruling lineage to the New World. These years were, within Latin America, a political golden age. Using the "moderative power" of the conservative 1824 Constitution, Pedro II counteracted the separatism and political inarticulateness of his nation by careful manipulation of elections, ministries and policy changes. Yet he never originated policies or intervened in the affairs of the two political parties. Joaquim Nabuco described him as merely making "soundings on either side of the channel being navigated." His power was rigorously exercised:

1st.) within the Constitution; 2nd.) in accord with the fictions and uses of the English parliamentary system, which were even observed by our parties themselves; 3rd.) in constant obedience to public opinion and sentiment.[25]

Beneath the parliamentary trappings one senses Thomistic vestiges. Pedro's legitimacy was unquestioningly recognized by the people, while he in turn felt morally, if not procedurally, responsible to them. So it is the republican coup d'état of 1889, rather than independence (as in Spanish America), which most clearly defines the post-Thomistic watershed. The presidential regime which supplanted the Emperor was, to be sure, more stable and constitutional and less a prey to disruptive localism than the Spanish American governments of two generations previous. Yet its slogans were those of a somewhat cynical positivism, and it signalized the triumph of city over country, of materialism over traditionalism, of industrialized coffee over patriarchal sugar, of European fashion over native custom. In the conscience of the new bourgeois generation that destroyed the paternal symbol one writer discovers a gnawing "complex of remorse."[26]

For the United States, Professor R. G. McCloskey has already shaped a perspective comparable to my own for Spanish America, one which refines the analysis of Northrop referred to at the start of this essay. McCloskey maintains that the American Constitution and Jeffersonian democracy drew upon "a diverse array of abstract doctrines, semireligious convictions, and economic motivations." This tradition enshrined economic freedom for individuals and Lockean sanctity of property rights without discarding the humane, Christian values derived also from Locke and from England's seventeenth-century leftist Puritans.[27] Just as in colonial Spanish America, moral rather than economic man was society's nuclear element.

An eloquent expression of this tradition is Calhoun's *A Disquisition on Government*.[28] Showing nostalgia for a monarchy in which a king's interests are hereditarily indentified with those of his subjects to form a kingdom-community, Calhoun affirms society to be organic and "man so constituted as to be a social being." A constitution:

... must spring from the bosom of the community, and be adapted to the intelligence and character of the people, and all the multifarious relations, internal and external, which distinguish one people from another.

Not from the will of a "numerical, or absolute majority," but from that alone of a *concurrent majority* may "the sense of the community" be taken. Only when the vox populi proceeds out of natural communities and through the permanently empowered "appropriate organ" of each one will anarchy and despotism cease to threaten, private and public morals become one, all elements of the nation-community achieve a "disposition to harmonize" and the people's voice become God's. With few changes Calhoun's principles become Thomistic, or those of modern Mexico.[29]

The Civil War is, symbolically at least, the watershed corresponding to Spanish American independence and the exile of Brazil's Emperor. It marks the dominance of industrial and monopolistic over mercantile capitalism, and the eclipse of Calhoun's agrarian, patriarchal South as a determinant in national policy. The moral, humane, Christian component of Locke becomes recessive; the Lockean sanction for atomistic economic individualism—which had been less strong in the earlier period than Northrop suggests—becomes dominant. Mc-Closkey writes that "a new conservative rationale develops on the moribund body of Jeffersonian liberalism."[30] He develops his case by examining three respresentatives of the late nineteenth century: William Graham Sumner, who as a sociologist urged "the frank espousal of a social norm based on material utility"; Stephen J. Field, who as a jurist argued "that democratic freedom and economic freedom are one"; Andrew Carnegie, who as a captain of industry, and despite his vaunted humanitarianism, felt that capitalism and democracy "cannot be disjoined."[31]

Henry Adams had received his mind-set by the 1860s and could never to his own satisfaction address these new conditions of post-bellum democracy. Of that period he later wrote:

The system of 1789 had broken down, and with it the eighteenth-century fabric of a priori, or moral, principles. Politicians had given it up. Grant's administration marked the avowal.... Darwinists ought to conclude that America was reverting to the stone age, but the theory of reversion was more absurd than that of evolution. Grant's administration reverted to nothing. One could not catch a trait of the past, still less of the future. It was not even sensibly American.[32]

With Lincoln Steffens, however, born a generation after Adams, we find a mind from the Far West, cast in the flux of the new period and with the self-confidence to cope with it. Steffens shrewdly perceived the disparity between constitutional morality and the structure and exercise of power to be no different in Europe than in the United States. The French, however, do not face the moral dilemma of American democracy because they "have not called good or right the evil that they have done, and so they have that charm which I felt always in 'bad men' in America, in the 'honest crooks' in politics and business."[33] Lincoln Steffens' lesson to America, to the Americas, is that a meaningful political morality issues only from American experience, that it is a lived morality and that it must be recognized as being lived.

Notes

1. F. S. C. Northrop, *The Meeting of East and West* (New York, 1946), chaps. III, IV. See also Merle Curti, "The Great Mr. Locke, America's Philosopher, 1783-1861," *The Huntington Library Bulletin* 11 (April 1937), 107-151.

2. S. A. Dunham, *Spain and Portugal,* 5 vols. (London, 1832-1835), IV, 109.

3. Luis Villoro, *Los grandes momentos del indigenismo en México* (Mexico City, 1950), 15-88.

4. The historic debate (1550-1) between the humanitarian "Protector of the Indies," Las Casas, and the erudite humanist, Sepúlveda, epitomized the issue as to whether the Spanish empire should continue to expand by force and enslavement. Though the disputants hardly objectified such nebulous abstractions as medieval and Renaissance outlooks, Las Casas' view that Indians should be treated *ab initio* as catechizable souls coincided with subsequent official theory. For conflicting interpretations of the debate see: Lewis Hanke, *The Spanish Struggle for Justice in the Conquest of America* (Philadelphia, 1949), 109-132, 187-189, and Edmundo O'Gorman, "Lewis Hanke on the Spanish Struggle for Justice in the Conquest of America," *The Hispanic American Historical Review* XXIX (1949), 563-571.

5. D. Valcárcel, *La rebelión de Túpac Amaru* (Mexico City, 1947), 180.

6. H. Keyserling, *South American Meditations* (New York, 1932), 103.

7. Manuel Díaz Rodríguez, *Sangre patricia* (Madrid, n.d.), 169.

8. José María Luis Mora, *Ensayos, ideas y retratos* (Mexico City, 1941), xx, 184.

9. Bernadino Rivadavia, *Páginas de un estadista* (Buenos Aires, 1945), 137 (letter to a politician of Upper Peru, 14 March 1830).

10. G. W. F. Hegel, *Lectures on the Philosophy of History* (London, 1894), 87-90.

11. Thomas Carlyle, *Critical and Miscellaneous Essays,* 5 vols. (London, n.d.), IV, 316.

12. José Antonio Páez, *Autobiografía,* 2 vols. (New York, 1946; re-issue of 1869 edition), I, 132.

13. Esteban Echeverría, *Dogma Socialista; Edición crítica y documentada* (La Plata, 1940), 206-212.

14. Harold A. Bierck, Jr. (ed.), *Selected Writings of Bolívar,* 2 vols. (New York, 1951), I, 267-268

(letter to F. de P. Santander, 13 June 1821).

15. *The Writings of Henry David Thoreau,* 20 vols. (Cambridge, 1906), IV, 376.

16. F. J. de Oliveira Vianna, *Instituições políticas brasileiras,* 2 vols. (Rio de Janeiro, 1949); T. Lynn Smith, "The Locality Group Structure of Brazil," *American Sociological Review,* IX (February, 1944), 41-49.

17. Luis E. Valcárcel, *Ruta cultural del Perú* (Mexico City, 1945), 143-144. See also Charles Gibson, *The Inca Concept of Sovereignty and the Spanish Administration in Peru* (Austin, 1948), 88-100.

18. José Carlos Mariátegui, *Siete ensayos de interpretación de la realidad peruana* (Lima, 1928).

19. H. H. Gerth and C. W. Mills (ed.), *From Max Weber: Essays in Sociology* (London, 1947), 78ff.

20. George I. Blanksten, *Ecuador: Constitutions and Caudillos* (Berkeley and Los Angeles, 1951), 35-36.

21. George S. Wise, *Caudillo, A Portrait of Antonio Guzmán Blanco* (New York, 1951), 161-163.

22. Frank Tannenbaum, *Mexico: The Struggle for Peace and Bread* (New York, 1950), 101, 118.

23. Ricardo Donoso, *Las ideas políticas en Chile* (Mexico City, 1946), 64-114; Alberto Edwards Vives, *La fronda aristocrática en Chile* (Santiago, 1936), 39-47.

24. The dictatorial interregnum of Carlos Ibáñez (1925-1931) can be considered as Chile's nearest approach to the first, or pure caudillo type of rule. His advent is partially explained by the post-World War I collapse of the world nitrate market, which impaired the mainspring of parliamentary, laissez-faire government and left Chile (since Alessandri had not yet given shape and momentum to his social democracy) in its primordial anarchy. Ibáñez, though sometimes referred to as a "man

on horseback," effectively used modern technocratic methods and was not a caudillo of the old stamp—to which his re-eiection in 1952 bears witness.

25. Joaquim Nabuco, *Um estadista do Império,* 4 vols. (Sao Paulo, 1949), IV, 108.

26. Luis Martins, "O patriarca e o bacharel," *Revista do Arquivo Municipal* (São Paulo) LXXXIII (1942), 7-36. For the anti-traditionalist spirit of the early republican period see Gilberto Freyre, "O período republicano," *Boletim bibliográfico* (São Paulo) I, 2 (1944), 61-72.

27. Robert Green McCloskey, *American Conservatism in the Age of Enterprise* (Cambridge, 1951), pp. 1-8.

28. John C. Calhoun, *A Disquisition on Government* (New York, 1854).

29. Like Argentina's Echeverría, Calhoun espoused a Machiavellian rather than an artificial social-contract theory of how governments are formed: "It would thus seem almost necessary that governments should commence in some one of the simple and absolute forms, which, however well suited to the community in its earlier stages, must, in its progress, lead to oppression and abuse of power, ... unless the conflicts to which it leads should be fortunately adjusted by a compromise, which will give to the respective parties a participation in the control of the government; and thereby lay the foundation of a constitutional government, to be afterwards matured and perfected. Such governments have been, emphatically, the product of circumstances. And hence, the difficulty of one people imitating the government of another." *(Ibid.,* 79.)

30. McCloskey, *op. cit.,* 15.

31. *Ibid.,* 167.

32. Henry Adams, *The Education of Henry Adams* (Cambridge, 1918), 266, 280-281.

33. Lincoln Steffens, *The Autobiography of Lincoln Steffens* (New York, 1931), 705-711.

On "Functional Groups," "Fragmentation," and "Pluralism" in Spanish American Political Society

Ronald C. Newton

The term "functional group"—sometimes rendered "interest group" or, to be on the safe side, "functional interest group"—has attained of late a certain modishness among Latin Americanists. At present, unfortunately, it serves as little more than a convenient catchall reference for the great *intereses,* the list of which, except for pride of place, has also become virtually standardized: the several officer corps, the university, landowner cliques or associations, *cámaras* of merchants and industrialists, the Church, the *entes autónomos,* organized labor, and so on. The fact that professional concern is increasingly being directed toward such structures is in itself significant, for it reflects a deep disenchantment with the more traditional methods of conceptualizing and analyzing Spanish American political society.

For some time, in fact, it has been apparent that a broad range of phenomena—most obtrusive in the repeated cycles of civic violence and civic paralysis, protracted incidences of dysfunction in which the great *intereses* have played prominent roles—simply do not respond to analysis and explanation in terms of constitutional dispositions and electoral and parliamentary behavior. Over the past decade or so this scholarly *inquietud* has generated numerous studies of national military establishments, student political movements, labor federations, and so on. Similarly, writers have amply described and analyzed the one Spanish American national system—Mexico—in which organized *functional* (as distinct from *territorial)* political groupings have been frankly accepted as agents of the political process.

"Functional interest groups" are thus by no means unfamiliar; the point is, however, that the conceptual armamentarium at present available to the investigator seeking to comprehend them *as a cul-ture-wide phenomenon* remains meager and imprecise. An adequate working definition of the Spanish American "functional interest group," considered both as a structure of social interaction and soli-darity and as a vehicle for the pursuit of political ends, is still lacking—indeed, even the terminology itself must be regarded as only pro-visional. Furthermore, we need a conceptual framework—a "model," if one wishes—by means of which a total Spanish American national system may be examined in terms of the interrelationships among its constituent functional groupings, and of their involvement in the political process. Hence this essay, whose purpose is to isolate and define the issues and to develop a vocabulary and a frame of refer-ence for their further study.

Because the discussion that follows breaks with many of the cate-gories and premises that have shaped North American thinking, it is instructive to turn first to the short interpretive passage from which the essay's title and its organizing principle are derived. Some years ago Arthur P. Whitaker observed, apropos the repeated failures of consensus in Argentine political life in the years following the over-throw of Juan D. Perón:[1]

Socially and politically, Argentina is a highly fragmented country. Its fragmentation *is different from the* pluralism *which many of us think is one of the best attributes of society in the United States. In Argentina, the divisions are sharper, deeper, and more numerous, and the several fragments either do not communicate with each other at all or else do so mainly to quarrel and fight. Hence the widespread feeling of frustration and loss of direction that embitters domestic differences and tends to perpetuate them.* [emphasis added.]

For the purposes of this paper, Argentina is merely the extreme or stylized case in the examination of the dysfunctional phenomena that Whitaker refers to as "fragmentation." Both the duration and the intensity of the crisis of unconsummated change that has beset Argentina since 1930 have worked with uncommon virulence to rend political society into mutually isolated and bitterly antagonistic *intereses creados,* concerned above all to maintain past gains in what is now conceived to be, relative to earlier expectations an economy of scarcity. In a complementary process, Argentina's once-vigorous parliamentary institutions and political party system had fallen into discredit and disarray long before they were swept away by military fiat in mid-1966. In the accelerating disintegration of these mechanisms for the achievement of consensus, the nation's demise as a political democracy was further hastened by the inability of successive executives to withstand the divisive importunities of organized interests. (In this respect Argentina stands at the opposite pole from Mexico, a viable "corporative centralism,"[2] whose institutions have proven adequate until now to maintain the PRI's functional "sectors" subordinate to the will of the party and national executives.) Nevertheless, while unique historical processes have thus thrown Argentina's essential configuration into a merciless high relief, analogous structures and processes have often enough been discernible in other Spanish American national systems, *most particularly those at a roughly comparable level of socio-political development.*

Three elementary propositions arise from the foregoing. In the first place, although large secondary groups are central to both, North American pluralism is indeed, as Whitaker indicates impressionistically, very different from the Spanish American phenomena in question. Both are culturally determined, which is to say historically determined: they rest upon theoretical and juridical bases, and manifest themselves in reiterated patterns of socio-political behavior, markedly at variance with one another. In the second place, however, the two are not direct opposites, for fragmentation is not, in any sense, a *system.* The term can only refer, rather, to the *dysfunction* of a system—one which, until relatively recently, has performed with tolerable efficiency. It is this traditional[3] set of arrangements—which lacks any universally-accepted descriptive label—that is the Spanish American counterpart of pluralism.

Thirdly, therefore, the fragmentation syndrome is to be correlated to the emergence of transitional modes of socio-political organization. This means, in its simplest terms, that as a given Spanish American national system acquires more fully the attributes of transitional society, and, in particular, as its political framework distends to accommodate newly-articulate and newly-exigent urban groups, the conjuncture of constitutional and informal structures through which, in traditional society, political demands were received, processed, and acted upon, grows increasingly unworkable, and may, as in Argentina, become directly obstructive. As will be suggested in the course of this essay, the remarkable tenacity with which traditional patterns resist alteration and/or supplantation draws strength not only from the Bourbon attitudes of the present holders of power, but also, to a degree not yet properly remarked, from the peculiar modalities of Spanish America's *pre-industrial* urban structure.[4] This implies, among other things, little reason to believe that Spanish America's transitional periods will be anything but protracted and agonized, or that the more complex configurations ultimately to emerge will bear much more resemblance to the North American variety of pluralism than they do at the present.

The first task of this essay is thus obviously to establish a conceptual baseline in North American pluralism.[5] The latter possesses two

characteristics of great relevance to the matter at hand. The first
is the *multiplicity of groups,* in which is implied also the unfettered
freedom to form such groups. That is, in the North American experience, pluralism has since the beginning been bound up with the
concept of the "voluntary association," the ad hoc banding together
of individuals for the accomplishment of (usually) limited ends:
political, educational, charitable, fraternal, religious, and so on.
Alexis de Tocqueville is certainly the shrewdest observer of the
Americans as joiners:[6]

> *Americans of all ages, all stations in life, and types of disposition
> are forever forming associations. There are not only commercial and
> industrial associations in which all take part, but others of a thousand
> different types—religious, moral, serious, futile, very general and
> very limited, immensely large and very minute. . . . In every case,
> at the head of any new undertaking, where in France you would find
> the government or in England some territorial magnate, in the United
> States you are sure to find an association. . . . I have often admired
> the extreme skill they show in proposing a common object for the
> exertions of very many and inducing them voluntarily to pursue it.*

De Tocqueville described the America of the 1830s. He was undoubtedly correct in emphasizing the long prior evolution of the
habit of voluntary association in the Anglo-American tradition, particularly within the context of the struggle for religious liberties.
Nevertheless, from the vantage point of more than a century it seems
clear today that the burgeoning group life he described was also
in large part due to a concatenation of circumstances unique to
time and place. These included: the optimistic faith that *any* social
end could be accomplished by the organized human will; the extreme fluidity—which on the frontier approached atomization—of
society in Jacksonian America, a fluidity which permitted individuals
to slough off the ascriptive ties of birth and thus more easily to
come together in temporary groupings for limited aims; the political liberty possible under governments whose own area of competence was rigidly circumscribed; the moderating effect of universal
suffrage on the "violence of faction." The North American reality
has, of course, since changed in many ways. The purview of government has grown, that of voluntary associations has contracted—but
the legal permissiveness, the habit, and the myth linger on.

North American pluralism possesses a second characteristic, however, of perhaps even greater significance: *multiplicity of affiliations,*
or, as Samuel, Kornhauser and others would have it, *"cross cutting
solidarities."*[7] A North American—a middle-class North American,
let us say—receives imperatives from, and senses allegiances to, a
great diversity of collectivities. These may include his local com-

munity, his regional community, and his national community; his church; his old school; his occupational group (perhaps in both local and national aspects); his political party (*idem*); possibly his fraternal order (although the decline of these once-flourishing associations seems irreversible); possibly his ethnic association (*idem*); the military (through a reserve unit); social clubs and public-service organizations; and so on. Such multiple affiliations undoubtedly place heavy demands on the intellect and sympathies, but the compensation is correspondingly great, for *"so long as no association claims or receives hegemony over many aspects of its members' lives, its power over the individual will be limited"* (italics added).[8]

Although the events of the 1960s leave little room for complacency about the efficacy of the "unseen hand," the presumed ability of the stystem to stabilize itself *automatically,* it is nevertheless true that the unique style of American politics continues to owe much to the two characteristics just discussed. In industrial, or post-industrial, society, the moil of competing groups, the exquisite web of personal allegiances, have long since replaced the conformism and occasional tyranny of the village community; except on its margins—in the central-city ghettos or the more traditional areas of the old Confederacy—society is not and cannot be cleaved into great monoliths to be captured by all-or-nothing political movements. Rather, even as James Madison foresaw, "extend the sphere, and you take in a greater variety of parties and interests; you make it less probable that a majority of the whole will have a common motive to invade the rights of other citizens. . . ."[9] There is little hindrance to the use of existing groups or the formation of new ones for the voicing of grievances, claims, demands for redress. So long as the system per se is regarded as legitimate and capable, however, the task of transmuting this input into output—legislation, policy, dispensation—is left to agencies specialized for the purpose: parties, legislatures, executives, bureaucracies. And because the defeat of a group's objectives at the hands of the system is seen neither as permanent nor as a rebuff to a total or inclusive way of life, it can be accepted, for the time being, with something like a good grace.

The Spanish American system whose symptoms of dissolution have here been labeled "fragmentation" is less well understood, and definitions must be approached more circuitously. To begin with, there are *at the moment* certain natural limits to fragmentation within Spanish America. It occurs only in simultaneous fulfillment of two general sets of conditions within a given national system (or at the point where two developmental scales intersect): first, a sufficient elaborateness of *urban* socio-economic structure to permit the emergence of a variety of modernizing, politically aggressive functional groups; and second, a commitment to representative political institutions—a conventional party system and legislature—which are, however, incapable either of processing and satisfying the groups' manifold political demands, or of barring the groups' direct access to the formal agencies of government. Provisionally, therefore, two distinct clusters of national systems fall outside the scope of the discussion, although it is perfectly conceivable that very soon the fragmentation syndrome may well make its appearance in either. In the first, comprising Paraguay and the Caribbean and Central American nations, the modernizing zone of society remains minute in size and influence. In the second, in which Chile, Uruguay, and Costa Rica hold somewhat precarious membership, the organized functional groups, although relatively well developed and politically exigent, must nevertheless interact with durable and viable structures of "interest aggregation," the party system and legislative bodies. The Cuban and Mexican systems are special cases. Both have incorporated functional structures; in both, however, the hegemony of a revolutionary elite remains without effective challenge; and few evidences of the type of dysfunction under discussion here are visible. It is thus in the sizeable remainder—Argentina, the Bolivarian republics, perhaps Guatemala—that the preconditions of fragmentation are most abundant.

It is a commonplace that the extent of change varies enormously within Spanish America. Whether one conceives of a given national system as a continuum, tending *in toto,* though unevenly in its parts, toward modern industrial society, or rather as discontinuous subsystems ("Urbia" and "Agraria"), it is clear that the greatest transformations have taken place in the great urban agglomerations, particularly those where industry has encroached upon older commercial, extractive, and bureaucratic interests. Here older modes of behavior have been diluted, older forms of face-to-face relationships modified, older allegiances to clan, commune, and *patrón* loosened. These primary relationships and traditional imperatives are supplanted by, or more commonly encysted within, the larger, more impersonal occupational structures and business concerns of the city. The *patria chica* syndrome, the *cofradía,* the artisan *taller,* the café circle, the informal monopoly of wholesalers and retailers, the intricate obligations of *amistad, relaciones,* and *compadrazgo,* still remain, though increasingly in simulacrum. Now, however, they subsist within or alongside the labor syndicate, the managerial cadre, the college of professionals, the association of merchants, the officer corps, the government bureau, the integrated factory.

In these modernizing zones the style of politics has altered. In the nineteenth century—which, taken as a cultural epoch, did not end in 1900—the political process was often enough little more than the equation derivable from the forces that could be commanded at a given moment by particularistic solidarities. It turned upon dynastic feuding among the great political clans and their retinues; *indiadas* or the threat of *indiadas;* city-state versus city-state; military factions pledged, for the moment, to General X as against those of General Y; clerical versus anticlerical sects; and the like. It must be emphasized that most of these solidarities lacked organizational forms for the sustained pursuit of political ends. The political capacity of which they disposed was, at best, latent, negative, inchoate, and intermittent. To operationalize that capacity, and to lend it some color or legitimacy, the more or less fortuitous appearance of a caudillo or *movimiento* was useful, if not indispensable. In the last one to three generations, however, demographic shifts and the centralization of administration, communications, and economic enterprise have caused the Spanish American city to regain its central role as the arbiter of political destinies. It is the natural home of larger, more complex secondary groups, able to exert their will on the political process through the modern devices of strategic work stoppages, bloc voting, public-relations campaigns, direct access through institutionalized channels to the councils of power, or, in the case of the military, monopolization of the use of force.

"Modern" as applied to the emergent functional interest groups is of course a relative term, for they are conjunctures of very disparate elements. Many of the *occupations* pursued within them have been "called into existence" by the requirements of a complex industrial age, and are highly modern in their narrow specialization and the formidable technical expertise they demand. This is as true of the clergyman trained as sociologist or social worker or the *militar de laboratorio,* as of the management consultant or automation expert. Still, on the principle of cumulativeness, as suggested above, the groups comprise intricate webs of personalistic, non-instrumental relationships. Moreover, the institutional matrix—the juridical principles involved, the ascription of individual and corporate status and roles, the devices of corporate self-government, the legitimation of political intervention in the larger system and frequently the mechanisms through which such intervention is exercised—is one which pertains to Spanish America's preindustrial urban past. For all of the anomalies involved, however, and for all the great disparities among functional interest groups with respect to the solidarity and political leverage they in actuality possess, it must be pointed out that *as a type* they dispose of certain inherent characteristics—permanence in time, internal systems of discipline and authority, legal status and a claim to political legitimacy, direct access to the decision-making levels of government—which make them, vis-à-vis the haphazard political sects of the past as well as the faltering party systems of the present, extremely effective vehicles for the achievement of their own ends.

For while it is perfectly comprehensible that newly emergent functional groups should seek a variety of ends on a more or less regular basis, the infrequency of their recourse to the traditional political institutions in doing so is worth remarking. In the extreme case, for which Argentina before 1966 provides the *locus classicus,* significant negotiations develop in personal confrontations between the leadership cadres of the groups, and the chief executive and/or his subordinates within the appropriate bureaucratic structures depending from his cabinet; the instituionalized apparatus of legislative chamber and party caucus is partially or wholly circumvented. One may safely follow Gabriel Almond, *et al.,*[10] in suggesting that this pattern of political interaction is highly deleterious to nations committed verbally to rapid development within the framework of conventional democratic institutions. If an organized group's demands on government are not subjected to the pulling and hauling, the deals and compromises of the legislative process, they then remain stark, unmodified, uncompromising. Should they be met, orderliness and continuity in overall developmental planning may have to be sacrificed—if not immediately, then as soon as competing groups have had the opportunity to make known *their* wants. On the other hand, the group that is rebuffed—because its demands are too outrageous or too inchoate to be processed or simply because of a weak tactical position—can easily persuade itself that it has been denied elemental social justice. Its *total* way of life, affective and rational elements both, has been offended; and the repercussions in public life may be severe. At the very least, neither the administration which has been pressured into concessions behind closed doors nor the regular party politicians, shown once again to be marginal to the serious business of politics, are likely to gain in public stature. At the worst, should a general stalemate ensue between administration and the key functional groups, the temptation to cut the Gordian Knot may well prove irresistible to a self-proclaimed "restorer of the people's liberties" or whatnot who commonly appears nowadays as the chairman of a military junta.

At this stage of the inquiry, an elaborate nomenclature is of little value; too much remains to be tested and verified. For purposes of rough classification, the most useful criteria are the simple, incisive ones of *solidarity* and *power.*[11] With them, it is possible to focus one's attention on the relatively small cluster of familiar *intereses* central to each national system. This is, after all, a common-sense approach for a cultural area in which, despite bloomin' buzzin' appearances, secondary-group formation is by no means as extensive as in a matured industrial system. It is apparent, for example, that monopolies and oligopolies limit the number of economic interests seeking representation; that economic "underdevelopment" itself poses rather strict limits to the variety and elaborateness of occupational structure (where no electronic industry exists, one does not find an Association of Electronic Manufacturers or a Syndicate of Electronic Engineers); that the Roman Catholic Church, although not homogeneous within itself, has yet to see its religious monopoly seriously challenged by other organized sects; that many potential groups of lower status and/or rural origin have until now been effectively prevented from acquiring the sinews of organization.

Although it has been used for convenience in this discussion, the term "interest group" is inappropriate for serious analysis. Even within the North American context, the concept has lost much of its validity. For Spanish America its connotation of "rationality" and "instrumentality" does not in the least accord with the totality of the affective as well as the cognitive involvement of the *latino*—or at least of the *latino* well placed enough to be considered, and to consider himself, part of the system. A more subtle problem is posed by the term "corporate group," which has also been applied of late. Because it calls up echoes of the antidemocratic experiments of the 1920s and 1930s, it is capable of provoking ideological resistance among those fearful of surrendering any part of their faith in the liberal-democratic ethos of Spanish America. Objections on analytical grounds, however, would seem to be better founded. For while one may indeed discern the existence in embryo of corporative regimes in several of the systems of the region (*e.g.,* Argentina, Ecuador), the fact remains that no such corporative regime (if one excepts Mexico) has as yet been formally founded. In the absence of a comprehensive corporative statute, one which would, presumably, provide the means of compulsion to membership and a rough equality of functional representation in social and economic councils or in a corporative chamber, the present configuration possesses none of the neat symmetry that would permit the indiscriminate application of the term "corporate" to its components; far from it. If "corporate" is to be used, after all, the touchstone must be the probability that corporate discipline[12] can be exerted in ordinary and extraordinary situations, and this probability varies greatly from one functional structure to the next. As will be suggested later, the probability also appears to vary according to broad occupational categories ("heterocephalous" and "autocephalous"), and according to class/status determinants. With all this, "corporate group" as a generalized label is of doubtful utility.

"Institutionalized functional group" is perhaps for the moment as unexceptionable a term as any. Despite its infelicity, the adjective "institutionalized" is desirable on several counts. Whereas a "functional group," in the bald meaning of the term, is a group organized functionally for the attainment of ends particular to itself—like the birth-control leagues or Communist Parties of Spanish America—the great *intereses* are as a matter of course accepted as socially legitimate. They are, in fact, institutions in that, to follow Germani, their ostensible ends "constitute the basis of the explicit recognition on the part of society at large" (just as their "latent functions may be related to forms of recognition that are also latent").[13] But aside from recognition by society at large, the *sine qua non* of social legitimacy in contemporary Spanish America is juridical recognition by, and nominal or decisive administrative subordination to, the State. This direct one-to-one political relationship—prior to and distinct from the sense in which *any* secondary body capable of making claims on the State is inherently political—serves *ab initio* to blur and confuse the difference between *social* and *political* function, between "society" and "polity."

The *intereses* are institutionalized in another important sense. They endure over time and come to comprise (again to follow Germani) conjunctures of "norms, values, cognitive elements, which tend to form a relatively unified *system,* by virtue of which the 'members' of the institution have defined for them their relationships and reciprocal expectations."[14] In the absence of multiple horizontal relationships, as in the pluralistic configuration described above, such a system, depending on its antiquity and elaborateness, and also its efficacy as a source of patronage and/or material and psychological satisfactions, tends toward *inclusiveness,* toward discreteness and impermeability by other systems. In this event individuals are largely unbeset by competing allegiancies or cross-cutting solidarities; they are, rather, afforded a dominant or unique constellation of imperatives for belief and behavior, a dominant or unique reference group of significant personal contacts. A political society characterized by a congeries of such inclusive groups reproduces Ortega y Gasset's classic image of invertebrate Spain: "a series of water-tight compartments (*gremios herméticamente cerrados*)," none of which feels "the least curiosity toward events in the domain of the others."[15]

The sources of group solidarity and political efficacy, and of the sharp differentiations among these structures as well, can be examined under three mutually reinforcing aspects. The institutionalized functional groups may, first, be conceived as pyramidal structures of patronage and clientage, the apices of which extend within the formal precincts of government, particularly the ministries and dependencies of the executive branch. This area in which bureaucratic functionaries and the leaders of functional groups interact (or to put it another way, in which society and polity overlap and fuse) is of crucial importance—although, unfortunately, journalists and researchers are rarely welcome guests there. The *intereses* are, almost without exception, nonautonomous. Not only do they stand administratively and juridically at the pleasure of the State; in practical matters, too, they require constant executive dispensation relating to appropriations, achievement and retention of monopolies, tariffs, social and tax policy, and so on. Save in Mexico and Cuba, however, where revolutionary *political* elites and *functional* elites have interpenetrated, and a decisive subordination of the policies of the *intereses* to those of the State has taken place, the relationship is far from authoritarian. On the contrary, in the transitional societies in which no such revolutionary *Gleichschaltung* (to use the Hitlerian term in a strict technical sense) has occurred, a capable functional group leadership remains free to deploy its considerable influence in an environment of subtle interaction and maneuver, pressure and counterpressure. Thus the mixed agencies through which the formal superordination of the State is expressed—the chambers of commerce and industry supervised by the Ministry of Economy; the mineral, coffee, sugar, cotton, meat, grain "boards" under the same; professional licensing bodies linked to the universities which in turn retain a precarious "autonomy"—except for finances—under the Ministry of Education; the administrative boards of *entes autónomos;* arbitration commissions under the Ministry of Labor; military cadres serving in the Ministry of War—serve as channels through which demands and claims ("input") flow in one direction, and commands, dispensations, patronage ("output") in the other. The struggle for control of these vital stopcocks of patronage, and for the relative advantage of one over another, is never-ending.

Although the pattern described so far is by no means unique to Spanish America, several of its elements pertain specifically to the transitional societies of the area. First, it is not yet common for institutionalized functional groups to seek political ends through specialized agencies or lobbies. While individuals of exceptional gifts as "contact men" are detailed to perform much of this work, in general the incidence of *personalismo,* face-to-face confrontations between public officials and functional elite members, appears to continue high. More important still, although such negotiations outside the framework of open electoral politics are facilitated by the decrepitude of the conventional agencies and processes, it has nevertheless grown increasingly difficult to reach lasting accommodations, even within the context of covert arrangements. As the sheer number of interests to be satisfied has increased, the horizontal solidarities and tactical alliances within a small, relatively homogeneous oligarchy which once made possible an effective sub rosa manipulation of affairs have become correspondingly more tenuous. Although their hegemony has been by no means dissipated, the great families no longer enjoy an *automatically accorded* political prestige. Simultaneously, as new functional structures have proliferated, new men, some of them of rather more obscure background, have emerged as candidates to the new functional elites. Although they may aspire to—or, indeed, have been born to—the trappings, insignia, and way of life of the traditional oligarchs, they are not free to base their public eminence on simple class/status (*i.e.,* largely ascriptive) determinants. Their stature, rather, derives in great measure directly from their day-to-day performance as *patrones* of their respective functional groupings. Therefore, the new functional elites, taken as a whole, comprise little more than an ill-defined social stratum, one possessed of fewer internal linkages and much less internal cohesion than the traditional elite whose status derived from the simpler and more nearly complementary triad of landholding, military, and ecclesiastical interests.

A second approach lies through the expectations and other attributes of the inclusive group environment. Except in extreme cases, such as that of the military, this environment is not necessarily continuous with that of the latino's rich primary solidarities, his family and intimates; it does, however, occupy much of the remainder of his social universe. In it he finds a broad range of psychological gratifications. For some—the young priest, or officer, or trade-union organizer—the deepest satisfaction lies in the sharing of an ascetic ideal. For most, it affords security: shared values, reasonably certain expectations concerning career chances, possibilities for marital alliances, criteria for identifying one's self in the social order (including the *carnets* and other documents and impedimenta demanded by officialdom), the sense—when justified—that the group looks after its own.

The material benefits available through the group qua group are, of course, a major factor for cohesion. These commonly include beneficial tax or wage legislation; the multiple *cajas,* pension and social security schemes; monopolies or quasi-monopolies (as, *e.g.,* when the number of tobacconists, pharmacies, notaries, etc., within a given district is stipulated by public authorities); low-cost housing; social and athletic clubs, dispensaries, resorts and sanatoria available to members only; the discounts on public transportation and cultural events enjoyed by students; and so on.

Group solidarity is manifested through other devices as well. Some groups—students, performing artists, and railwaymen and other skilled workers—utilize an elaborate argot. There are differential modes of dress: the several military, police, and civil service uniforms, the apprentice's smock, the workingman's blue coveralls, etc. Informal immunities, such as the *universitario's* latitude in "manifesting" and his recourse to the university as sanctuary, or the apparent immunity of the *militar* from customs regulations (or, indeed, the criminal law), have far-reaching implications for political life. Even more significant, however, are the partly or wholly autonomous systems of internal jurisdiction: in the Church, in the military, in some permanent bureaucracies, in stock exchanges and *cámaras,* in commercial and labor tribunals, in the university.

In the older and more traditional functional groups, the imperatives and expectations particular to the group are so pervasive, so hallowed by time, so easily and unreflectively internalized that the result is a markedly stereotyped personal style. The ample endowment of attitudes, values, patterns of behavior, which the individual receives on entering or being co-opted into the *ramo* or *gremio,* is naturally reinforced by the expectation of others that he will act in predictable ways deducible from his group affiliation. The army officer who has internalized the values of authority, formal hierarchy, and patriotism and his corporate role as guardian of the (written or unwritten) constitution or the professor who has internalized the very different values of skepticism, intellectual hierarchy, and the universality of knowledge and *his* corporate role as monitor of the public morality and national socio-economic evolution—these are "stock" figures, partially because they have fully absorbed the imperatives to belief and action of their own functional groups, and partially because colleagues and others *expect* them to be stock figures and so interact with them in ways conducive to eliciting stock responses. The North American observer, culturally conditioned to "open-mindedness" toward the infinity of human possibilities, is disturbed to find himself surrounded, in a Spanish American milieu, by highly disparate, sharply modeled, and reasonably predictable *types.* It is, however, an equally crude folk-wisdom that permits the latino to conduct his social affairs—and regularly to deduce on a one-to-one basis the political allegiance of individuals from their group affiliation—by departing from ascriptive assumptions.

A third route of approach lies through the controlling concepts of the traditional legal culture. Although much research and elucidation remain to be done in this area, it is nonetheless clear that juridical precepts are intimately bound up in functional group solidarity and are instrumental in furthering differentiation among such groups; they do so by exaggerating the one-to-one relationship between group and State, and by diluting the Liberal requirement for juridical equality of groups before the law. On the part of the State, the legal regime is one intensely hostile to the *autonomous* existence of intermediary bodies. Its origins lie deep in the Roman Law, in the Roman "concession" theory, of which it has been said, "groups existed only in the legal contemplation of the sovereign."[16] In this tradition, the State does not take cognizance of a group; it *creates* the group by endowing it with juridical personality. Therefore, in systems like those of Spanish America, in which the State's recognition and patronage are all-important for privilege, places, and institutional legitimacy, the unrecognized group drifts in an uncomfortable, harassed limbo. This hostility is manifested in similar fashion through the procedures of administrative centralism, an administrative centralism whose functionaries at all levels can only view the enthusiasms and irregularities of voluntary ad hoc groups as inimical to orderly government and threatening to the status and competences of bureaucrats.[17]

But if the State's dominance over inferior groups is incontestable, there exists nevertheless in the general legal culture a countervailing rationale, one which poses formidable obstacles to the arbitrariness and despoliations of government, and thus inhibits the smooth, efficient, and potentially authoritarian, articulation of functional groups to the policies of the State—the rationale of the *interés creado*. This diffuse concept has behind it in the Hispano-Roman legal tradition antecedents of weight and venerability equal to those of the concession theory, and stands in perpetual tension with the latter.[18] Shielded by it, functional groups from which sizeable numbers of persons—or, for that matter, small numbers of eminent persons—derive their livelihood, which have over time accreted prerogatives and immunities, hold themselves justified in levying particularistic claims of equity upon superior government. As suggested earlier, the assertion of these particularistic claims against the programs and policies of regimes committed to rapid modernization renders public argumentation of the issues tortuous, and conflict, inchoate. The possibility of reducing disputes to operational terms is lessened; the possibility of a total confrontation is increased.

The polarity of these opposing concepts is most often made manifest in the acrimonious negotiations over the concession or revision of the *estatuto básico* or *ley orgánica*. It is a struggle that generates much affect, and it is notable that this affect is thence often transferred to the objective symbol of corporate legitimacy, the *ley* or *estatuto* itself. This phenomenon is undoubtedly relative to class and status, for it may be assumed that the infrequent high-status group endowed with a comprehensive *ley orgánica*—a stockmen's association or a *cámara* of manufacturers—does not need to view its dispositions with the same jealousy as a newly-formed secondary-teachers' association, industrial union, or peasant league. For such as the latter, however, the document's detailed statement of rights, duties, immunities, internal governance and jurisdiction, financial liabilities, and formal relationship to administrative organs are specific points to be cherished most vigilantly; the regime may unilaterally alter or revoke them only with the greatest difficulty and in the face of the most determined resistance. For the historian, the sense of familiarity is strong, for the *ley* or *estatuto*, taken together with the heterogeny of custom-derived informal immunities and prerogatives, constitutes a special and differential juridical status very strongly reminiscent of the corporate *fuero* of the *ancien régime*.

The institutionalized functional groups under discussion are largely co-extensive with the so-called middle sectors and, of course, the new functional elites. The point is well illustrated by a sardonic passage on Chile from the pen of Oswaldo Sunkel:[19]

The new middle class and organized workers who lacked the ability of ruling groups to circumvent the law, to avoid taxes, to isolate themselves in exclusive circles, to behave in short, as if they enjoyed extraterritorial rights in their own country, have also been creating an elaborate structure of legal privileges, the extent of which has depended on the power of their respective political pressure groups. The forty or fifty different social security systems, special pay clauses and benefits, tax exemptions, duty-free territories and ports, etc., are clear proof of this activity.

The extremities of the social hierarchy are little involved in these phenomena, for obvious reasons. In the submerged portion of the population, both organization and legal and political recognition— the minimum requisites of a multi-faceted group existence—face formidable obstacles. Some are inherent in social determinants: isolation and illiteracy; attachment to the traditional primary solidarities of ethnic group, clan, commune, patria chica, *patrón*-client relationships; initial disorientation in the new urban environment; the high economic vulnerability and occupational mobility of the unskilled. Others are patently political—the resolute resistance of interested parties to the formation of cooperatives, peasant leagues, industrial unions. In this, there is little that is uniquely Spanish American.[29]

At the other end of the social spectrum, among the favored of fortune, the traditional elites, *formal* organization for the promotion and defense of status and interest has been unnecessary, if not unthinkable. In the less complex world of the nineteenth century, and in the minds of those who find it altogether too attractive an age to abandon, traditional elites straddled landowning, military, and ecclesiastical interests, and interacted more or less amicably with foreign promoters of extractive and commercial development. Communications flowed freely through informal channels: dynastic marriages and alliances, social clubs, ad hoc caucuses, *relaciones*. Status was highly ascriptive; authority and the deference due it were highly internalized. While intestine conflict over the fruits of power was endemic, resistance against the infrequent external threat to the serenity of status could easily enough be mobilized without recourse to the devices of corporate discipline. Indeed, except in the Church, little such corporate discipline existed, in either the late-medieval or the modern sense.

For reasons that were suggested earlier, particularly the growing emphasis on performance ("achievement") rather than ascription, today's functional elites find it much more difficult to insulate themselves as social entities from their respective constituencies. One is, in fact, struck by the ragged interpenetration, the constant seepage in both directions, between functional elites and the levels of the upper middle sectors immediately below them. To explore this phenomenon, a discrimination made earlier must be restated in a slightly different way. That is, the institutionalized functional group conceived as a structure of corporate solidarity tending toward inclusiveness pertains preeminently, under this aspect, to the lower and middle levels of the middle sectors—to unionized skilled labor, organized white-collar workers, school teachers, and so on. Higher in the social hierarchy, however, the characteristic of the group as an elaborate web or discrete system of patronage and clientage, personal relations and obligations, comes to predominate. At these levels— very simply, as an individual's contacts grow more influential—the dependence upon personal social agility and manipulative skills becomes greater. The aspirant comes, in fine, to adopt much of the operational style of the members of the functional elites. It is worth remarking, for example, that the "free" professions, particularly law and medicine, that have traditionally served as springboards to political careers and/or bureaucratic sinecures, possess relatively fewer corporate accouterments than lower-status groups whose members have little pretension to direct access to the mighty. Even at that, however, the North American observer—bemused, perhaps, by what seems to him the total anarchy of the medical profession— should not exaggerate the freedom of the "free" professions. They too have become intimately dependent on government, both for employment and for the retention of the partial or complete corporate monopolies operated through the degree-granting and licensing agencies of the national universities.

The social continuum that spans functional elites and upper middle sectors is related to the often-noted community of values that also unites them. Both undoubtedly derive in some large measure from the phenomenon of downward social mobility. It is suggestive to ponder the fate of generations of cadet branches of the great families, cadets evicted by the glacial pace of economic growth, by mismanagement, profligacy, and the destructive gyrations of the world economy from a truly upper-status way of life. While their numbers have not been large in absolute terms, they have, of course, long adorned—and overpopulated—the government service, diplomacy, the free professions, and of late communications and the more respectable of the technical specialties. To these professions and occupations they have brought their ancestral pretensions and values and the *cachet* conferred by name, manners, education, and personal contacts. They have thus created a style, an environment of attitudes and cues for behavior, to be emulated by their newly arrived upwardly mobile colleagues.

In the lower and middle reaches of the middle sectors, on the other hand, the enterprise of individuals is, by and large, less central to the functioning of the newly emergent secondary groups than the mechanisms for the achievement and maintenance of corporate solidarity. As it is apparent, however, that the extent and effectiveness of such organization vary greatly from one group to the next, it is useful here to apply still another rough discrimination. This is the Weberian continuum which stretches between the poles of "autocephalous" (self-organized and managing) and "heterocephalous" (organized and managed by others) occupations.[21] The more heterocephalous occupations—the military, the clergy, blue- and white-collar and technical specialties within large business concerns, primary and secondary teaching, bureaucratic trades—operate within relatively rigid frameworks of authority, and are thus easily susceptible to formal organization and further development in the direction of inclusiveness. In the more autocephalous occupations—the professions; the arts; independent accountants, draftsmen, and the like; independent small and medium businessmen in merchandising, manufacturing, artisanry, and the service trades—effective organization is less feasible. The extent of the sense of community among individuals pursuing, on an individual basis, the same craft, is problematical; the possibility that this can be translated into solidarity and power—through, for example, monopolistic agreements or through syndical trade associations articulated to government—is even more so. Nevertheless, the extreme limiting case—the mere statistical agglomeration of persons all earning a livelihood in the same way—is rare, and likely to grow rarer in middle-sector Spanish America.

Certain long-cherished illusions about the political future of the Spanish American middle sectors are at last, it seems, being allowed to expire quietly. Commentators—North Americans in particular—departing from a priori and/or culturally-derived premises concerning the "natural" behavior of matured middle classes, have been given to foreseeing the emergence from the bosom of the middle sectors of broad-based, "aggregative"—and presumably reformist or progressive—political movements. In the past quarter of a century or so, moreover, the measurable numerical expansion of the middle sectors, together with the precisely observed elaboration of levels and gra-

dations of socio-economic status within them, appeared to lend
weight to these prognostications. To date, however, these data
have been of greater service to the market analysts of U.S. firms
purveying consumer commodities than to the political analysts, for
these *levels* and *gradations* have not been, with any notable rapidity,
transmuted into horizontal *solidarities* possessing the potential for
mass political action in the conventional manner.

The efficacy of institutionalized functional groups as social solidarities and as vehicles for the satisfaction of political claims is a
major factor in explaining this rather puzzling phenomenon. For
middle-sector latinos integrated into the system, the group solidarity
into which they have been born or migrated serves multiple ends:
material and psychological satisfactions, a reference group of personal relations, a single fount of patronage, a single source of authority, a single focus of allegiance. Barring a situation of general societal dissolution and accelerated change—and the resources of the system for barring such a situation are massive—caudillos, *movimientos,*
and the discredited actors and agents of the formal game of politics
have little claim on their attention; the means to the attainment of
political ends are closer at hand. In marked contrast to the pervasiveness of *vertical* patterns, structures of *horizontal* consensus
and solidarity below the level of government itself remain at best
exiguous. The traditional agencies—the alliance of extended high-
status families, on occasion ad hoc councils of ecclesiastical authorities or the parish church organization—which once, in an unstructured
and intermittent manner, exercised this function, have declined in
authority and efficacy; the shortcomings of the traditional political
parties are too well known to require comment. Only to a slight
degree, and very unevenly throughout Spanish America, have they
been supplemented or supplanted by modernized parties or, infor-
mally, by social clubs, voluntary associations, and other vehicles of
cross-cutting solidarity.[22]

The historian is by temperament unable to let the matter rest
in the immediate present—or in the hands of the present-minded.
The conclusion seems inescapable that, taken as a whole, the congeries of institutionalized functional groups, the mutual isolation
and/or hostility that characterizes their extra-mural relations, and the
peculiar modalities of their articulation to the political apparatus of
the State bear more than a superficial resemblance to the corporate
system of the *ancien régime.* It seems too that, as there are very few
direct institutional continuities discernible, the configuration described here represents in some sense a *recrudescence,* with many
alterations of varying magnitude, of a socio-political system which,
it has usually been assumed, passed into oblivion with the disintegration of Spain's American empire. To make such a proposal is,

unhappily, to raise conceptual problems of daunting complexity to which, in the present state of research, there can be nothing like definitive answers, only tentative organizing hypotheses. The discussion can logically be divided into two parts. The first involves a consideration of the corporate structure of the Hispanic and Hispanic American *ancien régime;* the second, an attempt to conceptualize the virtual disappearance in the nineteenth century and the reappearance, *mutatis mutandis,* in the twentieth of pre-Independence socio-political and juridical concepts and organizational forms. This temporal division, it should be noted, corresponds to the two different senses in which, in strict logic, the term and concept "traditional" as applied to Spanish America must be understood.

It is convenient, if not quite conventional among North Americans, to consider the corporate structure of Spain and her American empire as a national variant on the themes pursued in the older European historiography of the *corps intermédiaries,* a historiography which sought to establish the evolving relationships in the states of early modern Europe between sovereignty and the intermediary bodies which separated the sovereign and the individual.[23] Within this conceptual context, it is possible to make out a particular period in time in which the Hispanic state was overtaken by a peculiar sort of political paralysis, and from this to hypothesize that the *ancien régime* of both Spain and Hispanic America rested upon an equilibrium of contradictory and opposing forces, the precipitate of the fateful arrest of socio-political evolution that occurred in the Spanish lands in the latter sixteenth and early seventeenth centuries. For in these lands the relationship between sovereignty and *corps intermédiaires* was in effect frozen in mid-passage from the forms of late-medieval Christendom to those of the burgeoning royal absolutism that elsewhere in Europe was to erect the institutional scaffolding of the modern Nation-State.

The achievement of Ferdinand and Isabel, and of their immediate successors of the House of Austria, rested in great part upon their ability to arrest and for a time to reverse the centrifugal tendencies in Spanish political society. Prior to their advent, although there was in theory no question about the locus of temporal authority, the Crown, in practice the feudal organization of Castile, was characterized by extreme decentralization: it consisted of little more than an unarticulated congeries of autonomous *señorios, municipios,* privileged jurisdictions, guilds and functional corporations, and the like. In the reign of the Catholic Monarchs, however, and through most of the sixteenth century, the accretion of royal power, greatly facilitated by the work of an ever-ramifying bureaucracy, was inexorable. The Crown succeeded in turn in curbing the waywardness of the great noble houses, the military orders, the towns, and the headstrong prelates of the Church. This process of centralization required the enlistment, by coercion if necessary, of functional elites into the Crown's administrative structure, and the yoking, for better or worse, of the fortunes of the *corps intermédiaires* to those of the Crown (a relationship symbolized by Isabel's personal emblem, the Yoke and the Arrows). Individuals sought and found places as royal administrators; institutions like the Church, the military orders, and the Mesta became coordinate arms of Crown administration and served as indispensable sources of royal revenue. But significantly, loss of autonomy did not bring great alterations in the economic and social prerogatives of the elites, nor did it demand gross internal restructuring of the *corps intermédiaires* themselves.

But for the mounting bankruptcy of funds and spirit at home, and the unrelieved disasters abroad in the latter sixteenth and seventeenth centuries, it is conceivable that the process toward a more or less harmoniously integrated national polity might well have been extended and consummated—Spain might, for example, have continued to follow a trajectory analogous to that of France. This, however, did not occur. In the seventeenth century the Crown's insatiable demands for revenue, coupled to rising doubts that Spain's far-flung commitments could save the Imperial mission from disaster, worked to effect an approximate stabilization between Crown and *corps intermédiaires*. As the Crown's capacity for leadership became more problematical, its expedients more threadbare, its concessions of places and privileges, titles and monopolies, placed more nakedly on a financial basis, it and the *corps intermédiaires* approached a parity based on interdependence and exchange. The latter entities, *although they were never to regain their former de facto political autonomy,* evolved into tough structures of solidarity and privilege, concerned primarily, in the *desengaño* of the close of the Siglo de Oro, to preserve past gains.

Francisco Suárez, the most lucid and accessible of the constellation of brilliant jurisconsults who adorned Spanish philosophy during the Siglo de Oro, is the central theorist of Spain's arrested sociopolitical development.[24] In asserting this, unfortunately, one must be prepared to sail close to the winds of polemic, for in recent years Suárez has often been invoked in the sputtering debate over the doctrines of "popular sovereignty" in the Independence movements, as well as—more plausibly—by writers who, unpersuaded of his direct influence on eighteenth-century ideologues, nevertheless see in his writings a major source for the understanding of the value-structure of Colonial thought. These broad and disputed issues are not central here: what are relevant are the closely-reasoned and authoritative rationales he provided for *both* of the countervailing elements in the emerging stasis of Spanish statecraft.

Suárez was not a seminal thinker but preeminently a codifier and expositor. As such, he responded sensitively to the conflicting drives of the overlapping historical epochs of his lifetime. In his political corpus are gathered together the older themes of Thomism and Hispanic consuetudinary law and the newer philosophical justifications for the dynamic state-building autocracy of the sixteenth century. Not surprisingly, his attempted reconciliation of these very contradictory traditions is only partly successful. The tension, for example, between the older rationalism and the newer voluntarism remains unresolved. His theoretical State is a fictive person, in accord with Scholastic precedent; yet in important ways it is an entity distinct from and superior to its constituent members. Similarly, the magistrate is a functional member of the State, yet above it.[25]

Nevertheless—and this is the crux of the argument—Suárez endowed his State with a remarkable stability, a stability achieved through the delicate balancing of opposing and ultimately antagonistic forces. On the part of the people, their privileges and institutions are shielded by the authority of custom, consuetudinary law. For the magistrate, on the other hand, power is irrevocably his unless and until he lapses into tyranny. But the definition of tyranny is narrow, and the means by which it may legitimately be resisted are closely circumscribed. In the important question of inferior groups *(societates imperfectae),* the power of the magistrate *(potestas jurisdictionis)* is indivisible; this power may be delegated to inferior groups, but it may not be shared with them—flatly, *minores civitates non habere potestatem ferendi proprias leges.*[26] Nevertheless, inferior groups may, with the magistrate's assent, govern themselves, and this assent need be nothing more than the tacit toleration of what has become custom. Custom is, indeed, the justification for the *interés creado,* for customary privileges have the force of law for groups (but not individuals) which have shown their utility in the furtherance of the common good. In order to abrogate such privilege, it is the magistrate's obligation to demonstrate, in written law, that the common good has not been served—a difficult proposition in logic.[27] Suárez' State is, it must be acknowledged, a system admirably designed, out of very disparate components and different traditions, for the preservation of the status quo.

An equilibrium similar to that in Spain was achieved in Spanish America. Upon a protean social organization, particularistic, potentially and dangerously centrifugal, more analogous to fifteenth- than to sixteenth-century Spain, was superimposed a heavily bureaucratized administrative regime, the viceregal system, that was, in sixteenth-century terms, the utmost in modernity. Given the newness of the American *intereses creados* and the lesser social eminence of their leaders, this was, perhaps, an easier task than in the Peninsula itself. Nevertheless, distributive justice and, more importantly, the economic exigencies demanded that the *beneméritos de Indias* be conceded, within the notoriously flexible framework of viceregal supervision, their economic and social prerogatives, which included, with time and the coming of the *hacienda,* a more extensive authority over more servile labor than had ever been available to any but the very mighty in Spain. From this uneasy compromise emerged *criollo* elites whose social and economic hegemony went largely unchallenged, but who lacked the autonomous political (and through most of the period, military) functions appropriate to a true feudal nobility.

In America, the development of a rigidly hierarchical structure of socio-legal castes diluted the sense, derived from the common late-medieval analogy of the human body, of organic functional organization.[28] Nevertheless, there in time emerged in the urban centers limited systems of cabildos, consulados, guilds, monopolies, and privileged jurisdictions, differentiated from one another by status, function, and law. Although many made use of direct channels of political communication with superior levels of administration, their capacity for autonomous action remained, under the wary vigilance of Crown officials, latent save in the event of acephaly or a general breakdown of administration. This conglomerate society was far from static: it suffered the vicissitudes of demographic change and alterations in economic patterns; the personal fortunes of *benemérito* families and newcomers underwent violent gyrations. Toward the end of the eighteenth century gross changes were impending, changes implied on the one side by the threats to privilege posed by the Bourbon reforms, and on the other by symptoms of increasing "bourgeoisification"—the substitution of economic for legal class/caste criteria in social mobility and the assignment of status—in urban environments.[29] Nevertheless, the social and political patterns and juridical legitimization of the corporate regime remained substantially intact to the eve of Independence.

The subsequent processes are a conundrum, though perhaps not a totally intractable one. There is, after all, nothing particularly novel in the suggestion that for Spanish America a special awareness of historical sequences is required. The perceptive observer whose senses have been assailed in the streets of Mexico, perhaps, or Guatemala, or Quito, or Lima, or many another urban center, by the physical juxtaposition, the *montage,* of the pre-Columbian millennia, the Colony, the turn-of-the-century *belle époque,* and today's glass- and chrome-bedizened mass cult, is not likely to conceive of Spanish America's movement toward modern and industrial society as inexorable—much less rectilinear or unilinear. One comes, rather, to think in terms of multiple currents of cultural evolution moving at different rates to uneven rhythms, regressing as well as advancing, submerging as well as predominating, intersecting and interacting fortuitously within the framework of a given metropolis, a given institution, or indeed, a given personality structure.

The disintegration of the corporate system of the *ancien régime* can therefore be considered to represent a regression to simpler forms of socio-political organization, for it was not for decades replaced by structures of comparable complexity. When "the settlers . . . , foiled by the Crown in the sixteenth century, were at last triumphant in the nineteenth,"[30] Spanish American political society reverted to its primary components: the clan, the tribe, the hacienda, the village or town, the armed band. Much more than Liberal ideological imperatives, social and political determinants, acting at varying speeds and in varying combinations according to area, were overriding in the disappearance of the corporate system: the loss of royal political and juridical legitimacy; the concurrent dismantling of the structures of royal patronage and the expulsion of Spanish-controlled monopolies; the dislocations and atomization of the years of armed conflict; the ruination of the artisanate by cheap European goods; the deflection of economic activity away from the cities of the interior and their subsequent stagnation and rustication; rationalization, largely by foreigners, of the exploitation of natural resources; the proletarianization of the countryside. It seems no exaggeration to suggest that, toward the middle or end of the nineteenth century, many areas of Spanish America more closely approached the "two-class" model—still belabored by too many journalists and academics—than they had done since the first century of conquest, or have done ever since.

The political reconstitution of Spanish America which took place in these circumstances was bound to be somewhat illusory. The oligarchic republics which emerged in the better-favored areas owed much, in outward form, to imported constitutionalisms, parliamentary procedures, and up-to-date European legal codes; and so long as social organization remained rudimentary, suffrage remained effectively restricted, the hegemony of the newly consolidated creole elites—the survivors and victors of the post-Independence anarchy—and their foreign associates remained uncontested, few anomalies were apparent. It was only with the turn of the present century that urban development—still in a mode much antecedent to that of the industrial city—permitted newly vocal social groups and economic interests to begin to exert pressures for the expansion of the framework of politics. This phenomenon was most marked in the Plata region, where, significantly, not only sizeable "middle-class" parties but also *entes autónomos* and the quasi-corporative devices of the University Reform made their appearance during the first three decades of the century. Simultaneously, but in a less distinguishably urban context, the institutions of the Mexican Revolution began slowly to acquire their distinctive characteristics in the years following the promulgation of the Constitution of 1917. Since then—notably during the 1930s—the *vigencia* of nineteenth-century liberalism and of the constitutional procedures associated with it has continued to recede. At the same time, the socio-political elaboration described in the earlier pages of this essay has accelerated, and has created an intricate though informal system of political interaction parallel to the formal. The two have interacted, and have, after a fashion, produced results. As suggested earlier, however, their continued coexistence in the more "advanced" transitional societies has come to be the structural/functional dimension of paralysis.

To summarize: with the quickening pace of urbanization and the roughly parallel increase in the complexity of social and economic organization, there has predictably appeared a new congeries of urban secondary groups based on occupation or social function. Many of these have rapidly attained a sophisticated level of formal organization; insofar as they are effective in creating a framework for creature satisfactions, material and psychological, they take on the character of partially closed social environments in which sizeable numbers of persons find a single fount of authority and a single focus of allegiance. They thus manifest a high degree of "inclusiveness," and correspondingly, of mutual isolation, characteristics of a more traditional, preindustrial order of secondary-group organization. Their mode of political behavior is profoundly conditioned by these social determinants; it is further characterized by a pattern of direct, one-to-one interaction with the permanent structures of government. This pattern intersects at points with, but is largely alternative to, the constitutionally-envisioned electoral and legislative process. The vertical nature of these relationships is in large part determined by the controlling concepts of a traditional politico-legal culture, one which is throughout antagonistic to the autonomous existence of secondary groups, but which conduces to the institutionalization of dependent, *non*-autonomous secondary groups. Because the articulation and subordination of non-autonomous groups to government is far from complete, however—this too has deep roots in the evolution or non-evolution of the Hispanic State—the constant febrile effort and atmosphere of struggle necessary to keep the system in some sort of equilibrium conduces to in-group solidarity, exacerbates the differentiations among groups, and strengthens the configuration of multiple lines of vertical interaction converging within the apparatus of government. In sharp contrast, horizontal solidarities at levels other than that of government are few and feeble.

For all its patent injustices and ceaseless commotion, the system is not unworkable *so long as* 1) the number of interests to be satisfied is relatively small; and 2) the elites who command and manipulate them remain a) relatively unified and homogeneous, and b) relatively well-insulated from the importunities of their constituents. But it is precisely these conditions that are now disappearing, and thus the system is growing ever less viable. The number of groups, the extravagance of their expectations, and the stridency of their political demands have all augmented; at the same time, the slow eclipse of the old elites, the fragmentation of the new, and the continuing (and in some areas, growing) debility of the conventional party systems and legislatures make it increasingly difficult, in a nonauthoritarian context, to adjust those demands to the requirements of overall national development. Because of the prevalence of the vertical patterns of political flow, because parties and legislatures serve poorly or not at all as buffers and instruments of aggregation, the competition for preferment can be resolved only within the framework of government itself. The result very often has the appearance of a muted civil war. To be sure, the obvious authoritarian solution has not escaped the organizers of recent military coups, and such internal conflict has been suppressed by fiat. However, whether these military regimes possess the internal resources of leadership, programs, and cohesion to permit them to transcend the limitations of the system that has borne them to their present eminence is one of the more interesting of the questions raised here, the answers to which should begin to become clear in the next decade or so.

Notes

1. Arthur P. Whitaker, "The Argentine Paradox," *Annals of the American Academy of Political and Social Sciences,* 334 (March 1961), 107. *Cf.* Kalman Silvert, "The Costs of Anti-Nationalism," in K. Silvert (ed.), *Expectant Peoples: Nationalism and Development* (New York, 1963), 347-372. On pp.358-359, Silvert acutely and suggestively characterizes the Argentine system as a variant on "Mediterranean syndicalism," although, as the present essay attempts to show, the term "syndicalism," with its implication of autonomy for intermediary groups, is perhaps not totally appropriate. More generally, in a "thinkpiece" such as this, it is impossible to acknowledge all one's intellectual debts. To be sure, only a corporal's guard of North Americans—Blanksten, Kling, McAlister, Morse, Phelan, Sarfatti, Scott, Silvert—have addressed themselves to any of the major questions raised here. The Latin American and especially the European historiography is, however, fertile; I have followed especially: Beneyto, Castro, J. H. Elliott, Góngora, Hernández y Sánchez Barba, Konetzke, Leonhard, Lohmann Villena, Lynch, Maravall, Miranda, Verlinden, Vicens Vives, Zavala, Zorra-

quín Becú. The concepts in political sociology are derived from standard authors: Almond, Bendix, Pye, Verba, and, in a more traditional vein, W. Y. Elliott, Kornhauser, Nisbet, E. Lewis, It has also been rewarding to turn directly to the classic authors, particularly Parsons, Durkheim, Weber, and, with reservations, Weber's teacher, Gierke.

2. Robert E. Scott, *Mexican Government in Transition* (Urbana, 1959), 162-176.

3. "Traditional" and "transitional" are to be understood here in the meanings and contexts developed in recent years by the writers of the Parsonian persuasion. Similarly, "primary" and "secondary," as applied to groups, structures, and relationships, follow standard sociological usage.

4. *Cf.* Gideon Sjoberg, who holds that the organization of the economically active population in discrete and mutually exclusive secondary occupational groups is a near universal characteristic of the world's preindustrial cities. *The Pre-Industrial City, Past and Present* (New York, 1960), 183-204. Richard Morse, in numerous works, and recently Claudio Véliz, in his Introduction to *Obstacles to Change in Latin America* (London, 1965), 2-5, have emphasized the premodern character of the Latin American city and the requirement this places upon the investigator to re-examine his own premises. See also the Introducción to Torcuato S. Di Tella *et al., Sindicato y comunidad: dos tipos de estructura sindical latinoamericana* (Buenos Aires, 1967), 21-45. In this important work, a methodology for the empirical study of the phenomena of "solidarity" and "inclusiveness" —central to the present essay—has at last begun to take shape.

5. To add to the already considerable semantic confusion, *"pluralismo"* has begun to appear in the works of Spanish American publicists, especially Christian Democrats. The premises from which they depart are different from those under consideration here. *Cf.* Goetz Briefs: "For Catholic social thought the crucial point is not, as it is for [late-liberal pluralistic theorists] the *diversity* of social structures, but rather the *unity* harmoniously embracing this diversity, and the structure, hierarchically ordered according to merit, of this unity." "Katholische Soziallehre," *Staats-Lexikon,* VI (1956), 300.

6. Alexis de Tocqueville, *Democracy in America* (New York, 1966), 485.

7. William Kornhauser, *The Politics of Mass Society* (New York, 1959), 78-83.

8. *Ibid.,* 81.

9. "Tenth Federalist," *The Federalist* (New York, 1941), 56.

10. "A Functional Approach to Comparative Politics," in G. A. Almond and J. Coleman (eds.), *The Politics of the Developing Areas* (Princeton, 1960), 38-45.

11. Robert Nisbet, *Community and Power* (New York, 1962). These concepts must be cast in Weberian, probabilistic, terms. Thus *power* is "the probability that one actor within a social relationship will be in a position to carry out his own will, regardless of the basis on which this probability rests," and *solidarity* is "the probability that the imperatives mobilizable through the constitution of the corporate group will prevail upon members, as against imperatives received from outside."

12. Max Weber, "The Concept of Corporate Group and its Types," *The Theory of Social and Economic Organization* (New York, 1947), 145-152.

13. Gino Germani, *Política y sociedad en una época de transición; de la sociedad tradicional a la sociedad de masas* (Buenos Aires, 1965), 31-32.

14. *Ibid.*
15. *Invertebrate Spain* (New York, 1937), 44.
16. Nisbet, *Community and Power,* 113. On this question I have followed: Rudolph Sohm, *The Institutes: A Textbook of the History and System of Roman Private Law* (Oxford, 1907), 135-150, 186-203; Otto von Gierke, "The Idea of Corporation," in T. Parsons *et al.* (eds.), *Theories of Society* (2 vols., New York, 1961), I, 611-626; Luis Recaséns Siches, *Vida humana, sociedad y derecho: fundamentación de la filosofía del derecho* (3rd ed., México, 1952), 258-277.
17. The evolution of the Hispanic law of association may be traced in: *Novísima Recopilación,* Libro XII, Título XII, Leyes 1, 2, 3, 10, 12, 13; VIII, XXIII, 1. Printed in Marcelo Martínez Alcubilla (comp.), *Códigos antiguos de España: colección completa de todos los códigos de España desde el Fuero Juzgo hasta la Novísima Recopilación* (2 vols., Madrid, 1885-1886). In America, the restrictions placed upon association were, predictably, even harsher than those obtaining in Spain. Cf. Libro I, Título IV, Ley 25, of the Leyes de Indias. Also: John Phelan, "Authority and Flexibility in the Spanish Imperial Bureaucracy," *Administrative Science Quarterly,* V (1960), 47-65.
18. On *uso, costumbre,* and *fuero,* see Primera Partida, Título IV, Leyes 1-8, as reprinted in Martínez Alcubilla, *Códigos antiguos,* or elsewhere. Corresponding to the restricted right of association in America, the authority accorded there to *uso, costumbre,* and *fuero* was less than in Spain. Cf. Libro II, Título II, Ley 21, of the Leyes de Indias.
19. "Change and Frustration in Chile," in Véliz, *Obstacles,* 131-132.
20. Charles Anderson has hypothesized a typical process whereby new political groups, including those of low status, are co-opted into the system and admitted to the contention for power. "Toward a Theory of Latin American Politics," Graduate Center for Latin American Studies, Vanderbilt University, Occasional Paper No. 2, 1964; reprinted in this volume.
21. Weber, "Concept," 250-254.
22. The most extensive empirical demonstration of this point may be found in the comparisons established between Mexico and Britain, the U.S., Germany, and Italy, in Gabriel A. Almond and Sidney Verba (eds.), *The Civic Culture: Political Attitudes and Democracy in Five Nations* (Princeton, 1963). See especially pp. 194, 263, 273-278, 301-302, 319.
23. E. Lousse, "État de la question," *La société d'ancien régime: organisations et réprésentations corporatives* (Louvain, 1943), 16-17. After reviewing the somewhat sparse historiography on Spain, Professor Lousse concludes that it is "un problème qui ... reste aussi controversé que celui du parlement anglais." However, since 1943 numerous writers—especially Vicens Vives, Maravall, Hernández y Sánchez Barba, Beneyto, and Elliott—have added substantially to the record. Among some writers, it should be noted, the term *corps intermédiaires* is reserved exclusively for *parliamentary* bodies, e.g., the Cortes of Castile and Aragón. It is used here in a less legalistic, more sociological sense.
24. On Suárez, I have followed principally Labrousse, Mesnard, Rommen, Gierke, Sánchez Agesta, and Recaséns Siches. The thesis that follows, although its thrust is in a different direction, owes much to Richard Morse, "Toward a Theory of Spanish American Government," *Journal of the History of Ideas,* XV (1954), 71-93; and his "The Heritage of Latin America," in L. Hartz (ed.), *The Founding of*

New Societies (New York, 1964), especially 151-159; both reprinted in this volume.

25. On rationalism versus voluntarism in Suárez, see: Roger Labrousse, *Essai sur la philosophie politique de l'ancienne Espagne: de la Raison et politique de la Foi* (Paris, 1938), 27. On the State as fictive person, see F. Suárez, *De Legibus ac Deo Legislatore,* I, VII, 7; III, II, 4. On the Prince as functional member of the State, see *De Legibus* . . . , III, XXXV, 6, 8; and III, IV, 6; also the commentary in H. Rommen, *Die Staatslehre des Franz Suarez, SJ* (München-Gladbach, 1926), 104-105.

26. *De Legibus* . . . , III, IX, 17. Cited by P. Mesnard, *El desarrollo*

de la filosofía política en el siglo XVI (Río Piedras, P. R., 1956), 607.

27. *De Legibus* . . . , VII, IV, 10; VII, II, 2-7; I, VII, 9-10. Cf. Gierke, *Natural Law and the Theory of Society, 1500-1800* (Boston, 1957), 272-274.

28. Pointed out by L. N. McAlister, "Social Structure and Social Change in New Spain," *HAHR,* XLIII (1963), 353-357.

29. *Ibid.,* 368-370. See also the important essay by Enrique Wedovoy which serves as the "Estudio preliminar" to Manuel de Lavardén, *Nuevo aspecto del comercio en el Río de la Plata* (Buenos Aires, 1955).

30. J. H. Elliott, "The Spanish Heritage," *Encounter,* XXV (September 1965), 40.

Part Three

Independence, Change, and the Special Nature of Latin American Development

Part 3 includes four essays that deal with the political implications of the independence of Latin America from the Iberian mother countries, analyze the beginning of the change process in the late nineteenth century, and show the special character of Latin American development in the twentieth. Building upon the historical analyses of the previous chapters, these essays show a traditional society's beginning adjustment to change, the complex mixtures of traditional and modern that resulted, the impact of foreign and domestic pressures, and the early fashioning of a distinct Latin American pattern and process of development. Although the traditional structures generally remained strong, these chapters show that they were forced to adapt and adjust to new social forces that modernization set loose. How they adapted and the sheer persistence of traditional institutions gave Latin American development some distinctive features.

In the first essay, Professor Dealy offers a strong challenge to the usual interpretations of Latin America's early nineteenth century history. Most of the interpretations, largely written from a United States viewpoint, argue that the "new nations" of Latin America in the nineteenth century adopted United States constitutional forms, did not live up to the liberal, democratic, and republican precepts, and that therefore their histories as nations have largely been "failures." Dealy argues, in contrast, that the Latin American "founding fathers" remained true to their own historical (authoritarian, monist, hierarchical) traditions, did not seek to emulate the United States constitutional features, and that therefore Latin American history showed important continuities both before 1810 and after it. In perhaps his most controversial assertion, Dealy suggests that Latin America did not aspire to democratic rule then—and still does not now!

Fredrick B. Pike, professor of history at Notre Dame, next traces the patterns of tradition and social innovation in Latin America from 1900 to 1970. Like Dealy, Pike shows the persistence and power of Latin America's traditional institutions—the family, religion, the hacienda—*but he also shows how they began to adjust to the newer realities of* modernization, such as capitalism, an emerging middle class, a growing trade union movement. While providing a historical overview, Professor Pike also describes the main ideologies of the time, the new social and economic forces at work, and how the traditional institutions accommodated themselves to the new pressures so that they survived instead of being swept away by revolution.

In like fashion, sociologist Claudio Véliz, a Chilean now teaching in Australia, emphasizes the continuities and persistence of the Latin American traditions of centralism and nationalism. These traditions persist in regimes of the left as well as those of the right, Véliz argues, suggesting provocatively that Castro's Cuba is a highly centralized, personalistic, caudillo-dominated state as much because it is Latin-Hispanic as because it is Marxist-Leninist. Véliz demonstrates the continuity of the centralizing, authoritarian, and imperial traditions, but also points to new elements of which we have recently become cognizant: the dependency of the Latin American nations economically and politically on the United States; the fact that their development has been retarded as well as stimulated by this dependency; and the increasingly nationalistic responses of the Latin Americans to this.

In the second essay by Professor Pike in this section, attention turns to the foundations of the cultural contrasts between the United States and Latin America. Though his focus is the Andean Republics, most of the author's arguments apply equally well to Latin America as a whole. In a fashion parallel to the earlier arguments of Professors Morse and Dealy, Pike contrasts the Lockean-liberalism and individualism of the United States with the Catholic-organicism, patronalism-clientelism, and corporatism of Latin America. He traces not only the historic roots of these Latin American features but also their implications for contemporary politics and the obstacles they present to United States-Latin American understanding. In sum, all the essays in Part 3 emphasize the persistence of the historical Latin American tradition, but they also show the newer social and ideological forces at work and the ways in which the traditional institutions have adopted to these changes.

Prolegomena on the Spanish American Political Tradition

Glen Dealy

It is the purpose of this essay to raise some questions about a central dogma held by many writers on Latin American politics. A typical interpretation asserts that "there is little doubt that the Latin American ideal of government for more than a century and a half has been that of political democracy."[1] This is largely taken for granted. While few members of the intellectual community now engaged in Latin American research are specifically studying political ideology, it appears to me that many of us, whether beginning with a consensus or a conflict model, implicitly assume Latin American approval of democracy.[2] In this we are following a long academic tradition, albeit with new methods.

Most Americans tend to believe that a stable, viable Latin America would be a democratic Latin America. They derive that conviction from scholarly perceptions of early nineteenth-century political thought in Latin America. And this democratic argument is based upon two propositions: that Latin Americans borrowed the form and substance of their government; and that they failed to implant the alien system because they lacked political preparation. Writers who make these assumptions see the United States and French polities evolving out of their past despite certain foreign borrowings of an ideological and institutional nature. By contrast they often portray Latin American political leaders as having not merely repeated the words of their late eighteenth-century teachers, but as having actually plagiarized from their fellow students on both continents.[3] Overwhelming scholarly opinion credits France and the United States as the ideological source of both the structure and the substance of Latin American government since 1810, while the influence of Spain, the mother country, is minimized or ignored.[4]

This belief is so extensively accepted that it would be difficult to find a textbook on Latin America in which the thesis is not somewhere stated. For example, one writer speaks of the independence movement as sweeping through Latin America "under ideological banners bor-

Reprinted from *Hispanic American Historical Review* 48, no. 1, February 1968, by permission of the publisher. Copyright 1969, Duke University Press, Durham, N.C.

rowed from the United States and France."[5] Another notes that the
Wars for Independence were "fought in the name of the same ideals and
aspirations that accompanied the American and French revolutions."[6]
A historian summarizes this theme: "The political ideals of liberty,
natural rights, equality before the law, and popular sovereignty, which
were developed in England, given irresistible literary expression in
France, and first put into practice in the United States . . . constituted
the great spiritual force back of the heroic struggle of Spanish America
for emancipation."[7]

Latin American nations are charged with having similarly borrowed
the structure and organization of their new governments. A modern
author asks: "What, then, are the sources of the material embodied in
most of the written constitutions of the area?" "The answer," he says, "is
that much of this material is derived, not from Spanish or Latin American experiences as one would expect, but rather from the constitutional
norms and practices of France and the United States."[8] One textbook
holds that "most of the states drew up liberal republican constitutions
based upon that of the United States or that of the defunct French
Republic,"[9] while another declares that "many of the earlier constitutions were copied after that of the United States . . . and frequently the
French pattern was followed."[10] A leading sociologist writes: "The new
South American nations, looking around for models to follow, found
ready at hand the philosophies of the French and American revolutions,"[11] and an economist holds that "the constitutions which were
adopted by the new Latin American states were largely inspired, if not
copied, from that of the United States, while the 'generous ideas of the
French Revolution' served as the ideological foundation for the new
republics."[12] The implication is that Latin America is running upon a
borrowed ideology and borrowed institutions. In addition, it is usually
observed that the ideology and institutions so appropriated were democratic, in contrast to Spanish authoritarian colonial tradition.

The second assumption usually made by scholars is that the initial
failure of borrowed democracy in Latin America can be traced to the
men who tried to implement this alien type of government. Such
scholars hold that the leaders of the revolutionary era were politically
naïve, inexperienced, and untutored in government. This idea is at least
as old as Lord Bryce. Regarding the revolutionary upper class he
observed that none of them had "any experience in civil administration."[13]

The belief was carried forward by leading historians during the first
half of this century. "Except for his membership in the comparatively
unimportant *cabildos,* or local councils, the Spanish American creole,
or native-born white, had almost no participation in the government of
the colonies," says one of these works.[14] In another essay one reads of
the postindependence period that "the turbulence was due to political

inexperience."[15] "From the political viewpoint, what was the heritage left to these new states by Spain?" asks still another writer. He answers that "in the first place, there was the negative condition of political inexperience."[16] And a textbook published in 1950 states: "The political inexperience of the ruling classes was another great obstacle to republican government."[17] A contemporary political scientist agrees: "Latin American politics lacks an adequate theory or rationale drawn from experience."[18] Finally, one may cite one of the more influential books on Latin America to appear in recent years: "The intellectuals had little more than a theoretical understanding of what they proposed to achieve. They had been so effectively excluded from participation in government by Spain and Portugal, in collaboration with the Catholic Church, that nearly all their knowledge of the art of government and politics was academic."[19]

Assuming that the revolutionaries lacked political experience, historians have often exculpated them for not having established a functioning democracy: "It was unreasonable to expect that the Spanish Americans, with no schooling in self-government, exhausted and brutalized by twelve years of warfare . . . should at once have understood the successful operation of free institutions."[20]

Thus there is widespread agreement over the Latin American preference for democratic government as well as the cause for its initial failure in that area. These two beliefs are at the center of present interpretations of Latin American politics. The conclusion which follows from these assumptions is that for the last century and a half there has existed a constant ambivalence between the "real" Latin American government somehow rooted in the colonial tradition, and the "unreal" governmental superstructure based upon borrowed constitutions and ideologies.[21] Thus constitutional government grounded in democratic principles is the persistent aspiration, the "unreal." But the "real" Latin America continually comes to the fore in the form of rigged elections, caudillos, and the general repression of individual rights.

In contemplating the dualism of "real" and "unreal," fact and theory, achievement and aspirations, scholars as well as political figures directly concerned with Latin America tend to agree that the hiatus between adopted democratic theory and contrary practices must be filled in. They have assumed that it is possible to join the "real" (the sordid reality of Latin American politics) and the "unreal" (the adopted democratic ideology) and that this juncture will inevitably lead toward democracy.[22]

This essay will examine some of these assumptions as they pertain to Spanish America. It will develop the thesis that there exists but a single Spanish American tradition, and that this tradition exhibits a rather close unity between theory and practice. While scholars may certainly have differing interpretations of just what comprises the tradition, they cannot seriously maintain that Spanish American governments are any more schizophrenic than are those of the United States, France, or any other nation of the Western world. Spanish Americans in 1810 did not sever themselves from the ideals and practices of their colonial past or reject three hundred years of Spanish colonial institutions. The assumption that the patriot leaders borrowed the bulk of their ideological concepts is subject to question. Many scholars hold that they primarily reflected French or North American liberal thought, despite what Spanish Americans themselves asserted in the early 1800s. Political tracts of the independence era show that their authors possessed a remarkable genius for adopting the language, style, and enthusiasm of the age while retaining their own nondemocratic heritage almost intact. Although some of the ideas utilized by the republicans had their genesis in French and North American eighteenth-century political thought, these foreign sources provided the patriots with a great catalog of ideas from which to choose. One may readily admit that the Spanish Americans referred extensively to these sources. Through selection, deletion, and rewriting it was quite possible, however, to appropriate a considerable amount of nondemocratic ideology from this ideological pool. An analysis of twenty-seven of the first constitutions written throughout Spanish America from 1810 through 1815 will demonstrate the discrepancy between Spanish American political thought and allegedly borrowed ideas.[23]

Eighteenth-century political liberalism was almost uniformly and overwhelmingly rejected by Spanish America's first statesmen. Though there is a wide variety in the form and content of the early charters, not one could be construed as embodying constitutional liberalism, however loosely that term may be defined. Spanish American constitutions of this early period all began with a view of human nature which paralleled that of our founding fathers. Man was seen as essentially Hobbesian. Experience had taught that one must "protect the public and individual liberty against the oppression of those that govern." Upon this premise they built their constitutional order. Essentially pessimistic, they sought to regularize men's activities and to eliminate the vicissitudes and uncertainties of politics.

The answer which they gave to the problem of order, however, was vastly different from that of Anglo-Saxon constitutionalists. Unlike them the Spanish Americans had no faith whatever in the possibility of neutralizing evil through institutional arrangements. At the heart of our own constitutionalism is the conviction, stated by Kant, "that it is only necessary to organize the state well (which is indeed within the ability of man) and to direct these forces against each other in such wise that one balances the other in its devastating effect, or even suspends it. Consequently the result for reason is as if both selfish forces were nonexistent. Thus man, although not a morally good man, is compelled to be a good citizen."[24] This assertion presupposes a confidence in the instrument which one has created, a belief that a particular type of organization or deployment of men will actually neutralize evil.

The Spanish Americans displayed none of this confidence. Their constitutionalism is identified with both Greek and Christian thought and separated from Machiavelli and from those who followed in one crucial respect—it was based upon a fundamental relationship between statecraft and soul-craft. The drafters of Spanish American constitutions were unable or unwilling to make a distinction between external conduct and the goods of the soul. Thus, at the center of these documents is the conviction that only the morally good man could be a good citizen. "Consequently, he who is not a good son, good father, good friend, good husband, good master, good servant, cannot be a good citizen."[25] They could not perceive politics as the satisfaction of interests in the style of Locke. Politics to them was the achievement of the common good. And this, in the tradition of Aquinas, had no automatic connection with private interest.

Subscribing to such a view, as one might suspect, they were also necessarily committed to other conclusions. If the rules and procedures of constitutional government could not be trusted to defeat self-interest, it seemed to follow that good government depended upon the recruitment of good men. The province of Barinas, Venezuela, provided in its *Plan de Gobierno* that officials must be of "known virtue, talent, and patriotism, proven in the community."[26] In Argentina, for another example, we find that the election of the executive "will fall of necessity on a person of known patriotism, integrity, public repute, good habits, and aptitude for the office."[27]

But of course, there could be no surer means of obtaining good men than by sanctifying the electoral process itself. Thus in order to thrust self-interest out of men's minds and thereby ensure the moral purity of the newly elected, some constitutions went so far as to provide that midway in the elections all of the voters should go as a group to attend Mass and hear a sermon: "For the success of the elections, divine help must be sought, and to this effect, the electors united in cabildo before voting will proceed to the church. They will hear a Mass of the Holy Spirit conducted by the priest, who will then intone the hymn *Veni Creator,* and will briefly exhort the electors to justice and impartiality in the election."[28] By such electoral procedures, it was hoped that "those that are to vote will put aside all passion and interest, friendship, etc., and will choose persons of honesty, of the best possible education, and of good public repute."[29]

Since most of the charters begin with a declaration of rights, commentators have assumed the existence of premises similar to those held in the United States and France. However, there is reason to suspect this conclusion. Spanish Americans, through a confusion in terminology, seem to have equated modern natural right doctrine with their own natural law tradition. The apparent similarities, perhaps coupled with a proclivity to perceive only those principles which the commentators wished to underscore, tended to hide from view the quite different assumptions underlying each constitutional system.

The most striking example of this confusion is the fact that a number of the constitutions provided that in their schools children should be taught the fundamentals of Roman Catholicism and some version of The Rights of Man and of the Citizen.[30] The writers do not seem to have recognized that the first presupposed a hierarchical view of society, the second an egalitarian view. They wished, at the same time, to preserve the past and to embrace the new. In this they saw no conflict. Thus, in framing their bills of rights, they found no contradiction in almost uniformly establishing Catholicism as the state religion and prohibiting the free exercise of all other "cults";[31] abridging, if not abolishing freedom of speech and of the press;[32] and in some cases even denying the right of peaceable assembly[33] or of presenting collective petitions to the government.[34]

But the contrast with modern Western constitutionalism is perhaps sharpest when we consider the matter of limitations upon power. Carl Friedrich defines a constitutional government as one based upon "the establishment and maintenance of effective restraints upon political and more especially upon governmental action."[35] And he considers these restraints to be rooted primarily in a division of power—between legislative, executive, and judicial and/or between central and local government. The notion of a limitation upon power was not new to the eighteenth century, but was firmly rooted in the medieval tradition. Yet, as Charles H. McIlwain has affirmed, there is no medieval doctrine of a separation of powers as the basis for limitation.[36]

Spanish Americans in 1810 were clearly thinking more in medieval terms. Limitation for them was not equivalent to separation of powers, although the constitutions formally provided for separation. A close reading shows that almost without exception overwhelming power was finally vested in one body. While others were more subtle, a Colombian constitution states with amazing frankness: "Only the Legislative Power has the authority to interpret, amplify, limit, or comment on the laws, always adhering, however, in these matters to the formalities that are required and which are prescribed for their establishment. The Executive and Judicial Powers must follow them to the letter and consult the Legislative Body in case of doubt."[37]

Restraints were not procedural but moral. Following the Romans, the makers of Spanish American constitutions were charmed by the possibility of establishing a government based upon virtue. In some cases they provided for a body of moral censors to interpret this principle: "there will be a Senate of censure and protection . . . in order to sustain this Constitution and the rights of the people, to the end that either officially or through requirement by any citizen, any infraction or usurpation of all or each one of the three Powers—Executive, Legislative and Judicial—that is against the tenor of the Constitution may be claimed."[38] In other constitutions it was left to moral education, sermons before elections, and elaborate tattle-tale procedures to hold men to a virtuous course of action.[39]

Political responsibility in a constitutional democracy is primarily exacted through the electoral process. These early constitutions by contrast demonstrated their distrust of elections by turning to a colonial practice, the residencia. Under this system government officials were subjected to a judicial inquiry at the end of their term of office. Anyone could make a charge, and it would be duly investigated. The sweeping breadth of possible accusation is suggested by the Mexican constitution of 1814 which provided prosecution "for the crimes of heresy and apostasy, and for crimes of state, especially for those of misfeasance, extortion, and the squandering of public funds."[40] Thus not the hope of re-election but the fear of legal action was believed to keep men moral while they exercised political responsibility.

Constitutional government in early Spanish America can be set in relief by a consideration of *Federalist* paper No. 10. Madison had declared that "there are two methods of curing the mischiefs of faction. The one, by removing its causes; the other, by controlling its effects." But only a brief examination of the proposition led him to conclude that the "*causes* of faction cannot be removed; and that relief is only to be sought in the means of controlling its *effects.*" The Spanish Americans soon came to the opposite conclusion—they believed that political diversity could be checked only by dealing with its causes. In pursuing this assumption to its logical conclusion, they fulfilled Madison's requisites amazingly well. He had suggested two methods by which the causes of faction might be removed, "the one, by destroying the liberty which is essential to its existence; the other, by giving to every citizen the same opinions, the same passions, and the same interests."

Certain provisions which tended to destroy liberty have already been described. For example, the establishment of a state church and the eradication or curbing of some basic political freedoms have been noted. But at the very core of the early constitutions was the attempt to achieve a uniformity of opinion, an attempt grounded in the belief that similar passions and interests were not only desirable but possible. The basis of this assumption was derived from a near unanimity in religious matters: "Since there can be no happiness without civil liberty, nor liberty without morality, nor morality without religion, the government is to look upon it (religion) as the strongest bond of society, its most precious interest, and the first law of the Republic."[41] This unanimity in religion was held to be a natural course of affairs and one which could be readily extended to other parts of the socio-political order. In the negative sense, no freedoms were allowed which might be contrary to good customs, either public or private.[42] On the positive side, a concerted effort was made to achieve unity through an active policy of political education. In Argentina, by way of illustration, a weekly news-sheet, the *Censor*, was to be established. Its principal object was "to reflect on all the procedures and unjust acts of the public functionaries and abuses in the country, showing the people their rights and true interests."[43] No private educational institutions were allowed, and state schools were usually to be minutely supervised by the national congresses. Finally, the concluding statements of a constitution itself were often an injunction toward political unanimity: "Read it, study it, and make your children learn it. May the Constitution be your second catechism. Sustain it with your zeal and vigilance. . . ."[44]

Although one might continue to enumerate these rather startling constitutional provisions, perhaps enough has been said to bring into question the conventional view that Spanish America engaged in wholesale borrowing of a liberal foreign ideology in its early governance. No attempt has been made to give a consistent outline of the political philosophy of Spanish America during the independence period. Rather, the goal has been to demonstrate that the preponderate weight of its political thought was derived from sources other than modern Western constitutional philosophy, broadly construed. The purpose has been to cast doubt upon the current notion that Spanish America lives as a split personality, ever striving to unify itself in the direction of its democratic superstructure adopted in 1810. This is a prescriptive myth. Democratic theory was not embraced at that time. The forms of government bore certain similarities to other constitutional democracies, and at times the language even sounded familiar, but the content was in many basic ways at the opposite pole.

The second argument—that the men who attempted to implant this allegedly alien type of government failed because they lacked political preparation—is also open to question. The founding fathers did have wide political experience prior to their wars for independence. During the first five years of the movement for independence in northern South America approximately twenty constitutional charters were drawn up in the provinces and capitals of the old viceroyalty of New Granada—present-day Ecuador, Colombia, Venezuela, and Panama.[45] A list of the men who signed these fundamental documents may be representative of all Spanish America. Extensive research in the colonial archives of New Granada indicates the degree to which these men were politically active prior to the independence movements.[46] Of the 468 men who signed these early charters, no fewer than 303 had served in the Spanish colonial government before the wars of independence began. Among these were 92 lawyers, 100 members of cabildos, 107 in lesser bureaucratic positions, 28 militiamen, and 104 clergymen.[47]

Not only lawyers, but clergymen and militiamen as well were politically influential in colonial politics. To appreciate the import of the clerical figures one should recall that colonial Spanish America had operated under an integrated church-state governmental bureaucracy. Because of certain papal bulls, Spanish kings near the beginning of the sixteenth century were granted the patronato real in perpetuity. Thus the clergy came to serve at the pleasure of the kings of Spain rather than directly under the papacy. They soon became perhaps the most politically minded body of men in the Spanish bureaucracy.[48]

Almost by definition lawyers were part of the political structure of Spanish colonial government. In order to practice law before the royal audiencia, they must have first received a degree in law from one of the state administered colleges. Here they were educated in Roman civil law and canon law as well as the *Leyes de Indias*. In addition, they were obliged to serve a four-year apprenticeship to another lawyer. This training gave them a thorough grounding in the intracacies of colonial public administration. At the end of the designated period of preparation they were required to pass an oral examination and then more often than not they became an integral part of the Spanish bureaucracy.[49] Frequently those following a military career were also deeply involved in political matters. It was by no means uncommon for them to be named to civil as well as military posts. Although as a group they tended to be less educated than the lawyers and clergy, normally they too had some formal education. Training in the *colegios* was geared toward the creation of future political elites, and those who chose a military career felt themselves to be a part of that elite group much as the lawyers and the clerics. Obviously the founders were experienced in the philosophy and intricacies of colonial government. The question is not only *how much* experience but *what kind* of experience they had. It is possible that the "failure" of Spanish American governments in 1810 as in 1966 is really not a failure to achieve democracy, but a triumph for the ideals and aspirations which were theirs since colonial days.

One must conclude, then, that neither lack of prior experience nor a borrowed political ideology can explain the failure of Spanish Americans to establish viable democracy as we know it. Rather, it would seem that they consciously chose to implement a system of government which in both theory and practice had much in common with their tradition. If this is the case, one may well hesitate before discarding contemporary Spanish American constitutionalism and philosophy as irrelevant to the "real" political process. We cannot operate upon the facile assertion that Spanish Americans have long suffered from the effects of their vain aspirations toward liberal constitutionalism. The revised premises raise many questions. Central to our consideration, however, is whether those peoples still aspire to the type of "democracy" envisaged in 1810.

A brief glance at contemporary Spanish American constitutions elic-

its some striking parallels to those first charters of 1810—and some
amazingly nonliberal, nondemocratic propositions. As constitutions
have come and gone during the past century and a half, the philosophic
beliefs of the documents have become at times clouded and less explicit.
Nevertheless, the direction of thought has maintained a most significant
continuity since 1810. Throughout these years the vision has been essentially nondemocratic; it still is.

For convenience let us assume the widest possible definition of democratic theory—that it "is concerned with processes by which ordinary
citizens exert a relatively high degree of control over leaders."[50] Applying this definition to contemporary Spanish American constitutions, one
cannot help concluding that they are essentially concerned with the
opposite—that is, the processes by which leaders may exert a relatively
high degree of control over ordinary citizens. From this generalization it
follows that there is a direct relationship between theory and practice in
contemporary Spanish America, not a dichotomy of "real" and
"unreal." The reality of Spanish American politics is supported at every
step by very real constitutional provisions which authorize, legitimize,
and enshrine undemocratic processes and continue the tradition of 1810.
Each of the present-day constitutions denies the proposition that men
have certain unalienable rights. Instead rights in Spanish America are
constitutionally qualified and relative—that is, no right is allowed to
stand as a point of unvarying reference. Necessity of State is a recognized doctrine.

One of the major qualifications to individual rights is that of public
order: "The free exercise of the rights which this Constitution establishes
is guaranteed, without other limitations than those which may derive
from the necessity of maintaining public and social order."[51] Another
qualification of basic rights, often directed at the practice of religion, is
that of good morals, or good customs. Costa Rica will not impede worship that "is not opposed to universal morality or good customs,"
Panama demands of all religions "respect for Christian morality," while
the constitution of Nicaragua insures the free exercise of all religions
that are "not opposed to morality, good customs, or public order."[52]

One may see in these qualifications the need for some body with the
authority to define these relative rights in practice. Spanish Americans
have provided such a body in Congress. Indeed, this is perhaps the
major function of their legislative bodies.

The bastion and safeguard of rights of religion, speech, and press
guaranteed by the First Amendment in our Constitution is not the
statement of these rights *per se,* but the words: "Congress shall make no
law . . . respecting . . . , prohibiting . . . , or abridging . . ." them. With
this prohibition the rights take on a fundamental, unchangeable personality. The law-making body is forbidden to make rules in this area. A
key to understanding Spanish American government by contrast is the

recognition that there is nothing in the way of rights or privileges that may not be constitutionally abridged by passage of a law. The constitution of Chile states, for example: "Only by virtue of a law is it possible to restrain personal liberty and freedom of the press or to suspend or restrict exercise of the right of assembly. . . ."[53] An accepted view is that "everyone has the right of association for lawful ends, in conformity with the law."[54] In place of the word "association," one might equally well substitute "religion," "petition," or "free speech" without misconstruing the philosophy of these constitutions.[55] Most significant is that these rights must be exercised "in conformity with the law." Hence, contrary to our contention that "Congress shall make no law" is the Spanish American view that Congress *must* make laws on these matters. A short review of the congressional debates in those countries would show just how often these questions arise and how much time is devoted to discussing the relations between church and state, the right of groups to assemble, the right to form associations, and the extent to which free speech will be guaranteed. Truly, these rights are a relative matter in that area of the world.

To recapitulate: first, rights are not unalienable in Spanish America; and second, congressional bodies are charged with the definition and qualification of these rights. Yet a third premise must be mentioned— the constitutional provision whereby the basic rights may be set aside altogether, usually by the chief executive. For example, in the Dominican Republic a state of siege may be declared "in the event of disturbance of the public peace or public disaster," and power is granted "to suspend, wherever the foregoing exist and for their duration, the human rights proclaimed. . . ."[56] Similar provisions appear in the other Spanish American constitutions. Again, it may be noted, public order or reason of state is an organizing concept for these governments. Rights are constitutionally qualified by their effect upon public order and may be entirely abridged when there is a threat to that order. We have here a clear indication of the possibilities for our "reverse" theory of democracy, i.e., the process by which leaders exert control over ordinary citizens. When rights of speech, assembly, and press are curtailed, the right of political opposition is in effect being quashed. For this reason the "ins" dominate the "outs": the constitution justifies the procedure.

Spanish American governments also differ from that of the United States in the matter of restraint upon power. As in the colonial and independence eras, the concept of limitation upon power is clear, while the notion of a separation of power to achieve this limitation is not a viable doctrine.[57] The General Assembly of Uruguay is competent "to interpret the Constitution"; and the Bolivian Legislative Power may "enact laws, repeal, amend, or interpret them." The charter of Ecuador is more explicit: "Congress alone has jurisdiction to declare whether a law or legislative decree is or is not unconstitutional."[58] Thus do congresses move within the judicial sphere. But the President's sweeping powers under the state-of-siege doctrine demonstrate that, as in the charters established soon after independence, these contemporary constitutions do not seriously contemplate a restrained use of power through the concept of tripartite government.

How then may limitation upon power be attained? Here Spanish Americans also rely on their colonial and independence traditions. They attempt to recruit qualified men in the hope, often vain, that good government will result. Spanish Americans are gradually turning from this emphasis to a more up-to-date focus upon the recruitment of men with education, training, and capacity. In practice, however, the traditional and the modern approach are almost indistinguishable in that they subordinate the supposed internal merits of the individual to public, external restraint.

Illustrating the more traditional Spanish American view of restraint, the Paraguayans seek a president who can "meet the moral and intellectual requirements of his office"; El Salvador requires its presidents to be "of well known morality and education." Nicaragua looks for a candidate for General Treasurer who is "of good reputation." Venezuela seeks school teachers "of recognized morality."[59]

The present Spanish American theory of limitation upon judicial power also clearly fits the definition of Latin American "democracy" suggested in this essay. Contemporary constitutions perpetuate a favorite practice of colonial and independence governments—they provide for the exclusive recruitment of judicial officials from among the educated and professional minorities, thus preventing the ordinary citizen from sharing or restraining that power.

Most constitutions of Spanish America look for the following characteristics in their judicial candidates: specialized education, an academic degree, experience, and (if possible) capability. With slightly elaborated details a majority of these documents resemble Article 166 of the constitution of Panama, which specifies that a magistrate of the Supreme Court be required: "to be a law graduate and to have completed a period of ten years in the practice of the profession of law or the position of magistrate, Attorney General of the Nation, attorney (fiscal) of a superior court, circuit judge, or professor of law in a public educational institution." One may question whether this is intrinsically an undemocratic provision. It is beyond debate, however, that when one adds to this concept of judicial office the lack of jury trial and the general absence of the doctrine of stare decisis, the way is open for the few to control the many, with precious little legal restraint.

Political responsibility in a constitutional democracy is primarily exercised through the electoral process. By contrast, contemporary Spanish American constitutions show a distrust of elections as a means of control. Most countries have specific constitutional provisions against the reelection of the president.

Present-day constitutional government in Spanish America can also be understood as the opposite of Madison's conclusions in *Federalist* No. 10. It presumes that diversity can be checked by dealing with its causes, i.e., by destroying the liberty which is essential to its existence and by giving to every citizen the same opinions, the same passions, and the same interests.

There are other ways of destroying liberty in most Spanish American countries than those already mentioned in the discussion of individual rights. Although it is no longer usual to establish an exclusive state church as in colonial and independence times, it would be an error to assume that people of different religions have the same degree of liberty in contemporary Spanish America. For example, the preamble of the Colombian constitution, added in 1957, begins: "In the name of God the supreme source of all authority, and for the purpose of strengthening the national unity, one of whose bases is the recognition by the political parties that the Apostolic and Roman Catholic Religion is that of the Nation, and that as such the public powers shall protect it and see that it is respected as an essential element of the social order. . . ."

Thus Latin American constitutions check diversity by assigning to every citizen the same opinion. Nowhere is this sort of restriction more obvious than in the field of education. Beginning with the assumption that moral education and the advancement of culture are proper spheres of the government, these charters soon reach the conclusion that all education, both private and public, must be controlled by the state. As one of them puts it, "education in all its degrees shall be subject to the guardianship of the State, exercised through the Minister of Education."[60]

At the heart of these charters is the endeavor to gain a uniformity of opinion premised upon the belief that similar passions and interests are both desirable and possible. Although the thesis is seldom stated clearly, there exists in Spanish America the medieval presumption that (as stated by Aquinas) "we differ in our particular interests and it is the common good that unites the community."[61] Modern Spanish America implements this tradition by asserting that in the event of conflict "the private interest must yield to the public or social interest."[62] Here again is an opportunity for those who govern to exercise constitutional restrictions over the governed. Politics is the achievement of the public good, which is in constant opposition to private interest. Hence the injunction that "the members of both houses represent the whole Nation, and must vote only in the interest of justice and the public good,"[63] or that deputies "represent the entire Nation, are not subject to any mandate, and obey only the dictates of their conscience."[64] Actually, this theory of representation closely reflects the reality of Spanish American politics. Deputies do in fact focus primarily upon the nation as a whole rather than their own districts, and it is obvious that in most cases they are listening to some voice other than that of their constituents.

Relevant to any consideration of popular control are the procedures for ratification and amendment of the constitution itself. Of the constitutions now in effect, it appears that only those of Venezuela and Uruguay were referred to the people. The Venezuelan Constituent Assembly submitted its constitution to the states, while Uruguay called for a plebiscite. The others were decreed. In this regard it is interesting to note the absence of a conception of fundamental law. While some of these documents were drawn up by constituent assemblies and others by congresses, there are almost no distinguishing differences between the character of this law and ordinary law in terms of popular sanction.[65]

This is also the case in the matter of amendments. Except for Mexico, Uruguay, and Venezuela, these documents may be amended almost as easily as ordinary laws are passed. By such means Spanish American countries can alter their constitutional charters with ease. In most cases the process has no relationship to the popular will, for by custom constitutions are not originally referred to the people, and by constitutional provisions amendments need not be so referred.

Finally, we might note that in some countries the armed forces have been placed in the position of defending the constitutional order. In a sense this regularizes the "higher law" position which Spanish American armed forces have long exercised. An armed force charged with ensuring "respect for the Constitution,"[66] "maintenance of constitutional order,"[67] or "defense of this Constitution,"[68] surely has some reason to intervene when it feels that a threat to the constitution exists.

In conclusion, Spanish America does not appear to suffer from a chronic pathological condition brought on by a fruitless aspiration toward democratic goals. Should this assertion be taken seriously, the ramifications are many. Yet the central issue is this: If they have not been the unfortunate losers in a vain struggle to achieve liberal constitutionalism, exactly what sort of government do they prefer? However one phrases the question, it is not clear at present whether Spanish American government has been a tremendous success or a dismal failure during the last 150 years of independence. The consensus is that it has been a failure, but those who hold to this position assume that Spanish Americans generally aspired then and aspire now to democratic goals. One may more cogently argue that this was, and still is, not the case.

Notes

1. Charles O. Porter and Robert
J. Alexander, *The Struggle for
Democracy in Latin America* (New
York, 1961), 4. While using here a
generalized terminology, my
research and my conclusions are
confined to *Spanish* America.

2. See for example, Seymour
Martin Lipset, "Some Social Requi-
sites of Democracy: Economic Devel-
opment and Political Legitimacy,"
*The American Political Science
Review*, LIII (March 1959), 69–105;
W. W. Pierson (ed.), "The Pathol-
ogy of Democracy in Latin America: A Symposium," *The American
Political Science Review*, XLIV
(March 1950), 100–149; Russell H.
Fitzgibbon, "A Statistical Evaluation of Latin-American Democracy," *Western Political Quarterly*,
IX (September 1956), 607–619; John
J. Johnson, *The Military and
Society in Latin America* (Stanford,
1964), 100: "But even in their more
radical moments, the leaders of the
middle sector always kept within the
framework of western representative
democracy. . . ."

3. In part, this concentration on
borrowed aspects of Latin American
ideology may be attributed to the
success of such works as Arthur P.
Whitaker (ed.), *Latin America and
the Enlightenment* (Ithaca, 1961),
and J. T. Lanning, *The Eighteenth-
Century Enlightenment in the University of San Carlos de Guatemala*
(Ithaca, 1956). In demonstrating the
impact of enlightenment philosophy
in Hispanoamerica prior to the revolution these works have contributed
to a historical oversimplification.
They have shown essentially the
presence of forbidden books and
ideas in Latin America. But these
writings have not demonstrated
what the Latin Americans did with
these ideas. It is one thing to have
the complete writings of Marx in

your bookcase; it is another to be a
Marxist.

4. A notable exception is the discussion by Woodrow Borah, Charles
Gibson, and Robert A. Potash in
separate articles on "Colonial Institutions and Contemporary Latin
America," *HAHR*, XLIII (August
1963), 371–394.

5. Kalman H. Silvert, *The Conflict Society: Reaction and Revolution in Latin America* (New Orleans,
1961), 12.

6. R. A. Gomez, *Government and
Politics in Latin America* (New
York, 1960), 20.

7. J. Fred Rippy, *Historical Evolution of Hispanic America* (New
York, 1932), 133.

8. George I. Blanksten, "Constitutions and the Structure of Power,"
in *Government and Politics in Latin
America*, ed. by Harold E. Davis
(New York, 1958), 228. "The republicanism of the constitutional arrangements which the new nations
now made was largely spurious and
existed in form only, having no
roots in the political experience of
the people." Donald M. Dozer,
*Latin America: An Interpretive His-
tory* (New York, 1962), 237.

9. Mary W. Williams, *The People
and Politics of Latin America* (New
York, 1945), 337. "They wrote constitutions fashioned chiefly on the
model of the United States. . . ."
Hubert Herring, *A History of Latin
America* (New York, 1961), 295.

10. A. Curtis Wilgus, *A History
of Hispanic America* (Washington,
1931), 508.

11. Kingsley Davis, "Political
Ambivalence in Latin America," in
*Readings in Latin American Social
Organization and Institutions*, ed. by
Olen E. Leonard and Charles P.
Loomis (East Lansing, 1953), 112.

12. Albert O. Hirschman, *Latin
American Issues* (New York, 1961),
5. William Rex Crawford observes
that "borrowed constitutions seemed
impotent to solve these problems."

A Century of Latin American Thought (Cambridge, Mass., 1961), 5.

13. James Bryce, *South America: Observations and Impressions* (New York, 1912), 571.

14. Charles E. Chapman, *Republican Hispanic America: A History* (New York, 1933), 16.

15. Herbert Eugene Bolton, "The Epic of Greater America," reprinted in Lewis Hanke (ed.), *Do the Americas Have a Common History?* (New York, 1964), 85. Hutton Webster, *History of Latin America* (Boston, 1941), 141, notes that "the Creoles who carried through the revolution lacked political experience."

16. Rippy, *Historical Evolution,* 168.

17. Dana Gardner Munro, *The Latin American Republics: A History* (New York, 1950), 153.

18. Harold E. Davis, "The Political Experience of Latin America," in Davis, *Government and Politics,* 17.

19. John J. Johnson, *Political Change in Latin America* (Stanford, 1958), 16.

20. Herman G. James and Percy A. Martin, *The Republics of Latin America* (New York, 1923), 106.

21. One must agree with Albert Hirschman that "this permanent and painful 'collision between theory and practice, between words and action, between content and form' has been described by virtually all observers of the Latin American scene. . . ." *Latin American Issues,* 6. Blanksten is possibly the most precise exponent of this view in his contrast of the "real" constitutions and their written constitutions arguing that "the real constitutions of the various states of the area originated in their own experiences, not only during the colonial period but also since the achievement of independence. Yet few aspects of this experience have been written into Latin American constitutions." Blanksten, "Constitutions," 228. The same theme, with a slightly different vocabulary, is developed by J. Lloyd Mecham, "Latin American Constitutions: Nominal and Real," *The Journal of Politics,* XXI (May 1959), 258–275.

22. Scholars in this country in large part owe this hope to a judgment which they make about the proclivities of Latin American authors. As an example one might cite the United States political scientist who states that Latin American constitutions "contain provisions expressing faith in the theory of political democracy," and adds "from independence to the present time, Latin American writers, mainly lawyers, have produced literally thousands of volumes recognizing the theory of political democracy. Every country has so many such books that it would require a bibliography of many pages to list them." William S. Stokes, *Latin American Politics* (New York, 1959), 269–270.

23. Provincial as well as national constitutions have been referred to in the belief that such a broad scope would give the best perspective upon the Spanish American mind during the formative years. Sources used for this study are as follows: On Argentina, "Reglamento orgánico de 22 de octubre de 1811"; "Estatuto provisional del gobierno superior de las Provincias Unidas del Río de la Plata a nombre del Sr. D. Fernando VII (1811)"; and "Estatuto provisional para dirección y administración del estado (1815)," all of which are found in Faustino J. Legón and Samuel W. Medrano, *Las constituciones de la República Argentina* (Madrid, 1953). The three Chilean constitutions: "Reglamento de la autoridad ejecutiva (1811)"; "Reglamento constitucional provisional (1812)"; and the "Reglamento para el gobierno provisional (1814)"; are contained in *Sesiones de los cuerpos legislativos de la República de Chile, 1811 a 1845* (Santiago, 1887), I. Colombian documents referred to are: "Consti-

tución de Cundinamarca (1811)"; "Acta de federación de las Provincias Unidas de la Nueva Granada (1811)"; "Constitución de la República Tunja (1811)"; "Constitución del Estado de Antioquia (1812)"; "Constitución de la República de Cundinamarca (1812)"; "Plan de reforma o revisión de la Constitución de la Provincia de Cundinamarca (1815)"; "Constitución del Estado de Mariquita (1815)"; and "Constitución provisional de la Provincia de Antioquia (1815)." These documents are collected in Manuel Antonio Pombo and José Joaquín Guerra, *Constituciones de Colombia* (Bogotá, 1951), I and II. Four Colombian charters referred to but not found in this work are: "Acta de Constitución del nuevo gobierno de la Provincia del Socorro," in Horacio Rodríguez Plata, "10 de Julio de 1810," *Boletín de historia y antigüedades,* XXVIII (December 1941), 1073–1077; *Constitución del Estado Libre de Neiva, 1815* (Bogotá, 1914); *Reglamento para el gobierno provisorio de la Provincia de Pamplona* (Tunja, 1815); and "Proyecto de la Constitución de la Provincia de Popayán (1814)," reprinted in *Boletín histórico del Valle,* No. 49 (1938), 35–60. On Ecuador: "Artículos del pacto solemne de sociedad y unión entre las provincias que forman el Estado de Quito," reprinted in *Museo histórico,* IX (1957), 85–103. The Mexican "Constitución de Apatzingán, 24 de octubre de 1814," is located in *Constituciones: a Collection of Constitutions of Mexico and Spain, 1811–1843* (Bancroft Library, University of California). Venezuelan provincial charters: "Constitución de la Provincia de Caracas (1812)"; "Constitución de la Provincia de Mérida (1811)"; "Constitución de la Provincia de Barcelona (1812)"; "Constitución de la Provincia de Trujillo (1811)"; and the "Plan de gobierno para la Provincia de Barinas (1811)." These are found in Biblioteca de la Academia Nacional de la Historia, *Las constituciones provinciales* (Caracas, 1959). The "Constitución Federal de 1811" of Venezuela may be referred to in José Gil Fortoul, *Historia constitucional de Venezuela* (3rd ed. Caracas, 1942), II, 370–415.

24. From "Eternal Peace" in Carl J. Friedrich (ed.), *The Philosophy of Kant* (New York, 1949), 453.

25. *Mérida* (1811), Capítulo 11, Art. 10. See also *Trujillo* (1811), Título I, Cap. 1; *Estatuto* (Argentina, 1815), Capítulo VI, Art. V; *Constitución Federal de 1811* (Venezuela), Capítulo VIII, Art. III, par. 4; *Antioquia* (1812), Título I, Sec. 3, Art. 4; *Antioquia* (1815), "Deberes del Ciudadano," Art. 4; *Cundinamarca* (1811), Título XIII, Art. 4; *Cundinamarca* (1812), "De los Derechos...," Art. 28; *Mariquita* (1815), Título II, Art. 6; *Neiva* (1815), "Deberes del Ciudadano," Art. 37; *Pamplona* (1815), Art. 147; *Tunja* (1811), Sec. I, Cap. II, Art. 3.

26. *Barinas* (1811), Art. 9.

27. *Estatuto* (1815), Sec. 3, Cap. I, Art. 2.

28. *Cundinamarca* (1812), Título XI, Art. 11. The Mexican Constitution of Apatzingán, Sec. II, Cap. V, Art. 69, provides: "The citizen electors and the president together, will pass to the principal church where there will be a solemn mass of the Holy Spirit, and the priest or other ecclesiastic will give a discourse relevant to the circumstances." Most constitutions, however, only asked that the clergy be on hand to supervise the elections.

29. *Mérida* (1811), Cap. II, Art. 10.

30. See as examples the following: *Popayán* (1814), Art. 193; *Antioquia* (1812), Título IX, Art. 1; *Cartagena* (1812), Título XII, Art. 2; *Tunja* (1811), Cap. VI, Sec. 6, Art. 1; *Cundinamarca* (1811), Título XI, Art. 3; *Cundinamarca* (1812), Título X, Art. 3.

31. *Estatuto* (Argentina, 1815),
Cap. II, Art. 1 and 2; *Reglamento*
(Chile, 1812), Art. 1; *Acta de Fede-
ración* (Colombia, 1811), Art. 4 and
42; *Antioquia* (1812), Título I, Sec. I,
Art. 1, Título III, Sec. I, Art. 8;
Antioquia (1815), Título I, Art. 7;
Cartagena (1812), Título III, Art. 1
and 2; *Cundinamarca* (1811), Título
I, Art. 1, Título II, Art. 1 and 2;
Cundinamarca (1812), Título I, Art.
1 and 4; *Mariquita* (1815), Título
III, Art. 1 and 2; *Neiva* (1815),
Título III, Art. 1 and 2; *Popayán*
(1814), Art. 1 and 12; *Tunja* (1811),
Sec. I, Cap. III, Art. 7; *Artículos*
(Ecuador, 1812), Art. 4; *Apatzingán*
(1814), Sec. I, Cap. I, Art. 1; *Consti-
tución Federal de 1811* (Venezuela),
Cap. I; *Barcelona* (1812), Título 14,
Art. 1; *Barinas* (1811), Art. 16; *Car-
acas* (1812), Art. 304; *Trujillo* (1811),
Título I, Cap. 1 and 2.
32. *Estatuto* (Argentina, 1811),
Art. 2–10; *Reglamento* (Chile, 1812),
Art. 23; *Antioquia* (1812), Título X,
Art. 12–15; *Cartagena* (1812), Título
II, Art. 14; *Cundinamarca* (1811),
Título I, Art. 16; *Cundinamarca*
(1812), Título II, Art. 8; *Mariquita*
(1815), Título I, Art. 9 and 10;
Pamplona (1815), Art. 115; *Popayán*
(1814), Art. 174; *Artículos* (Ecuador,
1812), Art. 20; *Constitución Federal
de 1811* (Venezuela), Cap. 8, Art. 2,
par. 31; *Apatzingán* (1814), Sec. I,
Cap. V, Art. 40.
33. *Antioquia* (1812), Título X,
Art. 13; *Cartagena* (1812), Título I,
Art. 26, Título XIII, Art. 10; *Cundinamarca* (1812), Título XII, Art. 6;
Pamplona (1815), Art. 161; *Popayán*
(1814), Art. 186; *Mariquita* (1815),
Título XXIII, Art. 11 and 13; *Neiva*
(1815), "Deberes del Ciudadano,"
Art. 43; *Constitución Federal de
1811* (Venezuela), Cap. 9, par. 15
and 17; *Barcelona* (1812), Título 14,
Art. 14; *Mérida* (1811), Cap. 12, Art.
14; *Mérida* (1811), Cap. 12, Art. 9
and 12; Trujillo (1811), Título 9,
Cap. 10.
34. *Cartagena* (1812), Título XIII,

Art. 11, Título I, Art. 27; *Cundinamarca* (1811), Título XIV, Art. 6;
Mérida (1811), Cap. 12, Art. 10;
Constitución Federal de 1811 (Vene-
zuela), Cap. 8, Art. 2, par. 32–34,
Cap. 9, par. 16.
35. Carl J. Friedrich, *Constitutional Government and Democracy*
(New York, 1950), 123.
36. Charles H. McIlwain, *Constitutionalism: Ancient and Modern*
(Ithaca, 1958), 142.
37. *Cundinamarca* (1811), Título
VI, Art. 20. Similar views are
expressed in the Mexican constitution of *Apatzingán* (1814), Sec. II,
Cap. VIII, Art. 106; *Reglamento*
(Argentina, 1811), Sec. 3, Art. 5;
Antioquia (1815), Título III, Sec. I,
Art. 10, Título XV, Art. 10; *Antio-
quia* (1812), Título III, Sec. I, Art.
11; *Cartagena* (1812), Título VI, Art.
15; *Cundinamarca* (1811), Título VI,
Art. 4; *Neiva* (1815), Título IV, Art.
5; *Tunja* (1811), Sec. I, Cap. III, Art.
10 and 22; *Pamplona* (1815), "Del
Cuerpo Legislativo," Art. 21;
Reglamento (Chile, 1811), Art. 1.
38. *Cundinamarca* (1811), Título
I, Art. 9. In addition see especially
Estatuto (Argentina, 1815), Sec. VII,
"Estatuto Provisional de la Junta de
Observación," Art. VII, *Barinas*
(1811), Art. 1. In many of the constitutions a *Senado Conservador* was
established to carry out this censorial
function.
39. One method of holding the
executive in check was to appoint
two "advisors" to stand at his elbow.
Like the little boy's admonition that
"I'll tell if . . . ," when the advisors
"note that the president wishes to
take or is taking measures subversive
to this Constitution, it is not enough
simply to cover their responsibility
by a contrary opinion, but under
this very responsibility they are
obliged to declare that they will give
an account to the Chamber of
Representatives, and if the president
does not desist, they will present it at
the earliest moment if the legislature

is in session." *Antioquia* (1812), Título IV, Sec. I, Art. 4. Another procedure used was to direct the executive to watch over all members of the three branches of government "in order that each one may fulfill the obligations of his position. In case of notorious infraction, he will accuse the members of the powers before the Senate. . . ." *Mariquita* (1815), Título XI, Art. 14.

40. *Apatzingán* (1814), Sec. II. Cap. III, Art. 59. See also *Reglamento* (Chile, 1811), Art. 16; *Reglamento* (Chile, 1812), Art. 11; *Antioquia* (1812), Título III, Sec. 2, Art. 34–37, Título IV, Sec. 2, Art. 2; *Antioquia* (1815), Título III, Sec. 3, Art. 1; *Cartagena* (1812), Título VIII, Sec. I, Art. 12; *Cundinamarca* (1811), Título I, Art. 10, Título V, Art. 39; *Cundinamarca* (1812), Título II, Art. 5 and 31, Título VII, 1–12; *Cundinamarca* (1815), Art. 118 and 119; *Mariquita* (1815), Título XI, Art. 9, Título XIX, Art. 1; *Neiva* (1815), Título VI, Art. 1–14; *Pamplona* (1815), Art. 35 and 79; *Popayán* (1814), Art. 62; *Tunja* (1811), Sec. I, Cap. II, Art. 9 and 10; *Artículos* (Ecuador, 1812), Art. 11 and 26; *Barinas* (1811), Art. 15; *Mérida* (1811), Cap. III, Art. 36; *Trujillo* (1811), Título 2, Cap. 8, Título 4, Cap. 6.

41. *Neiva* (1815), Título III, Art. 3. The Mexican constitution of *Apatzingán* (1814) stated: "The quality of citizenship is lost for crimes of heresy, apostasy, and *lesa-nación*." Sec. I, Cap. III, Art. 15.

42. See for example *Artículos* (Ecuador, 1812), Art. 20; *Caracas* (1812), Art. 187 and 282; *Tunja* (1811), Sec. I, Cap. III, Art. 8; *Trujillo* (1811), Título 5, Cap. 1; *Barcelona* (1812), Título 7, Art. 6, par. 9.

43. *Estatuto* (1815), Sec. 7, Cap. II, Art. VI.

44. *Cartagena* (1812).

45. For constitutional sources see the appropriate countries in footnote number 23.

46. A complete listing of the documentation is not feasible. I cite here only some of the more important published works. Concerning the signatories of Ecuador see the following: Camilo Destruge, *Álbum biográfico ecuatoriano* (Guayaquil, 1904); Roberto Andrade, *Historia del Ecuador* (Guayaquil, n.d.); Gustavo Arboleda, *Diccionario biográfico y genealógico del antiguo Departamento del Cauca* (Bogotá, 1962); Manuel de Jesús Andrade, *Ecuador. Próceres de la independencia* (Quito, 1909); Gustavo Arboleda, *Diccionario biográfico de la República del Ecuador* (Quito, 1910); B. Pérez Marchant, *Diccionario biográfico del Ecuador* (Quito, 1928); I. Toro Ruiz, *Más próceres de la independencia* (Latacunga, 1934).

On Colombian signatories see José María Restrepo Sáenz, *Neiva en la independencia* (Bogotá, 1919); José Restrepo Sáenz, *Gobernadores y próceres de Neiva* (Bogotá, 1941); Gustavo Arboleda, *Diccionario biográfico y genealógico*; Joaquín Ospina, *Diccionario biográfico y bibliográfico de Colombia* (Bogotá, 1927–1939); José P. Urueta, *Los martires de Cartagena* (Cartagena, 1886); M. Leonidas Scarpetta and Saturnino Vergara, *Diccionario biográfico de los campeones de la libertad de Nueva Granada, Venezuela, Ecuador i Perú* (Bogotá, 1879); José María Baraya, *Biografías militares* (Bogotá, 1874); Roberto Jaramillo Aragón, *El clero en la independencia* (Antioquia, 1946); Ramón C. Correa, ... *Monografías* (Tunja, 1930); José Joaquín García, *Crónicas de Bucaramanga* (Bogotá, 1896); José María Restrepo Sáenz, *Biografías de los mandatarios y ministros de la Real Audiencia, 1671 a 1819* (Bogotá, 1952); Ricardo Castro, *Páginas históricas colombianas* (Medellín, 1912); José P. Urueta, *Cartagena y sus cercanías* (Cartagena, 1912); José María Restrepo

Sáenz, *Gobernadores de Antioquia, 1579–1819* (Bogotá, 1931); José María Restrepo Sáenz, *Constituyentes de Tunja en 1811* (Bogotá, 1913); Roberto María Tisnes J., C.M.F., *Capítulos de historia zipaquireña, 1480–1830* (Bogotá, 1956). On Venezuelan signatories see Ramón Armando Rodríguez, *Diccionario biográfico, geográfico e histórico de Venezuela* (Madrid, 1957); Héctor García Chuecos, *Estudios de historia colonial Venezolana* (Caracas, 1937); Héctor Parra Márquez, *Historia del Colegio de Abogados de Caracas* (Caracas, 1952); Vicente Dávila, *Próceres trujillanos* (Caracas, 1921); M. Leonidas Scarpetta, *Diccionario*; Manuel Landaeta Rosales, *Sacerdotes que sirvieron a la causa de la independencia de Venezuela, de 1797 a 1823* (Caracas, 1911); Antonio Ramón Silva, *Recuerdo histórico. Patriotismo del clero de la diócesis de Mérida* (Mérida, 1911); Andrés F. Ponte, *La Revolución de Caracas y sus próceres* (Caracas, 1918); *Calendario manual y guía universal de forasteros en Venezuela para el año 1810* (Caracas, 1959); Ramón Azpurúa, *Biografías de hombres notables de Hispano-América* (Caracas, 1877); Vicente Dávila, *Próceres meridenos* (Caracas, 1918).

47. Because of overlapping of functions the numbers given add up to more than 303. I do not pretend that such totals are complete. For example, no information whatever regarding the background of some seventy-eight of the original 468 men has been found. One may be certain, however, that the information is on the conservative side—further research could only show further involvement. It would be an impossible task to read all of the relevant documents available on Spanish colonial administration in the years immediately preceding the Wars for Independence in the three nations.

48. However, I do not wish to convey the impression that clerical and secular officials always worked together harmoniously during the colonial days. A bibliography of the colonial church-state relationship may be found in Fredrick B. Pike, *The Conflict Between Church and State in Latin America* (New York, 1964), 233–235.

49. Read, for example, the "Primeros estatutos del Colegio de Abogados de Caracas," in Héctor Parra Márquez, *Historia del Colegio de Abogados* (Caracas, 1952), 337–360; or "Constituciones y Estatutos que se han de observar por el Ilustre Colegio de Abogados de esta Ciudad de Lima," in Aníbal Gálvez, *El Colegio de Abogados de Lima* (Lima, 1915), 179–217.

50. Robert A. Dahl, *A Preface to Democratic Theory* (New York, 1956), 3.

51. The constitutions cited below are those in effect as of June, 1966. *Guatemala,* Art. 44. See also *Bolivia,* Art. 6.c; *Chile,* Art. 10, par. 2; *Colombia,* Art. 42 and 44; *Costa Rica,* Art. 28; *Ecuador,* Art. 168; *Honduras,* Art. 87; *Dominican Republic,* Art. 8, par. 7; *México,* Art. 6 and 7; *Panamá,* Art. 38 and 40; *Paraguay,* Art. 3; *Nicaragua,* Art. 110; *Venezuela,* Art. 65.

52. *Costa Rica,* Art. 76; *Panamá,* Art. 35; *Nicaragua,* Art. 110. Essentially the same proposition is stated in the following: *Chile,* Art. 10, par. 2; *Colombia,* Art. 53; *Dominican Republic,* Art. 8, par. 5; *Ecuador,* Art. 168; *El Salvador,* Art. 158; *Guatemala,* Art. 66; *Honduras,* Art. 88; *Paraguay,* Art. 3; *Venezuela,* Art. 65.

53. *Chile,* Art. 44.

54. *Venezuela,* Art. 70.

55. By way of example see: *Chile,* Art. 10, par. 3; *Costa Rica,* Art. 29; *Ecuador,* Art. 187, par. 11; *Guatemala,* Art. 65; *Honduras,* Art. 85; *Nicaragua,* Art. 113; *Paraguay,* Art. 31; *Perú,* Art. 63 and 66; *Uruguay,* Art. 29; *Venezuela,* Art. 66; *Argen-*

tina, Art. 14; *Panama,* Art. 39.

56. *Dominican Republic,* Art. 38, par. 7.

57. Four of the constitutions suggest that the branches of government "collaborate harmoniously in the realization of the aims of the State." *Nicaragua,* Art. 13; *Panamá,* Art. 2; *Colombia,* Art. 55; and *Venezuela,* Art. 118.

58. *Uruguay,* Art. 85; *Bolivia,* Art. 57, par. 1; and *Ecuador,* Art. 189. See also *Colombia,* Art. 76, par. 1; *Ecuador,* Art. 53, par. 21; *El Salvador,* Art. 47, par. 14; *Costa Rica,* Art. 121, par. 1; *Honduras,* Art. 181, par. 4; *Perú,* Art. 26 and 123, par. 4.

59. *Paraguay,* Art. 46; *El Salvador,* Art. 66; *Nicaragua,* Art. 251; and *Venezuela,* Art. 81.

60. *Bolivia,* Art. 198. The constitution of Colombia says: "The State shall have . . . the supreme inspection and supervision of institutions of learning, public and private, in order to ensure the fulfilment of the social purposes of culture and the best intellectual, moral, and physical development of students." Art. 41. See *Chile,* Art. 10, par. 7; *Costa Rica,* Art. 79; *Ecuador,* Art. 171; *Guatemala,* Art. 95; *México,* Art. 3, pars. 2 and 3; *Nicaragua,* Art. 99 and 106; *Panamá,* Art. 79; *Paraguay,* Art. 20; *Venezuela,* Art. 79.

61. *Selected Political Writings,* ed. by A. Passerin D'Entrèves (London, 1959), 5.

62. *Panamá,* Art. 47. *Uruguay,* Art. 7. "El interés público primará sobre el interés privado." *El Salvador,* Art. 220. Also note *Colombia,* Art. 30; *Paraguay,* Art. 13.

63. *Colombia,* Art. 105.

64. *Panamá,* Art. 107. See *El Salvador,* Art. 44.

65. Latins have an old saw: "We have hundreds of laws but no law to obey the laws." Their constituent assemblies must have been listening. Five countries, Nicaragua, Bolivia, Guatemala, Ecuador, and Venezuela, now have constitutional provisions directing their citizens to obey the law. Ecuador (Art. 159) and Venezuela (Art. 52) even have constitutional provisions directing their citizens to obey the constitution.

66. *Venezuela,* Art. 132.

67. *Ecuador,* Art. 153.

68. *Paraguay,* Art. 18. By Art. 92 of the Dominican Republic's constitution, her armed forces are charged "to maintain public order, the Constitution, and the laws." El Salvador created her armed forces "to see that the laws are fulfilled, to maintain public order, and guarantee constitutional rights. The armed forces will especially watch to see that the norm of presidential alternation is not violated." Art. 112.

Spanish America, 1900–1970: Tradition and Social Innovation

Fredrick B. Pike

1. Turn of the Century Spanish America: Traditional Society and a Revolutionary Challenge

The most noteworthy feature about generation after generation of
Spanish American leaders has not been their inability to attain political
stability. Rather, it has been their awesome success in achieving what
they view as infinitely more important: social stability. This study examines the uncanny skill of the directing classes of Spanish America in preserving the traditional social order against the multiple forces of change.

By traditional society in Spanish America is meant a society divided
into two components with life styles and values so dissimilar that they
must be described as distinct cultures. At the top is a dominant culture,
vastly complex in its composition and frequently split by internal divisions. Beneath it lies a vast lower mass or subordinate culture, generally,
for the sake of brevity, referred to as a subculture. It too is made up of
many elements. Some of these, domestic servants and unskilled urban
manual labourers, for example, may be in intimate contact with the
dominant culture. Others, among them unassimilated Indians, are isolated and remote from the dominant culture.

Perhaps the most salient feature distinguishing the subculture is its lack
of a capitalist orientation. Its members are resigned to a subsistence
existence and are not motivated by a success myth that leads them to
expect a more affluent tomorrow as a result of competitive skills. They
live in the present and find it difficult to conceive of a future that is better
than or essentially different from the present. Relatively quarantined
against the incentives of individualistic, capitalist materialism, moreover,
men of the subculture tend to have a collectivist outlook. To many of
them, collectivist labour and land-utilization patterns are apt to seem
natural and congenial.

Another significant characteristic of the subculture, one closely associ-

Selection is reprinted from *Spanish America 1900–1970, Tradition and Social
Innovation,* by Fredrick B. Pike, with the permission of W. W. Norton & Company, Inc. Copyright © 1973 by Thames & Hudson, Ltd.

ated with its noncapitalist orientation, is the willingness of its members
to live in a state of dependence. Concerned with security rather than
independence, they rely on the paternalism of those above to keep them
from sinking beneath the level of subsistence. Whether this paternalism
is extended by the Church, a private *patrón* (owner-management) group
or the state is unimportant. All that matters is that privately or publicly
the men and institutions of the dominant culture assume the responsibilities and burdens involved in being depended upon by those below.

Among isolated Indian groups in such countries as Mexico, Guatemala, Ecuador, Bolivia and Peru, dependence is often less pronounced
than in the case of subculture groups living in more intimate contact
with higher social sectors. Indians dwelling in remote *comunidades*
(communities) are relatively self-sufficient, producing themselves the
goods that maintain them in a subsistence existence, whether these are
food products they consume themselves or commodities sold to a local
market to provide cash for the purchase of a few essentials. For whatever
cash income they receive, however, and for the few finished goods they
require, these Indians are dependent upon the mechanisms of a local,
regional or even national economy over which they have no control.
This situation is accepted because any endeavour to transform the
market place into a more benign agency would perforce entail increased
contact with the outside, non-Indian world. Suspicious of and sometimes
overtly hostile to that world, Indians tend to regard dependence on its
economic mechanisms, even when these are manifestly harsh, as infinitely
preferable to integration into it. Within their status of economic
dependence, then, they opt for maximum cultural freedom. By avoiding
integration, they maintain the freedom to live almost exclusively in the
domain of their own language, social habits, dress and eating styles,
beliefs, prejudices and myths. Decidedly missing from their world of
cultural values is a faith in steady progress towards individual mastery
of nature and control of destiny.

In stark contrast, members of the dominant culture live almost as
much in the future as in the present. They are motivated by the belief
that individual action taken in the present can render the future more
comfortable and secure. In short, they employ the perspectives associated
with capitalism. These perspectives persist regardless of how ambivalent,
ambiguous and unorthodox their attitudes towards capitalism often
are—attitudes that will be described in the course of this book. Appre-
ciating the value of individual capital accumulation in ensuring independence and self-reliance and in providing for the future, men of the
dominant culture are little inclined towards patterns of collective
ownership.

During the first two or three generations after independence had been
achieved in the second and third decades of the nineteenth century,
Spanish America's two cultures coexisted with at least the outward

appearance, and perhaps at most times the actual substance, of harmony. On the rare occasions when conflict—which critics of the traditional society maintain was endemic, albeit cunningly masked by subtle means of repression—became outwardly manifest, the directing classes resorted to overt suppression. By and large, however, they did not have to do so.

One reason for the infrequency of a total breakdown of peaceful social relations was that men of the dominant culture were on the whole content to leave those of the subculture alone; they did not intrude unduly into their world, interfere with them or question their life styles. As a result members of the subculture were permitted at least that sense of dignity that comes when there is little criticism of their way of life by the leaders of society. In addition, those at the top of society showed at least some willingness to accept the obligations of paternalism. The upper classes honoured their paternalistic obligations partly because, true to values that can be traced back at least as far as medieval Spain, they associated resignation and poverty with virtue rather than vice. In ministering to the needs of the masses, then, they were rewarding virtue, not indulging vice.

Attitudes among the dominant culture, inherited from the colonial past and continuing to prevail to some considerable extent even beyond the mid-twentieth century, help to explain the subtle manner in which racial discrimination has operated in Spanish America. The social structure has aptly been described as a "pigmentocracy," and the darker-skinned masses at the bottom were not expected to rise socially and economically, except in the case of certain extremely unusual individuals. Because they were not expected to rise, but were regarded as most virtuous when they uncomplainingly kept the lowly place in society regarded as proper for them, they were not dismissed as morally inferior when they failed to advance in social status and economic power. As a result a dark skin, generally associated with poverty, was not taken as a badge of vice, although it was as often as not associated with limited intellectual potential.

The situation changed when assertive liberal elements appeared among the dominant culture and began to intrude into the world of the subculture, hoping, in many instances, to reform and uplift that world. It was their contention that the masses below should be reformed by being pressured into acquiring the more individualistic, self-reliant, materialistic and capitalist orientation of bourgeois elements within the dominant culture.

In so far as they grew aware of efforts to transform them, men of the lower mass were deprived of the dignity that had been theirs when they were accepted as virtuous by society's leading elements. They were now asked to feel ashamed of what they had been and were, and to undergo a complete change in values and attitudes. Moreover, the new liberal approach contributed ultimately, even if unintentionally, to a hardening of racial prejudices, in so far as vice, joined now with poverty, came to be identified with a dark skin.

As a result of circumstances which lead the dominant culture to intrude in a new way upon the subculture or to discard time-honoured obligations towards it, a revolution—or an attempt at one—is unlikely to emerge. However complex and veiled its motivation, the revolution will probably initially assume the outer form—reflected by propaganda and sometimes by the sincere utterances of its leaders—of an endeavour to shape the structure of the dominant culture, allegedly corrupted by its liberal, bourgeois ways, in line with the noncapitalist life styles associated with the subculture. Revolutionary leadership will, most likely, be provided by alienated members of the dominant culture.

As the threat of social revolution intensifies, the leaders of the prevailing system can save themselves immediately by violent repression. If they are to survive in the long run, on the other hand, they must devise new methods to re-establish more harmonious relations between the two cultures and to restore unity among the different elements of the dominant culture. What follows is the story of the general success of the ruling classes of twentieth-century Spanish America in discovering the long-term methods necessary to calm revolutionary situations, and thereby to preserve tradition.

2. Ideology: The Challenge to and Defense of the Traditional Society

Three Positivist Philosophies Spanish America's romantic liberals of the immediate postindependence period, irrepressibly optimistic in their appraisal of human nature, had wished to remove restrictions and restraints in society in order to bring an equalitarian state into being. However, as they fell under the influence of positivism in the second half of the nineteenth century, liberals became increasingly pessimistic in assessing the potential of the vast majority of people inhabiting the new republics. Concerned more and more to encourage a natural élite, the liberals-turned-positivists wished to remove restrictions and restraints in society for the benefit of those allegedly fit to profit from the ensuing freedom. Eschewing the paternalism of Auguste Comte's pristine positivism, one important group of positivists accepted the concept of unrestricted struggle, or social Darwinism, associated with Herbert Spencer. The result was a rather unnatural union between the ideologies of Comte and Spencer.

Pensadores (literally, thinkers) such as Antonio García Cubas and

Francisco Bulnes in Mexico, the younger Carlos Octavio Bunge and José Ingenieros in Argentina, and Alcides Argüedas, Oyola Cuellar and Nicomedes Antelo in Bolivia insisted upon the inherent racial inferiority of the vast Indian-mestizo-mulatto masses of the national populaces. In their view, the proper way to deal with the Spanish American masses was to stop pampering them in a spirit of paternalism and leave them to die out in an unrestricted struggle with the fitter elements of society. At the same time most of the leading figures who subscribed to this racialist school of thought saw the need to encourage massive immigration from the countries of Western Europe that had presumably achieved a more advanced stage in the evolutionary process. Through the immigration of Caucasians they hoped to achieve their paramount goal of national economic development.

In spite of the prevalence of racialist positivism in Mexico, a formidable outcry of protest greeted a suggestion in the *New York Herald* in 1884 that all Indians, being incorrigible, should be exterminated in the interest of progress. The protest, which T. G. Powell described in the *Hispanic American Historical Review* in February 1968, arose in part because of the influence of Gabino Barreda, who had helped to bring into being a different, reformist school of positivism. Barreda and his followers conceded that the Indians, who constituted by far the largest part of Mexico's masses, were inferior in their present state and an impediment to national development. But through better feeding and education, they believed, the Indians could be converted into agents of progress. Basically, they argued that Indians could be reformed by being made self-reliant; they could be infused with ambitions for material, individual gain and then taught how to satisfy their new ambitions by acquiring productive skills and habits of thrift and foresight. The reformist positivists therefore set out to render the Indians worthy and virtuous by turning them into replicas of the individualistic, self-reliant, materialistic, capitalist-oriented elements within the middle and upper classes. One way to initiate the process of reform lay, they believed, in depriving Indian settlements of communal properties and turning each member into a private landowner.

Other Spanish American countries as well as Mexico produced prominent spokesmen for this type of reformism. In Peru, for example, Javier Prado y Ugarteche came to believe that the lower classes, both Indian and non-Indian, could be uplifted and transformed into instruments of national progress. In his book *Estado social del Perú durante la dominación española* (1894), Prado stressed that education must be used to awaken in the individual the desire for greater well-being; material ambition would in turn implant in individuals a higher degree of civic virtue and personal morality. "It is necessary," he insisted, "to educate, and to educate through labour, through industry, which is the greatest medium of moralization. There is nothing which will better elevate a man's character today, nothing which will make him interest himself more effectively in the future of his country, than to educate him to be practical and prudent and to acquire wealth by means of his personal efforts."

A similar position was taken by the Chilean Francisco Antonio Encina when, in his book *Nuestra inferioridad económica* (1912), he complained that the Latin American republics were becoming economic colonies of the United States. This he attributed to the economic inferiority, the lack of capitalist, productive virtues, that typified all too many Latin Americans. Encina demanded a new approach to education, one aimed at instilling in all members of society, from top to bottom, the productive, individualistic, self-reliant capitalist outlook that certain enlightened middle sectors had already acquired.

Whether the reason was the desire of the upper classes to eliminate them, or alternatively, to change and uplift them, the Spanish American masses began to experience new pressures around the turn of the century. Society no longer afforded them a secure and respectable place; it no longer recognized their dignity and virtue within their traditional world of values. These circumstances inevitably fostered bewilderment and resentment. In Mexico the Indian Emiliano Zapata raised the cry *Tierra y Libertad* ("Land and Liberty"), voicing the desire of the masses to regain security in their traditional patterns of collective landownership, to be left alone once more in their accustomed way of life and to regain freedom from the intrusion of an uncongenial world. Zapata also expressed the resentment of the Indians when, in a conversation with Pancho Villa in 1914, he exclaimed: "Those son-of-a-bitch politicians. . . . I can't stand them. . . . They're all a bunch of bastards." Much of Zapata's anger stemmed from the manner in which politicians, especially since the 1880s, had intruded into the world of the Indian subculture.

In Mexico many members of the ruling classes had also become alienated. Encouraged by the restlessness of the masses, engendered in part by the attempt to reform them on bourgeois lines, they began to raise the call to revolution. Their idea was to use the masses in order to force the upper classes to reform themselves in accordance with the noncapitalist values, traditions and general patterns of life of society's underlings. Not surprisingly, then, Zapata found in an alienated intellectual, Antonio Díaz Soto y Gama, a spokesman for a revolutionary change that would involve little less than imposing certain values of the Indian subculture upon the middle and upper classes. And in Chile, where Indians had long since been virtually eliminated, Luis Emilio Recabarren responded in a somewhat similar manner to the perplexity and resentment of the urban lower classes as the dominant groups either intensified their exploitation or insisted that the lower classes begin to emulate their betters. By the early 1920s Recabarren was preaching a revolution that would bring all society into line with the allegedly socialist, collectivist, noncapitalist, nonmaterialistic values of the masses.

Throughout Spanish America the old live-and-let-live relationship between the dominant and the subcultures was beginning to break down. The ruling classes had initiated the process by intruding more forcefully into the lives of the masses. The resulting tensions produced a favourable climate for numerous revolutionaries, among them radical socialists and anarchists, whose aim was to impose the values of the subculture upon the world of the dominant culture, and so, in fact, to destroy it.

Except in Mexico—and later in Bolivia and Cuba—the pressures generated by the ruling classes were decreased in the course of time and the potential for revolution was reduced. As a result the traditional society survived essentially intact. Just as some ideological factors had contributed to the creation of a revolutionary situation, so others helped to contain it by providing an intellectual climate conducive to preserving the established order.

A third group of intellectuals—the paternalistic positivists—always stressed social harmony and order above progress. They realized instinctively that national development based upon awakening the competitive instincts and materialistic aspirations of the masses portended the collapse of the traditional society. Their aim was to prevent such a collapse by inducing the masses to accept their place in a pattern of existence characterized by dependence, and in this way to defuse the revolutionary situation. Hence they called upon the privileged classes to assume new paternalistic obligations that would ensure social solidarity by guaranteeing economic security to the lower orders. At the same time the paternalistic positivists sought to provide the masses with nonmaterial rewards that would afford them spiritual contentment within their lowly economic status. In spiritual gratification combined with paternalistic protection, they saw the means of restoring a harmonious relationship among the various components of society.

This type of self-interested paternalism was proclaimed in Argentina by J. Alfredo Ferreira in an article published in the periodical *La Escuela Positiva* in 1899. Communism, Ferreira wrote, had played an understandable role in helping to awaken the labouring classes and to expand their horizons, but it was not acceptable as an ultimate solution to the social problem. Rather, the solution lay in a form of positivism that stressed the social duties of property. A similar approach was developed in Chile by Valentín Letelier, who defeated Enrique Mac-Iver, an advocate of Spencerian positivism, in the councils of the Chilean Radical Party in 1907; and from that time onwards the country's Radicals paid lip service to a form of government intervention in social questions which they described as socialism.

In Bolivia certain *pensadores,* among them Ignacio Prudencio Bustillo, began to urge that the state respect the distinctive features of Indian culture, including collective landownership, even though these features might not be conducive to material development in line with scientific laws of progress. And in Venezuela intellectuals such as Gil Fortoul and, later and far more directly, Laureano Vallenilla Lanz argued the case for paternalistic dictatorship, expressing doubt whether much could be accomplished in the way of reforming the masses.

The paternalistic positivists were not particularly concerned if the social costs of their programmes slowed the rate of economic development. They accepted this overhead as necessary to preserve social solidarity and order, without which there could be no long-term, sustained material development. What attracted them was the vision of an ideal society that had many points of similarity to that of the colonial period. Within this society—new, yet rooted in the past—the possibilities for overall economic development would be limited by the inability of the masses to acquire extensive purchasing power. The advantage of this society was that within it the directing classes would remain unchallenged because the masses were shielded against ambitions for economic, material self-reliance—ambitions that if fulfilled would give rise to demands for social and political independence.

In seeking to give the masses nonmaterial rewards and incentives so as to preserve social harmony, Spanish American paternalistic philosophers borrowed heavily from the teachings of a writer who, through his disciples, had an enormous posthumous influence on Spanish liberalism and positivism in the second half of the nineteenth century: Karl Christian Friedrich Krause.

The best-known Spanish translation of a work by Krause, *Ideal de la humanidad para la vida* (1860), reveals most of the essential features of his social philosophy. In it Krause lays down that every individual is placed on earth to pursue his end through his particular vocation. Moreover, however lowly his estate, each man should participate to some degree in "the higher callings of human nature." Thus, members of all social classes should be taught to appreciate the beauty of their physical surroundings and given a liberal education, including instruction in art, literature and music, intended to awaken in them a regard for the aesthetic world. By learning to perceive, however dimly, and to appreciate, however imperfectly, the higher truths and beauties of life, men would be liberated from obsession with material desires, from base passions and appetites, from selfish inclinations and resentment and rancour against others. Thus liberated, they would achieve a harmonious and fully developed character, while at the same time finding the solace and joys necessary to make them content and resigned in the stations in life to which they were called.

As they began in their limited way to interest themselves in the higher things of life the humble classes, according to Krause and his Spanish as well as his Spanish American disciples, would come to revere the hierarchy of values in which the artistic and spiritual and aesthetic took precedence over material considerations. They would come to revere this hierarchy because in their leisure time, when they enjoyed respite from the physical labour that gave "no nourishment to the spirit and that chilled the heart," they would find an exhilarating and rewarding world in the higher pleasures to which they had been introduced by their liberal education. Coming to appreciate a hierarchy of values, the labouring classes would tolerate and even welcome the existing social hierarchy, understanding that only better men were capable of fruitfully pursuing the better things in life and achieving new works of artistic creativity that would eventually add to the pleasure of the humble, non-creative classes.

The Argentinian positivist Manuel A. Bermudes clearly identified himself with the Krausist approach when he argued in 1897 in his article "Educación y socialismo" that through education the poor and humble could be made to understand that their situation was natural and that they could thereby be liberated from resentment against the rich and the mighty. In order to achieve this purpose, Bermudes affirmed, education had not merely to be vocational; it had also to be liberal, so as to acquaint the student with the wonders of the realms of the mind and soul.

Arielism The champions of paternalistic, harmonious positivism hoped to spiritualize both the masses and, at the same time, a bourgeoisie which was growing all too assertive within the dominant culture; they were also interested in the long-range economic development of their countries and inclined to believe that the laws of progress could be discovered through science. On the other hand they feared the social upheavals that might result from an exclusive obsession with development in the immediate future. In contrast, a new group of intellectuals, the Arielists, who appeared at the turn of the century, were vitally concerned with preserving the traditional social order and entertained considerable doubts about the value of national material development, questioning scientific methodology in general.

Arielism took its name from the book *Ariel*, written by the Uruguayan intellectual José Enrique Rodó and published in 1900. In this work, which became vastly influential throughout the Spanish-speaking world, Rodó depicted Ariel as the creature of intellectual and spiritual pursuits, concerned with art, beauty and moral development as ends in themselves, rather than with material progress. Ariel was used to symbolize what, for Rodó, was most authentic in Hispanic culture. Through the words he gave to Ariel, the author chided Spanish Americans, sometimes directly, sometimes by implication, for having abandoned the culture and values natural to them and having embraced the materialistic, utilitarian, mechanistic life styles associated with alien cultures, most specifically with Anglo-Saxon civilization.

Arielism coincided with and contributed to the growing hostility to the United States at the turn of the century, provoked by a fear of Yankee imperialism. To fear of political and economic imperialism, Arielism added a cultural dimension. Basic to the Arielist position was the conviction that the type of culture developed by Yankees would, if allowed to penetrate Spanish America, contribute to levelling social revolutions. Out of this conviction came the resolute determination of many Spanish Americans to return to and strengthen their own unique cultural traditions, to reassert their own specific national identities and immunize themselves against United States influence.

The basic flaw in United States culture, according to most Arielists and to the proponents of paternalistic, spiritual positivism as well, lay in its exclusive concern with the material development and progress of the individual and the nation. Only a materialistic society, they contended, could accept the madness of political democracy based upon the concept of one man, one vote. A materialistic society was characterized by an obsessive interest in things; because all men were capable of producing and consuming things—though not ideas—such a society granted them an equal political voice. Within a materialistic society whose hallmark was indifference to the provinces of mind and soul, it seemed suitable enough to permit, through the operation of egalitarian democracy, the destruction of the social hierarchies essential to preserving the hierarchy of values.

Within the United States proper, in the view of many Arielists and their ideological associates, some element of social solidarity and political stability could be maintained. A people by nature materialistic, as Yankees were assumed to be, could achieve institutional stability within a democratic order permeated throughout by individualistic, capitalist values. Such a people, of course, could never amount to much in the overall scale of human values. They could contribute little to art, to the spiritual development of men, to the nobler creations of which the human spirit was capable. They could, however, achieve remarkable results on the lower levels of human existence and in general satisfy the wants of a materialistic citizenry sufficiently to prevent anarchy and chronic disorder.

The real importance of the Arielists, however, lies in their analysis of Spanish America. They insisted that the transfer of the materialistic approach to life to a people and a cultural milieu marked by an overriding concern with the higher, more spiritual values of human existence, and accordingly organized in hierarchical fashion, must inevitably undermine the established order and pose the threat of social revolution. In their view the materialistic concept of life was fundamentally incompatible with one that was spiritual and humanistic; it could establish itself only by destroying the institutions and social order that had naturally developed in response to the needs and aspirations of a society that put intangible benefits first. Thus, when Spanish Americans denied their own nature and cultural identity, when they introduced democratic experiments and sought to disseminate throughout society the alien values of acquisitive, competitive, individualistic capitalism, they were, however unwittingly, serving the cause of social revolution.

The Catholic Church As a result of the Plenary Council of Latin American prelates, convoked in Rome by Pope Leo XIII in 1899, came an effort to reinvigorate the Church in Latin America and to improve its channels of communication with the Vatican. The Plenary Council also gave rise to a series of provincial councils within the various Latin American republics, one of the first of which was held in Caracas in 1904. The resurgence of the Catholic Church in Venezuela, dating from this provincial council, continued during the long dictatorship of Juan Vicente Gómez (1908–35).

The Plenary Council was also followed by a number of provincial councils in Colombia. The third of these, held in Bogotá in 1916, produced a joint pastoral in which the prelates instructed the faithful to vote only for political leaders who would protect the interests of the Church and allow the clergy a role of "moderate intervention" in the public life of the country. At the conclusion of the council a Spanish journalist writing in the Jesuit organ *Razón y Fe* in January 1917 complimented the bishops for their efforts which had, he said, increased the already appreciable strength of the Church in Colombia and established it as the most formidable "bulwark of the existing social order."

The Church's gradual acquisition of prestige and influence in Venezuela, following a period of rampant anticlericalism in the late nineteenth century, and the strengthening of its already considerable power in Colombia were signs of a general revival of Catholic influence in most parts of Spanish America. In an indirect way the resurgence of Catholicism can be traced back to the reaction of Arielism at the turn of the century against materialism and mechanistic utilitarianism. It is true that Arielism, initiated by men like Rodó who were indifferent to religion, shared with positivism a hearty, sometimes even a virulent, anticlericalism. Both Arielists and paternalistic, spiritual positivists believed that humanism afforded an adequate foundation upon which to base the higher values they extolled. But roughly between 1910 and 1930—though the situation differed considerably from country to country—a new pattern became discernible. Increasingly the leaders of the spiritual reaction against utilitarian and materialistic criteria began to return to the Catholic Church, persuaded that the higher human values, if they were to prevail against democratic, levelling, revolutionary impulses, required a basis in theology and revelation. The famous Peruvian intellectual José de la Riva Agüero stands as a symbol of this development. In his youth a leader of the Peruvian version of the Arielist movement and strongly influenced by liberal anticlericalism, Riva Agüero made a conspicuous return to the Catholic Church in 1932.

Not all countries, of course, shared to an equal degree in this type of cultural change. In Mexico, where after the Revolution of 1910 intellectuals preferred to flirt with radical anticlerical and sometimes atheistic doctrines, and in Uruguay, where the Church had never enjoyed more than a tenuous existence and where agnosticism was a significant intellectual force, the reaction against materialism failed to evolve into a major resurgence of Catholic influence. Even in Mexico, however, by the late 1920s José Vasconcelos and, more clearly still, Alfonso Junco typified a growing number of *pensadores* who emerged as apologists for Hispanic traditions, including Catholicism; and in the 1930s the ultra-Catholic *sinarquista* movement gained a large mass following among rural Mexicans as well as the backing of some intellectuals. Meanwhile, moreover, the Uruguayan Luis Alberto de Herrera was developing into perhaps the most eloquent lay spokesman of traditional Catholic values that his country has produced.

Early in the twentieth century, the Spanish American episcopacy launched an effort to organize the laity into Catholic Action, hoping thereby to capitalize on the increasingly favourable circumstances in which they found themselves and at the same time to ease social tensions. The primary purposes of Catholic Action were to win back the masses to the faith and to quicken the social conscience of the upper classes so as to induce them, under the hierarchy's supervision, to take paternalistic measures to mitigate the suffering and isolation of the masses. This little-studied development in Spanish American Catholicism undoubtedly helped to dissipate the pressures for revolutionary change.

Catholic spokesmen attributed the mounting social tensions in Spanish America to the secularization of society that had been under way since the eighteenth century. Unlike those positivists influenced by Krause, they denied that the masses could be persuaded through education and an appeal to reason alone to accept their inequality on this earth. Only when convinced of their equality in a life to come would they resign themselves to a temporal status of inequality. It followed, then, that all those who advocated secularism, among them liberals, positivists and the early Arielists, were, however contrary to their intentions, preparing the way for social revolution.

The spectre of social revolution contributed to a *rapprochement* between anticlericals and proponents of Catholic social doctrines. Faced with what appeared to be an immediate threat to the established order, anticlericals began to curb their demands for the total secularization of society and to present a common front with religious leaders against the forces of change. Even during the late nineteenth century Bolivia's traditionally anticlerical Liberals had managed to arrive at a mutually advantageous *modus vivendi* with the Church-affiliated Conservatives. By the late 1920s this pattern had established itself in Colombia, where the Liberals, out of office at the time, discovered a basis of co-operation with the incumbent Conservatives. By the early 1930s Chilean Liberals and Conservatives, discounting the issues that had divided them for decades, had joined together to form an alliance that would remain one of the country's most powerful political forces for the next thirty years.

Corporative Decentralization   Most Catholic observers of Spanish America at the turn of the century, and a good number of ardent secularists as well, expressed alarm at the degree to which the masses were becoming alienated from a social and political system that did not even permit them a minimal degree of participation. They also pointed with apprehension to a situation in which individual members of the labouring classes no longer enjoyed a secure sanctuary in society but were constrained to compete for their livelihood under conditions that rendered their chances of success minimal. To remedy this situation, which if ignored might result in revolution, they urged the decentralized and corporative organization of society. Their programme called for breaking down the monolithic, centralized social-political structure into its natural subdivisions (organisms or corporations) and granting to the masses some voice in governing the subdivisions appropriate to them.

Spanish American Catholics recognized at an early date what Erich Fromm later called the inherent contradiction between competition and "belongingness." In restoring to the masses of society a sense of belongingness, Catholic *pensadores* hoped to avoid social revolution. In their analysis they even found common ground with Karl Marx, although their prescriptions for the future differed in all respects from his. Marx saw corporative institutions as one of the means whereby social harmony had been maintained in medieval Europe; and he contended that the separation, specification and division of labour basic to industrial capitalism produced an estrangement in human relations that led to the fragmentation of society at all levels. It was precisely this fragmentation that alarmed Catholic thinkers and led them to advocate a return to the corporative structure.

According to its Catholic critics, the liberal, secular state—excessively individualistic and at the same time excessively centralized—had eliminated the possibility of hierarchical organization. Within such a state each individual operated as a free atom, participated by his vote in decisions at all levels, and was allowed and even encouraged to raise his voice on issues he was incapable of understanding. The democratic goals of this unnatural organization were seen as self-defeating. Eventually, most individuals, because of their inherent inability to understand the complex issues of national policy on which their votes were solicited, would retreat into their own narrow world of self-interest and abandon all concern with the republic. The Catholic advocates of decentralization argued that by replacing an atomistic with an organic or corporative structure it would be possible for each individual to find his way into a local political group, and in addition into a professional or functional organization, in the management of which he could safely and knowledgeably participate. Content within their own sphere of activity and active politically to the fullest extent their faculties permitted, the masses would happily leave decision-making on the higher, national level to an élite that would emerge through careful screening procedures.

By means of corporative decentralization Catholics hoped not only to preserve the hierarchical social order but also gradually to desecularize society. They envisaged the organization of labour and professional groups under strict Church dominance, relatively free from the control of a centralized state bureaucracy, which in their view was often tainted by liberal, secular, anticlerical, materialistic, Masonic errors, by Jewish and Marxist aberrations and even by Protestant heresies. In the final analysis, Spanish American Catholics tended to see excessive centralism arising from the same heretical assumptions that allegedly underlay democracy. They contended that from the heretical premise of the equality of all men—said to be an outgrowth, even if unforeseen, of the individualistic Protestant approach to religion—there had followed the conclusion that all citizens should be ruled by the same laws and institutions. As a result all local and regional "particularisms" had been repressed by a despotic central government that absorbed or eliminated all intermediary associations between itself and its citizens.

Many positivists and Arielists, and also members of other anticlerical and secularist groups, concurred with Catholic spokesmen on the desirability of a decentralized state that would alleviate revolutionary pressures by providing for popular political participation at the level of professional or local corporations. Still, however much inclined they may have been as the twentieth century advanced to co-operate with Catholics in waging a common struggle against basic social change, secularists were not prepared to accept any form of decentralization that increased the Catholic Church's temporal influence unnecessarily. This situation led to a split within the ranks of the secularist defenders of the *status quo*. Some continued to urge decentralization, but a large number decided to work through the existing centralized state structure over which anticlerical forces had gained control in most republics—a control which by and large they continued to maintain despite the twentieth-century resurgence of Catholic influence.

To a considerable extent, therefore, partisans of secularism abandoned the corporative cause to Catholics, opting instead for a centralized, nation-wide, state controlled system of paternalistic government administered by a secular bureaucracy. Such a system had the disadvantage of denying to the masses such satisfaction as comes from participating in the decisions of subsidiary corporations within the body politic. On the other hand, it was believed that a centralized, paternalistic government would stifle revolutionary impulses by guaranteeing economic security to the masses, thereby increasing their attachment to the established political and social system. Furthermore, they might be given a sense of dignity and participation if effectively persuaded that they were playing an essential role in advancing national progress. In this way a new secular religion of nationalism might take the place of traditional Catholicism and provide the spiritual, nonmaterial gratifications required to make the masses content to remain within their customary place in society.

In all these ways—by means of a secular, liberal education or a religious revival, by private or state controlled paternalism, by decentralization or through a highly centralized structure whose existence was justified by an appeal to nationalism—the dominant classes of Spanish America hoped to keep the masses dependent and isolate them from the values of laissez-faire capitalism and individualistic materialism. If assured of economic security, if given nonmaterial rewards in the form of art or religion, or participation in subsidiary groups natural and appropriate to them, or if they could be persuaded that they were playing a role in realizing their nation's destiny, the dependent classes would presumably not demand a revolutionary departure from the uses of the past. Instead, they would remain content within a system that took from them according to their abilities and gave to them according to their needs. They would remain, in short, basically noncapitalist. And they would tolerate the continued existence above them of a culture which was capitalist, at least in so far as its members expected from the system a great deal more than the satisfaction of their basic needs. In such circumstances, tradition would be secure.

3. Social and Economic Factors in Preserving the Traditional Society

The New Paternalism   The old system of paternalism in Spanish America, established in colonial times and reflecting in many ways the institutions of central and southern Spain, began to collapse in the nineteenth century. One reason for this can be traced to the declining power of the Church at that time. Buffeted in most republics by an onslaught of hard-hitting anticlerical legislation, the Church lost the lands on which it had provided security for large numbers of peasant labourers. It lost also the capital resources and income that had enabled it in

colonial times and at the outset of the independence period to be the
main supporter of charitable programmes.

More significant in causing the disruption of the old paternalism was
a population shift away from the countryside into the cities, a shift that
got under way in most Spanish American republics in the late nineteenth century. Some of the migrating rural masses were Indians whose
communal properties had been seized in the name of liberal reform. The
majority were peasants—both Indian and non-Indian, depending on the
country—who had laboured on large, privately owned rural estates. By
migrating these rural masses passed directly from a manorial setting—in
which they had been cared for paternalistically, had never learned to
protect themselves in a competitive society and had almost never
acquired an education—into new conditions of incipient industrial
urban life. Moreover, the recent arrivals in the cities knew nothing of
how to organize to protect their interests. Emerging urban capitalists
would have been more than human had they initially exhibited a spirit
of noblesse oblige similar to that which had prevailed in employer-
employee relationships in a rural setting. Inevitably these circumstances
produced a reaction as the burgeoning urban proletariat, responding
with mounting enthusiasm to revolutionary rhetoric, began to show
signs of striking back at an exploitative system.

From the early twentieth century governments took action to calm
the discontent of urban masses—their numbers dramatically swelled in
such countries as Argentina and Uruguay by foreign immigrants—by
extending to them vast new concessions, including employer liability
protection, accident and unemployment insurance, and virtual guarantees against dismissal, almost regardless of inefficiency and provocation
to management. Workers were also provided with medical clinics,
somewhat better working conditions, sports fields, parks, subsidized
housing, concerts, cheap holidays and excursions, as well as lavish spec-
tacles and parades on literally dozens of holidays; and the prices for the
more popular, mass-consumed alcoholic drinks were maintained at an
incredibly low level. By and large, however, workers did not receive
substantial increases in real wages. An increase in real wages would
have brought genuine power to the masses, whereas generous grants of
fringe benefits left them dependent upon, and hopefully grateful to, the
system that furnished the benefits. The masses remained, therefore,
essentially a subculture, free from the spirit of self-reliance assured by
individual control over capital surpluses.

The inflationary process in most Spanish American republics, reaching back in many instances as far as the late nineteenth century, also
had the effect of maintaining the masses in a condition of dependence—
by chance, probably, rather than design. Conditions of spiralling inflation discouraged the lower classes from acquiring the habits of thrift
and saving through which, in a stable economy, they could have gained

economic independence. They remained instead dependent upon the government to provide them at periodic intervals with cost-of-living adjustments which, while possibly compensating for losses in purchasing power caused by inflation, did not constitute an increment in real wages.

Many critics of the Spanish American ruling classes have suggested that the masses have been betrayed by the system on which they depend; it is arguable, however, that given the economic resources available to them, Spanish American governments have been proportionately more generous in dealing with the lower classes than the governments of many advanced economic powers. Through a new paternalism devised early in the century, Spanish America's urban proletariat has been spared at least some aspects of the brutal exploitation that characterized the industrial revolution in England, the United States and, for that matter, in Communist Russia. The degree of protection in Spanish America has conceivably impeded industrialization. But it has served the cause that is dearer to most Spanish American leadership groups: the preservation of the traditional, two-culture society. In this process, Spanish America discarded liberal political theory and moved back towards the political traditions of the past; a paternalistic, all-embracing central government re-emerged as the dominant factor in national politics.

In implementing vast and complex new programmes of paternalism, Spanish American states relied extensively upon government controlled labour unions. Labour leaders were absorbed into the established system and assigned the role of intermediaries between the rank and file union membership and the government. Their success in serving their constituencies depended upon their ability to wrest favours from the government for which they acted virtually as bureaucrats. Finding it expedient to abandon policies of militant confrontation with capital, a great number of union leaders happily settled for the benefits they could gain by maintaining a friendly working relationship with the political masters of their countries. Labour leaders thus co-opted were no more inclined to rise against governments in which they had a vital stake than were the major-domos on the large *haciendas* of colonial times to strike out against the estate owners whom, with advantage, they served. Some labour leaders, of course, resolutely refused to work within the established system. Espousing revolutionary ideals, especially those of socialism and anarchism, they sought to dismantle the traditional order. In most countries, however, their influence remained relatively slight and they were eclipsed by those leaders who had been co-opted.

Middle Sectors in a Two-Culture Society   Judged by purely economic criteria, a substantial middle class came into existence in Spanish America during the first half of the twentieth century. But, notwithstanding important divisions and cleavages, the various sectors of the middle class identified by and large with the upper classes (widely referred to, especially by critics, as the *oligarquía*), reflected their values, imitated their customs and patterns of behaviour and looked forward some day to entering their ranks. While they were waiting to enjoy a higher status, they did all in their power to safeguard the perquisites, privileges and immunities of the upper-class world so that its splendours would be undiminished when they finally rose into it. As a result, in spite of the emergence of sectors that on economic grounds have to be denominated middle class, Spanish America remained psychologically and in values and attitudes a two-culture society. For a time, it is true, at a point early in the twentieth century, an assertive bourgeoisie seemed as though it might impose its values throughout society. But when it became apparent that this could lead to a revolutionary situation, the bourgeois elements curbed their efforts to reform the subculture and at the same time reverted to their position as defenders, rather than modifiers, of upper-class life styles and values. Because of the general reluctance of Spanish America's bourgeoisie—at least until some time in the second half of the twentieth century—to regard themselves as members of a permanently distinct class, they are referred to most often in this book as middle sectors rather than as a middle class.

One factor explaining the attitudes of the middle sectors is that historically Spanish America's aristocracy (for the sake of simplicity, albeit at the sacrifice of total accuracy, the term is used synonymously with upper classes) has remained relatively open to new members. Thus it was by no means unrealistic for members of the middle sectors to look forward to climbing into the aristocracy. Throughout the nineteenth and early twentieth centuries many old and established aristocratic landowning families, heavily in debt because of the uneconomic management of their estates, welcomed alliances, often cemented through marriage, with affluent men of urban, industrial and commercial backgrounds. Once they had acquired the social status reserved in the Hispanic world to landownership, the fresh arrivals in upper-class families frequently abandoned their old business pursuits, now considered beneath their dignity, and took to the established aristocracy's uneconomic way of life. As a result, within a generation or two the new aristocrats found themselves in their turn in financial distress that could best be relieved by opening their ranks, again often through marriage, to a new generation of successful bourgeois capitalists.

This ever-recurring process, which had already become firmly established in the seventeenth-century colonial period, contributed significantly to social stability and to the preservation of the two-culture society. At the same time, it drained money from capital-generating urban enterprise and channelled it into largely nonproductive investments. The typical landowner in the Hispanic world regarded his real estate as a badge of social prestige and as a source of money for conspicuous consumption rather than as a means to bring about the growth of capital.

In order that the traditional society should remain secure, it was not enough for men of the middle sectors to cling to the dream of ascent to aristocratic status. They had, in addition, to be given sufficient means to allow them to wait in dignity and also to act, in many respects, as if they had already joined the upper-class world. A dramatic proliferation of the bureaucracy helped to create these conditions. Government salaries, as well as the many opportunities for graft that offered themselves to state functionaries, presented bureaucrats with the financial means to emulate the aristocracy's conspicuous consumption without having to lower themselves to money-grubbing, economically productive occupations.

The effects of an unnecessarily large bureaucracy whose corruption was almost institutionalized militated against economic development, while contributing to social stability. In all of this there was little that was fundamentally new. In the Hispanic world of the sixteenth and seventeenth centuries, in much of the peninsula and in the American colonies, a mushrooming bureaucracy, combined with opportunities for frequent new admissions into the titled and lesser nobility, had served to maintain the established social order. At the same time these circumstances had helped to produce economic stagnation.

Expansion of education further served to buttress the *status quo*. One of the most enduring and consequential effects of the University Reform movement that exploded in 1918 in Córdoba (Argentina), and simultaneously in other parts of Spanish America, was the opening of institutions of higher education to many middle-sector youths who had previously been excluded. Hereafter, more and more men of middle economic status had the chance to attend a university and acquire the law degree that was all important for gaining a post in the government bureaucracy or in other occupations that did not carry the social stigma attached to direct involvement in the primary, productive sector of the economy. Moreover, expansion of educational facilities below the university level, to which many republics devoted considerable expenditure from the beginning of the century onwards, helped to cement the loyalty of the lower classes.

The schools provided in increasing numbers for lower-class children were, of course, staffed by men and women who were products of the dominant culture—largely middle-sector individuals who identified with upper-class values. They knew little if anything of the life and style of the subculture from which the bulk of their students came. Speaking in terms that did not bridge the gulf separating the two cultures, the teachers failed to educate. Consequently a high percentage of children in the elementary public schools failed their courses. If they persevered in the school system, they were likely to repeat the lower two or three grades year after year. Their parents, grateful to the government for having presented them with the novel experience of sending their children to school, attributed the failure of their offspring to natural stupidity—many of the children actually were mentally retarded, not necessarily as a result of genetic factors but because of the high incidence of injuries at birth among the poor, malnutrition, sickness and accidents during the earliest years of life. In this process lower-class parents became all the more resigned to allowing men of presumed intelligence to direct affairs of state.

Richard M. Morse has provided a profound insight into the effects of the middle-sector orientation of the public school curricula in the rural zone of Córdoba, and his analysis may legitimately be extended to cover much of preuniversity public education throughout the rest of Spanish America. As Morse puts it, "The failure of children in school, a most frequent occurrence, [signified] the victory of community integration." In other words, the failed child was drawn back into his own cultural community, becoming thereby more fully than ever integrated into what the present study describes as a subculture.

The Dominant Culture, Industrialization and the Money of Power
The process of upward social mobility which siphoned men out of commerce and industry and projected them into an economically nonproductive realm interfered with the continuity of economic development in Spanish America. Certainly it slowed the rate of industrialization in most of the republics during the period from 1900 to the 1950s. At certain points in the twentieth century, however, when the flow of manufactured goods from the world's economically developed countries was interrupted, the Spanish American republics were forced to introduce massive import substitution programmes. This was particularly so at the time of the First World War, when because of military involvement the leading world powers could no longer supply Spanish America with finished products, and again during the years of the great Depression, when the area was unable to finance the importation of manufactured goods owing to low world prices for its raw products.

During these times of crisis Spanish American governments had to counteract ingrained social prejudices against industrial entrepreneurship and to cajole men with surplus capital into becoming industrialists. In the process, governments resorted to monopolistic concessions, tax exemptions, tariff protection and other privileges and incentives. The resulting industrial élite owed its existence and opportunities for future aggrandizement to government. In a way, the new industrialists were as dependent upon government as the leaders of organized labour. Furthermore, their emergence, like that of labour leaders, did not pose a challenge to the established system of which government was a servant, but instead strengthened that system.

Claudio Véliz, the Chilean historian, has pointed out that in England and much of Western Europe industrialization was the marginal result of a new way of life, a part of a complex cultural whole which included attitudes towards art and literature, education, and also public and private morality. An industrial bourgeoisie identifying with the new cultural values challenged tradition and triumphed. In contrast to the spontaneous, natural process of industrialization in much of the Western world, the unnatural, forced industrialization of Spanish America perpetuated the existing social structure.

Véliz's analysis may be supplemented by that which the Spanish intellectual and statesman Ramiro de Maeztu developed in the *Revista de las Españas* in 1927. Fascinated throughout his life by the differences between Spanish and Anglo-Saxon culture (both his mother and wife were English and he lived for many years in England), Maeztu argued that English-speaking men generally sought the power of money, while, by contrast, in the Hispanic world both Spaniards and Spanish Americans pursued the money of power. By this Maeztu meant that Anglo Saxons were inclined unabashedly to throw themselves into economic enterprise and, having thereby acquired money, to exult in the individual power that it gave them. On the other hand, in the Hispanic world there was a tendency to avoid involvement in direct economic enterprise which, it was believed, dehumanized people and stifled appreciation of higher aesthetic and cultural values. When in quest of money the typical product of Hispanic culture turned to those in power in government and garnered concessions from them that assured economic success without really having to work for it. Such a person was concerned with the money of power.

This approach seems to have been deeply ingrained in Hispanic, especially Castilian, culture. Ideally, according to its standards, money, like happiness, is not to be won in direct pursuit. When it comes, well and good: it is the result of benign providence or of *buena suerte* (good luck). Acquired in this way, money can confer honour and distinction, whereas if it is accumulated through direct pursuit it attests to a person's greed.

In the realm of traditional Castilian values, within which, in spite of frequent protestations to the contrary, the New World's Spanish-speaking republics largely continue to function, the prosperous capitalist feels constrained to apologize for his success. He can do so by attempting to demonstrate that his wealth came not from seeking it directly in demeaning economic enterprise but instead was the product of good fortune. The corrupt bureaucrat can acquire a fortune in dignity by using the power of his office, asking all to believe that his financial success is the result of fortuitous circumstances, not of personal acquisitiveness. The prosperous industrialist whose wealth depends on favours from those in power rather than on direct and avaricious pursuit of money can also justify his affluence on the grounds that it is all simply a matter of luck that is very surprising to him. In the Anglo-Saxon world, on the other hand, the capitalist who amasses a fortune through his connections with the wielders of political power tries to mask the fact and to pretend that his success resulted from indefatigable enterprise in the conscious quest of money.

Possession of capital is of course vitally important to members of the dominant culture in Spanish America. Capital provides them with the economic basis for independence, for the individualism and self-reliance that are badges of gentlemanly status. Beyond this, capital is essential if one is to seek fulfilment in the world of aesthetic pleasure and artistic creativity. It is indispensable, moreover, if a man is to prove he is not covetous by indulging in conspicuous consumption, lavish display and all the various acts of prodigality which within the Hispanic culture have traditionally been taken as signs of virtue.

Once the bourgeois assertiveness of the turn of the century had been bridled, Spanish American governments succeeded remarkably in providing men of the dominant culture, whether they were of true upper-class status or only psychologically members of the upper class while economically of the middle level, with the sort of world they desired. The rewards of successful capitalists were made available to them without their having to acquire the skills and attitudes commonly considered prerequisite for the creation and accumulation of wealth.

Meanwhile, the masses were pacified by a system of fringe benefits that left them thoroughly dependent upon a *patrón* sector and at the same time economically inefficient and nonproductive. Because the new paternalism saddled government with huge burdens of social expenditure, a considerable price naturally had to be paid for the pacification of the masses.

How could a two-culture society endure economically when its survival seemed to depend upon pampering the semicapitalists of the dominant culture with all the fruits generally reserved for fully fledged capitalists? How could it endure economically when concomitantly its survival seemed to depend upon preventing the masses from acquiring the capitalist mentality and aspiring to become independent by husbanding capital surpluses? For many years foreign capital in Spanish America played an important role, often totally unperceived by foreign capitalists, in preserving a social structure that economically was not viable.

Foreign Capital and the Preservation of the Traditional Society In their endeavour to conserve the sort of social structure inherited from the colonial past, the privileged classes in Spanish America sensed that they could combine their traditional ideals and values with the advantages of foreign capital. Instinctively, they rejected the validity of the dichotomy presented by Ramón Valle-Inclán in his novel *Tirano Banderas,* published in 1922. In this work the distinguished Spanish writer sketched a scene in which a member of the Spanish colony in a mythical Spanish American country conversed with a United States businessman. The Spaniard insisted that the ruling classes realized that in order to avoid social upheaval they had "to turn their eyes once more towards the *madre patria*" and steep themselves in its social, economic and ethical values and traditions. With considerable scorn the Yankee businessman replied: "If the *criollo* [white, Spanish-origin] elements survive as the directing classes it will be owing to the ships and cannons of North America."

Whether by intuition or conscious rational analysis, Spanish Americans understood that preservation of their social system required both of the elements alluded to by Valle-Inclán. It depended not only upon bolstering the ideals and values of the *madre patria* but also upon the capital and technology of the United States.

To begin with, the social services—by means of which Spanish American governments won the allegiance of the labouring classes, or at least bought their quiescence—had to be financed. As the new paternalism developed and ramified, soaring social overheads seriously reduced the capital that might otherwise have been available for economic development. Had the pressures for investment in economic development not been relieved by foreign capital, Spanish American governments would probably not have been able to fund their social programmes.

For many years, moreover, taxes collected on foreign business allowed the Spanish American élite to remain virtually free from direct taxation; thus the traditions of the colonial period and of preconquest Spain were maintained, according to which freedom from many forms of direct taxation was a perquisite of aristocratic status. The propensity of Latin American governments to compel foreign, especially North American, subsidiaries to pay a disproportionately large share of the area's public revenue—even though the sums initially exacted were relatively modest—is indicated in a study entitled *United States Business Investments in Foreign Countries,* published in 1960 by the United States Department of Commerce. According to this, United States companies, while employing a little over 1 percent of the labour force in Latin America (Brazil included), account for roughly 10 percent of the area's gross national product and pay one-fifth of all taxes and one-third of all direct assessments on income.

The period immediately following the First World War witnessed an enormous increase in the importance of United States capital within the Spanish American economies. It was then that North Americans achieved the long cherished goal of taking over the role originally played by British, and to a lesser extent by German, Italian and French investors and lenders. The extent of United States economic penetration is revealed by statistics.

Between 1919 and 1929, United States investment, direct and indirect, in the five Bolivarian republics (Venezuela, Colombia, Ecuador, Peru and Bolivia) increased from $10 million to $316 million. Between 1920 and 1929, United States direct investment in Chile rose from roughly $200 million to $592 million. Furthermore, in the 1920s, when many Spanish American republics were setting up the machinery of the new paternalism; foreign loans were in abundant supply. In Peru, for example, foreign indebtedness soared from approximately $10 million to $100 million between 1918 and 1929, and most of the foreign loans were obtained from international banking firms incorporated in the United States.

Foreign loans, foreign investment and taxation of foreign business, as well as deficit financing, enabled the Spanish American governing classes to avoid social upheaval while maintaining the traditional ideals bequeathed by the *madre patria*. In order to remain loyal to these ideals, however, the élite had to accept dependence on the capital and technological expertise of the United States.

The result was that Spanish America's dominant culture, while continuing to be dominant *vis-à-vis* the subculture, became in turn a subculture in relation to United States and other foreign capitalists. Within the Spanish American republics the subculture is characterized by a mentality of dependence, by a tendency to live in the present and to avoid preoccupation with accumulating capital to provide for the future; its members are confident that the *patrón*, private or public, will always supply what is required to maintain security in the customary way of life. In its relations to the world of foreign capital, the internally dominant culture of Spanish America showed the same traits. Its members accepted a role of dependence, and in so doing took on the psychological traits that characterize that role. Paradoxically, however, their dependence makes them more vulnerable than the domestic subculture within their countries. When dealing with the subcultures of their own countries, the upper classes of Spanish America are under greater compulsion to be paternalistic than are foreign capitalists in their dealings with the Spanish Americans who are dependent upon them.

Economists and historians may never be able to resolve whether or not the effects of foreign capitalism have been to drain off Spanish America's economic resources without adequate compensation. Many, however, would agree that it has had a draining effect morally, by undermining the character of Spanish America's directing classes. This view, of course, implies a negative appraisal of the traditional values of the Hispanic world. The élites of Spanish America, on the other hand, find no difficulty in justifying their dependence on foreign capital. They use similar arguments to justify their dependence on the labour of serfs and peons. Like the native lower classes, foreign capitalists are regarded as incapable of adding to humanity's cultural treasure. Hence, it is considered a natural division of talent for a dominant culture to accept dependence on the manual labour of a subculture and on the capital of foreigners in order to liberate its members from material care and enable them to enrich the realm of the mind and spirit.

Dependence can thus be seen as strengthening rather than draining the character of the Spanish American élite, and there is no doubt that foreign capital, however unwittingly, has made a vital contribution to the preservation of Spanish America's two-culture society. Critics of the traditional society argue endlessly over who bears the major share of responsibility for its perpetuation: the foreign capitalists or the natives who have been willing to become dependent upon them. In either case, it is virtually certain that both foreign capitalists and the dominant Spanish American élite, because of their symbiotic relationship, will receive little mercy at the hands of revolutionary groups seeking to destroy the traditional social relationships.

Even without major revolutionary upheavals, a deterioration in the customary relationship between foreign capital and Spanish Americans seems likely to occur, if historical experience is any guide. In colonial times and in the period immediately following independence, the main source of monetary loans to a noneconomic upper class was the Catholic Church, an institution which, in spite of its frequent denunciations of capitalist values, ran some of the most successful economic operations in Spanish America. The indebtedness of the Spanish American upper classes to the Church was endemic, but eventually they repudiated their debts and in many republics confiscated the properties and capital wealth of the Church and sought to curtail or eliminate its remaining power and temporal influence. It is hardly likely that those who replaced the Church as the principal suppliers of capital to noneconomic, semicapitalist groups will escape a similar fate.

Such conclusions can obviously only be conjectural. On the other hand, historical evidence shows clearly the tenacity of the traditional institutions and social forms. Their preservation has been achieved in different ways in the different Spanish American republics, but it is a basic fact in the contemporary situation. Even in Mexico and Bolivia, countries which experienced successful social revolutions, the traditional two-culture society has largely been restored. Elsewhere, only since the 1950s have new challenges become clearly evident. In Cuba under Fidel Castro there emerged for the first time in Spanish American history a society radically different from the traditional one; but it is still not clear whether it will set an example or remain an exception. Developments during the first dozen years following Castro's seizure of power make the second of these possibilities seem the likelier.

Centralism
and Nationalism
in Latin America

Claudio Véliz

For the last century and a half, Latin America has been a faithful echoing chamber for every political noise uttered in the more civilized regions of the northern hemisphere. It now appears that this period may be drawing to a close, partly as a result of domestic developments, and partly because the source of models deemed worthy of imitation is drying up. This is not the end of ideology, but it certainly suggests that the era in which Latin America accepted blindly the political experiences, aspirations and recommendations issuing from the shores of the North Atlantic is coming to an end.

Practically every major political ideology which found a sympathetic echo in Latin America during the last hundred years was produced by the impact of the Industrial Revolution upon a European social structure which in turn was fundamentally modified by historical events like Feudalism and the Reformation that had no counterpart in the Luso-Hispanic tradition. Thus, under different names and guises, conservatism, liberalism, radicalism, communism and social democracy (and its Christian Democratic variant), all with deep European roots, have dominated the political life of this part of the world. Even conservatism, which could perhaps claim to be timeless and pre-industrial, never succeeded in clearing the awesome frontier of 1810; it retained a distinct republican flavor which placed it closer to modern European convervatism than to any irredentist monarchial movement with Hispanic roots.

The European origins of liberalism, radicalism and communism of course need no documentation. The aura of modernity and originality which currently adorns the Christian Democratic and Christian Socialist movements in Latin America is more than faintly similar to that which graced their European precursors, not only in recent times but also when they provided Chancellor Bismarck with some of his livelier political difficulties or when they shattered the com-

Reprinted from *Foreign Affairs,* October 1968. Copyright © by the Council of Foreign Relations, Inc., New York City, New York.

placency of the Bishops' Conference of 1908 at Lambeth.

The modern political arrangements of the so-called Western world—which most certainly includes the Soviet Union—are to an important degree the offspring of the transformations brought about by industry during the nineteenth century. But Latin America has been bypassed by the Industrial Revolution: industry has indeed come to these countries, but without the great changes which attended its earlier appearance on the shores of the North Atlantic. Moreover, the Latin American social structure, which has received the benefits of modern industrial technology, is different in essence from the European one which produced it.

The complex of cultural differences makes it hard if not impossible to establish priorities or hierarchies of significance. Nevertheless, I would like to suggest three fundamental differences which may account for the apparent inability of Latin America at present to provide a fertile soil for European ideological models and which indicate the type of development likely to dominate its domestic and international political life in the near future. The three differences are the absence in Latin America's historical experience of feudalism, of religious nonconformity and of industrial development which is individually initiated as opposed to that which is centrally encouraged. Conversely, I would suggest that it is precisely in the vertebral centralism of the Latin American tradition that an explanation of recent developments and perhaps even the key to the political future of the region will most probably be discovered.

2

The feudal experience is not part of the cultural tradition of Latin America. Of course the word has often been used pejoratively to describe the relationship between landlord and peasant in Latin America as elsewhere, but in fact feudalism as a political structure never existed in this part of the world. It is important to realize this, because the balance of power between a weak center and a strong periphery, which was characteristic of feudalism, was evidently a major ingredient of European liberalism and all its social-democratic variants.

In spite of the quaint efforts by Mexican revolutionaries, the founders of APRA and others to establish direct lines of descent from the centuries before the coming of the Spaniards, the fact is that Latin America was born into the modern world during the sixteenth century, at least three hundred years after feudalism had disappeared from Western Europe; its institutional structure was fashioned whole-sale in Madrid by the strongest monarchy in Christendom and on the Renaissance model of a centrally controlled polity. It hardly needs pointing out that Columbus discovered the New World pre-cisely the year that the last Moorish stronghold of Granada was taken by the Spaniards, bringing to an end a military campaign which had lasted, with varying intensity, for seven centuries. The victorious Catholic kings ruled unchallenged and the faint attempts by regional military orders or aspiring warlords to contest their authority are of no more than anecdotal value. A full generation before Henry VIII started his quarrels with the Vatican, Ferdinand of Aragon secured from Pope Julius II the famous bull *Universalis ecclesiae regimini* which, together with earlier generosities of Rome, laid the legal basis for the absolute power, temporal and ecclesias-tical, which the Spanish rulers were to exercise with considerable efficiency over their vast American territories.

The institutional structure devised for the Indies naturally re-flected this unqualified centralism, and no effort was spared to en-sure that distance would not facilitate the development of peripheral sites of political power; even to fill a minor post at the Viceroyalty of Peru, consultation with Spain was required, and whoever attempted to depart from the strictest reading of the colonial legislation was punished with severity. Even the most exalted colonial rulers had at the end of their mandate to make the lengthy voyage to Spain to sit at the dreaded *juicio de residencia*. Madrid's power gave muscle to the longest administrative arms in Christendom.

This system survived for three centuries and when it finally col-lapsed, its legalistic, centralist and authoritarian tradition passed on undiminished to the republican régimes, which had the advantage of shorter lines of communication. It must be remembered that the revolutions of 1810 were not popular uprisings but rather indepen-dence movements after the fashion of the one led by Mr. Ian Smith for a time in Rhodesia.

The institutional habit of compromise between alternative centers of political power is not, then, part of the Latin American tradition. The feudal experience of northern Europe, where the central mon-archy had to negotiate with a number of lesser centers of power, is simply not known in this part of the world. Here the center has never been decisively challenged and even its major revolutionary experi-ence—that of 1810—was initiated in the name of legitimacy and against the French, who by then represented egalitarianism.

Political centralism remained virtually unassailed during the nineteenth century. No doubt instances can be found of uprisings by local chieftains but, apart from the fact that these were generally unsuccessful, close examination will show that even the most outspoken regional *caciques* were often feeding on the crumbs of political power which fell from the table of the central government.

The centralism of the past four centuries has survived well into our times. The three major modern revolutions in Latin America—perhaps the only real ones—have reconstructed society according to strikingly different ideas, yet they have all resulted in single-party systems: the Mexican PRI is unique in the ramifications of its centralist control; the Cuban government party, I would suggest, rules from an authoritarian center because it is Cuban rather than because it is communist; and the Bolivian MNR, although eventually unsuccessful, made a determined attempt to monopolize political power and was later replaced by another régime at least as centralist. The trend that can be perceived in other countries—without considering the outright tyrannies—is clearly toward the establishment of a dominant political party identified with the government. This is seen even in the most sophisticated and democratic states in the region.

The weight of this historical tradition has lately been reinforced by the well-nigh universal trend toward increased participation or intervention by the central government in all aspects of national life. While in, say, Britain, the United States or Sweden, this trend clashes with the prevailing pluralistic and generally liberal concept of political responsibility, in Latin America it reinforces the existing drive for greater central control.

If political centralism has worn well over the last few centuries, the same can also be said of the Catholic Church. It is a moot point whether nonconformity is, or is not, a basic ingredient of European liberalism, but it is difficult to imagine political liberalism in Britain, France or the United States, for instance, without a concomitant attitude in matters of religion. In Latin America the problem would hardly arise: there has never been anything which could reasonably be equated with nonconformity; the religious authority of the Catholic Church has never been challenged from within. No doubt priests have been shot, churches burned and anticlericalism has become an established political and social attitude, but the spiritual authority of the Catholic Establishment remains untouched. Even in a country like Mexico, where from Juárez to Zapata the major revolutionary movements have been staunchly anticlerical and where it is easier to sustain normal diplomatic relations with Cuba than with the Vatican, the Catholic Church remains the only significant national religion.

There is, of course, ample evidence of dissent within the Catholic Church in Latin America today, but this stems from anxiety over social and political issues, not over the fundamental religious tenets of official Catholicism. The inroads of Protestantism are also not to be minimized, but so far, even in Chile, where they have been most noticeable, less than 10 percent of the population is registered as belonging to the numerous Protestant sects.

In Europe and North America it was but a short step from religious dissent to political dissent; it does not take exceptional scholarship to trace the nonconformist ancestry of many of the most active reformist parties.

3

As might be expected, political and religious centralism was accompanied by economic centralism, which is not only the product of a long Hispanic tradition but also the result of the way in which industry came to this part of the world. In Europe, industrial activity arose out of a complex cultural situation which resulted in the conscious accumulation of industrial capital over a long period of time. This process owed little or nothing to the intervention of the central government and it led to a dispersion of power. That the central state later came to represent these industrial interests is beside the point; for it to happen, the new industrialists had to challenge the traditional ruling groups and wrest power from them.

Further, the growth of industry ran almost parallel with the growth of cities, and urbanization was a consequence of industrial activity. Industry then was labor intensive and for it to function efficiently a sizeable labor force had to be organized in urban centers. As a result the workers acquired a new political consciousness. Thus it can be said that the impact of industry on traditional European society was revolutionary at least in that it was spearheaded by a newly formed industrial bourgeoisie and it resulted in the formation of a new industrial proletariat.

None of these considerations would seem to apply to the industrialization of Latin America. Here industry has been stimulated largely by external factors such as the great crisis of 1929 (principally affecting Brazil) and the Second World War, which began the process of import substitution. It owed relatively little to domestic determinants. And urbanization in Latin America did not wait for industrialization, which was instead grafted onto a sophisticated, self-conscious, relatively urbanized society. A remarkably large proportion of the population was already living in cities for reasons other than the development of industry. More important perhaps, industrialization owed a very great deal to the direct intervention of the central state—through tariff protection, subsidies, credit policies or straightforward programs of industrial development carried out directly under the aegis of public development corporations. Lastly, the social changes generally associated with industrialization have not occurred in Latin America; there have been many changes but not the ones that scholars and politicians were prepared for.

Latin America has industrialized rapidly, but this has not been the result of the exertions of an industrial bourgeoisie; nor has it produced an industrial proletariat. In the 1870s, Britain was the first industrial power on earth and was producing her first million tons of steel. To achieve this, over 370,000 workers were employed. In Latin America today, Argentina, Brazil and Mexico are well over the million-ton mark (Brazil is moving close to four million tons per year) and a rough estimate shows that only seven or eight thousand workers are needed to produce each million tons of steel. Peru is the first fishing nation on earth, but the total labor force engaged in the fisheries and processing plants does not exceed thirty thousand men. Such examples abound and they all point to a fairly obvious development: industrial technology has changed; it is now more capital than labor intensive. The industrial labor force in Latin America is not the modern equivalent of the traditional proletariat. Working with an advanced industrial technology, it is smaller, better trained and better paid. It is in fact an aristocracy of labor with incomes which all too often rise above those of vast numbers of white collar workers in the tertiary sector.

As the capacity of industry to absorb large numbers of workers is limited, the massive transformation of peasants into industrial workers has not come to pass. With luck, the average migrant to the cities will find employment in the building industry, but more often than not he will somehow drift into the service sector, which is by far the best organized as well as the most politically active. The coming of industry resulted in a sharp decrease of self-employed artisans and craftsmen and a spectacular rise in the number of people in service occupations, but this increase was only the continuation of a process that had been going on for well over a century. These professionals, white collar employees, bureaucrats and domestic and service workers are not the Latin American equivalent of, say, the rising English middle class of 1832; for the most part they are directly or indirectly associated with, or dependent upon, either the central government or the traditional social structure. Few are involved in industry, and their political activities have been directed principally toward securing greater participation in the existing social organization rather than in seeking to demolish it and replace it with another.

The pre-industrial urbanization of Latin America is a significant phenomenon in its own right; its intensification during the last three decades has resulted in the steady depopulation of an already sparsely settled countryside. At present Latin America has a greater proportion of its urban inhabitants living in cities of 100,000 or more than does Europe; in Argentina, Cuba, Chile, Uruguay and Venezuela the proportion of the population that is urban is well over 40 percent. It is neither the "landless peasant" nor the "exploited" industrial worker who epitomizes the politically significant Latin American; it rather the underpaid bank clerk with social aspirations.

As for the Latin American equivalent of the traditional industrial bourgeoisie—forward-looking, adventurous, willing to take risks, ready to innovate, anti-aristocratic and reformist—it simply does not exist. The force for dynamic change has been the central government. Domestic private enterprise has seldom performed with distinction except when instigated and assisted by the government. If all state subsidies and financial commitments were to be withdrawn from private industry, precious little would remain in operation. This has come about partly by default; the so-called industrial bourgeoisie and their clientele have been agile opportunists and mediocre imitators rather than adventurous challengers or originators of new ideas. With remarkably few exceptions—mostly foreign immigrants—they owe their newly achieved economic prosperity more to their social or political proximity to the government cornucopia in the years between 1940 and 1960 than to any impressive exertions on their own part.

For them, industry is just one of many ways of making money: they own industrial capital, they often have a controlling interest, but they are not industrialists in the meaningful sense of the word. More often than not they are prepared to exchange the risks inherent in effective responsibility for an agreement with a foreign company which will guarantee royalties, expert advice and a numbered bank account in Europe. Their docility has prevented them from becoming an effective pressure group except in a negative sense. This is shown, for instance, in the opposition of Ecuadorian and Venezuelan businessmen to plans for regional integration. There is in Latin America no counterpart to European industrial liberalism.

In Europe and the United States it was the dynamic industrial groups that for various reasons became the mainstay—both political and economic—of a development policy aimed at the satisfaction of national aspirations; in Latin America, however, the owners of industry are largely responsible for increasing our external dependence. They have not been innovators, nor have they challenged the established social order or provided political alternatives. Instead they have fallen with remarkable ease into the patterns of imitation and emulation characteristic of social climbing. In fact, it would not be surprising if their major contribution to the contemporary life of

Latin America turns out to be the efficient institutionalization of this process; far from weakening the traditional structure, they have become its most loyal and enthusiastic upholders.

In summary, then, there appears to be no substantial evidence indicating that the tradition of centralism characteristic of Latin American culture is in any significant way being challenged from within. Furthermore, the pressure groups which in Europe and the United States played such an important role in forcing through the changes demanded by the incorporation of industrial technology are either not fitted or not prepared to play a comparable role in Latin America. What sector of society, then, is likely to fulfill this function in the future?

4

Marx and Lenin have not been the only ones to accept the notion that the state is an instrument, a tool to be used by one group or another to defend its own interests. This concept of the state has figured prominently in the historical tradition of Western Europe (though perhaps more significantly in Britain and the United States). From it derives the conceptual framework which informs much of contemporary sociological and historical analysis—including the study of Latin America. Learned northern observers of the Latin American situation have thus spent much time identifying the pressure groups which are expected to be vying with each other for the control of that supposedly inert instrument, the central state. In their writings, various groups are favored as most likely to assume the leadership of the process that is vaguely described as modernization. Some place their bets on the rising urban bourgeoisie; others hope or fear that the peasantry will march on the cities and transform everything; others are impressed by the vociferous political activity of the students; while others still stress the reformist aspirations of the Nasserist groups in the armed forces.

This type of analysis does not seem to me helpful, largely because it starts from the mistaken premise that the central government in Latin America is at least as instrumental as that typical of the European tradition and as likely to respond to the pressures, civilized or not, coming from more or less powerful groups. In Latin America the central government itself is the most powerful pressure group. It extends its power and influence through a highly centralized civil service and through complex and all-embracing systems of social security and patronage which have transformed most of the vast urban service sector into an institutionalized clientele; it controls the major centers of learning and is capable of exercising almost unrestricted control over economic life. The only institutions which could perhaps be regarded as likely rivals, because of their relatively self-contained nature, are the Church and the armed forces, but in either case the rivalry would not be counterbalancing or pluralistic; rather it would tend to emphasize the central and national responsibilities of the government. Whenever pressures from these two sectors are exerted, they encourage the state to exercise still more all-embracing power from the center.

If this powerful and self-conscious pressure group did not earlier exert its potential force to the fullest, it was because the domestic and international conditions prevailing during the hundred years which preceded 1929 were such as to discourage or at least make unnecessary an activist role for the state. Conflicting interests were few. The ruling groups of the time enjoyed a more than reasonable degree of prosperity; those influential in forming political and intellectual attitudes were clearly identified with European liberalism, while the expansion of world trade and a growing demand for the primary commodities of Latin America tended to make acceptance of the tenets of laissez faire financially profitable as well as socially and intellectually agreeable.

It was not external pressures, therefore, which forced the state to accept an apparently passive role, but rather a decision made for reasons of expediency. It is worthwhile remembering that the same uncritical admiration of everything European which contributed to making Manchester liberalism so attractive to the exporters of mineral and agricultural products also eased the introduction into Latin America of English fashions, German militarism and French positivism, European tastes and methods of education. Sarmiento was not alone in thinking that for Latin America to become truly civilized, it had to become European.

The crisis of 1929 and the Second World War marked the end of the lengthy period of prosperity based on the export of commodities. It also established the conditions for the massive introduction of industrial technology, if only through the doubtful channels of indiscriminate import substitution. Yet the full political impact of the ensuing changes was postponed as a result of circumstances imposed by the Second World War and the pressures of the cold war.

Apart from other important considerations, the Second World War introduced a virtual moratorium on political development in Latin America. With the world divided into warring factions and the countries of the region more or less in the Allied camp, traditional alignments were redrawn to fit external demands. Even the communist parties and their close associates of the time postponed their

struggles against capitalism and loyally collaborated in the efforts
to keep the Allies well supplied with raw materials. The hope was
also widely entertained that the end of the conflict would bring, as a
well-earned reward, a veritable flood of assistance, which would in
some undefined way bring back the plentiful days of the past.

Although the nationalistic movements in Latin America had little
or nothing in common with Germany save a shared suspicion of the
United States or Britain, they were often sympathetic to the Axis,
and it required considerable coaxing before they declared for the
Allies. It would be facile and mistaken to think that Villarroel in
Bolivia, Ibañez in Chile, Vargas in Brazil, Perón in Argentina,
Arnulfo Arias in Panama and so many others were simply stooges
of an international Nazi conspiracy. It would be closer to the truth
to say that these various nationalist movements were essentially
domestic and reflected the basic aspirations or dissatisfactions of
important urban sectors. The issue of the Canal Zone was foremost
in the minds of those who supported Arnulfo Arias at that time;
economic imperialism and the Falkland Islands were ever present
in Perón's oratory; Villarroel came to power as a result of the frustrations of the Chaco War but also on the assurance that Bolivia
would not remain forever a colonial appendage of the tin industry;
Vargas represented the drive toward industrialization and economic
autonomy. These movements, under whatever name, represented a
nationalist alternative to the traditional programs presented by the
established parties of Right and Left. At their most successful, they
provided the basis for what in the postwar period has generally been
described as Latin American populism—perhaps the most revealing
portent of the political future of the region.

The widespread feeling that rampant nationalism was the ultimate
cause of World War II tended to make the domestic nationalist
movements in Latin America appear like the villains of a new black
legend. Internationalism became the new religion and international
cooperation the accepted morality. But with the slaughter and destruction of the war still fresh in mind, a weary world plunged into
yet another total struggle. Mr. Truman's doctrinal declaration di-
viding the world into two oddly defined camps presented Latin
America with a formidable false dilemma. It was clear that Mr.
Truman had not really meant each country to choose between democracy and tyranny; there were enough despotic régimes on the side
of the angels to make this a doubtful proposition. On the other hand
it was apparent even then—and it has since become obvious—that
the communist parties in the Latin American countries had no intention of leading revolutionary movements to overthrow their respective governments. In this respect they reflected the pragmatic attitude of the Soviet Union, which accepted Latin America's being

within the sphere of influence of the United States. Yet the urgencies of the international situation forced a decision, and anti-communism was raised to the status of dogma by able politicians; although these men were well aware that the local communists did not constitute a serious threat, they kept their eyes fixed on the flow of aid which was invariably directed toward those countries whose loyalty to the Western world was beyond dispute.[1]

In the anxiety of the Soviet Union and the United States to marshal their allies into supranational political and military arrangements, the Organization of American States was created. The OAS, which became the Latin American branch of the cold-war policy of the United States, can validly claim to be one of the least impressive of the many postwar pacts. For a time internationalism apparently was defined in Washington and Moscow as a willingness to accept the validity of these arrangements, and the good favor of the superpowers depended on the degree of zeal with which these treaty organizations were supported. But to those Latin Americans who were not absolutely committed, the cold war was less an ideological confrontation than a struggle between two obsessively nationalistic powers intent on defending or extending their respective spheres of influence. Neither was seen as a particularly attractive model and neither received more than tepid gestures of popular support—except from the notoriously servile tyrannies.

Yet a most important consequence of the coming of the cold war to Latin America was the emphasis it placed on the dependent nature of both domestic and international political life. Political activity became largely subordinated to the vagaries of the great world confrontation; neutralism was unacceptable and nationalism severely frowned upon, while friendly internationalism was most definitely encouraged. Any reformist program, any criticism of the United States, however justified, any attempt to steer an independent policy became suspect, and more often than not was publicly tinged in deepest red. It finally required an initiative by the United States to make agrarian, fiscal and administrative reform respectable political aspirations.

5

The feeling of utter dependence has grown deep roots during the years of the cold war. But as the confrontation becomes attenuated by the challenge of France and China to the leadership of the United States and the Soviet Union, by the growth of polycentrism

on both sides of the Iron Curtain and by a measure of détente between the two great powers, a resurgence of nationalism is apparent
in Latin America. "A plague on both your houses" is becoming a
common attitude; as the tide of cold-war loyalties recedes, Latin
Americans are becoming increasingly conscious of national aspirations submerged for too long.

The time may now be ripe for the centralist state to come into its
own, fired with a new nationalism fed on an awareness that the increasing cultural and economic dependence of the region is one of
its principal problems. Had circumstances even faintly similar to the
present ones occurred, say, half a century ago, a fashionable European ideology would no doubt have been promptly imported by the
latest batch of Latin American intellectuals returning home from
their grand tour. Today this is no longer possible, partly because the
mood is emphatically nationalistic and partly because the prevailing
feeling is that the northern hemisphere has precious little guidance
to offer: the United States and the Soviet Union are living through
critical times themselves and have abandoned much of their ideological fervor in order to adopt pragmatic and short-term solutions.
Even those who until recently were willing to grant the benefit of the
doubt to some tired old horses—e.g., socialism, capitalism and their
variants—are now conscious that their application to Latin America
is at least questionable. Indeed, Latin America may for the first time
in its history become an exporter of political symbols and ideas. This
is suggested by the enthusiastic adoption of Ché Guevara by students in Europe and the United States, while here his political appeal
is largely restricted to a genuine admiration for his integrity and
heroism.

In the absence of a more elaborate framework within which to fit
political action, men tend to fall back on elemental loyalties—tribe,
family or, as in Latin America today, straightforward nationalism.
Besides being undemanding intellectually, nationalism draws support
from all the people, regardless of other interests.

A nationalistic ideology can perhaps get us from a confused present to a more satisfactory future, but the risks cannot be ignored.
Nationalism tends to magnify the impact of external factors on domestic situations. Even if it is based on a reasonably civilized understanding of what constitutes the national interest, it courts international friction. In this kind of mood, affecting the major nations of
Latin America simultaneously, rearmament, for example, assumes an
importance which cannot be overlooked.

At the same time it should be emphasized that the major objective
of Latin American nationalism is to reverse the present trend toward
cultural and economic dependence on the United States. This, to be
fair, is apparently also an objective of enlightened U.S. policy, as

shown in numerous official pronouncements calling for a determined effort in Latin America to shoulder a greater part of the burden of its own development. The financial difficulties of the United States may of course make this objective mandatory. At any rate, it must be remembered that independent behavior in nations, as in human beings, cannot easily be confined to some things, excluding others. If the countries of Latin America are to act with greater independence in the planning and implementation of truly national development policies, it should not surprise anybody if they become independent in foreign policy and other fields as well. The military, for example, which until recently have been the most loyal allies of the United States, are now beginning to see the penetration and interference of the great northern power in the same light in which they formerly viewed communism—as an international threat to national sovereignty and integrity. Their indignant reaction to the efforts of the United States to stem their growing purchases of armaments is a significant example of the new attitude.

Although the numerous Latin American student movements operate from strikingly varied backgrounds, under various political auspices and with very varied purposes, they do seem to share a preoccupation with the need to encourage national research and scholarship as a means to escape the cultural penetration of the United States. These students are not necessarily militants of extreme left-wing parties; more often than is realized they are politically non-aligned or represent middle-of-the-road political movements. They themselves, of course, come predominantly from the middle and upper classes of society.

There is a widespread feeling, especially in the academic community, that Latin American integration is in difficulties partly because it is too closely associated with the United States. One of the informal conclusions of a major conference which met earlier this year [1968] in Chile to examine the problems of integration was that what was needed was a truly American process of integration instead of the present Inter-American scheme which allows the United States to play too important a role.

Until a few months ago there were three principal organizations interested in the process of integration: the Latin American Free Trade Association (LAFTA), the Inter-American Development Bank and the Inter-American Committee of the Alliance for Progress. Of these, the last two are based in Washington and depend on the financial support of the United States; LAFTA is strictly a Latin American organization but also the least successful so far. This anomalous situation has not gone unnoticed, and it may be that the move to create truly Latin American sub-regional organizations like the Andean Group or the Plata Basin Group is at least indirectly a consequence of this awareness.

Amidst the debris left behind by the quiet failure of the Alliance for Progress will be found a number of social-democratic movements which feel—with or without justification—that the United States did less than it could have done to assist their reformist efforts, after giving them decisive early encouragement. Their frustration is minimal, however, compared with that of the right-wing parties, which feel that after decades of giving their loyal support to every political move made by the United States and facing the domestic onslaught of the left-wing opposition to such unpopular policies as the overthrow of the Arbenz régime in Guatemala or the Bay of Pigs invasion, the Kennedy Administration stabbed them in the back by putting forward a program like the Alliance for Progress, whose principal objective was precisely to undermine the very basis of their economic and political position.

Such examples could be multiplied. The important fact is that the growing isolation of the United States in the world, whatever its causes, is now being reflected in Latin America. It is not easy to find a significant political group or sector of society willing to stand up and be counted on the side of the great northern neighbor.

Given these indicators and the concomitant resurgence of nationalism in Latin America, it is likely that relations with the United States will become difficult in the future. Moreover, the challenge to U.S. hegemony will probably come not from the extreme left wing but rather from the state itself, supported by sizeable sectors of the urban population. The United States is likely to be more vulnerable to this type of confrontation than is usually imagined. Seen from Latin America, it will resemble the fortress of Singapore on the eve of the Japanese invasion: all guns facing the sea but virtually defenseless against a land attack.

However important the negative dynamism generated by aggressive independence of the United States, I would suggest that this is not the principal feature of contemporary Latin American nationalism. Rather it is the return to a style of political behavior firmly rooted in an autocthonous centralist tradition. On this tradition is founded the structure of institutions and political habits of Latin Americans; on it, as well, are based the organizational successes of the past decades. Latin Americans are increasingly conscious that in harnessing the momentum of this tradition to the needs of national development they will acquire understanding and mastery of the problems of their nations.

Although this novel process of self-discovery is scarcely a few years old it has already offered promising first results in various fields. The original, successful and growing participation of the central government in the Mexican economy; the plans for public multinational corporations which will operate within the sub-regional schemes; the remarkable history of growth and consolidation of the enterprises fathered by the Chilean Development Corporation—all afford evidence of the vitality of this trend. At the same time, the writings of historians, economists and political analysts reflect both a generalized dissatisfaction with foreign imitation and an endeavor to create a new political architecture, using the materials at hand instead of importing them ready-made from elsewhere.

Latin America has been prodigal in the arts and letters—perhaps the world's best contemporary novels have been written during the past decade by Colombians, Peruvians and Argentines—but it has not distinguished itself in the field of political and social ideas. It is not unduly optimistic to think that this is due at least in part to the diligence with which its intelligentsia has in the past looked to the northern hemisphere not only for political answers but for the questions as well. It would be surprising indeed if a reversal of this trend does not prove extremely rewarding.

Note

1. "In other parts of the world it may be merely ridiculous to claim that the communists are not revolutionaries, but in Latin America it is a fact that the communist movement has no vigorous revolutionary tradition. There is probably no conservative or liberal party in all of Latin America that has not staged more insurrections and incited more civil wars than the communists. In a continent racked by civil strife the communists' record has been one of remarkable quiescence. Their one major attempt to seize power by force was the 1935 insurrection led by Luiz Carlos Prestes in Brazil, apart from which there have been only some instances of communist participation in risings by noncommunist groups." Ernst Halperin, *Nationalism and Communism in Chile* (Cambridge, Mass.: Massachusetts Institute of Technology, 1965), p. 13.

The United States and the Andean Republics: Perspectives of Cultural Contrasts

Fredrick B. Pike

1. Introduction: Capitalism, Socialism, Corporatism

Shaped by reinforcing Hispanic and Indian influences, Andean society continues to this day to function in a manner calculated to blunt the individual egotisms of a great majority of the populace. Crucially important in accomplishing this objective are networks of intermediate groups. Encapsulated within these groups, constantly seeking peer-group reinforcement and ever sensitive to peer displeasure, the individual develops basic attitudes of dependence and deference. Generally, the closer to the bottom of the social pyramid the individual is, the more pronounced are the dependence-deference characteristics. Moreover, these characteristics are manifested not only in relationships with the group to which the person is most intimately tied, be it functional, local, or regional, but also in relationships with more powerful personages located at higher levels within the vertically structured society. Having learned to subordinate private desires to group pressures, individuals are predisposed to sacrifice self-reliance in any number of interpersonal associations. Above all, they are predisposed to expect the allocation of goods and services by power domains lying beyond their control.

Such, at least, has been the great idol of Andean elites from preconquest times up to the present. Like any great ideal, this one has at best been no more than approximated in reality. But the hard facts of reality have never dimmed the appeal of the ideal; and except for several brief moments in the nineteenth and twentieth centuries when a few Andean leaders were beguiled by the rival charms of liberalism, elites have clung to their traditional ideal, no matter how sorely divided on other issues. Nor have nonelites waged any consistent challenge to this ideal. In their moments of protest it has not been the ideal to which they object. Rather, they have protested the failure of the system as currently functioning to bestow security in exchange for dependence and deference.

From Fredrick Pike, *The United States and the Andean Republics* (Cambridge: Harvard University Press, 1977). Copyright © 1977 by the President and Fellows of Harvard College. Reprinted by permission.

The term corporativism is used in this study to designate the type of social-political structure prevalent in and apparently natural to Andean America. Many North Americans might prefer to use the implicitly pejorative terms primitive and premodern. In twentieth-century Andean countries, however, political leaders from virtually all positions on the ideological spectrum are convinced that the corporative society offers the best means for attaining modernity—without sacrificing the stabilizing and disciplining mechanisms of the traditional order.

Bolivia embarked on its version of a twentieth-century modernizing, corporativist revolution in 1952, after having flirted, along with Ecuador, with a similar transformation in the 1930s. Then in 1968 Peru began its widely publicized revolution under the direction of the military. In all these instances, corporativist movements of national regeneration were justified ideologically on the grounds that they offered the best means for combining the most desirable features of premodern and modern life, while avoiding the undesirable aspects of socialism on one hand and capitalism on the other.

As 1976 drew to a close, Andean corporativism was functioning poorly, particularly in Peru, the country that had been the most aggressive in attempting to adapt the system to contemporary needs. At the end of 1976, in fact, the prospects for Peru's revolutionary corporativism seemed decidedly dimmer than when the year began and when this manuscript was completed. It is possible that by the time this study appears in print the death knell for the most recent specimen of Peruvian corporativism will have sounded. It is further possible that the demise of revolutionary, military corporativism will have been hastened by the dictates of international bankers under circumstances suggesting that dependence on private capitalists may be more onerous than traditional dependence on the State Department and other arms of the United States government. Even if corporativism in its latest guise escapes extinction in Peru and elsewhere in the Andes, it will hardly have contributed to one of its most heralded objectives: attainment of economic, political, and cultural independence.

However dim its immediate prospects, Andean corporativism will survive as a great ideal. It has already assumed mythic qualities that place it in the company of the two other systems whose myths and mystiques also guarantee longevity regardless of the failures of human beings to live in accordance with their respective myths. I refer, of course, to capitalism and socialism.

Capitalism has promised to raise the human condition to almost unimaginable splendors by means that are primarily material and quantifiable—hence its claim to modernity. That it has not yet perfected human existence to a degree even remotely approximating what has been promised does not dismay true believers. They contend that capitalism has not had the chance to show what it can deliver because it has never been properly practiced. Nor have the failures of socialism to achieve development—while at the same time avoiding the alienation assumed to be associated with the capitalist pursuit of progress—caused abandonment of the socialist myth. Socialism's true believers await one more opportunity to apply their belief system, confident that this time the blunders of the past can be avoided. With good reason Robert G. Wesson has given to his recent book on Marxism the subtitle: *The Continuing Success of a Failed Theory.*

Peter Berger, in *The Public Interest* (Summer 1976), attributes the indestructibleness of the socialist myth to its promise to synthesize features of modernity and premodernity. (Neither Berger nor I use the term myth in a pejorative sense or necessarily question the truth content of the visions and ideals of myths.) According to its myth, socialism will bring about development without destroying the sense of community associated with the middle ages and with many primitive societies. Even as it is accomplishing prodigies of progress, socialism allegedly will nourish fraternity, persuading people happily to subordinate their desires to group interests and decisions of national leaders.

Just as much as socialism, corporativism promises to weave the warp of modernity with the woof of traditionalism to produce a new social fabric. And corporativists, at least of the contemporary Andean variety, have at their disposal certain lures denied to socialists. These corporativists promise to weave a cloth ample enough to encompass private capitalists. Thus the bourgeoisie does not experience with Andean corporativism the difficulties they encounter with socialism.

With problems of crime, alcoholism, drug abuse, and family breakup becoming ever more menacing in the United States, the corporativist myth takes on an added attractiveness in the lands to the south. Only corporativism, the believers of the myth profess, will foster the mental-spiritual habits of obedience and abnegation needed to check the excessive concern for individual gratification said to cause social disintegration in capitalist countries. At the same time corporativism will purportedly avoid the complete crushing of the human will presumed to occur in socialist nations. With a common denunciation of many aspects of modernity and a common assurance as to the feasibility of tempering modernity with traditionalism, corporativism and socialism have far more to share than do corporativism and capitalism—a fact that is bound to color Andean attitudes toward the United States.

In yet another significant way corporativism reveals greater affinity to socialism than to capitalism. For capitalists of ideological purity, if any exist, the sole source of political legitimacy must be the ability of the system to get things done, in other words to accomplish material progress. Socialists, however, are able to hedge. They can rest their claims to legitimacy on the ability of the system to get things done and also to preserve for citizens the contentments of social belongingness and group participation within a style of life that does not equate pursuit of happiness with gratification of the acquisitive instincts of possessive individualism. Corporativists also can hedge. Like socialists, they can justify their regime, whenever indices of material development falter, on the grounds that it provides certain essential nonmaterial rewards. It is as difficult to hold such claims up to verification as it was to substantiate the claims of the priestly class in premodern societies that they and their allies of the secular aristocracy were creating circumstances most conducive to the eternal salvation of the masses. What matters is that for decades and centuries the masses believed the priestly assertions, a lesson that has duly impressed modern socialists and corporativists.

In premodern societies with their conditions of physical adversity myths helped make life bearable. And they are just as important in modern times, especially in those areas where adversity stubbornly refuses to yield to the exorcisms of prophets of progress. Corporativists share with socialists a sense of awe before the power of nonmaterial forces and an appreciation of what myths can accomplish in mobilizing those forces in support of a political regime. In this they enjoy a certain advantage over capitalists. Their advantage lies in a broader view of human existence. Their political vision encompasses a world far more vast than the physical features that tend to blind archetype capitalists, inordinately proud of their demythologizing modernity, to all other facets of the human condition.

The tendency of the United States to see in a modern sense contrasts with the Andean habit of seeing in a traditional, medieval manner that takes in the real world of spirit as well as the real world of matter. From the contrast ensues a great deal of the incompatibility between the two regions. Prospects for reducing the incompatibility are slight, precisely because it has been formed by circumstances far more basic than the heedless or vicious acts of individual fools or knaves on either side. But if reduction should occur, it probably will not be because Andeans narrow their vision so as to see in the same way as most North Americans. More likely the day of greater compatibility waits upon the ability of North Americans to broaden their vision of human existence, as indeed they may very well be forced to begin to do in a postmodern era.

2. Cultural Contrasts: The United States and Latin America

Concepts of national character may belong more to the realm of myth than of reality. But people live more by myth than facts. Thus the prevailing conviction that there is a United States national character and

that individualism is—or has been—a principal ingredient deserves careful consideration in any study intended to explain North American relations with other countries, such as those of Andean America, which
have rejected society-wide individualism. In the 1970s, when shortages
of resources and concern about environmental pollution counsel greater
state control over private conduct, individualism is increasingly under
criticism in the United States. No matter: individualism still remains one
of the favorite yardsticks of North Americans for measuring their own
virtue and that of foreign peoples.[1] In fact, even as they become increasingly unattainable, the ideal of individualistic self-determination and the
desire to be masterless grow ever more hallowed.

Individualism and the determination to be masterless have "expressed
the universalism and idealism most characteristic of the [American]
national consciousness."[2] And, far more than in most countries, these
qualities have been nourished from a tender age within the typical family. Erik H. Erikson demonstrates that children in the American family
are brought up to value their freedom of choice, rather than to seek
security and emotional support through dependence on parents. "The
American family . . . tends to guard the right of the individual member
. . . not to be dominated." This type of family situation, Erikson con-
tends, breeds "undogmatic people, ready to drive a bargain and then to
compromise."[3] All of this is associated with the American dream to be
free from subordination and to bargain, as equals, with those whose
authority to command (that is, parents, employers, and so forth) is
calmly accepted in other cultures.

Associated with individualism, from which basically they all derive,
have been such other American characteristics, commented upon by virtually all observers of the national scene, as compulsive competitiveness,
the need for private achievement,[4] and intolerance of economic failure.[5]
Also associated with individualism has been basic suspicion of government, arising from the conviction that individual men in their immediate situations could always act best in their own interests and thereby
best serve the common good.[6] Understandably, the great American
dream has envisioned a final stage of human progress that would be
achieved "in a spontaneously cohesive society of equal individual
rights."[7]

Ironically, it was an Englishman, Herbert Spencer, who was to
provide—especially in his book *Man Versus the State*—one of the most
complete rationales of American individualism and of the paramount
characteristic sired by it, suspicion of the state. Spencer maintained, at
least with regard to the economic phase of social life, that men "have
been blest with an automatic, self-regulating mechanism which operated
so that the pursuit by each individual of his own self-interest and private
ends would result in the greatest possible satisfaction of the wants of all.
All that was necessary was to remove the obstacles to the operation of

this mechanism."[8] Convinced that the state did not have to intervene to assure a harmony that was self-assured, Spencer urged each man to dedicate himself to his own maintenance through his own work, free from "the direction of society in its totality." What is more, he believed that the social regulatory role of the state would grow "narrower and narrower, for it would have no other object than that of keeping individuals from disturbing and harming one another."[9]

The price that Americans have had to pay for their devotion to individualism has been enormous, as a large number of social commentators have recognized. In the quest of individualism Americans have snuffed out the desire for community, "the wish to live in trust and fraternal cooperation with one's fellows." Also sacrificed has been the desire for dependence, "the wish to share responsibility for the control of one's impulses and the direction of one's life."[10] Summarizing the case against the national trait lauded uncritically by most American liberals only a few years ago, Richard N. Goodwin wrote in 1974:

We live under the domination of an individualism whose conquest has been so complete that it has torn the thread of individual life from the fabric of humanity. We have been sundered from the wholes which gave us life.... For the ideology of individualism is so powerful that we still look on bonds as restraints; values as opinions or prejudices; customs as impositions. The remaining structures of shared existence, the restraints which make it possible for people to live with, and through, and not merely alongside one another, are assaulted as unjust restraints on liberty, impediments to the free assertion of self.[11]

Individualism has been pursued also at the cost of self-delusion and hypocrisy. Those who seek escape from the crushing competitiveness of freedom try to mask the fact, for acceptance of dependence on others is regarded somehow as un-American, as unmanly, and today as unwomanly. The psychological strains resulting from not being able to admit openly the need for dependence are enormous.

As much opposed to the individualistic credo as the open acceptance of dependence is the overt attempt to dominate others. Thus the ambition to command and dominate is carefully disguised and even the means used to persuade others must be hidden from the public gaze. North Americans, it has been written, no longer curtail and conceal their sexual urges but instead their "inner drives for power and status. They can never be mentioned or acknowledged without shame or embarrassment. Just as the Christian prohibitions were the source of innumerable hypocrisies about sex and individual conduct, so our new ethic gives rise to endless hypocrisies in politics and social life."[12]

Individualism and Rising Expectations American individualism stems from "strong confidence in self, or reliance upon one's own exertion and resources"; it stems also from belief in "the strife of all our citizens for wealth and distinction *of their own,* and their contempt of reflected honors."[13] Making feasible the competition for distinction of their own and their insistence upon "parity in competition"—which has been the real essence of the American belief in equality,[14] at least until the late 1960s when certain writers began to urge parity of results—has been the great abundance of the United States. This abundance, present in the frontier in the nineteenth century but even more in evidence in the cities which provided greater opportunities for mobility than the wilderness, can be viewed as the true wellspring of United States attitudes.[15] Only unique abundance, combined with a small population, made it possible for persons to compete for ever greater wealth and distinction without destroying all mechanisms of social and political control.

Dealing with these themes, Stuart Bruchey refers to "a quality of alertness to the possibility of material betterment" that either inheres or fails to inhere in a cultural value system. He argues persuasively that that quality "came with the first Americans to these shores, . . . and that with the progressively greater market opportunities provided by both government and private business during the late eighteenth and early nineteenth centuries, it seems increasingly to have permeated the American people."[16]

At the heart of Bruchey's analysis lies the conviction that the United States has fostered a belief in unlimited material progress, both for the individual and the nation. Certainly the belief in progress seemed well justified in the early nineteenth century. Between 1800 and 1840 real per capita domestic product increased about 60 percent.[17] To men of religious fervor, abundance and unparalleled progress indicated that God had singled out the people of the United States: they were his chosen people, destined to effect the sort of temporal progress that would result in the highest degree of human virtue and perfection that mankind could achieve. In short, progress as achieved by the American people would complete the work begun by the Reformation and usher in the millennium. No less a person than John Adams was among those caught up in belief in the providentially ordained role of the United States to bring about the millennium through temporal progress.[18]

To those inspired by this belief, achievement in the City of Man pointed to high rank in the City of God; for material progress automatically brought with it moral progress. From its infancy, then, the United States was acquiring the "spirit of capitalism," that is, a set of attitudes that strongly endorsed "the acquisition of money and the activities involved in it."[19] Earlier societies in their formative periods had tended to regard materialistic, acquisitive instincts as a necessary evil. In contrast, the United States exalted the spirit of capitalism, which accords approbation to acquisitive activities, holding them up as both the result and the source of virtue.

In the United States, persons entertained rising material expectations, initially at least, because fulfillment of such expectations brought them not only comfort and security in this life but constituted in addition an augury of salvation in the next world.[20] Any number of beliefs, values, and prejudices originate in religious convictions, and then are retained long after the religious origins have been forgotten. And so, long after secularism suppressed religiously inspired concern with the millennium, the acquisitive instincts remained, undiminished in strength, to guide America's business society.[21]

Given this background, it is understandable that success in America has been judged not so much in terms of the wealth or position one possesses but rather by what one has gained.[22] The all-important determinant of success is how far one progresses from the starting point. Owing to these values and attitudes, social and political stability has depended upon the ability of a fairly high percentage of people—an ability that is either real or imagined, it doesn't really matter which so far as consequences are concerned—to fulfill their ever-rising expectations.[23]

How is it that the United States has managed in the perception of most citizens, at least in the past, to provide sufficient fulfillment of rising expectations to maintain stability? The question is particularly significant in view of the abundant literature that questions whether there has been any significant redistribution of income at all in the twentieth century.[24] One answer points to the American standard of living, "higher than that of any other country for many generations." This standard of living "has permitted the large majority of the population greatly to improve their living standards from one generation to the next, and has narrowed the gap in consumption standards among the classes,"[25] without occasioning the need for a more equalitarian distribution of income.

Patronalism-Clientalism, Corporativism, and Andean Cultural Patterns The cultural patterns of Andean America have permitted the desire to be masterless to extend only to a tiny segment of the population. Historically, only this minority has exhibited the traits of individualism. In contrast, the vast majority has hoped to attain security through dependence upon some more powerful personage. Those in positions of dependence did not take part in the individualistic pursuit of happiness; rather, they solicited happiness, along with security, from those patrons to whom they acknowledged ties of subordination.

Andean America of the colonial period, and even of the nineteenth and twentieth centuries, affords a classic example of a patronalist-clientelist society. Within this type of society there exists an endless variety of asymmetrical relationships (relationships between nonequals) characterized by the relative power of patron elements on one hand, the deference and dependence of clients on the other. Patrons are those persons who because of their authority, prestige, status, and wealth, or a combination of all these elements, can fulfill their will against the resistance of others. In fulfilling their own will, they can defend not only themselves but also those who are dependent upon them. In contrast, clients are those who, recognizing their inability to shift for themselves, seek out others to provide protection.[26]

The social structure under discussion may be described in terms of a continuum. At one end is the pole of most complete independence and power, and about this pole cluster the tiny minority of individuals who neither defer to nor acknowledge dependence upon any persons more exalted than they. At the opposite extreme of the continuum is the pole of unattenuated dependence, and here are assembled those members of society who rely exclusively on more exalted beings for their security and subsistence and who can claim no clients who are dependent upon them. In between the two poles there stretches an endless number of vertical, asymmetrical relationships involving those who are patrons for certain individuals of lesser status while in turn the clients of persons outranking them in status. In the patronalist-clientelist setting, the status that society ascribes to the individual is determined to some degree by how closely he approaches the patron pole of the continuum, and by the number of clients who acknowledge dependence upon him. In these circumstances, the lust to dominate others, regarded as antisocial behavior in the United States, is the normal determinant of conduct for society's upper sectors.

Patronalist-clientelist ties often are based upon kinship, whether created by blood or by the spiritual bonds of *compadrazgo* or co-parenthood. In many instances those who lack the resources to maintain themselves independently are related by blood to their patrons. In addition, many who feel inadequate to protect their own interests seek out someone more powerful as their *compadre* or co-parent. In the resultant relationship of *compadrazgo* the more powerful person becomes the godfather of the child of the less powerful, and in return for the ties of deference which the child's father assumes toward him, he assumes obligations to protect both the child and the child's father, who has become his *compadre*. This situation is one of "vertical *compadrazgo*," in contrast to the "horizonal *compadrazgo*" that exists when *compadres* are social equals.[27] Through vertical *compadrazgo*, social hierarchy acquires added legitimacy because it is "dressed in spiritual rhetoric and ritual."[28]

For its harmonious functioning, the patronalist-clientelist system requires acceptance by the overwhelming majority of their inability to initiate action on their own and recognition of the need to appeal to patrons to initiate desired actions. Attempts to obtain action, however, are seldom confined to relations between just one patron-client unit. More often than not a patron cannot himself initiate the action desired by his client; instead, he can only appeal to someone more powerful than he, someone who is his patron, to take the desired action. Thus the role of the intermediary, acting as a broker between the more and the less powerful, has been all important and all pervasive in society.

What was true of the temporal order was true also of the relations of humans with God. Only the most audacious mystic could conceive of going directly to God with a request to bring about some desired action on earth. For the vast majority of persons, God could only be approached through the brokerage of saints or of the Virgin. In the process, religious beliefs and practices reinforced the conviction that human beings, on their own, were generally incapable of mastering their destiny. Action was not the result of the individual's willing it or of coalition and alliance among subordinates; instead, it resulted from an appeal to a superior being.

The supernatural reinforcement of the belief that it was necessary to rely on others in seeking the means of survival derived not only from Spanish Catholicism and the place of honor accorded by it to the saints and the Virgin. Reinforcement derived also from preconquest Indian faiths. In Inca times, Indians had recourse to numerous gods from whom they sought the temporal conditions they felt powerless to bring about on their own. In more recent times, an Indian with a problem is likely to seek out a witch because of the latter's presumed power to influence or control supernatural forces.[29]

Acceptance through the years of the patronalist-clientelist society in Andean America has rested in no small part upon the harmony in the relationships between those who dominate and those who are dependent. There has existed, at least as the great social ideal, a give-and-take relationship beneficial both to patrons and clients. Whether animated by considerations of Christian charity, or simply by enlightened self-interest and the desire to preserve social stability, patrons have, in return for their clients' performance of duties to them, assumed with some degree of willingness the burdens of paternalism. Moreover, if clients may occasionally feel frustrated in their dependence upon a patron, they can, in the vast majority of instances, find compensation in the fact that they in turn are patrons over others less powerful than they. Those in society who have absolutely no one to dominate are relatively few. Even those males toward the very bottom of the class structure have, more often than not, a woman whom they expect to command, while the women have children to dominate, and the children often have a dog to dominate and abuse—in vivid contrast to the United States family which is an association of equals and in which the dog is often accepted as a family member almost on a basis of equality.

A basic prerequisite through the years for a harmonious relationship between patrons and clients has been, in addition to paternalism, the universal belief that a state of dependency by no means detracts from human dignity or impedes realization of human potential—a belief that in Andean America goes back even beyond the Spanish colonial period to the great pre-Columbian civilizations. One of the most striking indications of this belief is the prevalence of Marianism (*Marianismo,* or the cult of the Virgin Mary), not only in Andean America but in other parts of Latin America as well. Marianism entails belief in the spiritual superiority of women, specifically upper-class women. To a very considerable degree, Marianism finds its origin in the concept that persons liberated from competitive, individualistic struggle for survival can attain to the highest degree of human perfection. In Andean culture the upper-class woman is expected to accept dependence upon her husband as the family patriarch who must concern himself with providing materially for all its members. Freed from material concerns, the woman can dedicate herself to the life of the spirit, while the husband-patron must allow himself, for the well-being of the family, to be distracted by material pursuits, succumbing inevitably to temptations of improper conduct. Quite possibly it is owing to the superior virtue ascribed to her, in her role of dependence, that the upper-class Latin American woman shows greater acceptance of her role in society than does her United States counterpart.[30]

The role of lower-class women in Andean society, and the role assessment made by their social superiors, is an altogether different matter. Women of lower social circumstances often avoid marriage, recognizing it as more often than not an institution that simply enables men to exploit women while giving little if anything in return; and they are resigned to making their way through their own initiative and competitive hustle. According to the standards that society has set for the poor in general, lower-class women are guilty of deviant behavior because of their individualism. This is one of the reasons they are so often dismissed by respectable society as *sin vergüenzas* (without shame), or shameless hussies.

The poor who accept their dependence on others are regarded by society as virtuous, and from this very fact originates some considerable degree of the self-satisfaction and dignity which can brighten the lives of social underlings. Dependence is widely recognized as conducive to moral progress, and from this stems the belief that poverty, which is always associated with dependence, is one source of virtue in this life and of salvation in the next.

In the cultural setting shaped by United States liberalism, dignity has inevitably been viewed as unattainable by those lacking freedom. Andean Americans, however, see no necessary connection between dignity and freedom. Thus they find it perfectly natural to assume that even in the status of slavery a person was not necessarily altogether deprived of human dignity.

In the antebellum South of the United States, largely unaffected—like

Andean America—by liberalism's view of the human condition, certain defenders of the "peculiar institution" insisted that a social organization of domination and subordination was natural to and inevitable in human existence, and that dependence did not deprive a person of dignity. One of these southerners, Henry Hughes, tried to persuade northern capitalists of the advantages of establishing what amounted to patronalist command domains over their workers in the interest of rationalizing employer-employee relationships. Southerners, of course, failed ignominiously to win northern converts to their belief in the need for a society dichotomized between those who were dominant and those who were subordinate. The spirit of independent, individualistic capitalism in the North, as well as the absence of a large nonwhite labor force, doomed the southern arguments.[31]

The southern slaveocracy desired, in effect, to establish a dual society throughout the United States. Increasingly motivated themselves by an individualistic, bourgeois, capitalist ethic, they hoped to prevent the spread of this ethic among slaves; and they doubted their ability to achieve this purpose unless northern capitalists could also be enlisted in an effort to snuff out individualistic, self-reliant competitiveness among their laboring classes. What the southerners desired was a society based on self-reliance for those at the top, dependence for those below. Northerners did not go along, and they won the Civil War. In Latin America, however, as Richard M. Morse has observed in one of the most profound sentences ever written about that area, "The 'South' seems always to have won the 'Civil War.' "[32]

In order to provide a broader structural framework which would encompass and rationalize the countless dyadic relationships throughout society between patrons and clients, Spain introduced in its American colonies a system of corporativism based on models developed in Castile. The breakdown of the body politic into semiautonomous corporations or guilds provided an institutional basis for bringing together into one vertically structured association all those patrons and clients concerned with performance of a particular function in society, or all of those occupying a particular, narrowly circumscribed geographic area, such as a municipality. Each corporation was in turn linked through bureaucratic apparatus to the central government mechanism. While joined to a central government, corporations were not connected to each other.[33] Consequently, class consciousness at any level of society was virtually impossible to achieve, and no general sense of citizenship could develop.[34] Instead, all persons saw themselves as patrons, or as clients, within a particular functionally or geographically determined community.

In spite of all attempts in the postindependence era to eliminate corporativist structures, corporativism has retained its appeal in Andean America and was clearly reemerging in new guises during the 1960s and

1970s. Helping to explain the enduring strength of corporativist traditions in Andean America is the fact that they are the products not just of the Spanish but also of the Indian heritage. Preconquest Inca society was divided into *ayllus,* or agrarian communities whose members originally at least were related and who worked in common the land they held in usufruct, and also into various functional associations such as those of the silversmiths, the weavers, and the like. This corporative division of Indian society impeded social mobility, and consequently parents could calculate at birth their children's life chances. Moreover, Inca corporativism, even as its Spanish counterpart, placed a decided curb on the thrust of dynamic individualism and bred in most members of society a sense of dependence and reliance upon the collectivity to which they belonged.

The great French sociologist Emile Durkheim has provided, indirectly at least, one of the most compelling rationales for the type of corporativism that has prevailed in Andean America since pre-Hispanic times. According to him, a nation can be maintained "only if, between the State and the individual, there is intercalated a whole series of secondary groups near enough to the individuals to attract them strongly in their sphere of action and drag them, in this way, into the general torrent of social life."[35] The great advantage that Durkheim recognized in corporate organization is that functional associations "subordinate . . . private utility to common utility" and attach a moral character to individual subordination by necessarily associating it with "sacrifice and abnegation."[36] The corporative association was seen as having a further advantage in that from it "comes a warmth which animates its members, making them intensely human, destroying their egotisms."[37]

Down through history, the ultimate objective of Andean corporativism—whether shaped by Indian or Iberian traditions—has been, in effect, to combine the individualism hailed by Spencer with the collectivist spirit lauded by Durkheim. Within each corporation patron elements, although hedged about by commitments of paternalism to client segments, have behaved to some degree in accordance with the value and goals of competitive individualism. The directing or patron groups represent their particular corporation in the rest of society that exists outside the corporate confines; and they compete for maximum advantage in that outside world. What is more, within their own corporation, their exalted status, resulting from wealth, prestige, and authority, provides the basis for some element of self-reliance. Above all, the patrons, in the exercise of their individual wills, set the collective policies of each corporation. Also present within each corporative entity is a clientelist sector, made up of collectivist beings whose egotisms are curbed by unmitigated dependence upon their group and also upon the patrons who command it. Thus the corporative society is a projection of the basic social unit, the patronalist-clientelist extended family—just as United States society is, or at least used to aim at being, an extension of the family of bargaining equals.

In Andean corporativism the disciplining mechanism which attaches a moral character to subordination applies, obviously, mainly to the client sector. Subordination to the group represents, in fact, the basic source of the dependency mentality of the masses. With the instincts of dependency once firmly established among the collectivized majorities, in consequence of their group consciousness, the more individualistic patron sectors can proceed to forge the interpersonal links of domination-subordination between themselves and clients. Corporativist collectivism, therefore, is not only the means for providing the broad structural framework necessary to rationalize the myriad relationships throughout society between patrons and clients; corporativist collectivism is also the origin of the dependency attitudes of the masses, of their willingness to be dominated, that is the bedrock of the patronalist-clientelist society.

Patronalist-Clientelist Corporativism and the Image of the Limited Good   In the interpersonal relationships between patron and client, harmony depends to some measure, as has been noted, upon the willingness of the patron to assume the burdens of paternalism. Similarly, within each corporation solidarity depends upon the willingness of patron segments to shoulder responsibility for the security of underlings. The paternalism practiced by society's better-off elements was inspired and also frequently augmented by an institution that cut across all corporative boundaries and was omnipresent in society, the Catholic Church.

In addition to paternalism, harmony in the corporative society depended upon what anthropologist George Foster has described as the image of the limited good.[38] There existed, that is, within this society the well-nigh universal agreement that the available amount of wealth, goods, and resources was relatively fixed and that it was beyond human power vastly to expand the total. This being the case, persons acted not in response to motivations of rising expectations; rather, their actions were guided by the assumption that those with power and those dependent upon them had always to interact in harmony, for stability could not endure in the face of competitive drives that threatened to bring about any basic reallocation of the limited good.

Although challenged on some occasions, the limited-good image has endured in Andean America through the ages—pre-Hispanic, colonial, and postindependence. Its survival explains why the person who has progressed notably from his or her point of departure in the accumulation of worldly goods is regarded as immoral; for whoever augments wealth is thought to do so by depriving others of their former share of goods. In the society where the limited-good image prevails, the person who succeeds too spectacularly in the City of Man offers proof thereby of alienation from the City of God.

The concept of the limited good throws much light on the dramatic differences that distinguish Andean heroes from United States heroes. In the history of Andean America one looks almost in vain for heroes of the Horatio Alger type. One finds instead heroes of failure, beginning with Rumiñavi, the commander of the Indian forces who conducted opposition to the Spanish conquerors engaged, under Francisco Pizarro, in subjugating the Inca empire. In the end, Rumiñavi was captured and executed in the main square of Quito. It was the same with Manco Inca, "the Great Rebel," who led a vain uprising against the Spaniards in 1536, and with Túpac Amaru I who some thirty years later took up the same cause, and with Túpac Amaru II who according to popular myth assumed the form of the sacred bird, the Condor, following his execution by the Spaniards in 1781. The heroes of failure continue through the years; with Simón Bolívar, the Venezuelan-born Liberator of much of Andean America who died convinced he had ploughed the sea; with the Ecuadorans Gabriel García Moreno who died at the hands of assassins, Juan Montalvo who died of cancer in poverty and self-imposed exile convinced like Bolívar of the failure of his life-long struggle to improve the worldly ambiance, and Eloy Alfaro who was lynched by a once-adoring populace; with the Peruvians Miguel Grau and Francisco Bolognesi who despite their astonishing valor met death in the course of military defeat administered by Chile; with the Bolivians Andrés Santa Cruz who died in exile and ill repute, Manuel Belzu who although the idol of the masses was gunned down by an alcoholic rival, Germán Busch who committed suicide in the face of overwhelming adversity, and Gualberto Villarroel who was hanged from a lamppost. In general, the heroes of Andean America have shown Seneca-like resignation before hostile circumstances they could not possibly master. Their lives provide useful examples for impressing upon the masses the folly of seeking personal, material success. Andean American heroes have also been, most generally, kind, generous, affectionate father-symbol types, men who have shunned the quest of personal wealth in the desire to allocate fairly and equitably among their fellow citizens (often referred to as their children) the limited good available to the nation.[39]

There have been successful, Horatio Alger types in Andean history, men who on the basis of entrepreneurial skill, daring, vision, and hard work, and sometimes on the basis also of vicious, individualistic competitiveness, have accumulated vast personal fortunes as they advanced spectacularly beyond their starting points. In this connection, one thinks especially of the Bolivian tycoon Simón Patiño. Such persons, however, have never become national heroes. Instead, they stand as examples of the bad aristocracy, of the "oligarchy," whose members are character-ized by their individualism, their refusal to be burdened by paternalistic ties to clients, and, in consequence of all of this, by their heedless upset-ting of the delicate balance in the distribution of the limited good.

The difference between United States and Andean hero types extends even to contrasting views on the "good" Indian. In the United States, once the Indian menace had been dealt with by extermination and by confining the relatively few surviving Red Men to reservations, there began to enter into folklore the legendary, heroic Indian hunter who symbolized the virtues of resourcefulness and self-reliance, who lived in accordance with the "free exercise of natural impulses and power of men," and who refused steadfastly to accept fetters other than those imposed by his own nature.[40] In Andean America, on the other hand, the Indian most commonly glorified—at least by mainstream, estab-lishment society—is the collectivized Indian, liberated, because of his dependence on group and state, from the socially disruptive drive of the individual will, patiently resigned to an environment whose adversity can be no more than slightly mitigated, and developing inward, spiritual strength as a result of his stoicism.

Understandably, in light of the preceding material, Andean Ameri-cans have traditionally viewed the businessman with suspicion. In a society that subscribes to the limited-good concept, the businessman is seen as a predatory exploiter who amasses wealth not by creating it, but by bringing about a redistribution of wealth to the disadvantage of oth-ers. Throughout most of Andean America's history, moreover, religion has sanctioned and reinforced the hostility to businessmen.

The preconquest Indian past and also the colonial past were ages of faith, during which it was assumed that supernatural forces had fixed the amount of wealth and resources available to mankind. By their own efforts, mortals could not increase this wealth. However, by appealing to the deities they might gain an increase in overall wealth in such manner that should they thereby be benefited they would not at the same time damage the interests of their fellow beings. Therefore, appre-ciable increase in one's material well-being could be obtained legiti-mately only by "the favor of the saints . . . , certainly not by thrift, work and enterprise."[41] In order to remain socially acceptable within this sort of cultural environment, a person who inclined toward the deviant behavior patterns of seeking wealth through thrift, hard work, and enterprise had to do all in his power to disguise this conscious pursuit of material success and to pretend that good fortune had come about unexpectedly, altogether fortuitously, and could only be attributed to providence. The callous businessman who did not take pains to disguise his activities was, at best, merely tolerated by elites because of his sheer usefulness. But the greater his success, the more of a pariah he became. Little wonder that during much of the colonial period applicants to the

University of San Gregorio in Quito had to prove that none of their ancestors engaged in trade.[42]

In stark contrast to the situation in Andean America, cultural values in the young United States were influenced by a deistic concept of the relationship of God to mortals. The almighty, it was assumed, left persons alone to pursue in their own way the expansion of the means originally entrusted to them—permitting these mortals all the while to enhance sanctity by means of augmenting the resources placed in their care. In this society the successful businessman was originally a saint and later, as the age became more secular, a culture hero. Undoubtedly, the dimensions of the United States development experience would have been far less dramatic had it not been for the nearly universal interest in and admiration of business that permeated the social structure.[43]

Faith that the good was not limited, but could be endlessly expanded through the actions of man, particularly the businessman, helped create a situation which amazed an English mission sent in 1853 to study the sources of United States industrial success. The mission concluded: "the real secret of American productivity is that American society is imbued through and through with the desirability, the rightness, the morality of production. Man serves God in America, in all seriousness and sincerity, through striving for economic efficiency."[44]

The outlook observed by the English mission also accounts for the premium that the Americans attached to science and technology. Obsessed with increasing their already bountiful wealth and resources, Americans were interested in ideas that would produce practical, tangible results in the physical environment, results that could be measured in terms of increased affluence, private and national. For Americans, it soon became axiomatic that ideas led to action and produced results in the real world.

In Andean America, ideas were less directed toward producing actions and quantifiable results in the physical environment; for the environment was regarded as a fixed good that man could not decisively alter. As a result, ideas were seen mainly as a source of inward gratification. Ideas were nonetheless terribly important, for inward realms were widely regarded as more important than the outer world—a situation which materialistic societies have always regarded condescendingly as typical of primitive people. In addition to being terribly important, ideas in Andean society also became the playthings of the upper classes; and their display served to increase prestige just as much as did the conspicuous flaunting by rich North Americans of their material playthings.

Because ideas were not associated with producing actions in the temporal order or changing the environment, society in Andean America became accustomed in the postindependence era to tolerating bizarre and even subversive ideologies. At least until quite recent times, those who propounded such ideologies were generally engaging in the conspicuous display of harmless playthings; they seldom expected their ideas to produce concrete social results, in spite of the bombast with which they propounded these ideas. Tolerance of ideas markedly at odds with mainstream consensus has been a characteristic of Andean culture. In contrast, North Americans, accustomed by their attitudes toward science and progress to associate ideas automatically with action and results in the social order, have been little inclined to put up with "un-American" ideologies.

The Nature of Government American individualism, as already noted, has fostered an ingrained suspiciousness of government. For a society that placed its faith in individualism, logic demanded that interference with the private bargaining process be kept to an absolute minimum. Americans came to believe that theirs was a "self-maintaining" social and political system;[45] and in this they were one with John Locke, to whom it never occurred that "public good might not always be compatible with . . . the [private] rights of property. . . . A century later the possibility did occur to Adam Smith, and was waived aside by his 'harmony of interests' theory."[46]

By the time of the immediate post-World War I era, faith in uncurbed private bargaining had given way to a new faith, no less firm, in the miraculous results of collective bargaining and interest-group pluralism.[47] According to the new faith, the public interest is determined through the unchecked competition of interest groups. Given the fact that the country's roots were sunk deep in individualism, it is scarcely surprising that interpretations of political processes based on collective bargaining, countervailing forces, and interest-group pluralism proved totally "congenial to national sentiment."[48]

Pluralist theories of politics, even as the earlier creed of Spencerian individualism, narrowly circumscribed the role of government. In fact, the "zeal of pluralism for the group and its belief in a natural harmony of group competition tended to break down the very ethic of government by reducing the essential conception of government to nothing more than another set of mere interest groups." In the view of the pluralists, government was not an entity distinct and separate from the countervailing group forces that determined the public interest; instead, "government was nothing but an extension of the 'political process.' "[49]

Always, just outside the mainstream of American political ideology, there has existed a significant group of thinkers and leaders who have challenged the optimistic faith in the working of the "unseen hand." These persons have been fearful "that man's weakness would betray the nation," and they have sought a balance between liberty and order that stresses the second element.[50] Certain observers of the social and political scene have remained pessimistic about the ability of the self-regulating system to find, spontaneously, the public interest and they contend that there has always been present a far greater degree of planned control than is commonly recognized. They point to the president as virtually an uncrowned monarch and to his power, rather than to an unseen hand, they attribute what success the American political system has enjoyed.

Especially since the 1950s, a growing number of thoughtful persons have drawn attention to the failure of interest-group pluralism to achieve what they construe to be the true objectives of democracy. In their view, important political decisions have long ceased to be the result of free competition among a vast number of roughly equal groups. Instead, a few corporate giants are said to control the system and in the process to deny to the citizenry in general any meaningful participation.[51] Yet, despite the broadening perception of the weaknesses of the political system, Americans, who are perhaps more than most people the products of their past because all of that past is so recent, remain peculiarly loathe to seek to cure the failures of democracy through government intervention. In few areas is the contrast between the political cultures of the United States and Andean America so glaring.

Basically ill-disposed toward "unseen hand" theories, Andean Americans do not regard as best a government that intervenes the least. To them, it seems natural for the state to "impose its power upon individual wills, in order to serve as the mobilizing force within a responsible, obedient, and at times passive people." The Andean political theorist "tends to separate, analytically, the command from above from the spontaneous initiatives and pressures from below, and to proclaim the virtues of the former." Consequently, he is "suspicious of attempts of the civil sectors to define themselves in spontaneous action."[52] To him, "the idea that the existence of a plurality of competing interests could lead anywhere except to anarchy is almost beyond comprehension."[53] The roots of these attitudes must be sought not only in the Spanish but also in the Indian background.

Among the higher preconquest civilizations of Andean America, government was something altogether apart from the people, something that totally transcended them because, at the very highest level, the powers of government were wielded by rulers who were divine as well as human. At the top, for example, of the Inca Empire of Tahuantinsuyo was the "Sapa Inca, head and heart of the empire, God himself, made man, absolute sovereign, with total political, administrative and legislative powers."[54] Not only for the Incas but for all the high pre-Columbian Andean civilizations there existed a "religiopolitical system." Government was headed, that is, by a personage assumed to be endowed with divine attributes; and from the divinity of the ruler, government derived its legitimacy.[55]

Certain of the features of a religiopolitical system were continued, perhaps even strengthened, during the Spanish colonial period. More than the popes, the Spanish kings were the administrative heads of the Catholic Church throughout the Hispanic world. As such they were enveloped in an aura of divinity, and the interpenetration of religion and politics was evident in virtually all phases of temporal existence. Sovereignty was conferred upon the ruler not by the people, directly (as in the Lockean view), but only by the people as the instrument of God. And, once the people had conferred sovereignty, it passed altogether from their possession unless the king should prove himself to be an unmitigated tyrant. As a result, royal power rendered its holder superior to the community of citizens. In the words of the Spanish Jesuit Francisco Suárez (1548–1617), one of his country's most important political theorists: "Once power has been transferred to the king, he is at once the vicar of God and by natural law must be obeyed . . . the transference of power from the community to the prince is not a delegation but almost an abrogation, that is, a total grant of power which was formerly in the community."[56]

Until the very end of the colonial period, Spanish kings were secure in their legitimacy because they possessed charisma, in the sense in which Max Weber used the word: "It [charisma] is the quality which attaches to men and things by virtue of their relations with the 'supernatural,' that is, with the nonempirical aspects of reality in so far as they lend theological meaning to men's acts and the events of the world. . . . Legitimacy is thus institutional application or embodiment of charisma."[57] Accustomed by the colonial experience to obey their ruler because of his charisma or sacredness, Andean Americans retained intact, on the very eve of independence, a traditional religiopolitical system.

If democracy is to take root, the assumption must prevail that truth and proper norms of conduct can be discovered by citizens, largely on their own. According to the Lockean analysis that was so influential in shaping United States values, each person was capable of acquiring individually, through the use of his or her own reason, a knowledge of the natural law. However, in the Hispanic colonial world, the cradle in which Andean America developed its political culture, the natural law was strange and mysterious, in part because it was inseparably interwoven with the divine positive law which was incomprehensible to all save those trained in theology and canon law. Thus the intelligentsia, a group apart, separate from and above the masses, had to advise and consult with rulers in order to assist them in applying the interpenetrated divine and natural laws to any particular situation. In these circumstances, justification for monarchy derived from what has been termed "transcendental metaphysics."[58]

Even after monarchy came formally to an end with the attainment of independence, it remained latent in Andean America's political attitudes. Governments continued to concern themselves with transcendental metaphysics, the only difference being that now, as the age became more secular, the sources of transcendent truth ceased to be the revelations found in the writings of saints and doctors of the Catholic Church and became instead the pronouncements of such prophets and lawgivers as Bentham, Saint-Simon, Comte, and Spencer. Later, for those who were seeking to topple incumbent governments, the sources of transcendental metaphysics came to be such prophets as Bakunin, Marx, and Lenin.

Belief that law had necessarily to proceed from a highly complex and mysterious fusion of divine and natural sources and could only be formulated and interpreted by specially trained groups set apart from ordinary mortals contributed to the reverence in which the legal profession was traditionally held in the Spanish-speaking world. In Andean America, as elsewhere in that world, the masses turned to the lawyer as an absolutely essential mediator before a higher power. Popular attitudes and the need for government bureaucracies to be staffed by persons trained in law, given the incredible confusion arising from the existence of numerous corporative entities each with its own legal immunities and court of law, contributed to the enormous prestige of legal study. The law faculty became from the very outset the heart of the university structure in colonial Andean America. And it retained this status at least until the post-World War II era when suddenly the demand for development began to transfer reverence to another breed of persons apart, the technicians.

In notable contrast, the people of colonial English America and of the young United States "cherished . . . an ingrained hostility to the law as a profession." Lawyers were accepted, if at all, only on the premise that they might have a kind of nuts-and-bolts expertise acquired through practice, but never in the belief that they had through long training somehow gained initiation into a world that the common man could not hope to enter. For this reason law schools made their way in the United States "against widespread popular suspicion." [59]

Within the framework of Andean American political attitudes, shaped by the conviction that government and even its legal advisers are removed from the people by possession of charismatic qualities, the interventionist, omnipresent state is taken for granted. The corporativist traditions of the colonial past contribute strongly to this outlook. Within the colonial corporativist structure one of the most important prerogatives attaching to the ruler's sovereignty was the exercise of a moderating power.[60] Through this power, the ruler could regulate activities both within and among the various functional and local compartments into which society was divided. Traditionally, the political ideology of corporativism has denied to the vast majority the right to share in the exercise of the moderating power. Their energies absorbed and their interests confined by their local and functional groups, average persons could not—the reasoning goes—see society in its totality. It followed that only the ruler and the ruler's advisers who were removed from and above the rest of society could acquire the overall view necessary for the rational pursuit of the common welfare.

Within Andean America's political culture, it has proved extremely difficult to introduce collective bargaining. Instead of by this process, labor relations are shaped by what has been termed political bargaining. In political bargaining, labor appeals directly to government for protection of its interests. Frequently, labor resorts to violence in order to dramatize its appeal. This violence may be misinterpreted by foreign observers as a challenge to the government. Actually, at least in many instances, it is simply a part of the ritual by which labor, accepting its role of dependent clientelism, brings its pleas before the state.[61]

Democracy in the United States may be viewed as based upon the conflict of laterally interacting organized groups as they compete first for the backing of other groups, then for concessions from government, and ultimately, if need be, for the support of the electorate. In the patronalist-clientelist, corporativist setting of Andean America, where the important social ties are vertical rather than lateral and where government is something apart and transcendent, organized groups compete for the benevolent attention of those in power. This is the ultimate weapon in their arsenal, short of revolution. What passes for justice is determined by direct relations between government, the super-patron, and the petitioning group. The number of people supporting the petitioning group is often irrelevant. It would be demeaning to the group and insulting to the patron to suggest that matters of justice should be influenced by the viewpoint of the half plus one.

Obstacles to United States—Andean Understanding At the conclusion of an influential book, Louis Hartz asks: "Can a people 'born equal' ever understand peoples elsewhere that have to become so?"[62] If slightly rephrased, this question probes at some of the most basic aspects of United States relations with Andean America. Can a people born affluent and equal ever understand peoples elsewhere that are poor and unfree and, with the exception of minorities in their midst, not terribly interested in becoming rich and free?

Comparing themselves to Andean Americans, the people of the United States traditionally have seen the contrast of modernity (good) with traditionalism (evil). Modernity they have equated with technology, industrialism, democracy, secularism, individualism, progress, and equalitarianism. For them the modern society, being the good society, merits the adjectives civilized and developed. In contrast, traditionalism—in the eyes of the North Americans who pride themselves on their modernity—is characterized by backwardness and primitivism which in turn derive from excessive concern with kinship and honor, from the sacred or religious view of life, from corporativism, hierarchism, localism or particularism, and the like.[63]

From the United States viewpoint, Andean America has remained mired in traditionalism.[64] All the more disconcerting in North American eyes is Andean rediscovery and unabashed glorification in the twentieth century of the historical tradition of corporativism, associated not only with the Spanish past but also with the pre-Hispanic background.

Erikson tells us that for every positive identity, both for individuals and for nations, there must be a negative identity, embodying all the opposite values—all of the objects of the positive identity's scorn and derision. The positive identity "must ever fortify itself by drawing the line against undesirables, even as it must mark itself off against those negative potentials which each man must confine and repress, deny and expel, brand and torture, within himself."[65]

Prominent among the traits of the United States positive identity has been devotion to society-wide equalitarianism. The contrasting negative identity, that is, commitment to corporativism, is perceived as the badge of uncivilized people. For other aspects of the negative identity, even stronger revulsion obtains. Lack of concern with progress, for example, was actually attributed by many nineteenth-century North Americans to the influence of satan.[66] Thus North America's quarrel with the life style of its Andean neighbors initially rested in some measure on religious grounds.[67]

Also conspicuous among the features of the United States positive identity has been the already-alluded-to need to achieve. Francis G. Grund, a German observer who lived in the United States in the early 1830s, noted the general contempt for a person who remained poor and who was not animated by the desire to attain success. Such demeanor was taken as a sign of irresponsibility and bad character.[68] The same judgment has been assessed against the Andean Americans who, in this instance, exhibit yet another trait of the negative identity.

The struggle of the positive identity always to triumph over the negative was involved in the attitudes shown by the dominant culture toward the counterculture that surfaced in the United States during the 1960s. One author suggests that the virulence manifested by defenders of the dominant culture may have sprung from inner misgivings about the cult of individualism and achievement, and from fear of finding something to admire in the counterculture.[69] Perhaps inner misgivings and fear have often been present as North Americans observed in Andean Americans the personification of their negative identity.

Heaping opprobrium on those who personify the negative identity is by no means a one-sided undertaking in hemisphere relations. Through the years, the majority of cultured Andeans seem to have been in agreement with the assessment that the renowned Peruvian intellectual José Carlos Mariátegui made of human liberty. For Mariátegui, individual liberty was the root cause of the evil that had befallen mankind in modern times. In the quest of individual liberty, human beings had set themselves against one another; and, in the obsessive pursuit of private material gain they had suffered alienation.[70] Although Mariátegui stood far to the left in the ideological spectrum, his views on the effects of obsession with individual liberty have been shared by most right-wing Andean ideologists. For left and right alike, negative identity is embodied in North Americans.

If United States opinion has generally shown concern and even dismay over Andean Americans as they are perceived to be, hope has sprung eternal that they could be transformed and uplifted. Thus Americans have always been encouraged when they detected, as the United States minister assigned to La Paz thought he detected among Bolivians in 1879, signs that their neighbors were moving "as fast as possible" to fashion "their form of government after our own."[71]

However much North Americans have grasped at the hope that Andeans were eager to embrace new and allegedly better ways and beliefs, the truth is that they have clung to their traditional modes of existence with remarkable tenacity. Their identity has, after all, been shaped by factors reaching far back into their history.

3. Epilogue: Some Implications

This study has been based on the conviction that corporativism is the system most congenial to Andean cultural traditions and, beyond this, that it is a system suitable to late-developing nations in their struggle to retain political viability in the postmodern era. However, there are any number of different varieties of corporativism,[72] ranging from fascism (whatever that is) to anarchism with its autonomous communes. Each variety contains sources of serious internal tensions and weaknesses. For corporativism is, after all, a system—a political-social-economic system and sometimes a religiopolitical system. And no system really works, except during brief and rare moments in history when fortuitous circumstances operate in a particularly benign manner. Prevailing circumstances in Andean America's immediate future seem likely to be harsh, and thus corporativism cannot be viewed as a panacea. Among many other factors, the persistent though shifting patterns of a deeply ingrained elitism, combined with the lack of a homogeneous population base, strongly suggest a continuing story of strife.

It must be stressed that no system, even if not forced to contend against unfavorable circumstances in the general economic, ecological, and demographic environment, can of itself solve the problems of alienation and class tension resulting from the need for management in any kind of enterprise. In the economic sphere, even if workers to some degree own, share in the profits, and participate in the direction of firms, friction and frustration can still arise out of the relationships with their associates who in the final instance perform the function of management in the interests of efficiency. Thus in matters of alienation and class and division-of-labor conflicts, individual human equations, rather than overall systems, will remain the determinants of paramount importance.[73]

Nevertheless, Andean Americans, having at last turned a blind eye toward the fading enticements of liberalism, are on the right approach to finding a political system more likely to be congenial than counterproductive in the light of changing needs and challenges. In this regard, they may even be on a more promising approach than the United States. This possibility arises out of the fact that exceptionalism, equated with bringing into being some sort of millennialist existence perhaps reaching worldwide dimensions, has seldom been a major factor in the myth-fantasies that have helped shape Andean culture. Unlike North Americans, then, Andeans are not faced with having to adjust to the loss of a vital ingredient of their traditional culture. In postmodern times, as recognition of defeat and failure begins to curb the Western world's expectations of triumph and glory, Andean Americans may find it easier than their neighbors of the north to accept themselves for what they are and must be.

Notes

1. See Clyde Kluckhohn, "Have There Been Discernible Shifts in American Values During the Past Generation?" in Elting E. Morison, ed., *The American Style* (New York, 1958), p. 149, and Walter Gordon Merritt, *The Struggle for Industrial Liberty* (New York, 1922), p. 4. On the issue see also Alan F. Westin, ed., *Views of America* (New York, 1966).

2. Yehoshua Arieli, *Individualism and Nationalism in American Ideology* (Cambridge, Mass., 1964), pp. 345–346.

3. Erikson, *Childhood and Society*, 2d ed. (New York, 1963), pp. 316–318.

4. See the classic study by David C. McClelland, *The Achieving Society* (New York, 1961).

5. See Gabriel Almond, *The American People and Foreign Policy*, rev. ed. (New York, 1960), p. 42, and Henry Steele Commager, ed., *America in Perspective* (New York, 1947), p. x.

6. See Robert Kelley, *The Transatlantic Persuasion: The Liberal-Democratic Mind in the Age of Gladstone* (New York, 1967), p. 67.

7. Steven Lukes, *Individualism* (New York, 1973), p. 27. In his excellent study *The Mind of America, 1820–1860* (New York, 1975), Rush Welter finds that one of the four basic attitudes among average, literate antebellum Americans was a view of society that reduced order to

the self-interest of its individual members.

8. Talcott Parsons, *The Structure of Social Action*, 2 vols., 2d ed. (New York, 1968), I, 4.

9. Emile Durkheim, *The Division of Labor in Society,* trans. George Simpson (New York, 1964), p. 200. The English translation of this work, a classic refutation of Spencer, first published in France in 1893, appeared initially in 1933.

10. Philip Slater, *The Pursuit of Loneliness: American Culture at the Breaking Point* (Boston, 1970), p. 5.

11. Goodwin, *The American Condition* (Garden City, 1974), p. 75. Among the many writers in addition to Goodwin who in recent years have lamented the absence of a sense of community in America, Glenn Tinder figures prominently. See, for example, his book *Tolerance* (Amherst, Mass., 1976). In "Learning about Crime—the Japanese Experience," *The Public Interest,* no. 44 (1976), 55–68, David H. Bayley argues persuasively that the reason for Japan's declining crime rate during the past twenty-five years, in such dramatic contrast to the situation in the United States, lies in the preservation of intermediate groups which curb individualism and bolster respect for authority.

12. Paul Starr, "Who Are They Now?" *New York Times Magazine,* October 13, 1974, p. 110.

13. Editorial from an 1841 edition of the *Boston Globe,* quoted in Lukes, *Individualism,* p. 27.

14. See David Potter, *People of Plenty: Economic Abundance and the American Character* (Chicago, 1954), p. 92.

15. See ibid., p. 67 et passim. By 1840 the young republic had a gross national product per capita that was 40 to 65 percent larger than France's and was rapidly approaching Great Britain's. See Robert Gallman, "Gross National Product

1834–1909," in National Bureau of Economic Research, *Output, Employment and Productivity in the United States After 1800* (New York, 1969), pp. 5–7.

16. Bruchey, *The Roots of American Economic Growth 1707–1861: An Essay in Social Causation* (New York, 1965), p. 209. Making still more explicit the interconnection between American "character" and environment, Bruchey observes (p. 194): "While few if any men wished not to improve their circumstances, the latitude of their opportunities to do so necessarily influenced both the value and quality of economic effort."

17. Paul A. David, "New Light on a Statistical Dark Age: U.S. Real Product Growth Before 1840," *American Economic Review,* 57 (1967), 294–306.

18. See Ernest Lee Tuveson, *Redeemer Nation: The Idea of America's Millennial Role* (Chicago, 1968), p. 25 et passim.

19. Parsons, *Structure of Social Action,* II, 513.

20. In a review that appeared in the AHR, 74 (1973), 1130, Yale University historian Sydney E. Ahlstrom records his impression of "the remarkable degree to which the changes in Protestant thinking seemed to intensify rather than weaken the ways in which the Protestant ethic encouraged the growth of an unregulated capitalist society" in the United States.

21. Enlightening on this matter is Thomas C. Cochran, "Cultural Factors in Economic Growth," *Journal of Economic History,* 20 (1960), 512–530.

22. See Margaret Mead, *And Keep Your Powder Dry* (New York, 1942), pp. 31, 40–41, 50–53.

23. Stephan Thernstrom in the concluding section of his *The Other Bostonians: Poverty and Progress in the American Metropolis, 1860–1970* (Cambridge, Mass., 1973)

compares his findings with those of other recent urban studies. He concludes that a high degree of fluidity had indeed characterized United States urban life, even though various ethnic groups and most especially blacks stand as exceptions.

24. On this controversial matter see Herbert Gans, *More Equality* (New York, 1974), Richard Hamilton, *Restraining Myths: Critical Studies of U.S. Social Structure and Politics* (New York, 1975), Gabriel Kolko, *Wealth and Power in America* (New York, 1962), Robert Lampman, *The Share of the Top-Wealth-Holders in National Wealth, 1922–1956* (Princeton, 1962), Oscar Ornati, *Poverty Amid Affluence* (New York, 1966), and Richard Parker, *The Myth of the Middle Class* (New York, 1972).

25. Seymour Martin Lipset, *Revolution and Counter-revolution: Change and Persistence in Social Structures,* rev. ed (Garden City, 1970), p. 20.

26. See Richard N. Adams, "Brokers and Career Mobility Systems in the Structure of Complex Societies," in Dwight B. Heath, ed., *Contemporary Cultures and Societies of Latin America,* 2d ed. (New York, 1974), p. 84, and *The Second Sowing: Power and Secondary Development in Latin America* (San Francisco, 1967), esp. pp. 39, 257.

27. See George M. Foster, "Cofradía and Compadrazgo in Spain and Spanish America," *Southwestern Journal of Anthropology,* 9 (1953), 1–28, John M. Ingham, "The Asymetrical Implications of Godparenthood in Tlayacapan, Morelos," *Man,* n.s., 5 (1970), 281–292, Sidney Mintz and Eric Wolf, "An Analysis of Ritual Co-Parenthood (Compadrazgo)," *Southwestern Journal of Anthropology,* 6 (1950), 341–368, and Arnold Strickon and Sidney M. Greenfield, eds., *Structure and Process in Latin America: Patronage,*

Clientage and Power Systems (Albuquerque, 1972).

28. Ingham, "Asymetrical Implications," p. 290.

29. See Gabriel Escobar, *Organización social y cultural del sur del Perú* (Mexico, 1967), esp. pp. 51–53, and John Gillin, *Moche: A Peruvian Coastal Community* (Washington, 1945), p. 27.

30. For thoughtful essays on the role of women in Latin America, essays which have been used as the principal point of departure for the treatment of Marianism, see Ann Pescatello, ed., *Female and Male in Latin America* (Pittsburgh, 1973), and Rosa Signorelli de Martí, "Spanish America," in Raphael Patai, ed., *Women in the Modern World* (New York, 1967). An exhaustive bibliographical study is Meri Knaster, "Women in Latin America: The State of Research, 1975," *LARR,* 11 (1976), 3–74.

31. Louis Hartz, *The Liberal Tradition in America* (New York, 1955) pp. 185–196, provides a brilliant description of the unsuccessful appeal of southern slaveowners to northern capitalists and employers.

32. See the introduction by Morse to the work which he edited, with Michael L. Conniff and John Wibel, *The Urban Development of Latin America, 1750–1920* (Stanford, 1971), p. 13. For other probing essays on Latin American culture and values as contrasted to those of the United States see Morse, "The Heritage of Latin America," in Louis Hartz, and others, *The Founding of New Societies* (New York, 1964), pp. 123–177, and "Toward a Theory of Spanish American Government," *Journal of the History of Ideas,* 25 (1954), 71–93. [Both articles are reprinted in this volume.] See also Robert Kern and Ronald Dolkhart, eds., *The Caciques: Oligarchical Politics and the System of Caciquismo in the Luso-Hispanic World* (Albuquer-

que, 1973), K. H. Silvert, "National Values, Development, and Leaders and Followers," *International Social Science Journal,* 15 (1963), 560–570, and Howard J. Wiarda, ed., *Politics and Social Change in Latin America: The Distinct Tradition* (Amherst, Mass., 1974; 2d rev. ed, 1982, this volume).

33. See Magali Sarfatti, *Spanish Bureaucratic-Patrimonialism in America* (Berkeley, 1966). She describes society as divided into compartments among which virtually all lateral relationships were mediated through the imperial apparatus.

34. For pertinent observations on how the highly fragmented society of the corporativist model could safeguard hierarchical rule by preventing the "half-plus-one" type of decision making see David Apter, "Notes for a Theory of Nondemocratic Representation," in his *Some Conceptual Approaches to the Study of Modernization* (Englewood Cliffs, 1968).

35. Durkheim, *Division of Labor,* p. 28.

36. Ibid., p. 13.

37. Ibid., p. 26.

38. Foster applied the limited-good image to peasant society. See especially his "Peasant Society and the Image of the Limited Good," *American Anthropologist,* 67 (1965), 293–315.

39. There is a strong connection between the type of heroes most widely venerated, especially by the masses, in Andean America and the Suffering Christ, one of the most important religious symbols to the area's Indian and mestizo multitudes. See Miles Richardson, Marta Eugenia Pardo, and Barbara Bode, "The Image of Christ in Spanish America as a Model for Suffering," *JIAS,* 13 (1971), 246–257.

40. See Richard Slotkin, *Regeneration Through Violence: The Mythology of the American Frontier, 1600–1860* (Middletown, Conn.,

1974), pp. 47, 264.

41. This description by Edward C. Banfield of a southern Italian village is equally applicable to Andean America. See his *The Moral Basis of a Backward Society* (New York, 1958), p. 109. Also helpful in providing perspective is Alexander Gerschenkron, *Economic Backwardness in Historical Perspective* (Cambridge, Mass., 1962).

42. See Harold Benjamin, *Higher Education in the American Republics* (New York, 1965), p. 16. For an excellent review of some of the literature pertaining to the contrasts in United States and Latin American perceptions of business and businessmen see Lipset, *Revolution and Counter-revolution,* pp. 77–140.

43. See Thomas C. Cochran, "The Business Revolution," *AHR,* 79 (1974), p. 1465.

44. Quoted in Lynn White, Jr., "Technology Assessments from the Stance of a Medieval Historian," *AHR,* 79 (1974), p. 2.

45. See Alvin W. Gouldner, *The Coming Crisis of Western Sociology* (New York, 1970), pp. 346, 348.

46. Edwin Corwin, *The "Higher Law" Background of American Constitutional Law* (Ithaca, 1959), p. 71.

47. Mark E. Neely, Jr., argues convincingly that pluralism scored its definitive triumph among United States intellectuals only in the 1920s. Prior to that, currents of elitism and organicism and of partiality to the powerful state had retained considerable appeal. Thus Neely challenges the Louis Hartz thesis on the uninterrupted devotion in the United States to Lockean principles of liberal individualism. See Neely, "The Organic Theory of the State in America, 1838–1918," Ph.D. diss., Yale University, 1973.

48. See Milton Derber, *The American Idea of Industrial Democracy, 1865–1965* (Urbana, 1970), p. 521.

49. Theodore J. Lowi, *The End of Liberalism* (New York, 1969), pp. 48–49.

50. See Paul S. Nagel, *This Sacred Trust: American Nationality 1798–1898* (New York, 1971), p. vii.

51. Among the writers who criticize the way in which pluralism has operated to impede democracy and who urge correctives aimed at achieving greater equality are Peter Bachrach, Corine Lathrop Gilb, Michael Harrington, Christopher Jencks, Grant McConnell, Kenneth A. Megill, Carole Pateman, and John Rawls.

52. Sakari Sariola, *Power and Resistance: The Colonial Heritage in Latin America* (Ithaca, 1972), pp. 99–100.

53. Glen C. Dealy, "The Tradition of Monistic Democracy in Latin America," *Journal of the History of Ideas*, 35 (1974), 640. Reprinted in Wiarda, *Politics and Social Change in Latin America* (see n. 32 above).

54. José Fellman Velarde, *Historia de Bolivia*, 3 vols. (La Paz, Cochabamba, 1968–1970), I, 53.

55. See Donald E. Smith, *Religion and Political Development* (Boston, 1970), p. 115.

56. Quoted in Peggy K. Liss, "Jesuit Contributions to the Ideology of Spanish America in Mexico, Part I," *TA*, 29 (1973), 320.

57. This is Talcott Parsons' description of Weber's concept of legitimacy, in *Structure of Social Action*, II, 669.

58. Robert Michels, *Political Parties: A Sociological Study of the Oligarchical Tendencies of Modern Democracy*, trans. Eden and Cedar Paul (Glencoe, 1915), p. 17.

59. Perry Miller, *The Life of the Mind in America from the Revolution to the Civil War* (New York, 1965), pp. 102, 110.

60. On the moderating power see Frank Jay Moreno, "The Spanish Colonial System: A Functional Approach," *The Western Political Quarterly*, 20 (1967), 308–320.

61. See James Payne, *Labor and Politics in Peru: The System of Political Bargaining* (New Haven, 1965), p. 3 et passim. On the clientelist mentality of organized labor see Henry A. Landsberger, "The Labor Elite: Is It Revolutionary?" in S. M. Lipset and Aldo Solari, eds., *Latin American Elites* (New York, 1967), pp. 256–300.

62. Hartz, *The Liberal Tradition*, p. 309.

63. See Robert A. Nisbet, *Social Change and History: Aspects of the Western Theory of Development* (New York, 1969), p. 191. In an important article that indirectly sheds much light on the identity quest of the Spanish-speaking world in the eighteenth and nineteenth centuries, Marc Raeff, "The Well-Ordered Police State and the Development of Modernity in Seventeenth- and Eighteenth-Century Europe: An Attempt at a Comparative Approach," *AHR*, 80 (1975), 1222, writes: "I would suggest the following as conveying the essence of what we call 'modern,' as opposed to earlier, 'traditional' . . . patterns of culture: . . . society's conscious desire to maximize all its resources and to use this new potential dynamically for the enlargement and improvement of its way of life." See also Joseph R. Gusfield, "Tradition and Modernity: Misplaced Polarities in the Study of Social Change," *American Journal of Sociology*, 72 (1967), 351–362.

64. For a good general discussion of the persistence of traditional political culture in spite of major socioeconomic innovations see Robert Levine, "Political Socialization and Culture Change," in Clifford Geertz, ed., *Old Societies and New States* (Glencoe, Ill., 1963), esp. p. 289.

65. Erik H. Erikson, *Dimensions of a New Identity* (New York, 1974), pp. 70–71.

66. Tuveson, *Redeemer Nation,* pp. 76–77.

67. See William Gribbin, "A Matter of Faith: North America's Religion and South America's Independence," *TA,* 31 (1975), 470–487. For valuable comparative insights see Nathan O. Hatch, "The Origins of Civil Millennialism in America: New England Clergymen, War with France, and the Revolution," *William and Mary Quarterly,* 31 (1974), 407–430. The study shows that at the time of the Seven Years' War, New England clergymen described the struggle against Frenchmen in terms of the confrontation of liberty and tyranny, of heaven and hell. They condemned the French enemy both on the grounds of their religious tyranny ("popishness") and their civil tyranny, and depicted the two forms of tyranny as inseparably intertwined. The same attitudes were evident in the initial appraisals formed by many U.S. leaders of the newly independent republics of Spanish America.

68. Grund, *The Americans* (New York, 1837), pp. 173–174.

69. Slater, *The Pursuit of Loneliness,* p. 2.

70. See John M. Baines, *Revolution in Peru: Mariátegui and the Myth* (Tuscaloosa, 1972), p. 95.

71. September 29, 1879 letter of S. Newton Pettis to Secretary of State William Evarts, in *Message from the President of the United States, . . . Relating to the War in South America* (Washington, 1882), p. 19.

72. See Philippe C. Schmitter, "Still the Century of Corporatism?" in F. B. Pike and Thomas J. Stritch, eds., *The New Corporatism: Social-Political Structures in the Iberian World* (Notre Dame, 1974), pp. 85–131.

73. Peter F. Drucker, "Pension Fund 'Socialism,' " *The Public Interest,* no. 42 (1976), p. 44, puts the matter this way: "No 'system' can create harmonious or even stable industrial relations and human relations. Industrial relations and human relations are not primarily macro-phenomena. They are primarily micro-phenomena—the results of the management of work by management and the management of the job by the worker. Both can be affected only at the workplace, by redefining the relationship of a specific worker to a specific job. The problems of work and job cannot be remedied by changing the 'system.' "

Part Four

Latin America:
Toward a Framework for Analysis and Understanding

The essays in Part 4 begin the process of pulling together the diverse themes presented earlier into a coherent, unified theory. They serve to tie the several threads together, to look at the patterns and intermeshing of the concepts previously developed, to elaborate a fuller and more detailed model and framework for the analysis and understanding of Latin American development that takes account of the area's unique and distinctive features. For up to this point and in developing the contrasts with the United States, we have said a good deal about what the development process in Latin America is not; now it remains for us to determine more explicitly what the Latin American model is and how it works. The historical and the contemporary interpretations of Latin America need to be brought together.

The first essay, "Law and Political Development in Latin America: Toward a Framework for Analysis," is a summary statement that synthesizes much of the literature in the field and tries to draw out the common themes that go to help make up a unified theory of Latin American development. Though the particular focus of this essay is on law and the constitutional system, its main thrust is toward explaining Latin American socio-political development in general.

In Lawrence S. Graham's work, "Latin America: Illusion or Reality?," we find a parallel statement and series of propositions regarding the distinct political-administrative features of Latin American development. But Professor Graham adds these further dimensions: that our studies and comparisons should be concerned with a broader culture-area approach that encompasses the "Latin" or "Mediterranean" nations of Southern Europe as well as those within the geographic area of Latin America; that at the same time we must look at these countries individually both because they are quite different nations and in order to see where the general and theoretical comments presented in this book apply to a greater or lesser extent; and that United States policy must also be shaped in accord with these newer and more complex understandings.

Finally, in Charles W. Anderson's essay, "Toward a Theory of Latin American Politics," we have one of the most sophisticated and most widely influential efforts yet made to fashion a full-fledged framework and theoretical model for the analysis of the Latin American political systems and their change processes. Professor Anderson emphasizes the systematic *nature of Latin American politics, however distinctive that system is from that of the United States, and demonstrates its dynamic processes of change and modernization, again illustrating Latin America's divergencies from the United States model. His work too is based on the rich literature that has gone before and draws its various components together into a coherent, logical, and orderly theory. In a recent survey Anderson's work was rated the most widely read by Latin Americanists in the United States; and along with the other essays presented here, his study carries important policy implications.*

Law and
Political Development
in Latin America:
Toward a Framework
for Analysis

Howard J. Wiarda

Legal scholars have long been concerned with exploring the historical emergence of national law. And more recently sociologists and
political scientists have fashioned an already extensive body of literature dealing comparatively with the question of national development and modernization. Yet there has been relatively little attention by either legal scholars, sociologists, or political scientists to the
relations between law and the socio-political structure, the role of
law in the development process, and the impact that development
and national modernization, in turn, have on the law.[1] This essay represents a modest effort to try to begin filling that gap, with particular
reference to law and political development in Latin America.

At this stage of our knowledge, it is clear, the ideas and themes
explored here must be advanced not as final truths but as a set of hypotheses and propositions which are intended to be exploratory and
suggestive rather than definitive and which require a great deal of further investigation, explication, and qualification. We must begin in-
vestigating these relationships further, however, for it has already
become obvious that the impact of law upon the political culture, the
style of political behavior, the social and political institutional structure, and the entire development process in Latin America is far too
important to be ignored on the one hand or compartmentalized strictly according to the traditional disciplines on the other. If the study of
law is too fundamental to be left solely to lawyers, to add a new twist
to an old adage, it is equally certain that it cannot be left to the sociologists and political scientists either, for they have conspicuously
denegated the significance of law for the development process by all

Reprinted from *The American Journal of Comparative Law* 19, no. 3, Summer 1971. Copyright © by the American Association for the Comparative
Study of Law, Inc.

but ignoring it. Indeed, given the crucial role of law in the Latin American tradition and the overriding contemporary concern on the part of the nations of the hemisphere with stimulating development, the study of law and development in Latin America would seem to offer a particularly apt—and important—subject area for inter-disciplinary study and cross-fertilization between legal scholars, political scientists, sociologists, and their various hybrids.[2]

In the discussion that follows an effort will be made to suggest what is unique about the Latin American development process, to fashion a rough and as yet preliminary framework for the study and analysis of development in Latin America, and to relate law and the legal system to the process of overall socio-political development there. Our focus will be on the sociology of law in the Latin American context, on comparative jurisprudence, broadly defined, or what might be termed the legal aspects of the political culture, and also on the relationship of the legal structures to the nature of the Latin American systems more generally. It is hoped that the discussion will prove provocative, will suggest new lines of possible research, will help stimulate some greater cross-disciplinary analyses, and will thus help enhance our comprehension of the broader Latin American development process.

Law and the Development Process in Latin America: Toward a Framework for Analysis[3]

Few of the theoretical frameworks for the study of national development put forward in recent years have much relevance or usefulness for the study of socio-political (including legal) change in Latin America. With some 150 years of independent life behind them, the Latin American nations could hardly be classified as "new nations." By and large, the Latin American nations have by this time resolved the major development-related dilemmas attendant upon new nationhood—the determining of national boundaries, the devising of new institutional forms, the creation of a genuine nation state where only tribal, ethnic, or regional loyalties existed before, etc. Nor is the Western-non-Western continuum of much use in studying these semi-feudal extensions of Western, albeit Iberic, Europe, *circa* 1500. To be sure, there are still isolated Indian elements in many of the Latin American countries who have not as yet been wholly "Westernized," but it is clear that the dominant socio-politico-cultural strain throughout Latin America, even in the so-called Indian countries, is Hispanic (or Iberic) and Latin.[4]

Marxian theory has provided us with a useful general theory for comprehending better at least some aspects of the Latin American development process, particularly as the political systems of the region have in recent decades become increasingly class-, issue-, and interest-oriented. But as a general theory of analysis the Marxian framework still leaves too many questions unsatisfactorily answered, in the eyes of many Latin America scholars, and it is probably too narrow, restrictive, and closed to encompass fully the complex dimensions of national development. Though a more extensive discussion is required and though so brief a statement as this runs the risk of merely knocking down straw men, it may be suggested that the Marxian framework misses the mark by positing that class and ideological position must be consonant, that class is the motor force behind the Latin American political development process, that the peasants and workers are becoming increasingly revolutionary, and that Latin America is about to explode in violent revolution. In most countries, however, the evidence seems to point to the continuing conservatism of the bulk of the peasantry and much of the working class, to the continued capacity of the old elites to adapt to change rather than being overwhelmed by it, and to the fact that revolutionary movements in Latin America have met with neither widespread support nor great success. Class analysis has proved inadequate even in explaining Latin American "class" behavior, nor has it been of much assistance in helping students of the area comprehend the special role played by the state or by such corporate interests as the Church, the military, or even, as we shall see, the trade unions. Class considerations, of course, play a major part in any examination of Latin America. But class is not the mirror reflection of social and economic history, nor can political, ideological, and other variables be neatly subordinated to class determinants.[5]

But if the Marxian "power elite" and "class conflict" approach, while useful in some regards, is in others somewhat foreign to the Latin American ambience, so too is the non-Marxian "stages of growth" or "stages of development" framework. The "stages" approach tends to posit a unilinear path to national development, fails to take into consideration the in many ways unique experiences of Southern Europe, particularly Spain and Portugal and their New World fragments, builds into the model a bias in favor of equilibrium and stability, and is, like the Marxian model, somewhat narrow and ethnocentric and certainly far less universal than its proponents claim.[6] Indeed, the case may be made that both the Marxian and non-Marxian "developmental" models are based largely upon the experiences of the Northern European and Anglo-American countries and may thus be inapplicable and inappropriate for comprehending the special nature of the development process in Latin America. Both these general frameworks have their usefulness in exploring *some* aspects of Latin American development; but—and the argument demands more detailed attention of course—neither of these two models is fully satisfactory by itself, neither provides complete explanations or a set of general propositions that would enable scholars to analyze the full range and ramifications of the questions at issue, and neither adequately comes to grips with the question of what makes Latin American development (or the lack thereof) distinctive.[7]

If the point is granted that both Marxian analysis and the non-Marxian "stages of growth" approach have but limited utility for the study of development and its vicissitudes in Latin America, can one fashion a general analytical framework that *does* seem to correspond more closely to the realities of Latin America and the peculiarities of its change process? Within the confines of the present paper it is of course impossible to construct a full-blown and all-encompassing theory of Latin American development.[8] Nevertheless, some of the major parameters and components of such a schema may be outlined, for this will enable us to assess the relationship between law and legal institutions and the overall process of development.

A good starting point for the study of Latin American society and polity—not just of its traditional order but of much of its present-day style and structure as well—is to think in terms of a fairly well-defined, rigid yet adaptable, hierarchically and vertically segmented pattern of class and caste stratifications, social rank orders, estates, juridical groupings, guilds, corporate bodies, and *intereses*. The various groups and sectors revolve around, are tied to, and derive legitimacy from the authority of the central state or its patrimonial leader.[9] The historic origins of this system lie in the remote Iberic-Latin past, most particularly the late medieval and early modern era (roughly the fifteenth and sixteenth centuries), and in the early attempts to blend and accommodate the medieval-Catholic concepts of hierarchy, natural law, and estates with the newer requisites of centralization, absolute monarchy, and the Conquest. Given the context of the times, it should not be surprising that such a grand reconciliation was achieved, for example in the work of Suárez, Spain's great sixteenth-century political philosopher and perhaps the most seminally important thinker in the Hispanic-Latin tradition, but that this scheme would prove as durable as it has. Spain, Portugal, and the colonies they established in the New World have long been—and in many respects remain today—based upon a social and political order that is authoritarian, patrimonial, Catholic, stratified, corporate, and semifeudal to its core. As Ronald C. Newton writes, "Suárez endowed his State with a remarkable stability, a stability achieved through the delicate balancing of opposing and ultimately antagonistic forces . . . Suárez' state is . . . a system admirably designed, out of very disparate components and different traditions, for the preservation of the status quo."[10]

The legal-institutional base of Spain at the time of the conquest was the *Siete Partidas,* drawn up in about 1260 and formally promulgated in 1348. Naturally, the Spanish view and philosophy of law in this period were closely intertwined with Spanish social and political philosophy in general. As Richard M. Morse points out, the *Partidas* were not so much rules *for* conduct in the Roman sense but rather medieval types of principles *of* proper conduct and *of* the well-ordered society and polity that approached the sanctity and status of being moral treatises. Reflecting the strong Catholic-Thomistic-natural law world view that has always been so influential in the Latin-Hispanic tradition, the *Partidas* assumed the nuclear element of society to be not Lockean atomistic man as in the Anglo-American tradition, but social and organic man. Each person's station in life was thus determined by mutual obligations with and responsibilities toward his fellow men, in accordance with God's immutable law and the principles of hierarchy, rank, and order as set forth by Aquinas and other late medieval and early modern Catholic political theorists. Governance, therefore, took the form of the dispensing of immanent justice on the part of the Crown and the ceding and protection of special privileges, or *fueros,* to the major corporate entities—the Church, the Army, the nobility, the merchant guilds, and so forth.[11] It is Suárez who blends these peculiarly feudal, medieval, and Christian aspects of the Hispanic tradition with the sixteenth century imperatives of more modern statecraft. Characteristic of the Spanish tradition, however, he does so through the assimilation of the newer ingredients and their accommodation with and grafting on to the older tradition rather than the replacement of the one by the other.

Each "class" or corporate estate had its own privileges as well as obligations, its own code of conduct as well as, frequently, its own courts and judges. Particularly in the New World, classes and castes were strictly segregated; justice was similarly dispensed on a sectoral and not an egalitarian basis. When men talked of "rights" they were not referring to any abstract Lockean "natural" or individual rights but rather seeking to guarantee and frequently enhance the *fueros* or special privileges that were inherently theirs because of their or their group's place and status in the society. Though there has thus far been relatively little historical examination of the whole system of corporate estates in colonial times and of the juridical structure of *fueros* on which it was largely based, and though Latin man is also profoundly individualistic, the legacy of the feudal-corporate group system remains strong even in contemporary Latin America. One need only cite as examples the fact that criminal and other forms of justice are still being dispensed largely on a "class" basis; the intense

preoccupation on the part of such traditional corporate interests as
the landed interests, the Church, and the military with preserving and
protecting their special place in the system and on the part of the
newer rising groups, such as the new industrialists, the middle sectors, and organized labor, with having their "rights" recognized and
legitimized; and the fact that even today special law (that is, law or
statutes designed for and aimed at benefiting a single interest or individual) often prevails over more general law. The Thomistic-Catho-
lic-feudal structure is still omnipresent in the Latin countries, not only
in their systems of law but also in the fundamental order of society
and polity as well.[12]

Some change took place within the traditional Latin American
colonial structure, of course, as new laws and new institutions were
added on, as royal authority waxed and waned, and as both the
Iberic nations and their American colonies adapted themselves to
new concepts and pressures. But the basic structure of society and
polity remained largely intact. Indeed, since Latin America was
largely bypassed by the great revolutions that we associate with the
early stirrings of the modern order—the Protestant Reformation and
the emergence of religious pluralism, the growth of capitalism and
the industrial revolution and the accelerated social change to which
this gave rise, the scientific revolution and the enlightenment, the
growth of limited representative government—much of the subsequent
history of Latin America to the present may be understood in terms
of the institutions and behavioral patterns first established by Spain
and Portugal in the Western Hemisphere during those definitive
decades of conquest and colonization in the sixteenth century. So
durable, in fact, were the Iberian social structure and political-
institutional framework that they survived not only some three centuries of colonial rule, but also, with some readjustments, the wars
of independence from Spain and, in the case of Brazil, the separation from Portugal. In many respects they have survived even the
long-delayed acceleration of the development-modernization process
in the late nineteenth and twentieth centuries.[13]

To be sure, there was some modification of the original system and
some reordering occurred, but such change as did occur came from
the top down and was ordinarily carefully controlled and regulated.
As Morse writes, furthermore, this was not so much a matter of
"fundamental change" in the Western European or North American
sense (that is, implying revolutionary transformations, a reconstruction of the socio-political base, self-transcendence, or the oblit-
eration of the past) as it was the mediating and gradual accommodating of the accouterments and rallying cries of modern, Western
industrial civilization to a way of life that remained in essence Ibero-
Catholic, highly structured and corporate, creole or New World

feudal, and patrimonial.[14] Capitalistic entrepreneurs and industrialists and their associations eventually emerged alongside of the ancient merchants and their guilds, but the pattern of a separate commercial code and of special *fueros* for the "merchant class" remained intact—at a time when these essentially feudal and corporate bodies were beginning to decline in Britain and in other of the more developed societies. At present in Latin America, therefore, one finds for example the maintenance of the older *fueros* or laws of guilds at the same time that more modern commercial and other kinds of codes have been imposed on top of them, and also when newer concepts of "socialist law," broadly defined, are also beginning to come to the fore. Similarly in the political sphere, new institutional apparati were also grafted on, largely to help fill the legitimacy vacuum left by the withdrawal of the Crown, which had formed the vortex of the Hispanic, corporate pyramid. But the underlying base, the socio-economic structure, the Church, the institution of the *patrón,* the system of *latifundia,* all remained stable as in the past. Moreover, through adaptation, accommodation, and cooptation on the part of the ruling elites, much of this same underlying structure has continued on into the present, though clearly the pressures for change have now become somewhat more intense.

Among the institutions grafted on during this early period were the constitutions written for these newly independent nations, as well as one or another version of the French *Code Napoléon.* It is practically a truism to point out that both the new constitutions and the new codes were ill-suited to the countries which adapted them and that the "grafts," hence, failed to "take." The constitutions, for example, provided for representative and democratic institutions, separation of powers, bills of rights, etc., in societies where these traditions were largely lacking and where the dominant structures had always been closed, authoritarian, centralized, and highly personalistic. The constitutions thus failed to serve as a check on those in power. Similarly, the law codes derived from France were in many ways inappropriate in Latin America. The Napoleonic Code was in essence anti-feudal and highly individualistic, while Latin America remained essentially a corporate-feudal area. The French law was utopian and revolutionary, built not only on the dramatic concepts of the Enlightenment and the French Revolution but also on the gradual and frequently less dramatic revolutionary modernizing movements that had been occurring in Western Europe in the two or three centuries prior to the promulgation of Napoleon's famous code. In Latin America, however, these movements had had only a limited effect. A legal system derived from them was bound to be largely irrelevant.[15] One finds, for example, a rejection of the old order in the constitutions and codes but not in the way Latin America continued to be governed and its group or corporate sector interrelations managed. There was a rationalization of the law but not a concomitant rationalization and modernization of society and polity. Of course, both the new constitutions and the new codes were based upon a series of abstract universal formulas—just as were Latin America's own earlier Roman and Thomistic "basic laws"—and, though irrelevant in many ways, they could thus be grafted on rather easily without altering either the socio-political or even the philosophical bases of the society. As a further result, however, a truly national and functional legal system never developed in the Latin American countries; the constitutions and systems of law remained isolated from the societies they were intended to serve.[16]

There has been a great deal of nonsense written about the inappropriateness and the supposed dysfunctionality of the legal-constitutional models adopted by the Latin American nations in the nineteenth century. First, one must keep in mind the very few alternatives open to Latin America's early "nation builders." Second, one must note the intentions of the men who drafted these fundamental charters. They were not, as Glen Dealy's research has shown, naive and inexperienced men, seeking unrealistically to emulate the French or North American constitutional-legal models and to impose them on societies where they did not fit.[17] Nor did this quite give rise to such a strict separation of "theory" from "practice" as is supposed to characterize the Latin American political tradition. In point of fact, the men who drafted these codes were eminently reasonable and highly qualified men. Nor did they seek to divorce themselves from 300 years of colonial rule and a Hispanic-Latin tradition that stretched back even further. Rather, they consistently tried to adapt the new laws to prevailing custom and history, showing what Dealy calls a "remarkable genius" for incorporating the republican forms and language of the day while retaining their non-democratic and non-revolutionary heritage almost intact. One need only examine the view of human nature found in these new constitutions (Thomistic, not Lockean), the distinctive meaning given the word "rights" (implying privileges or special *fueros,* group rights rather than natural individual rights), the privileged place accorded the Church and other corporate elites, the subordinate position of the legislature and judiciary, the role of the military as the "moderating power," the extensive authority of the executive, etc., to demonstrate that these founding fathers did not wish to repudiate the past but to preserve it, while at the same time assimilating some elements that were new. Democratic theory was not really embraced at that time, for even though to North Americans the language may have sounded familiar, the content and meaning were decidedly Latin-Hispanic and authoritarian. The former colonies of Spain and Portugal in the early nineteenth century were still essentially thinking more in medieval terms, of guilds and privileges, of hierarchy and authority, than they were in modern, democratic concepts; and the content of their laws and constitutions was similarly derived more from their own experiences than from others'. They did not simply take over, as numerous legal and political commentators have proclaimed, the frameworks of the West, but consciously sought to borrow what was useful in these newer schemes and largely rejected the rest. They chose, as Dealy concludes, to implement a system of government and of laws which in *both theory and practice* had much in common with their own tradition and was consistent with it.[18]

The independence period, thus, did not mark such a sharp change from the past as is often believed. Scholars have long pointed out that the wars of independence in Latin America were not "true" revolutions because there was little change in the socio-economic substructure. Now it appears there was precious little change in the political-constitutional-legal sphere as well. The garb was changed, to be sure, as new liberal, democratic, and representative dressing was added on, but the character of the political society underneath remained much the same. In fact, the dominant tradition of the past, one which was Catholic, authoritarian, stratified, semi-feudal, corporate, and patrimonialist, was retained; moreover, this tradition continued to exhibit a rather close (though sometimes disguised) unity between theory and practice. The vision of society and polity held by the leaders of that time was essentially non-democratic and it remains so today. The direction of political thought, Dealy again reminds us, has maintained a remarkable continuity since 1810 as well as before that date. At virtually every step of the way the reality of Latin American society and politics has been supported by constitutional and statutory provisions that authorize, legitimize, and enshrine authoritarian, hierarchical, and corporate practices and thus continue the venerated tradition. In short, Latin America does not seem to suffer, as so many North American writers have proclaimed, the "pathological condition" brought on by a relentless but frustrated search for democracy, by its effort to bring theory and practice together. The writers who hold that position are necessarily bound to consider Latin American history to the present largely a failure, for the democratic quest which they suppose Latin America embarked upon has not been accomplished. But that evaluation rests on the assumption that democracy "North American style" was and is the goal to which Latin America aspires. The argument of the present essay, however, is that that was not the case in the 1820s—and probably still is not today. Thus, it would seem, to paraphrase Dealy once more, that the supposed "failure" of the Latin American countries to achieve democracy a century and a half ago, and again in the 1960s, was not really a failure, but in fact a triumph for the major ideals and aspirations that had been theirs since the sixteenth century—however *undemocratic* these might be.[19]

In more recent decades accelerated change has taken place throughout Latin America and the strains upon the traditional structures and institutions have multiplied. Considerable economic growth has occurred, new social forces have emerged, new governmental institutions have been added, new ideologies have had their impact, and the pressures emanating from the outside world have intensified. But in many respects the traditional order and institutions and the time-honored way of managing change have been retained. The same *patrón-clientela* system persists, for example, also frequently dressed up in new and more modern forms but retaining much of its traditional substance. The state or one of its agencies has simply taken over the role previously held by the landowner or other *patrón* and is performing many of the same functions in much the same authoritarian and paternalistic way.[20] Moreover, the same Thomistic, hierarchical, elitist, and corporate outlook and organization which so strongly shaped Latin America's past history is also still present today, modified by the pressures of change but not destroyed by them. Indeed, the presence of these traditional features, not only in the most backward but also in the most "modern" or "developed" of the Latin American countries—from Paraguay's functionally representative Council of State to Brazil's system of officially-sanctioned labor syndicates, Mexico's corporately-organized *Partido Revolucionario Institucional,* and Venezuela's agrarian reform and peasant associations—is so all-pervasive that one cannot possibly even begin to list all the illustrations or analyze their influences. Suffice it to say for the moment that much of the Latin American socio-political structure is still based upon the old, hierarchically organized system of corporate bodies and groups, now expanded somewhat to encompass some of the newer social forces, but still highly segmented and vertically structured and linked to the government at the highest level.

The government tends to control and direct all associations and corporate units, with the result that the lines of command and influence go directly to the top without being filtered through and moderated by various intermediaries (strong and independent parties, trade unions, legislatures, and the like). It is the state, after all, that must pass on the group's or association's *estatuto básico* or *ley orgánica,* that in the process grants or withholds official recognition and thus determines whether that particular group or sector shall be accorded legitimacy or not, that thereby regulates the admission of new groups to the system and seeks to maintain that delicate balance between traditional and modern that is so fundamental in the Latin-

Hispanic tradition, and that ultimately is responsible not only for the good of society but also its individual members. Ideally, of course, the system works best within a context of mutually-accepted values and where the number of groups or *intereses* to be satisfied are small, but it is not necessarily incompatible with a growing pluralism of ideologies and associations.[21]

How may one describe this set of peculiar political structures and the unique nature of the development (or stagnation) process in Latin America? And why does the Latin American pattern seem to correspond so imperfectly to either the Marxian or non-Marxian "stages of growth" models? Though other terms may be used, I have found it helpful in my research and writing to conceive and analyze the Latin American systems from the viewpoint of what I have called the "corporative framework" of socio-political change.[22] Corporatism refers to a system in which the political culture and institutions reflect a historic hierarchical, authoritarian, organic view of man, society, and polity.[23] In such a system the "general will" prevails over particular interests; and group rights, or *fueros,* usually take precedence over individual liberties. To illustrate, there is widespread acceptance even at the constitutional level of Duguit's "social function of property" theory. It is society or the state that retains the rights to sub-soil natural wealth, not the individual property holder. Similarly, since the good of the whole social organism takes precedence over that of any individual part of it, the state may confiscate or expropriate private property, suspend civil liberties, or take any one of a number of other actions which are considered to enhance the general good, frequently at the expense of so-called individual rights. The state serves as the arbiter over a network of countervailing elites and corporate interests, organized hierarchically and segmented vertically according to considerations of formal-legal status, economic functions, or estates. Cooperation and accommodation are emphasized over conflict and disorder. Political issues tend to be adjudicated rather than arbitrated, with principle taking precedence over "politics."

An effort is thus made to deal with political issues bureaucratically; in both theory and practice administration supersedes politics. In the corporate system politics *per se* (implying log-rolling, give-and-take, the pragmatic compromise, etc.) is looked upon as degrading; hence, it becomes necessary to govern in an apolitical fashion (contradictory though that may sound) through the bureaucratic organization of society and the integration of the various social forces into the state apparatus.[24] This of course is not to deny the importance of politics in Latin America but to stress that the whole context in which politics takes place is quite different from the Anglo-American tradition. The stress is on each man's acceptance of his place in the corporate and hierarchical system along with its attendant privileges and responsibilities. Conflicts may thus be dealt with by denying they exist, through the harmonization of the points of view of the various elites and *intereses* rather than through class strife or an "unseemly" public controversy involving economic and political power plays. It is the duty of the state and its *líder* to organize opinion and maintain the proper balance among the various groups in the society through this corporate structure. Decisions, therefore, are usually made by a small coterie of elite group representatives, usually linked by formal and informal ties to the highest pinnacles of the administrative hierarchy and centering, ordinarily, in one man who, ideally, inculcates the national values, knows the "general will," and is the best and most qualified leader—the ablest and most skilled *caudillo* who is also the personification of the nation.

If this framework accurately represents some of the more salient features of the Latin American political process, then it would seem that instead of exclusively searching for and researching the instruments of change and / or revolution, we might better study the forces maintaining the status quo. We must study not only change but also continuity, with the latter—at least in the Latin American case—probably the more important. Why and how do the traditional social and political forms—and the legal and constitutional frameworks that help give them legitimacy—hang on so tenaciously? One important answer, it would seem, is the maintenance, even in the present and increasingly modern era in Latin America, of corporate social and political structures, reinforced by a political culture that stresses hierarchy, authority, status, and patronage. The corporative framework helps maintain this traditional structure, but at the same time provides for change through the process of cooptation of new social and political units into the administrative units of the corporate system. The corporative way of achieving change thus helps preserve the status quo while at the same time defusing discontent through gradualist and incremental accommodation to new pressures. It helps keep the pressures for change within check by minimizing the possibilities for disruption or revolution. The corporate framework may respond to modernization and adopt some of its ways, but it also provides for the preservation of traditional attitudes and traditional institutions.[25]

It should perhaps be reemphasized that the corporate structure and ideology is nothing new in Latin America. It has been rebaptized many times and under many names—Vargas' *"Estado Novo,"* Perón's "Justicialism," Trujillo's "Neo-Democracy," Mexico's sectorally-organized one-party system, today's military "Nasserism" and Christian democracy—but the roots of the system lie deep in the Hispanic-Latin past. At present it may take the form of official trade unionism or the granting of recognition to a new professional or employers' association, but this is not altogether different from the ancient system of royal recognition of and patronage over the medieval guilds and estates. Currently the crisis of Latin American corporatism involves the question of the integration of the lower or popular classes into the dominant system, but this does not differ greatly from the earlier efforts to assimilate and absorb other elites or the rising middle sectors. The corporate structure and theory did not, then, originate in the 1920s or 1930s, when "corporatism" and "fascism" acquired a sense of self-consciousness and a full-blown ideology; rather, the origins of the corporatist system stretch back to the ancient and medieval theory and structure of society and to the values and institutions initially carried over by Spain and Portugal to the New World.

The role of law in this system is exceedingly important, for it is legal recognition that gives legitimacy to a group and makes its existence formally recognized. Legal recognition by the government is the *sine qua non* for the activities of any organized interest, be it in the form of the acknowledgment of the juridical status of a labor organization or professional association or the granting of a charter to a university or municipality. The government regulates the whole process of group activities, elite integration, and national development through its powers of recognition and non-recognition, as well as through its power over the purse and the careful management of official subsidies. At the same time, any group that aspires to a more important place in the system and the right to bargain in it, as well as access to official funds and favors, must first have its "juridical personality" acknowledged and legal recognition to organize and carry on its activities granted. This is quite different from the Lockean-liberal tradition, in that individual, unorganized, atomized man cannot exert much pressure on the system; indeed, without inscription on the rolls and formal recognition of his group by the government, he is virtually a non-man. This power of recognition, formalized in the laws and sometimes even in the constitution, of course gives the state and the administrative and other elites that control it immense power over individual and group life and, in fact, the capacity to regulate and manage the pace as well as the direction of virtually the entire development-modernization process.

Characteristically, Latin American political systems seek to ameliorate social conflict rather than to meet it head on. Face-to-face conflicts are avoided by channeling problems through the offices of the administrative system. Socio-political issues are thus dealt with bureaucratically and usually through the process of elite integration and assimilation, rather than through program implementation. Patronage instead of concrete benefits is the chief medium of currency;

it is exchanged for acquiescence in official policies by elements in the society who might otherwise attempt organized opposition to such policies.[26] The government seeks to maintain an equilibrium among the contending forces and is thus highly centralized and bureaucratized. Solidarity, allegiance, and acceptance of the rules of the game are absolutely required; there can be no divided loyalties, at least as regards the fundamental structure and workings of the system. The personnel of government may change, coups or elections may occur, and new groups and new ideas may be absorbed, but the essential nature of the socio-political order and the base on which it rests must remain steadfast. New groups may be assimilated into the system, but before they are legitimized, they must be socialized into accepting its traditional *mores;* they cannot challenge the system *per se* or seek to topple it. Those that do must expect to and will be crushed until they too have made their accommodation with the prevailing system. Witness the differences, for example, between those groups and parties that managed such an accommodation and were thereby enabled to preside over a generally successful period of (to borrow Albert Hirschman's apt term) develop-mongering—*Acción Democrática* in Venezuela, the *Colorados* for a considerable period in Uruguay, and perhaps even the Christian Democrats in Chile—as opposed to those who either failed to reach such a compromise or were forced by the traditional elite to remain outside the system and who hence failed in their developmental goals—the *Apristas* in Peru, Bosch and his Revolutionary Party in the Dominican Republic, and Goulart and the now-defunct Brazilian Labor Party. Short of a full-scale social revolution, as in Mexico, Bolivia, and Cuba, one "plays" by the system's rules, or one doesn't "play" at all.[27]

In the corporative conception, society is thought of as an organic whole, a "family" with a profoundly moral purpose. One is bound to accept his station in life, the status to which society has assigned him. Ideally, however, through personal and family ties and various linkage mechanisms, all are integrated and made to "fit" into the system and their needs taken care of. This has tended to give even the most "progressive" and "democratic" regimes in Latin America a particularly tutelary and paternalistic form, guided from above. An attempt is thus made to transfer the prevailing traditional and elitist values to the rising new groups through example and "education." First the rising commercial and manufacturing elements were "civilized" and absorbed in this fashion, then the emerging middle sectors, and now the urban workers and even the peasants.[28] This helps explain why so frequently in Latin America one finds state-supported and officially-sanctioned political parties, trade unions, peasant associations, professional "colleges" or "classes," etc. It also helps explain why such "progressive" programs as agrarian reform have had so little impact in terms of fundamentally reordering the socio-political structure, for programs such as these have frequently been used as instruments of social control rather than of social change. Middle and now lower class people are thus offered marginal benefits and at least a partial stake in the system, both as a means of defusing possible discontent and of placing them directly under the paternalistic hegemony of the state, which is still dominated in so many ways by the traditional elitist and middle sector groups who often share a traditional elitist outlook. Whatever the surface and short-term manifestations of instability, therefore, in the form of frequent barracks revolts and palace "revolutions," systemic stability in the long run has generally been preserved. And in this fashion the traditional order in Latin America has proved to be remarkably resilient, bending to change where it had to but retaining its fundamental essence. One cannot help but be reminded of Japan, where many traditional patterns have similarly been retained at the same time that modern techniques have been absorbed.

It is characteristic of the political process in Latin America, therefore, that new social groups, new power contenders, new ideologies, and new institutional arrangements may be added on to the system but, owing to the absence of genuine social revolution in Latin America's past history, old ones are seldom discarded. Only in Mexico, Cuba, Bolivia, and Nicaragua have there been full-scale social revolutions which signified a sharp break with the past by destroying the power and position of the traditionally privileged elites and the socio-economic structure on which they rested. In the rest of the countries, however, as Charles W. Anderson puts it, Latin America remains something of a "living museum" of virtually all the systems of society and polity that have ever ordered the affairs of men and nations, a blend of feudalism, divine right monarchy, oligarchism, republicanism, absolutism, liberalism, positivism, capitalism, populism, fascism, democracy, socialism, and others, all existing side by side, no one of them any more with an absolute or definitive claim to legitimacy but with none of them being cast off either. Behavioral norms and organizational forms and institutions which have died off or been discarded elsewhere in the West continue in Latin America to coexist with those characteristic of more modern and industrialized nations.[29] Moreover, even in those countries that have had a genuine revolution—and one thinks particularly of Mexico in this regard—the corporate style and structure remain strong.

As a result of the singular tenacity of these traditional socio-political organizations, therefore, there has been remarkably limited "development" in most of the countries of Latin America, in either

a Marxian or a non-Marxian sense, but rather a trend toward stagnation, atrophy, anomie, and fragmentation. The future of Latin
America may not, therefore, lie in Bolivia, Cuba, Mexico, Peru, or
any of the other countries that have been cited as developmental
models, but in Argentina, by almost any index one of the most
"developed" and most "modern" of the Latin American nations,
but which, precisely because it is so "modern" in terms of its social
and political differentiations, has fragmented, polarized, disinte-
grated, and broken down. In a justly famous passage Arthur P.
Whitaker has emphasized that socially and politically Argentina is a
highly fragmented nation. Such fragmentation implies far deeper,
sharper, and more numerous cleavages than we think of as characteristic of pluralist societies, for the various sectors of society share
little consensus on the ends or means of political action and they
seldom communicate with each other except in conflict. Hence there
arises, in Whitaker's view, the widespread sense of frustration and
loss of direction that embitters domestic politics and serves to perpetuate the national differences.[30] In Argentina, indeed, the process
of social and political fragmentation has proceeded so far and endured so long that since 1930 the country has existed in virtually a
permanent state of crisis and disintegration. Kalman Silvert aptly
referred to it as a "conflict society" and Kenneth F. Johnson described its politics as a "mosaic of discord."[31]

The Latin American political process often involves not so much
the transcendence of one class or social order over another but the
combination of diverse elements pertaining to quite different eras
in some kind of tentative working arrangement. Again, the issue is
not so much one of "development" as it is that of reconciling, in
Morse's words, the static and vegetative features of the patrimonial,
corporate state and the creole-feudal society with the imperatives
of a modern, urban, industrial world.[32] The traditional order has
proved to be not nearly so rigid and immutable as we sometimes
imagine but, in fact, flexible, permeable, and almost infinitely
malleable, bending enough to absorb such features of "modernity"
as were required without in the process undermining the basic
order itself. It has assimilated the features of modernity that were
necessary and that could be contained within the traditional
framework, but it has rejected the rest.[33] It did so, as we said, chiefly
through the process of elite integration and the assimilation of newer
elements into the system. Up until recently this whole process of
elite integration, assimilation, and systemic adaptation took place
relatively smoothly, almost naturally, and without provoking systemic breakdowns (as distinct from the numerous coups and barracks revolts that dot the history of Latin America). At present, however, under the increasing pressures of the contemporary period,

with the change process speeded up enormously, and with the number of *intereses* or corporate entities rapidly expanding, the traditional style and structure has become far more tenuous and the capacity of the socio-political system to cope with and manage these changes far more uncertain.

It is useful, perhaps, to think of the Latin American systems in terms of a series of layers, or "stages," each superimposed upon the other, with new elements continuously being appended on and adapted to an older tradition, but without that older tradition being sloughed off or eliminated or even undergoing very many fundamental transformations. These layers originate in eras that are widely separated in time and content, but which are somehow fused in most of the Latin American systems. If one prefers the Marxian lexicon, one can refer to these layers as feudal, bourgeois, and socialist. Now, in Western Europe each of these stages more or less replaced or superseded its predecessor; in Latin America, however, the coexistence of the one with the others remains the rule. Though it represents something of an oversimplification, perhaps the 1970 Chilean presidential elections help illustrate that point. In Chile one can almost conceive of the three presidential candidates as representative of these three epochs—Alessandri a representative of an older traditional order, Tomic of a newer liberal bourgeois order, and Allende of the newest socialist order. Each layer or sector is currently about equal in voter strength, and hence no one of the three can command an absolute majority any more, while all three are coexistent within a single political system. Chile is, like Argentina, one of the more "modern" and socially differentiated of the Latin American countries and certainly one of the Hemisphere's most politically sophisticated nations. But in recent years, like Argentina, it has become increasingly divided and politically fragmented. Allowing for variations related to their level of modernization and social differentiation, one can observe similarly tiered patterns—though perhaps seldom as neat as in Chile—together with the increased social and political fragmentation and disintegration that seems to accompany the modernization process, in the other Latin American nations as well.

If one prefers different criteria, then the progression from two-class to multi-class societies or, better said, from systems of relatively few corporate interests or elites to systems of multiple interests and elites may also be an instructive way to picture the Latin American socio-political change process. Or, to use political terms, the continuum may run from authoritarian-patrimonialist to liberal-representative to populist-participatory. In this sense, the corporate framework that we have here used, even though it has demonstrated remarkable tenaciousness, has also seen the superimposition upon it of the representative institutions of a liberal, democratic, and constitutional sort and now, increasingly, the early stirrings of the trend toward greater popular sharing in the national wealth and involvement in decision-making. As we have emphasized, however, even with these newer layers added on, the corporate ideal remains strong and all-pervasive—although, under the pressures of change from the society at large, it too is changing. In law, also, one may trace the successive influences, from the scholasticism and Thomistic natural law of the colonial period, to the "rational" natural law of the Napoleonic codes and of the liberal and representative constitutions of the independence era, to the legal positivism of the late nineteenth and early twentieth centuries, to the neo-Thomism and "pure theory of law" philosophy of Kelsen in the period between the Great Wars and even beyond, and to the sociological jurisprudence and increasingly development-oriented legal concerns of today.[34] These paradigms of course are oversimplified and one may well disagree on the categories or descriptive labels used. But the important point is that in all these areas of Latin American life—the economic, the society, the political system, the legal-constitutional framework —one finds illustration of some of the major themes here discussed: namely, the perseverance of traditional structures at the same time that newer structures and functions have been repeatedly grafted on, the capacity of the ancient system of corporate estates, elites, and authoritarian structures to absorb and assimilate the newer currents without in the process itself being destroyed, the incredibly mixed, overlapping, heterogeneous character of contemporary Latin American society, behavioral norms, and political institutions.

In an attempt to explain and come to grips with these peculiar aspects of the change process in Latin America, Richard N. Adams has fashioned a theory of what he terms "secondary development."[35] Secondary development, in Adams' formulation, refers to the course which development takes when it enters an area that was formerly isolated from and a hinterland of the industrial revolution and of the modern Western world. Development in Latin America, therefore, does not *follow,* as a matter of successive stages, the development patterns of Western Europe or North America but involves the *adaptation* of an older order to newer forces. This is a process of derivation, assimilation, and reorganization, not of innovation. Secondary development thus implies the importation and adaptation of more modern social and political organizations and techniques and their superimposition on top of an older, already established socio-political order, not the replacement of the one by the other.

In such a system politics involves, in Anderson's words, the effort to reach tentative and conditional agreement among heterogeneous "power contenders" whose strength is unequal and whose interests are almost totally incompatible, because they pertain to quite different epochs.[36] Because these various elites and *intereses*—landowners, Church, Army, business or industrial groups, middle sectors, labor, peasants, etc.—emerged from distinct eras with distinct values and ideologies and with decidedly uneven legal-juridical bases for their legitimacy as a group, the attempt to fashion an accommodation and working arrangement among them has usually involved what to North Americans have always seemed some incredible marriages of convenience, alliances that appear to defy any "rational" person's sense of ideological consistency, or the fantastic twisting and stretching of the law or constitution so as to render them all but unrecognizable. Yet it is precisely these features that help account for the uniqueness of the Latin American development process and that give it its dynamism and its capacity to respond to new pressures—again, while keeping much of its traditional essence intact.

One comes to think, writes Ronald C. Newton, in terms of "multiple currents of cultural evolution, moving at different rates to uneven rhythms, regressing as well as advancing, submerging as well as predominating, intersecting and interacting fortuitously within the framework of a given metropolis, a given institution, or indeed, a given personality structure."[31] It is the task of the Latin American political leader or state apparatus somehow to reconcile these "multiple currents," to bring these quite diverse groups and concepts into harmony. Needless to say this is often an incredibly difficult juggling and balancing act, not only because of the increasingly diverse interests represented but also because no common consensus or bases of legitimacy any longer exist. The mixture of feudal traditions and modern codes, the overlap of distinct eras and socio-political arrangements and the absence of any single, dominant, surviving tradition help explain why, in fact, the law and the constitution *must* be so elastic, why such incredible juridical gymnastics *must* be engaged in, and why there are so many legalisms that seemingly have little to do with reality. With interests and ideologies pertaining to different epochs, with economies and social systems reflective of both the earlier feudal and the modern eras and of various hybrids of them, with political attitudes and institutions shaped by such a great variety of successive influences, with life styles, indeed, that are representative of completely separate worlds—and with all of these distinct interests, attitudes, ideologies, economic arrangements, institutions, social forces, social systems, and life styles superimposed successively in layers, the one upon the other in a mosaic of uneven, imbalanced, and overlapping patterns—it is small wonder that the politics of Latin America and its legal-constitutional arrangements have been as disjointed, as dysfunctional, and as discontinuous as they have.

Kalman Silvert's description of what he calls the "Mediterranean ethos" or "syndicalism" also closely parallels the present framework.[33] The nations which are a part of or which stem from this Mediterranean ethos (encompassing, thus, Greece, Italy, Spain, Portugal, the latter two's New World colonies, perhaps other countries to a lesser degree) are grounded upon a social order and value system that emphasizes order, hierarchy, and corporate organization. The organization of men by estate, status, and functions, in Silvert's words, actualizes the love of order and hierarchy, serves to contain divisive class conflict, avoids the foreign liberal and materialistic values, leaves inviolate the power and privileges of the esteemed traditional order, and at the same time provides for the slow and at least partial adaptation of traditional and patrimonial society to urbanization, industrialization, and modernization. Much of Latin American political life, therefore, involves the effort to bring into harmonious coexistence what is valuable in the modern Western nations—e.g., industry, greater affluence, etc.—along with those traditions and institutions considered valuable from the past—the family and religion, humanism and personalism, the corporate structure, and so forth.

The "good" society, therefore, is ordinarily pictured as one where each individual is rooted and secure in his station, where representation is determined by status or function and not as a result of certain "inalienable" rights of citizenship, and where decision-making is based upon a number of well-integrated corporate elites, all of whom agree on certain primary values, accept the operating "rules of the game," and are harmonized and coordinated into an organic whole.[39] The various elites (or "estates" or "classes") are connected directly and vertically to the central authority rather than having their interests channeled through a variety of secondary groups, or organized horizontally and impersonally across group boundaries. The state, in turn, is expected—even required—to exercise firm but paternalistic authority over this whole national "family."

The corporate framework is of course a fundamentally conservative way of managing changes. "Conservatism" as here used implies general correspondence to the system's prevailing and historical norms and the maintenance of essentially traditional institutions rather than their overthrow and replacement. The corporate structure, after all, serves the interests of the dominant elites and the power structures they control by subordinating the new groups and interests to the authority of the central state. For instance, the extension of official recognition to the trade unions, the bureaucratic organization of labor into a system of government-sanctioned and often controlled syndicates, and the creation of a labor ministry and of a hierarchy of labor courts all help avoid conflict and the possibilities of class struggle, provide for the cooptation of labor into the administrative apparatus of the corporate state, and thus help preserve the status quo. The corporate framework serves to preserve as much as possible of the traditional order during this period of accelerated social change. It does so by incorporating the newer forces generated by the modernization-development process into the prevailing system and by structuring their participation under its own (i.e., the state's or the elitist structure's) control and direction.[40]

Though the pattern of elite integration and cooptation stretches back for centuries, the newer and more complex corporate forms have arisen as a result of the emergence of new social and political groups in the national arena. The traditional elites have attempted to cope with this by establishing new integrating institutions controlled by the elites and oriented towards stability. Change and even some modernization are thus possible within the corporate framework but only within fairly circumscribed limits, since the condition for the absorption and accommodation of such new power contenders into the system is their acceptance of its prevailing norms. Within this context, it has proved to be virtually impossible to achieve more fundamental change, for the new groups are either "bought off" in this fashion, or they are suppressed. The change process in Latin America has thus been a fundamentally conservative one; but then, Latin America itself has thus far also been a fundamentally conservative and unrevolutionary area—one could argue, almost inherently so.[41]

By being flexible and by accommodating new groups and new ideas, we have said, the Latin American systems and their authoritarian-corporate socio-political structures have proved to be remarkably durable. More recently, however, the pressures upon the prevailing system have intensified and the possibilities for genuinely transcendent and "structural," or revolutionary change have greatly increased. Allowing for considerable variation from country to country, some of the older power bases in Latin America—the *hacienda,* the village community, the landed oligarchy, the traditional elitist cadre parties, etc.—are in the process of decline. At the same time, the number of interests to be accommodated within the traditional system has multiplied. Moreover the shared basis of ideas and values on which the old order rests has been undermined as new concerns and new ideologies have gained prominence. External pressures for change have similarly increased. These changes have placed great stress on the legal system and on political institutions more generally. It seems clear that the traditional mechanisms for adaptation and assimilation—such as family favoritism, patronage, the *jeito,* etc.— are, in themselves, no longer wholly adequate. As Latin American politics has become increasingly class-, issue-, and interest-oriented, and as the Latin American societies have become more complex, differentiated, and modern, the capacity of the traditional structure to cope with the new pressures thrust upon it has declined. But while such changes have increased the possibilities for a radical restructuring of the society on the one hand, they have additionally intensified the tenacious attempt of the status quo-oriented forces to preserve the traditional order on the other. In many countries of Latin America, therefore, the result of the process of the decline of the old order and the rise of an as yet unconsolidated new one has been not a more or less peaceful transformation from traditional to modern, but, instead, an increase in tensions and conflicts, a deterioration in the capability of the traditional mechanisms to manage and accommodate to change in the classic fashion, and a spiraling long-term crisis characterized by institutional decay, societal disintegration, praetorianism, and in some cases even complete national breakdowns.[42]

The corporate framework, we may conclude this general discussion of the change process in Latin America, has demonstrated enormous vitality and it may yet have considerable longevity—provided it proves capable of resolving the participation crisis brought on by the emergence of the organized masses into the national political arena and of managing the discordant influences that in the contemporary period threaten to undermine it. At the same time one must keep in mind that the Latin American nations are now at best only semi-corporate systems, that new layers have been added on, and that within this overlapping configuration there is room for a great deal of variation and internal conflict and contradiction. In Erickson's excellent case study of labor in the political process in Brazil, for example, the author shows both the mutual dependence and the mutual antagonisms that have come to characterize labor's relations with the state and its official trade union structure. On the one hand the corporate institutions of Brazil make the labor leaders dependent on the state in the traditional fashion, while on the other the growth of liberal democracy and the eventual emergence of populism enabled them to seek greater power *vis-à-vis* the state. Electoral democracy, populism, the strike technique, etc., all tend to work at cross purposes with the control function of the corporate system. Thus in the first stage of union organization in Brazil the masses were mobilized by established political elites and under the control of the government so as to restrict labor activities to the achievement of short-term material gains. In the later stages, particularly during the Goulart era, labor tried to get genuine participation in the political process. To this end it used its control of the labor ministry and the classic techniques of patronage not for the usual goal of achieving modest wage increases but to build a mass following and to try to effect fundamental social and political re-structuring. The use of the strike together with Leftist mobilization of the masses threatened to spell the end of the traditional *patrão-clientela* relationship.[43]

These changes regarding labor's relationship *vis-à-vis* the government were reflective of the changes taking place within Brazil more generally. As a result of industrialization, social mobilization, and overall modernization, there was a tendency toward increased populism of a participatory sort. Previously, the lower classes had been dependent upon the *patrões* and on the government, without a strong organization or even a strong sense of class consciousness. The system of official syndicates, in fact, was used by the government and the elites who controlled it to prevent such consciousness from growing and to rule out autonomous labor organizations that might have constituted a potential threat to the system. In the early 1960s, however, there began to occur the transformation from what Erickson calls amorphous, individualized clienteles held together by personal contacts and patronage into functionally more specific interest groups. As populism became more important and as the strike was used more effectively, the traditional paternalistic-administrative-corporate-patronage system underwent considerable modification, while power, concurrently, began to slip from the hands of the traditional elites. Had these new Leftist-nationalist labor leaders not violated the rules of the traditional game by threatening to "discard" the military and the older elites from the classic corporate coalition, it is possible that Brazil might have been able over time to assimilate its lower class labor and peasant elements into the prevailing system. Brazil would have continued with its corporate structure, to be sure, but some new social forces would have been grafted on and incorporated into it. As is was, however, the older elites felt threatened and they hence rebelled, subsequently suppressing labor and reinstituting the traditional system—with a vengeance! In Brazil as in Argentina, Chile, Peru, the Dominican Republic, and elsewhere in Latin America, some new patterns are rising up alongside and challenging the traditional corporate structure; and in Brazil, as in these others, the failure of the old reconciliationist system has tended to pave the way for increased conflict, breakdown, and military authoritarianism.[44]

Conclusion

Most studies of Latin American politics and government and of the

legal-constitutional frameworks that undergird them have emphasized the vast chasm which is seen to exist between the "ought"
and the "is," between what the formal-written rules call for and the
way the Latin American systems actually operate, or between the enactment of a law and its implementation. It matters little whether
one examines the literature regarding Latin American law, constitutionalism, the traditional tri-partite division of powers (executive,
legislative, judicial), elections, public administration, or more recently agrarian reform, tax reform, or any of a number of newer
areas of public policy, one finds the same preoccupation with these
same gaps, usually accompanied by the same prescriptive admonition that they should be closed, that some greater correspondence
must be forged between what the law and the constitution say and
actual operating practices. Implicit in this prescription, ordinarily,
is the idea that once these gaps have been closed, the Latin American countries will begin living up to the liberal, representative, and
democratic norms expressed in their laws and constitutions. In short,
they will become "just like us."

Much of the thrust of the present essay, however, points toward
the inadequacy of that kind of normative, prescriptive, and essentially ethnocentric approach. It is not that the goals of liberal, representative, democratic government are not good and proper goals,
particularly in the Anglo-American context, but that these normative judgments should not serve to cloud and prejudice scholarly research. For if the argument of this paper has merit, it is precisely
these gaps and lags, the patterns of sporadic, disjointed, discontinuous, and uneven modernization, the phenomenon of mixed, overlapping, and heterogeneous social groups, ideologies, norms, legal
philosophies, and governmental institutions pertaining to quite different epochs that are at the heart of the Latin American development process and that, it seems to me, should form the core of scholarly focus. In the literature, usually the ideal types at either end
of the continuum are stressed—be it in terms of indicators of social,
political, or legal-constitutional development—while the hodge-podge
and frequently crazy-quilt patterns that lie in between are dismissed
with a qualifying phrase. Such mixed and out-of-joint patterns, the
cross-currents of both traditional and modern coexisting side by
side, are, however, at the heart of the transitional process in which
all the Latin American nations currently find themselves. They may
be disjointed and frequently unstable, they may represent a hodge-
podge mixture of old and new, of feudal traditions and modern
codes, and there may be considerable gap between the principles
set forth in their constitutions and the way politics actually takes
place; but that, after all, reflects the mixed and overlapping social,
economic, and behavioral structures on which the contemporary

Latin American political systems are based. Furthermore, the fact that the law may seldom be applied, or may be applied more to some than to others, or the fact that constitutional niceties are not always observed, tells us a great deal about the nature and workings of the Latin American socio-political systems.[45] Finally, given the peculiar Latin-Hispanic tradition and the particular level of development of the Latin American nations, which, in varying degrees, to be sure, are neither wholly traditional nor wholly modern, this same heterogeneous and modified corporate-elitist system may be both far more flexible and far more functional than we ordinarily think.

Obviously it was easier in the "sleepy," nineteenth-century past for the Latin American nations to function with their in many ways antiquated structures and practices and with such huge disparities between legal and constitutional provisions and actual operating practices than is the case at present, when new challenges are being increasingly felt and when growing complexity and new demands upon the system seem to require its modernization and the narrowing, or at least the better bridging, of this gap between theory and practice. But one should not overstate this argument. First, as Dealy and others have demonstrated, the gap that is supposed to exist between the niceties of the legal-constitutional structures and the harsh realities of political life may not be so wide as North American observers are prone to believe; and second, it may well be that even under the pressures of the present the traditional Latin American structures and mechanisms for adapting to change may once again prove themselves permeable and capable of survival. It would seem, thus, that as scholars concerned with the process of Latin American development—including the place of law and legal institutions in that process—we should be concerned not so much with devising schemes to close these supposed "gaps" or with providing prescriptive remedies for the real or imagined "ills" of the Latin American nations that are usually based on some Western European or Anglo-American conception of the way the development process *ought* to proceed. Instead, we must recognize and come to grips with the dilemmas of Latin American underdevelopment realistically, on its own terms and in its own context. We must explore the way the Latin American systems function regardless of the supposed gaps that exist, comprehend how in Latin America these "gaps" can be bridged, glossed over, or even ignored altogether, and examine the various devices that exist for doing so, the frequently ingenious patchwork solutions that are devised, and the way a little "grease" here or a little cement there can hold the system together temporarily or enable it to slide through from one crisis to the next. A primary focus of scholarly research, it may be suggested, should be toward answering such questions as how the corporate structure of society and polity and the traditional institutions based upon it can adapt to modernization, as well as how such modern agencies as a trade union movement can adapt to the traditional structures and use traditional techniques (e.g., the way the Brazilian unionists used patronage and their position *within* the traditional corporate structure to advance their cause). These kinds of studies have become increasingly prevalent in sociology and political science in recent years, and in the sociological study of Latin American law and legal institutions as well. Such examples as Professor Kenneth Karst's study of adaptation and assimilation in the *barrios* of Caracas, Professors Karst's and Clement's work on the Mexican *ejidos,* Professor Thome's studies of agrarian reform, and Professor Rosenn's essay on the Brazilian *jeito* (*American Journal of Comparative Law,* Summer, 1971) come quickly to mind.

In undertaking such studies one must, I believe, always keep in mind the special nature of the Latin American change process. The precedents of Western Europe or North America are of limited usefulness in understanding this. Change in Latin America, we have emphasized, has ordinarily occurred gradually and incrementally—at times sporadically and most unevenly and frequently all but imperceptibly—through adaptation and assimilation, within a framework that combines and seeks to reconcile traditional and modern rather than implying the triumph or transcendence of the one over the other, or of one class or "stage" or epoch over another. As regards law, for example, we know that the experience of the North American or Western European countries—that is, historically of constantly adopting new legal principles from current needs at one end and tending to slough off the old and outdated ones at the other—does not really apply in Latin America, for while new rules and regulations have been repeatedly tacked on, the old ones have seldom been discarded. One should not overstate this argument, for here as in other regards, the differences are matters of degree rather than of absolutes. Nevertheless, the contrasts are striking. Similarly "private" or "special interest" law does not seem to be on the decline in Latin America as the modernization process proceeds; in fact, quite the opposite may be the case. It seems doubtful, indeed, whether any of the supposedly universal patterns of national legal development posited by the few scholars who have written from a comparative perspective on this subject have much relevance for the study of Latin American law and legal institutions,[46] or even that there are very many "common directions" in the development process.[47] To be sure, the legal landscape has changed significantly over the course of the last century and a half, and new areas of law have increasingly grown and received attention. But even today, I would argue, the continuities with the historical tradition are at least as important, and particularly given the heavy hand of tradition in Latin America, perhaps more important than are these newer currents.

In the past most change in Latin America has come discontinuously and disjointedly, not usually as the result of any profound or "glorious" revolution—or even, or so it seems, through much purposeful action. Change has, instead, ordinarily come by fits and starts and through the repeated crises and alternations of government that the Latin American nations are popularly known for, through shifting coalitions, barracks revolts, cabinet changes, new realignments, and the accommodation of new groups and ideas, from disintegration and *ad hoc* rebuilding, from day-to-day decisions and non-decisions, from the demonstration of new power contenders of their power capability and willingness to abide by the rules and hence their absorption into the system, from various forms of structured and unstructured violence that most often falls short of full-scale revolution.[48] This may not be a very glorious or soul-satisfying way of achieving development but it is development nevertheless, cumulative and thus perhaps eventually of a "structural" sort, and it does correspond more realistically with the present organization of power and society in Latin America, as well as being in accord with the peculiar nature of the Latin American development process.

Notes

1. For some parallel comments see Wallace Mendelson, "Law and the Development of Nations," *Journal of Politics,* XXXII (May, 1970) 223-38.

2. A pioneering effort in this direction is Kenneth L. Karst, "The Study of Latin American Law and Legal Institutions," in Charles Wagley (ed.), *Social Science Research on Latin America* (1964) 290-333. See also Karst's *Latin American Legal Institutions: Problems for Comparative Study* (1966). Two attempts to fashion a general model that links law to the development process are Mendelson, supra note 1; and Marc Galanter, "The Modernization of Law," in Myron Weiner (ed.), *Modernization: The Dynamics of Growth* (1966) 153-65. Though their focus is somewhat

different from the present essay, a number of political scientists have also begun to move in the direction of exploring "comparative judicial politics." See, for example, Theodore L. Becker, *Comparative Judicial Politics: The Political Functioning of Courts* (1970); and Glendon Schubert and David J. Danelsky (eds.), *Comparative Judicial Behavior: Cross-Cultural Studies of Political Decision-Making in East and West* (1969).

3. Some of the ideas in this section are also explored in Howard J. Wiarda, "Toward a Framework for the Study of Political Change in the Iberic-Latin Tradition: The Corporative Model," *World Politics,* XXV (January, 1973); Wiarda, "Elites in Crisis: The Decline of the Old Order and the Fragmentation of the New in Latin America," in Jack W. Hopkins (ed.), *Studies*

of Latin American Elites (New York, 1973); and Wiarda, "The Latin American Development Process and the New Developmental Alternatives: Military 'Nasserism' and 'Dictatorship with Popular Support,'" *Western Political Quarterly,* XXV (September, 1972). The present paper is thus part of a larger study which seeks to develop a general framework for the analysis of socio-political change in Latin America.

4. See John D. Martz, "The Place of Latin America in the Study of Comparative Politics," *Journal of Politics,* XXVII (February, 1966) 57-80.

5. Those who employ the Marxian framework are of course extremely varied in their perspectives, and any discussion that lumps them all together necessarily oversimplifies greatly. Two stimulating general discussions are Paul A. Baran, *The Political Economy of Growth* (1957); and Barrington Moore, Jr., *Social Origins of Dictatorship and Democracy: Lord and Peasant in the Making of the Modern World* (1966). For Latin America see the collections in James Petras and Maurice Zeitlin (eds.), *Latin America: Reform or Revolution?* (1968); and Irving Louis Horowitz, Josué de Castro, and John Gerassi (eds.), *Latin American Radicalism* (1969). For some discussion see Milton I. Vanger, "Politics and Class in Twentieth-Century Latin America," *Hispanic American Historical Review,* XLIX (February, 1969) 80-93; John Mander, *The Unrevolutionary Society: The Power of Latin American Conservatism in a Changing World* (1969); and Luis Mercier Vega, *Roads to Power in Latin America* (1969).

6. A few of the more outstanding volumes in this tradition include W. W. Rostow, *The Stages of Economic Growth: A Non-Communist Manifesto* (1960); Gabriel A. Almond and James S. Coleman (eds.),

The Politics of the Developing Areas (1960); David E. Apter, *The Politics of Modernization* (1965); A. F. K. Organski, *The Stages of Political Development* (1965); C. E. Black, *The Dynamics of Modernization* (1967); and Samuel P. Huntington, *Political Order in Changing Societies* (1968). For the application of this framework to Latin America see, for example, John J. Johnson, *Political Change in Latin America* (1958); and Martin C. Needler, *Political Development in Latin America* (1968). For some critiques of this approach see Alfred Stepan, "Political Development: The Latin American Experience," *Journal of International Affairs,* XX, No. 2 (1966) 223-34; Claudio Véliz (ed.), *The Politics of Conformity in Latin America* (1967) Introduction; and Juan Marsal, *Cambio Social en América Latina: Crítica de Algunas Interpretaciones Dominantes en las Ciencias Sociales* (1967).

7. These points are discussed at greater length in Wiarda, "Elites in Crisis ...," supra note 3.

8. See the references cited in note 3, as well as Howard J. Wiarda, *Dictatorship, Development, and Disintegration: The Political System of the Dominican Republic* (forthcoming). Another attempt at applying the model is the author's "The Catholic Labor Movement in Brazil: Corporatism, Paternalism, Populism, and Change," in H. Jon Rosenbaum and William G. Tyler (eds.), *Contemporary Brazil: Issues in Economic and Political Development* (New York, 1972).

9. Lyle N. McAlister, "Social Structure and Social Change in New Spain," *Hispanic American Historical Review,* XLIII (August, 1963) 349-70; Richard M. Morse, "The Heritage of Latin America," in Louis Hartz *et al., The Founding of New Societies* (1964) 123-77, reprinted in this volume; and Magali Sarfatti, *Spanish Bureaucratic-Patrimonialism in*

America (1968). Patrimonialism, it may be recalled, was one of Weber's forms of traditional domination.

10. "On 'Functional Groups,' 'Fragmentation,' and 'Pluralism' in Spanish American Political Society," *Hispanic American Historical Review*, L (February, 1970) 25; reprinted in this volume.

11. Paraphrased from Richard M. Morse, "Toward a Theory of Spanish American Government" *Journal of the History of Ideas*, XV (January, 1954) 71-93; reprinted in this volume. See also Hans Kirchberger, "The Significance of Roman Law for the Americas and Its Importance to Inter-American Relations," *Wisconsin Law Review* (July, 1944) 249-73; and Guenter Lewy, *Constitutionalism and Statecraft During the Golden Age of Spain: A Study of the Political Philosophy of Juan de Mariana, S. J.* (1960).

12. Two important studies in these regards are Lyle N. McAlister, *The "Fuero Militar" in New Spain* (1957); and Charles A. Hale, *Mexican Liberalism in the Age of Mora, 1821-1853* (1968) esp. Chapters 2 and 4. See also Karst, "The Study of Latin American Law . . .," supra note 2 at 299-302.

13. See, for example, Donald E. Worcester, "The Spanish American Past: Enemy of Change," *Journal of Inter-American Studies*, XI (January, 1969) 66-75; and Joseph Maier and Richard W. Weatherhead (eds.), *Politics of Change in Latin America* (1964) Introduction.

14. Richard M. Morse, "Recent Research on Latin American Urbanization: A Selective Survey with Commentary," *Latin American Research Review*, I (Fall, 1965) 41.

15. On the irrelevance of the French codes, given the Latin American tradition, see John Henry Merryman, *The Civil Law Tradition: An Introduction to the Legal Systems of Western Europe and Latin America* (1969) Chapters III-V. The parallel view of the inap-

propriateness for Latin America of the republican-democratic constitutional arrangements is a theme that runs through virtually all the traditional histories and government texts, particularly those written by North Americans.

16. Though somewhat outside the scope of this essay, a topic that needs a great deal of further explication is the impact of the code law legal system on political behavior and the political process. It seems likely that the code law system helped to reinforce and perpetuate the absolutist, rigid and unyielding, authoritarian, and paternalistic character of the political process in Latin America and that this remains true today. These and other political implications of the code law system, however, need to be examined in far greater detail. For some starting points see Herbert J. Spiro, *Government by Constitution: The Political Systems of Democracy* (1959); William S. Stokes, *Latin American Politics* (1959) Chapter 19; and Merryman, supra note 15 *passim*. I have tried also to come to grips with at least some of these issues in my research on the Dominican Republic—see Chapters XV and XVI of *Dictatorship, Development, and Disintegration*, supra note 8.

17. Dealy, "Prolegomena on the Spanish American Political Tradition," *Hispanic American Historical Review*, XLVIII (February, 1968) 37-58.

18. Ibid., 51-2. See also James L. Busey, "Observations on Latin American Constitutionalism," *The Americas*, XXIV (1967).

19. Op. cit., 51, 52, 58. Though Dealy's research dealt chiefly with constitutional arrangements, it is likely similar conclusions would be reached from an examination of the codes and the way they were adapted to fit the Latin American *ambiente*.

20. See, for example, John D. Powell, "Peasant Society and

Clientelist Politics," *American Political Science Review*, LXIV (June, 1970) 411-25; and Kenneth L. Karst and Norris C. Clement, "Legal Institutions and Development: Lessons from the Mexican *Ejido*," *UCLA Law Review*, XVI (February, 1969) 281-303.

21. See the discussion in James Petras, *Political and Social Forces in Chilean Development* (1969).

22. See the references cited in notes 3 and 8, as well as Wiarda, *The Brazilian Catholic Labor Movement: The Dilemmas of National Development* (1969).

23. The definitions and discussion here follow that of Kenneth P. Erickson, *Labor in the Political Process in Brazil: Corporatism in a Modernizing Nation* (Unpublished Ph. D. dissertation: Department of Political Science, Columbia University, 1970).

24. See especially Michel Crozier, *The Bureaucratic Phenomenon* (1964).

25. Erickson, supra note 23, Abstract and Chapters I-II. See also Mander, supra note 5, *passim*.

26. Erickson, supra note 23, at 54, 94.

27. Petras, supra note 21, *passim*.

28. See, among others, Warren Dean, *The Industrialization of São Paulo, 1880-1945* (1969) Chapter V; Anthony Leeds, "Brazilian Careers and Social Structures: A Case History and Model," *American Anthropologist*, LXVI (1964) 1321-47; and Erickson, supra note 23.

29. Anderson, "Toward a Theory of Latin American Politics," Occasional Paper No. 2, Graduate Center for Latin American Studies, Vanderbilt University, Nashville, Tennessee (February, 1964), reprinted in this volume; also Chapter IV of his *Politics and Economic Change in Latin America* (1967).

30. "The Argentine Paradox" *Annals of the American Academy of Political and Social Sciences*, 334 (March, 1961) 107.

31. Silvert, *The Conflict Society: Reaction and Revolution in Latin America* (1966) esp. Chapters 1, 2, and 17; and Johnson, *Argentina's Mosaic of Discord, 1966-1968* (1969).

32. Morse, supra note 11.

33. Economic Commission for Latin America (ECLA) *Social Development of Latin America in the Post-War Period* (New York: United Nations Economic and Social Council, April 15, 1964) 4-7, reprinted in this volume. This seldom-cited study is one of the earliest and best statements of the uniqueness of the Latin American development process.

34. Josef L. Kunz (ed.), *Latin American Legal Philosophy* (1948); Kunz, *Latin American Philosophy of Law in the Twentieth Century* (1950); and Karst, *Latin American Legal Institutions . . .*, supra note 2.

35. Adams, *The Second Sowing: Power and Secondary Development in Latin America* (1967).

36. Anderson "Toward a Theory . . . ." supra note 29, *passim*.

37. Newton, supra note 10 at 27.

38. Silvert, "National Values, Development, and Leaders and Followers," *International Social Science Journal*, XVI (1964) 560-70; "The Politics of Social and Economic Change in Latin America," in Paul Halmos (ed.), *The Sociological Review Monograph 11: Latin American Sociological Studies* (1967) 47-58; *Expectant Peoples: Nationalism and Development* (1967) 358-61, and in this volume; and *The Conflict Society*, supra note 31, Chapters 1, 2, and 17. For a similar argument see Lawrence S. Graham, "Latin America—Illusion or Reality? A Case for a new Analytical Framework for the Region," in this volume.

39. Derived also from Silvert's writings, supra note 37.

40. Erickson, supra note 23 at 3, 26, 98, 339.

41. Mander, supra note 5; Mercier Vega, ibid.; and Véliz, ibid.

42. Adams, supra note 34. On the praetorian society see Huntington, supra note 6, Chapter 4; and Amos Perlmutter, "The Praetorian State and the Praetorian Army: Toward a Taxonomy of Civil-Military Relations in Developing Polities," *Comparative Politics,* I (April, 1969) 382-404. For an application to Latin America see Riordan Roett, "The Quest for Legitimacy in Brazil: The Dilemma of a Praetorian Army," Paper prepared for the 1970 Annual Conference of the Midwest Association for Latin American Studies, University of Nebraska, Lincoln, Nebraska (October 1-3, 1970).

43. Erickson, supra note 23, esp. Chapter V; and Wiarda, *The Brazilian Catholic Labor Movement* . . . , supra note 22.

44. This paragraph relies heavily on Erickson's analysis, esp. Chapter V; as well as drawing on my own research and writing.

45. Karst, "The Study of Latin American Law . . . ," supra note 2 at 292; as well as the discussion in Robert F. Adie and Guy E. Poitras, *The Politics of Immobility in Latin America* (Unpublished manuscript, 1970) Chapter I.

46. Mendelson, supra note 1 at 234.

47. As social scientists we may have been guilty of too hasty generalization in seeking to erect all-encompassing and all-inclusive models of the national development process. See the remarks in J. P. Nettl and Karl von Vorys, "The Politics of Development," *Commentary,* XLVI (July, 1968) 52-9.

48. See especially Douglas A. Chalmers, "Crisis and Change in Latin America," *Journal of International Affairs,* XXIII, No. 1 (1969) 76-88; Anderson, *Politics and Economic Change* . . . , supra note 29, *passim;* and Albert O.

Hirschman, *Journeys Toward Progress: Studies of Economic Policy-Making in Latin America* (1965).

Latin America: Illusion or Reality? A Case for a New Analytic Framework for the Region

Lawrence S. Graham

The Cultural Unity Thesis

Several decades ago Luis Alberto Sánchez, a Peruvian Aprista, published a book with the title *Does Latin America Exist?*[1] in which he concluded that as a concept the term "Latin America" did not mean much if one focused on the national realities of each of the countries making up this region. While his attention was directed towards the primacy of the city over the countryside and the alienation existing between urban culture and rural Latin America, where the heart of the nation resided, his observations and the question he raised then are no less relevant today. While much has been written about Latin America in English, Spanish, Portuguese, and French from numerous disciplinary perspectives, we often find the frame of reference used as abstract and ill defined today as it has been in the past.

Within academic as well as governmental circles in North America, Latin America, and Western Europe the views articulated have usually fluctuated between those who see an underlying cultural unity in the region and those who would emphasize distinctive national experiences within individual nation-states. The proponents of cultural unity have customarily drawn attention to such factors as a common historical past, a similar cultural tradition, and a dependency relationship with financial centers and markets located in the United States and Western Europe. In Latin America much of the action, both in academic analysis and foreign policy making, has centered around the attempt to project an image of a relatively cohesive bloc of nations to counterpose the overwhelming political and economic power demonstrated by the United States in this area of the world since the 1890s.

Within the United States academic community, the range covered by the cultural unity thesis can be illustrated by the works of two widely respected writers, William Lytle Schurz and Charles W. Anderson.

In his preface to *Latin America,* Schurz sums up this thesis in terms
accepted and shared by many historians:

> *In this book I have endeavored to consider Latin America as a unit.*
> *I have not ignored the factors of differentiation, which often are very*
> *great but yet not sufficient to break the essential unity that causes a*
> *Colombian and a Uruguayan to meet the same situation in much the*
> *same way. To have treated the twenty republics in any other way*
> *would only have created in the reader's mind the confusion that comes*
> *from an effort to follow the separate fortunes of the Saxon kingdoms*
> *of early England or the city-states of medieval Italy.*[2]

Starting from a different perspective—one that is based within the
discipline of political science—Anderson also speaks of Latin America
as a distinct unit, one that for purposes of economic policy analysis
can best be approached through the use of a model that focuses on
regional policy procedures and processes which depart from accepted
Western experience. Like Schurz, and many other academicians concerned with Latin America, Anderson recognizes the difficulties of
generalizing about the diverse nations constituting this area. Nevertheless, underlying this diversity, he sees a common set of political
patterns which he would subsume within the framework of a Latin
American political systems model which he contrasts with the norms
and expectations present in the policy process of advanced Western
nations.[3]

In governmental circles the cultural unity thesis is to be found historically in the various attempts by this country to construct a Latin
American policy for the region. During the Taft administration such
a policy was called Dollar Diplomacy; during the presidency of Franklin D. Roosevelt it was known as the Good Neighbor Policy; during
the thousand days of the Kennedy administration the catchphrase
used was the Alliance for Progress. While the objectives in each instance varied considerably, the approach was similar: what was required was a common policy for this bloc of countries. The Taft administration saw the relationship between the United States and Latin America essentially in terms of the expanding investments of North
American firms and conceived of the government's role as one of protecting these investments and encouraging a favorable environment
for business. Recognizing the deterioration of United States-Latin
American relations and later the need for Latin American support of
the United States position as the war in Europe brought the United
States into greater involvement, the Roosevelt administration sought
to ameliorate hemispheric relations by converting the Monroe Doctrine from a unilateral declaration of policy into a multilateral statement of common interests among the American states. Thus, between

1933 (when Cordell Hull at the Montevideo Conference stated the
United States acceptance of the nonintervention principle and
eschewed intervention in the internal affairs of the American states)
and 1940, the United States embarked upon a course which ultimately ended in bringing amicable relations within the hemisphere
to an all-time high.

Following the end of World War II, the state of relations between
the United States and the Latin American republics underwent marked
change. Events in Western Europe, the Middle East, and Southeast
Asia assumed primacy for the United States policy maker. And it was
not until the emergence of Castro in Cuba and the fear of similar
revolutions throughout Latin America that the United States responded with a new regional policy, which attempted to reshape the
cultural unity thesis to fit changed conditions. In March 1961, with
the inauguration of the Alliance for Progress, President Kennedy
undertook the task of effecting a policy change designed to foster
peaceful and evolutionary development in Latin America and to meet
the challenge of violent revolution as the only alternative to breaking
the hold of the traditional order. But by 1969 that policy had come
to a dead end.

As the United States entered the decade of the seventies, it became increasingly clear that an era had ended: no longer could we
take for granted the primacy of our influence in the Western Hemisphere while we directed our attention to more pressing areas of the
globe. The illusion of a harmony of interests, founded on the Good
Neighbor Policy and cooperation during the Second World War and
revived by the Alliance for Progress was gone.[4] The isolation of the
region from the politics of the major powers had ended. And the
United States no longer monopolized its trade and credit.

In this context many observers have singled out the phenomenon
of nationalism as the origin of a growing diversity among these countries and have called attention to great differences among regimes
within a contiguous geographic area. As a consequence we have been
moving away from a regional focus towards an unannounced policy
of dealing with individual states in the region on the basis of the force
of immediate circumstance. In lieu of the Latin American policy of
the Kennedy-Johnson years we seem to have ended up with a null
policy as characteristic of the Nixon administration.

Counterposing these Anglo-American views of Latin America there
remains strong support for the cultural unity thesis within Latin
America. One frequently hears it stated that above particular dis-
agreements and conflicts there is a larger community which is best
expressed in the Bolivarian ideal of a unified Latin America as opposed to Anglo-America. Today, perhaps, its political content has

lessened considerably, but culturally and economically it is very much
alive. Those articulating this thesis usually emphasize the dichotomy
between the two Americas, the one Latin, the other Anglo-Saxon.
Probably the most popularized version of this orientation is that expressed by José Enrique Rodó in his symbols of Ariel and Calibán:
Ariel representing the lofty spirit of Latin American culture; Calibán, the grosser, more materialistic United States.[5]

While Rodó's essay first appeared at the turn of the century, it has
remained an important force in shaping an image of what the cultural
contrasts are between Latin America and the United States. Tied in
with this concept of shared cultural experience is the idea of a common religion, expressed in fidelity to the Roman Catholic Church and
given a distinctive form by ideas developed in Counter-Reformation
Europe. Another is the unity of language, since all but two of these
republics—Brazil and Haiti—are Spanish speaking. Even here differences are frequently minimized by pointing out that Portuguese is not
that different from Spanish, particularly if one goes back to the dia-
lects spoken several centuries ago on the Iberian Peninsula. Joined
to all this is the idea of a common historical experience, shaped by
the colonial powers of Spain and Portugal, and the nonrevolutionary character of the independence period out of which an elitist socio-
economic and political structure based on the trilogy of large landholders, the military, and the Church emerged.

None of these observations, however, is confined exclusively to
Latin American intellectual circles; they appear also frequently in
the literature on Latin America in Western Europe and North America. For example, in the writing on politics the proponents of the cultural unity thesis in all three areas have long identified as shared traits
the predominance of strong executives, weak legislatures, poorly developed national party systems, faction-oriented politics, a penchant
for new constitutions, and governmental instability. Much of this writing can be grouped into two schools: those who feel that revolution
or basic change is inevitable because of the inability of the existing
power structure to continue to limit the services of government to
the needs of a few, and those who feel somewhat pessimistically that
the hope for radical change in the area neither has had nor presents a
very bright future, except for a few fortunate areas such as Mexico,
Bolivia, and Cuba (although many would now exclude the former
two cases). Time and time again when area specialists have generalized about Latin America in regional terms, they have described
politics as being dominated by a relatively small power elite, pervert-
ing the ends of society to serve its own needs in opposition to a vast
nonparticipant majority. In sociological terms, these are said to be
societies that share in common dual social structures.

Difficulties with the Cultural Unity Thesis

The problem with observations such as these is that when they are held up for rigorous analysis and compared with what we know about politics and society in other areas of the world, they do not contribute much to precise thinking. What they do, instead, is to combine social and political patterns common to other traditional and transitional societies with organizational forms and attitudes peculiar to individual countries within Latin America. Yet the opposite viewpoint which seeks to point out the distinctiveness of each republic as part of a larger developing world is not much more satisfying. This is because once common economic conditions are left aside—those factors which distinguish developing countries from developed ones with industrialized economics and commercialized agricultures—one still encounters distinctive cultural patterns which while they transcend national boundaries are less than universal. While most contemporary political analysis usually minimizes cultural variables as having a bearing on cross-national comparison and opts for identifying contrasting political regime types, the cultural unity thesis is very much alive in the humanities where specialists in Latin American literature and art would emphasize a distinctive set of preoccupations and themes for the region. For reasons such as these Sánchez's question is still a valid one to ask.

Nevertheless, what is clear is that the old basis for generalization about Latin American cultural unity is no longer tenable. One of the effects of nationalism has been to maximize the development of symbols and beliefs which lead growing numbers of individuals within the region to identify with their own nation-state before they think in terms of a more amorphous land mass called Latin America. Among essayists in countries like Mexico, Peru, and Argentina this preoccupation is to be seen in concern with such concepts as *mejicanidad, peruanidad,* and *argentinidad.* Nor can one any longer really refer to common fidelity to the Roman Catholic Church as determining special unity for the region. Fidelity to the Church and its alternatives—agnosticism, anticlericalism, and indifference—are attitudes to be found in and shared with many other countries outside the region. Added to this is the fact that the historic unity imposed by the Church as a conservative force in Southern Europe and Latin America is undergoing tremendous change in the aftermath of Vatican II. On the Continent as well as throughout Spanish- and Portuguese-speaking areas of the Western Hemisphere a great debate is under way between conservative elements adhering to ideas developed out of the Council of Trent and reformist or revolutionary elements concerned with social justice and with updating the Church to make it more relevant to contemporary life. If we look at language, there, too, are signs of increasing diversity not only in the colloquial differences among the Spanish-speaking republics reflecting the emergence of distinctive national traditions, but also in the divergence between Spanish- and Portuguese-speaking areas which involves both Latin America and the Iberian Peninsula. And once we have moved into the European context through Spain and Portugal, considered the similarities and differences between Spanish and Portuguese, and examined the crosscurrents in literary concept and style, then we must face the question of why should we characterize Italian and French as languages articulating a world view that is markedly different from that of Spanish and Portuguese.

As we look at the evolution of politics across time within the Latin American region, additional examples can be cited of the limitations on the cultural unity thesis. The sharing of a common historical experience by the twenty republics has receded into the background as each has begun to act as an independent nation-state. This is to be seen in the smaller states in the region as much as it is in the larger ones. There is perhaps no better example in recent times than the conflict between Honduras and El Salvador, for it points to the continuation of marked national differences regardless of the advances made toward economic integration through the development of a Central American Common Market. At the same time, differences among the republics such as these are not new, but of long standing. What is true is that they have tended to be minimized in the twentieth century under the impact of United States influence and the all-pervasive gringo presence. If we look, for example, at nineteenth-century South America, a period during which the area was relatively removed from great power politics, we find instances of a very intricate set of balance of power relationships developing among recently formed nation-states.[6] In the twentieth century these differences have increased rather than decreased; but faced with North American economic, political, and military power, Latin American leaders have usually preferred to minimize them, keep them behind the scenes, and confine them to informal diplomatic discussions. Internally, the power components shared in common among these states have also changed as we have seen the classic trilogy formed by the large landowner, the military, and the Church replaced by more diversified socioeconomic and political elites reflecting a greater plurality of interests as traditional sources of influence have waned.

In a comparative politics grown conscious of extensive world areas, scholars have repeatedly pointed out that political characteristics such as strong executives, weak legislatures, poorly developed national party systems, faction ridden politics, frequency in the writing of new constitutions, and governmental instability are no more peculiar to the Latin American states than they are to the new states of

Africa and Asia or the older nations of Southern Europe. Comparative analysis has also led to a greater realization that the attitude towards change as fundamental and revolutionary in Latin America, as opposed to the preference for incrementalism so common to the Anglo-American world, can be extended beyond regional geographical boundaries to parallels with other political systems.[7] The prevalence of dual social structures in comparative perspective becomes not a characteristic peculiar to Latin America, but simply a phenomenon common to all partially modernized political systems where there is an elite-mass dichotomy.

Simultaneously it has become commonplace to refer to the great variation among political and social systems throughout Latin America, whether our comparisons be made from within the region or with political experience outside. The range between a Haiti or a Paraguay, where participation is limited and a marked dual structure exists, and a mass movement regime, such as a Mexico or a Chile, is, we are aware, as great as any to be found in any other area of the world. Yet to say there is no unity, no common set of ties, does not provide a solution to this issue, for parallels continue to assert themselves which go beyond political regime similarities (viz., Anderson's preoccupation with restating the thesis to fit changing circumstances and the concern with economic development).

The Concept of Cultural Area in Middle-Range Theory Building

In contrast to the rather sterile search for a more effective way to explain the uniqueness of Latin America in isolation, the theme of cultural unity within the region can be demonstrated to have validity, but only if it is approached as a comparative problem involving other groups of countries outside the region. Such an approach leads in this direction: many of the patterns of politics and social organization linking nation-state developments in Latin America together point also to similar patterns in Southern Europe which can be set aside from Northern Europe and the rest of the developing world. In both areas problems presented by partial modernization are acute;[8] both share in common a Western cultural tradition predating that held by countries of the North Atlantic.[9] An alternative way of stating this is to say that just as Gabriel Almond defined over a decade ago a distinct Anglo-American model as a basis for comparing politics among the various English-speaking nations (the United States, Britain, Canada, Australia, and New Zealand) so likewise his identification of a continental European set of politics can be expanded to include the Latin American area. The proposition I would offer for testing by field research is this: the distinctiveness of Latin American politics, when compared with the industrial states of the North Atlantic, resides not in the uniqueness of Latin American experience apart from Western tradition, but in divergent concepts of the nation-state and contrasting governmental experience which these countries share with the Southern European states. This is not to deny the uniqueness of the American experience—the confrontation of the European with a new world—but rather to state that the basis for cross-national comparison must begin from a European point of reference.

There are two dimensions of politics and administration that should be kept in mind, then, as we look at these republics and as we ask what are the origins of their cultural unity from the perspective provided by political science. First are those elements common to Southern Europe and Latin America which lead in the direction of a single governmental paradigm. Second are those factors allowing us to distinguish variations in political and administrative patterns as we compare the ways in which countries accepting this paradigm have met and handled issues pertaining to economic, social, and political change.

The nation-states to be included within this framework are nineteen of the twenty Latin American republics, Spain, Portugal, and Italy. While Greece and most of the countries of North Africa share a common Mediterranean ethos that has influenced political behavior in many similar ways, they are excluded because of the saliency there of a distinct political culture based on the impact of the Ottoman Turk and bureaucratic institutions identified with the Ottoman Empire. France is excluded because of its involvement in the politics of the North European states and the fact that its governmental institutions and the state model adhered to have developed in response to internal dynamics, whereas the developmental models utilized within Southern Europe and Latin America have arisen in response to exogenous forces. Cuba since the revolution is best handled in the category of communist or socialist systems and analyzed through the state model that has become salient in Central Europe. It is in this sense the only revolutionary state in this culture area, for it alone has attempted to break once and for all with the historico-cultural tradition of governance dominant in Southern Europe and Latin America. Likewise, cases such as those of the Philippines and Puerto Rico are not considered because of the overlay of other cultural traditions which have reshaped the original Latin ethos in quite different ways.

The objective behind a theory of this sort and the attempt here to identify it with specific countries is to direct attention to the saliency of distinct culture areas within the world where the social psychology of supranational groups of people suggest common patterns of behavior and perceptions of government which are neither exclusively national nor universal. Middle-range theory building within comparative politics might be greatly enriched if the identification of cultural area concepts with contiguous geographic regions could cease and if the perceptions available in the literature on social psychology and comparative linguistics were incorporated into the analysis of middle-range comparative problems in political science.

This group of countries shares six characteristics. First, they constitute a group of older nation-states who for most of their experience over the last century or century and a half have adhered to the model of a centralized hierarchically structured nation-state. Second, patterns of elite dissensus predominate (i.e., much of the struggle for political power is couched in terms of competition among mutually exclusive elite groups). Third, the disagreement over the rules to apply in processing conflict and change is tied in with the prevalence of fragmented political cultures that reflect a mosaic of divergent life styles, contrasting economic organizations, and marked regional disparities. Fourth, values and traditions to be identified with the pre-industrial urban culture of the Mediterranean world not only have survived in the small towns of Southern Italy, Spain, and Portugal but can be found also in the towns of Hispanic America where they have demonstrated the same tenacity as they have in the European context. Fifth, governmental and social organizations demonstrate a mausoleum effect in that previous organizational forms identified with earlier historical experience continue to exist side by side with those characteristic of modern industrial orders. Sixth, patterns of political change are characterized by alternation between faction-dominated parliamentary systems where considerable constraints are placed on executive power and strong executive-centered regimes in which politics is centered in a bureaucratic arena and corporatist thinking predominates. Within these governments public bureaucracies are well institutionalized and provide continuity between order-maintaining regimes and periodic breakthroughs of revolutionary movements designed to readjust socio-economic and political relations.

At the same time, variations in the response to political, social, and economic changes among these countries is marked. One way to handle these variations is to map out briefly some change oriented continua common to all nation-states. In this respect, a useful model to begin with is that provided by Fred Riggs.[10] Building on and re-shaping his concepts to fit the purposes here, three continua for comparative purposes may be identified: first, an economic continuum represented by highly industrialized societies at one extreme, characterized by increasingly rapid change and stable agrarian societies at the other; second, a social continuum characterized by elite pluralism at one end of the continuum and a concentrated, unified power structure at the other extreme; and, third, a political continuum with a mass-based political system at one pole and an elitist system at the other where political participation is limited to a small ruling class. Following Riggs's initiative it is important not to speak in this context of a typology which dichotomizes existing countries into categories of industrialized as opposed to agrarian societies, developed versus underdeveloped nation-states, mass-participant political systems against elitist oriented ones; but, to consider to what extent individual nation-states approach one pole or another on these continua.

Nevertheless, variations such as these in the response to socioeconomic and political change must be weighed against characteristics which can be singled out as constituting a common basis for comparison among the Southern European and Latin American states and which set them aside from other political systems. Of the six elements identified, most important is the prevalence of a particular type of bureaucratic organization in which impersonal rules predominate, but individuals maintain their status independently of organizational determinants; decision-making authority is centralized; public employees find themselves isolated in distinct hierarchical levels; cliques and personal ties continue but rarely cut across the various strata of the organization; and parallel power relationships, centered in distinct organizational units, develop.[11] In order to understand why public bureaucracies in these countries constitute a distinct genre, it is essential to approach governmental organization in a way that will include the central ministries and independent agencies as integral parts of the political process. Crucial to an identification or an understanding of the characteristics shared by the Southern European and Latin America states, then, is to begin with the decision-making core focused on the cabinet and the way in which administrative organizations and their participants interact with political institutions and party and interest group representatives around this center.

Let us now examine in some detail the six elements previously mentioned. The first directs attention to the continued vitality of the concept of the centralized state in the context of corporative political theory. The dominant role given to the state in regulating group relations, their access to governmental resources, and their influence over the allocation of public resources leads to a role for interest groups quite distinct from that to be found in the United States.[12] In contrast to developments in Northern Europe and in particular in the British Isles, these countries adhere to a civil law system, based on the revival given to Roman law by Napoleon and emphasizing the importance of codified law. The parallel in the approaches taken to public administration among these countries springs from this common legal system and the perception of policy formulation and implementation largely in legalistic terms. In this instance a basic value shared by these countries is the aspiration for an administrative system possessing a clear hierarchy of command and rationalized formal structures minimizing conflict. Yet in all these countries administrative reality is quite different: barriers among central ministries are marked; organizational disputes, frequent; and communications networks, diffuse.

The prevalence of the norm of strong central state control as a way of transcending organizational, regional, and interest group divisions is related to why patterns of regional and local government are similar throughout Southern Europe and Latin America. The dominant form for organizing state power at the subnational level is the prefect-governor system. In each case the prefect-governor (and here the individual terminology varies from country to country) is considered the personal representative of the central government in the provinces; he is responsible for maintaining political order and, while he does not have extensive control over the administrative activities carried out by numerous governmental agencies in the region, as a nineteenth-century French prefectural model might suggest, he can play an important role in articulating and representing those local interests affected by them. To give a concrete example, while the Mexican and Italian political systems are markedly different in party formation and the roles expected of the chief executive, there are some striking parallels in the administrative arena, if we move beyond formal institutional titles and look at bureaucratic behavior and practice. Both the Italian prefect and the Mexican governor carry out roles as representatives of the central government which emphasize an important administrative input to a much higher degree than occurs in Anglo-American practice. In both instances provincial and municipal government functions more as an administrative appendage of the national government than as an effective autonomous or semiautonomous political subsystem.[13] Finally, corporate state ideas are present in the interlocking structures of the governmental system and the networks which link together governmental and business groups through the mechanisms of state capitalism and interlocking directorates which guarantee the dominance of the state over individual interests.[14]

The second and third elements are related. The prevalence of segmented elites and fragmented patterns of political culture are tied in with the evolution of nonconsensual political styles.[15] In contrast to the political systems of the Anglo-American world which maximize policy outcomes that reflect adjustments reached among competing interests in a laissez-faire style, the dominant political tradition in Southern Europe and Latin America emphasizes the announcement and defense of public policy by the government (the executive and his ministers) in a manner that is conducive neither to bargaining on essentials nor to the accommodation of opposing interests. The point to emphasize here is not that the one carries with it a minimization of political conflict and the other a maximization of such, but rather that the former provides greater agreement on the rules of the game. Agreement on the form the state should take by a majority of the major political contenders in these countries is rare indeed. Political conflict more often revolves around competing groups attempting to seize control of power to impose their own particular concept of what the state should be, while excluding other groups from active participation.

The fourth element refers to the survival in parts of Southern Europe and the transferral to the Western Hemisphere of values and traditions identified with the preindustrial urban culture of the Mediterranean world. The close identity between middle class and upper class values and, hence, the absence of a distinctive middle class ethos is linked to the survival of this tradition. Throughout Italy, Portugal, Spain, and nineteen of the twenty Latin American republics there are important middle-class elements which are to be identified not with industrial development, but with a preindustrial urban culture oriented toward commerce and government and identified with the liberal professions of law, medicine, and engineering. To use a Castilian distinction, these are the *clases médias* as opposed to the bourgeoisie.

The fifth element, the mausoleum effect of political and social organization, expands on an idea advanced by Charles Anderson in defining the nature of the Latin American political system as a distinct phenomenon. He points out that in all but a few instances countries in this region share in common a type of politics that minimizes revolutionary impact. By providing for representation of a wide variety of groups, the Latin American political system becomes a "living museum" reflecting the whole history of political experience in this area of the world.[16] His identification of political power contenders and his explanation of how various political elements are admitted into the political system, while applicable to Latin American cases, are equally valid for political analysis in Spain, Portugal, and Italy. As a matter of fact, in no other country in Western Europe has the weight of the past hung so heavily over the present as it has in Spain. In the present diversity of political opinion and groupings that runs from strong monarchical sentiment to revolutionary socialism is written the whole history of political change in Spain since the

303
Lawrence S.
Graham

first decade of the nineteenth century. To a lesser extent this is true of Italy and Portugal where issues unresolved during the nineteenth century interact with management-labor disputes of the twentieth. Even in cases of social revolution, such as Mexico's, prerevolutionary forms of organization and attitudes have demonstrated an amazing vitality.

The sixth element directs attention to the alternation between faction-dominated party systems, with weak executives, and executive-centered regimes, where bureaucratic institutions dominate the governmental arena. It points out that unstable multiparty systems, weak legislatures, strong executives, frequent cabinet reorganizations, and crisis politics are not characteristics peculiar just to Latin American politics but are dimensions of politics shared also by Italy, Spain, and Portugal. The current stalemate in Italy has its parallels with Brazil before 1964 and with Chile prior to the election of Allende. At the same time, one should be aware of the fact that there is considerable variation in the time spans separating those cycles in which faction-dominated party systems with limited executive power predominate from those characterized by strong executives governing primarily through bureaucratic institutions. For example, in the case of Italy since unification in 1861, the periods in which the country has been governed by a faction-ridden parliamentary system with a weak executive far outweigh in length of duration the experience with authoritarian government under Mussolini and his attempt to institutionalize state corporatism. In contrast, in the case of Spain, a multiparty system and parliamentary predominance is limited to a relatively brief period of six years during the ill-fated Second Republic, while the thirty-five-year-rule of Franco, through a bureaucratic regime, has seemed interminable. The same patterns of variation are to be observed in Latin America. For example, the experience of Mexico since the revolution has essentially been one of strong executive rule through the mechanism of bureaucratic governmental organizations, represented by the PRI party structure and an elaborate administrative system. In contrast, Chile has established a functional multiparty system of long duration in which it has been extremely difficult for strong executive leadership to emerge.

If, then, these two perspectives could be adopted in dealing with the Latin American republics, that is, a comparison of variations in the response to social, political, and economic change with a more precise identification of the governmental paradigm shared by almost all of the Latin American republics and the countries of Southern Europe, we might be able to clarify more effectively our thinking about what the basis for comparison should be when we seek to generalize about Latin America as a whole.

Implications for Policy

Recognizing the fact that the preceding discussion has served essentially a heuristic purpose, is oriented primarily toward emphasizing the European basis behind the nation-state phenomenon in Latin America, and has minimized intraregional differences, there are some implications of this approach for those concerned with inter-American relations which go beyond the purely academic. But, such a statement should not be read as advocating abandoning a Latin American policy for a "Latin" one; rather, it is that we should be prepared to deal more effectively with distinct regional groupings within Latin America and to take into account the very different development problems which these states face individually. The identification of an underlying Latin American-Mediterranean cultural unity, which attempts to go beyond the work of Kalman Silvert,[17] is intended to point up the fact that generalizations regarding Latin American government, if checked out carefully, apply to an area much larger than a geographical one confined to the Western Hemisphere. What generalizations are made within the area must occur at a subregional level where one takes into account such factors as distinct geographic regions and culture groups (viz., the pampas and the gaucho of Argentina and southern Brazil, or the Andean region with its Aymará- and Quechua-speaking Indian populations), the importance of the larger states (for example, Brazil, Argentina, and Mexico), and regional groupings of nations (such as the Central American states and the Andean group). In United States policy analysis what this points to is the futility of continuing to search for a pan-Latin American policy capable of handling social, economic, and political change in this area as a single phenomenon.

In the 1940s Arthur Whitaker analyzed the death of the idea that the Western Hemisphere constituted a distinct unit and pointed out the divergent interests existing between the United States and Latin America in an extended essay, *The Western Hemisphere Idea: Its Rise and Decline*.[18] As we enter the 1970s it is time to advance one step further: move beyond recognition of the divergent interests between the United States and Latin America towards a greater understanding of the range of interests among the Latin American states themselves, within the context of subregional groupings, such as the Caribbean, southern South America, the Andean region, and Central America. Greater consciousness of these subregional disparities and of the contrast involved among large nation-states such as Brazil, Argentina, and Mexico; medium-sized republics such as Chile, Colombia, and Peru; and smaller national entities such as Uruguay, Panama, and El Salvador might help us to increase our awareness that, as attempts at modernization increase which break with an image of United States tutelage, they need not necessarily be identified with a decline in United States prestige or influence. What happens in Cuba or Mexico may well be of immediate concern to the United States because of geographical proximity. Yet, even in this instance, we have learned to live with a Cuban government far from our liking, and the United States and Mexico long ago buried their enmity. What occurs in Brazil or Argentina or Chile or Peru is even farther removed from immediate United States interests and might consequently be relegated to the same level as events in other parts of the world. If anything, the preferences for independent foreign policies in these countries might well be related to a policy of the United States in the 1970s of disengagement from the southern portion of the hemisphere, while these countries consolidate strong national governments capable of making the fundamental structural changes essential to modernization. In the final analysis the crossing of the ill-defined frontier between economies tied to a world market centered in the United States and Western Europe and those capable of self-sustaining growth is dependent on how independent national governments utilize their own domestic and foreign resources.

In this connection the case of Mexico warrants closer attention. Relations between the United States and Mexico have improved to the degree that a viable national economy controlled by a strong central government, capable of independent action, has emerged in that country. However, during the period when Mexico created and consolidated its own distinctive national government, capable of resisting foreign influence, relations with the United States remained abysmal.

The foundations for the economic growth Mexico has experienced since World War II have grown out of Mexican solutions to Mexican problems of land tenure (through the destruction earlier of an agrarian elite), education (through the development of literacy campaigns and a national system of primary, secondary, preparatory, technical, and trade schools), inadequate communications (through the emergence of a national system of highways, railroads, and airlines), insufficient investment in commercial and industrial enterprises (through state capitalism and the channeling of foreign capital into joint ventures), and the transfer of political power (through the institution of a dominant one-party system). As effective national government and sustained economic growth have become fixed, relations between the two countries have improved, trade has increased, and foreign capital has found Mexico to be a fertile area for investment.

None of this, however, should be construed to say that Mexico has solved all its problems, for in each of the areas singled out as examples grave difficulties remain. The difference lies in the fact that few of the countries in the region, outside Mexico, have been able to establish a government capable of instituting fundamental change in such areas as land reform and education, of providing a framework for handling management-labor-peasant conflict, and of establishing meaningful control over the uses of foreign private capital.

Aside from the fact that the United States and Mexico have learned to live with each other, the problem is that the important questions in hemispheric relations remain unanswered. Since the end of the nineteenth century the United States has considered its political, economic, and military interests to be preeminent in the Western Hemisphere. To date only Cuba has been successful in breaking completely with this sphere of influence, and this has been done at a cost few other nations will be willing to undergo. Will it be possible, now that all indications seem to point in the direction of increasing pressure for independent foreign policies among the larger, more developed Latin American states, for the United States to accept the situation? Can the United States contribute to the development of strong economic and political systems which, while within a Western cultural tradition, may well express values and orientations quite different from those of the United States? Even though the desire of the Latin American states to present a common front to the United States is certainly understandable, the question also must be raised as to whether or not this stance will facilitate the revision of United States policy toward the area and allow for the development of a foreign policy more cognizant of the divergent desires of each of these republics.

Notes

1. *Existe América Latina?* (México: Fondo de Cultura Económica, 1945).

2. William Lytle Schurz, *Latin America: A Descriptive Survey* (New York: E. P. Dutton and Co., 1964), p. vi.

3. Charles W. Anderson, *Politics and Economic Change in Latin America: The Governing of Restless Nations* (Princeton: D. Van Nostrand Co., 1967), pp. 87-114.

4. For a critique of the illusion of the harmony of interests theme in the United States-Latin American relations, see James Petras, "U.S.-Latin American Studies: A Critical Assessment," *Science and Society,* XXXII, no. 2, Spring 1968.

5. José Enrique Rodó, *Ariel* (Chicago: The University of Chicago Press, 1929).

6. This has been well documented in studies by Robert Burr. See, for example, "The Balance of Power in Nineteenth Century South America: An Exploratory Essay," *The Hispanic American Historical Review,* 25 (February 1955), pp. 37-60.

7. In this context, for example, the comparative analysis of violence and the structuring of conflict points to common perceptions in such cases as Michel Crozier's *The Bureaucratic Phenomenon* (Chicago: The University of Chicago

Press, 1964) and James L. Payne's analysis of *Labor and Politics in Peru: The System of Political Bargaining* (New Haven: Yale University Press, 1965).

8. Juan Linz and Amando de Miguel have suggested the utility of using A. O. Hirschman's analysis of economic development in Latin America in handling economic change in Spain. From that basis they go on to identify the problems of partial modernization which are characteristic of Southern Europe and Latin America as an area meriting distinct concern in comparative analysis. See Juan J. Linz and Armando de Miguel, "Within-Nation Differences and Comparisons: The Eight Spains," in *Comparing Nations,* ed. Richard L. Merritt and Stein Rokkan (New Haven: Yale University Press, 1966), pp. 267-319.

9. Both Kalman H. Silvert and Louis Hartz have addressed themselves to this phenomenon. In *Man's Power: A Biased Guide to Political Thought and Action* (New York: The Viking Press, 1970), Silvert discusses the distinctive political experience of Latin Catholic Europe and the prevalence of similar political problems in Latin America and Southern Europe. Taking a different tack, Louis Hartz suggests handling political systems in the New World as fragments of European civilization by linking Canadian and United States political experience with England's and that of Latin America with continental Europe's. See Louis Hartz, *The Founding of New Societies: Studies in the History of the United States, Latin America, South Africa, Canada, and Australia* (New York: Harcourt, Brace, and World, 1964).

10. *Administration in Developing Countries: The Theory of Prismatic Society* (Boston: Houghton Mifflin Co., 1964).

11. These ideas are adapted from Crozier, *The Bureaucratic Phenomenon,* pp. 187-94. The distinction between French bureaucratic experience and that of Southern Europe and Latin America lies in the fact that for the latter the bureaucratic model utilized is exogenous in origin and bureaucratic behavior is heavily weighted in the direction of the saliency of traditional norms and values mixed with technocratic skills.

12. An illustration of the contrasts to be found in interest group behavior in Anglo-American political cultures as opposed to Southern European and Latin American ones can be seen by comparing Theodore J. Lowi, *The End of Liberalism: Ideology, Policy, and the Crisis of Public Authority* (New York: W. W. Norton and Co., 1969) and Philippe C. Schmitter, *Interest Conflict and Political Change in Brazil* (Stanford: Stanford University Press, 1971). While Schmitter limits his comparison largely to contrasting United States and Brazilian experience, the model he uses, which emphasizes the impact of the policy process on interest group activity, is equally valid for interest group politics in Spanish-speaking countries as well as in Portugal and Italy.

13. For a more detailed analysis of these parallels, see Lawrence S. Graham, *Mexican State Government: A Prefectural System in Action* (Austin: Institute of Public Affairs, University of Texas, 1971).

14. As an example of this pattern of cohesive economic relations between private and public management in the context of a fragmented multiparty parliamentarian system, see F. Roy Willis's discussion of industrial decision makers and industrial and agricultural interest groups in *Italy Chooses Europe* (New York: Oxford University Press, 1971), pp. 178-220.

15. The most detailed national study of this pattern of elite fragmentation is to be found in volumes 2 and 3 in the MIT-CENDES-sponsored research project in Venezuela. See Frank Bonilla, *The Failure of Elites* and José A. Silva Michelena, *The Illusion of Democracy in Dependent Nations*, Vols. II and III in *The Politics of Change in Venezuela* (Cambridge: MIT Press, 1970 and 1971).

16. Anderson, *Politics and Economic Change*, pp. 104-14.

17. While Silvert has dealt with the theme repeatedly over the years, his most complete statement of this concept in broad, comparative terms is to be found in *Man's Power*, pp. 58-65, 132-43.

18. (Ithaca, New York: Cornell University Press, 1954.)

Toward a
Theory of
Latin American
Politics

Charles W. Anderson

For some, it may appear quite bizarre and quixotic to speak about the
"political system" of Latin America. Social system refers to pattern,
persistence, and regularity in human behavior. Latin American politics appear to be whimsical, unstable, crisis ridden, and unpredictable.
It would appear that what is at issue in the political life of this region
is failure to establish political systems, the hardening of a state of
crisis when all rules are suspended into a way of life.

However, though the patterns be unfamiliar to the observer who
identifies political system with the processes of constitutional democracy, there do seem to be certain recurrent and persistent patterns
in Latin American political life. The intervention of the military in
politics, the technique of the *coup d'etat,* the use of violence and terror
as political instruments, insecurity of tenure for constitutionally established governments, are all phenomena that appear over and over
again in the political history of the region. As K. H. Silvert puts it:

*"Unpredictable" and "unstable" are the two adjectives most often
applied to Latin American politics. The implications of both pejora-
tives are partially erroneous. First, to be "unstable" is not necessarily to be "unpredictable." As a matter of fact, one of the easiest
things to predict is instability itself. And second, some types of revolutionary disturbance do not indicate instability. If the normal way of
rotating the executive in a given country is by revolution, and there
have been a hundred such changes in a century, then it is not face-
tious to remark that revolutions are a sign of stability—that events are
marching along as they always have.*[1]

Still more enticingly, we are aware that certain patterns of Latin
American politics, such as the generally respected rights of exile and
asylum for losers in power struggles, may indicate that there are rules

Reprinted from Occasional Paper No. 2, February 1964, The Graduate Center
for Latin American Studies, Vanderbilt University, Nashville, Tennessee.

of political activity generally understood by the participants, which are effective in regulating political conduct even where formal, constitutional commitments do not apply. It may be that those versed in the skills of Latin American politics have not yet stated the nature of this art. Perhaps it is not that the term "political system" is inapplicable to Latin American politics, but rather, that we, the outsiders, do not yet know how that system operates.

A second objection to the effort to describe the "rules of the game" of politics in Latin America will be raised. I have been using the term "political system" in the singular. Surely, the same set of propositions cannot be applied to the heterogeneous circumstances of the twenty Latin American nations. Obviously, Costa Rica and Paraguay, Brazil and Uruguay, Bolivia and Mexico reflect quite different forms of political life. On the other hand, on close examination, it is clear that the simple label "constitutional democracy" does not account precisely for the political history of Costa Rica which has thrice had recourse to violent techniques of adjusting power relations in the twentieth century, nor does the appelative "military dictatorship" reflect the subtleties and complexities of the technique of rule of the Somoza family in Nicaragua. There would seem to be a need for a body of theory, a set of statements sufficiently general to enable us to compare Latin American governments in similar terms, and which could be adjusted to the characteristics of specific situations. Hence, what we shall say is not meant to refer only to the "typical" Latin American political situation, and to exclude such deviant cases as Uruguay or the Dominican Republic during the era of Trujillo. Rather, it is hoped that by adjusting the value of such variables as the "power capabilities" included in this theory, these statements can be applied generally to political life throughout Latin America.

A frequent point of departure for analysis of Latin American politics is to note that in this region there is imperfect consensus on the nature of the political regime, that the "legitimacy" of the formal political order is weak.[2] Political legitimacy is that characteristic of a society which enables men to disagree vigorously over the policies that government should pursue or the personnel that should occupy decision-making posts, yet to support common notions of the locus of decision-making authority, the techniques by which decisions are to be made, and the means by which rulers are to be empowered. For the American student of Latin American politics, the sublime counter-theme that ran below shock and grief at the assassination of the President of the United States was the sure knowledge that the system would survive, the republic would prevail. In lands where political legitimacy is weak, the end of a government brings into question not only the person of the successor, but the very form of government that will emerge.

However, imperfect consensus on the nature of political regime is
not a problem of politics peculiar to Latin America, nor does it account for the distinctiveness of Latin American politics. Rather, it
is on a further dimension of the problem of political legitimacy that
we must concentrate. For in Latin America, no particular techniques
of mobilizing political power, no specific political resources, are
deemed more appropriate to political activity than others. No specific
sources of political power are legitimate for all contenders for power.

Of course, this is to some extent the case in every society. In the
United States, despite the fact that our own political ideology prescribes the aggregation and mobilization of consent as the only legitimate means of structuring power relationships, we do recognize that
possessors of certain power capabilities, economic wealth, or control
of armed force, have particular influence in decision making. However, in democratic society, the organization of consent according to
prescribed norms is generally reinforced by holders of other power
capabilities, and, in the long run, democratic processes serve as a
court of last resort in structuring power relationships. In contrast, in
Latin America generally, democratic processes are *alternative* to other
means of mobilizing power.

The problem of Latin American politics, then, is that of finding some
formula for creating agreement between power contenders whose
power capabilities are neither comparable (as one measures the relative power of groups in democratic society by reference to votes cast)
nor compatible.[3] The political system of Latin America may be described
as the pattern by which Latin American statesmen conventionally attempt to cope with this variety of political resources used in their societies, and the way in which holders of these diverse power capabilities characteristically interact one with another.

In restructuring our frame of reference to cope with this unfamiliar
state of affairs, we might begin by suggesting that the techniques used
in advanced Western nations as means of ratifying power relationships more frequently appear in Latin America as means of demonstrating a power capability. The significance of this can best be seen
by examining three prominent techniques which we commonly assume are means of ratifying power relationships (that is, of structuring a regime or government) and reflect on where they fit in the
Latin American political scheme of things. These would be: election,
revolution, and military dictatorship.

Elections are not definitive in many parts of Latin America. However, they are conscientiously and consistently held, and just as conscientiously and consistently annulled. Few Latin American nations
can demonstrate an unbroken sequence of elected governments over

any substantial period of time. In a sense, our real question is not that of why elections are ignored, but why they are held at all given their inconclusive character.

Latin American political instability is more comprehensible if we do not view election as definitive, but as part of an ongoing process of structuring power relationships, in which election is important to some contenders, but not to all. Democratic election is really only relevant to those who have specific skills and support, who rely on their capacity to aggregate mass consent through parties and movements and interest groups for participation in the political process. Insofar as such contenders cannot be ignored by other holders of power capabilities, election, which is the device that "demonstrates" this power capability, measures and confirms it, is part of the political process. But since there are other contenders in the political process, whose power is not contingent on this type of support, elections do not define political relationships. Rather, the results of an election are tentative, pending the outcome of negotiations between other power contenders and the groups that have demonstrated a power capability through election.

Thus, when a new political movement which has amassed sufficient electoral power that other contenders must take it into account appears in the political arena, judgments must be made by other political contenders as to whether, on balance, the threat posed by this movement to the position of existing contenders is greater than the cost of its suppression, whether the stability of the system would be better insured by accommodating the power contender into that circle of elites that negotiate for control of the resources of the state or by its suppression.

Similarly, it is conventional to distinguish between "real" revolutions and "typical" revolutions in Latin America. Again, the "real" revolution, in the Western sense of the term, is a technique of ratifying power relationships, of structuring a new regime. The "typical" Latin American revolution, on the other hand, does not demolish the previous structure of power relationships, but adds to it that of the revolutionaries, who may be said to have demonstrated a power capability that other power contenders had found it advisable or necessary to recognize and accommodate into the power structure of the society.

Finally, we generally say that Latin American military dictatorship is to be distinguished from European military totalitarianism. With the possible exception of Perón, political intervention by the military in Latin America does not seem to have the effect of overhauling the power system of the society. Rather, under military governments in Latin America, holders of important power capabilities in the society are assured that their position in the society will not be endangered and are permitted some participation in the political process. (Certainly, military governments may brutally restrict entrance of other new power contenders into the political arena, and in some nations, they are supported by other power contenders for just this reason.) In general, the effect of military *coup* in Latin America is to add a new power contender to the "inner circle" of political elites, but one whose control is not exclusive or definitive.

One may say that the most persistent political phenomenon in Latin America is the effort of contenders for power to demonstrate a power capability sufficient to be recognized by other power contenders, and that the political process consists of manipulation and negotiation among power contenders reciprocally recognizing each other's power capability.

It is apparent that it is often not necessary for a power contender actually to use a power capability, but merely to demonstrate possession of it. For example, Latin American armies often prove incredibly inept when actually called upon to use armed force in a combat situation. One recalls the fate of Batista's well-equipped military force during the events of 1958. However, except in "real revolutionary" situations, Latin American armies are seldom called upon actually to use armed force. What is at issue is the demonstration and recognition of a *transfer* in the control of the military institution. This may be accomplished by the announcement of a shift in allegiance of certain critical garrisons. That one of the primary targets in a *coup* is control of a radio transmitter so that the insurgents can *inform* the populace of the change in loyalties is a vivid example of what is in fact going on.

Similarly, "manifestation" or "demonstration" is a means of demonstrating the implicit power capability of the mob. Seldom does mob action actually become manifest (as it did in the Bogotazo of 1948); rather, the presence of the multitude assembled before the national palace is generally adequate for existing power contenders to recognize and seek to placate or accommodate the new power capability that has emerged in their midst.

Even the use of noninstitutionalized violence and terror is often designed to show possession of a power capability rather than to use it directly for political ends. More true to the Latin American tradition in such matters than the political assassination or widespread destruction of property or life is the symbolic act of terrorism or violence. For example, the theft of an art collection in Caracas in 1962, the kidnapping and release unharmed of a U.S. Officer, as components of a rather consistent strategy of the FALN terrorists in Venezuela, were designed to produce the largest dramatic appeal and embarrassment to the regime, without large-scale devastation of property.

While the Latin American political process is becoming more complex, and such acts of civic disruption and violence are growing more serious and threatening in intent, in the classic pattern of Latin American political life, such techniques of demonstrating a power capability seem generally accepted as appropriate to the political system. Thus, when such techniques as manifestation, strike, and even violence are used symbolically, that is, as the demonstration and not the use of a power capability, there would seem to be an *a priori* case that the appropriate response of government leaders should be conciliation and bargaining. However, when use of such techniques actually degenerates into important destruction of life or property, it seems more generally felt that the rules have been transgressed, and that the use of sanctions is called for. Brutal police suppression, with the loss of life and widespread arrests, in the face of a student riot, even one that may have culminated in the burning of automobiles or the breaking of windows, may breed an ugly public mood. On the other hand, persistent agitation that actually disrupts the way of life of the society and is not dealt with firmly by constituted authority may lead quickly to agitation for a stronger, "no nonsense" government.

The characteristic political process of Latin America may then be described as one of manipulation and negotiation among power contenders with reciprocally recognized power capabilities. Seldom is this process overt or public. Often it does not consist of a formal situation of "negotiation" at all, but is rather implicit in the statements of a new government as it takes office, and carefully announces a policy format that accounts for the interests of all prominent elites, or as it delicately pursues a policy which takes account of dominant power contenders.

The character of the system is perhaps most strikingly illustrated in the "learning process" which Latin American reformist movements undergo when they come to power. While "outside" the effective political arena, they build consent on the promise of radical and sweeping reforms. The power of the military will be reduced, large foreign economic interests will be nationalized, a thoroughgoing agrarian reform will be carried out. Having created and demonstrated a power capability on this basis, having assumed political power perhaps on the basis of an election, their attitude changes. They become proponents of "evolutionary change," of "gradual, reasonable, reforms," in which "all social forces must participate and contribute to the welfare of the nation." The army is confirmed in its perquisites. Economic policy becomes more moderate. Strong action contemplated against existing elites is modified or abandoned.

What is at issue is less political cynicism, or the difference between campaign oratory and actual statesmanship, than it is a process by which these newly accepted power contenders learn the conditions of their own rule. In some cases, this learning experience is quite overt and apparent in public pronouncements made before and after entering office. In others, such contenders learn only by hard experience, by being deposed, and subsequently readmitted to power as more docile contenders. Of the former type, Arturo Frondizi of Argentina is a prime example. A fire-eating reformer out of office, committed economic nationalist, and defender of the rights of labor, he became an economic moderate in office, once instructed in the economic "facts of life" of post-Perón Argentina, quite eager to accept the stabilization recommendations of the International Monetary Fund, to invite in foreign petroleum firms, to hold the line on labor wage increases. Of the latter case, the *Acción Democrática* movement in Venezuela is revealing. Coming to power in 1945 on a program of reform, suggestions of action against both the military and foreign oil interests contributed to their replacement in 1948 by a harsh military government. The party returned to power in 1958 chastened and wiser, now seeking a "reasonable relationship" with the petroleum industry, and suggesting no diminution of the power of the army in national life.

The Latin American political system is "tentative." Unlike nations where constitutional provision and the legitimacy of election guarantees a specified tenure for any government, in Latin America, government is based on a flexible coalition among diverse power contenders which is subject to revision at any time if the terms under which the original government was formed are deemed violated. Revision occurs primarily when an existing holder of an important power capability feels threatened by action of government. Thus, in 1954, when the government of Jacobo Arbenz, the second consecutively elected government in recent Guatemalan history, attempted to carry out an extensive agrarian reform, diluted the army's power through creation of a "people's militia," and permitted overt Communist activity in collaboration with the government, it was overthrown by threatened holders of important power capabilities. Similarly, in Argentina, the government of Arturo Frondizi was deposed when Frondizi appeared prepared to permit *Peronista* electoral participation, adjudged a serious violation of previous "understandings" by important power contenders.

The Latin American political system, therefore, accounts for change, and permits change, but only within a rather rigorous context. New contenders are admitted to the political arena of reciprocally recognizing elites in Latin America when they demonstrate a significant power capability, and when they provide assurances that they will not jeopardize the ability of any existing power contender to similarly participate in political activity. Thus, with the exception of "real revolutionary" situations, the normal rule of Latin American political change is that new power contenders may be added to the system, but old ones may not be eliminated.

It is this characteristic of the system that gives Latin American politics its distinctive flavor. While, in the history of the West, revolutionary experiences or secular change have sequentially eliminated various forms of power capability, contemporary Latin American politics is something of a "living museum," in which all the forms of political authority of the Western historic experience continue to exist and operate, interacting one with another in a pageant that seems to violate all the rules of sequence and change involved in our understanding of the growth of Western civilization. Politically pragmatic, democratic movements, devoted to the constitutional and welfare state ideals of the mid-twentieth century, stand side by side with a traditional, and virtually semi-feudal, landed aristocracy. "Social technocrats" and economic planners of the most modern outlook confer and interact with an institutionalized Church which in some countries is favored with a political position not far removed from the "two swords" tradition of Medieval political thought. Military *caudillos* cast in a role set in the early nineteenth century, and little changed with the passage of time, confront an organized trade union movement, a growing middle class, a new entrepreneurial elite.

The rule that new power contenders will be admitted to the system only when they do not jeopardize the position of established contenders contributes to the tentativeness of the system in operation. Neither the accommodation of a new power contender (such as a reformist political party) nor its suppression is final. There is a marked reticence in the classic pattern of Latin American politics to define for all time who may and may not participate in the political process, illustrated by the rule that exile rather than purge is the appropriate way of coping with an antagonistic power contender. If a suppressed power contender can survive long years of banishment from the political forum, the chances are good that at some future date the patterns of coalition and alliance among established contenders will be revised in such a way that the contender will again be able to participate in political activity, to redemonstrate its power capability in an environment more hospitable to its admission to that inner circle of forces that reciprocally recognize each other's right to be part of the political system. The long and tragic history of the Peruvian APRA party, suppressed and underground for long periods, yet recurrently admitted to the political arena by virtue of its capacity to demonstrate large-scale mass consent to its leadership and program, is illustrative.

New contenders are admitted to the political system when they fulfill two conditions in the eyes of existing power contenders. First, they must demonstrate possession of a power capability sufficient to pose a threat to existing contenders. Second, they must be perceived by other contenders as willing to abide by the rules of the game, to permit existing contenders to continue to exist and operate in the political system. If the first condition is not fulfilled, the power contender will be ignored, no matter what the merits of his case may be. (For example, a strike by a few hundred students over a penny increase in bus fares may bring on a full-scale governmental crisis and immediate concessions to the students, while a full-scale agrarian revolt in some remote province may merely be noted and deplored by decision makers in the capital city. Given the urban bias of the Latin American political system, the former affects the conditions of power in the system, the latter does not.) If the second condition is not fulfilled, efforts will be made to suppress the new power contender.

The ability of established elites effectively to suppress a new power contender depends on a variety of circumstances. Some established contenders are not loathe to support a new contender to strengthen their bargaining position in the political process. Hence, in recent years, some military leaders in Latin America, reading the handwriting on the wall, have adopted a "reformist" or "democratic" posture, seeking alliances with mass movements or middle class parties. Increasingly, the Catholic Church is abandoning its old bases of political alliance, and throwing in its lot with the "modern" political forces. In addition, the basic style of the political process, which resembles a complex game of chess between political forces with reciprocally recognized power capabilites, implies a certain level of conflict and competition between the established power contenders. When such inner circle elites are in conflict or stalemate, a new contender may enter the process by the back door. For example, in 1945 in Peru, the APRA party, for years suppressed by dominant elites, was permitted to participate in an electoral contest. The election itself was in many respects the outcome of a deadlock between the established elites.

When disunity or deadlock among established contenders threatens to admit a potentially dangerous power contender to the political arena, military dictatorship is often the most satisfactory remedy to preserve the system intact. Without jeopardizing the status of existing contenders, the *caudillo* replaces bickering, conflict, and "politicking" among the dominant political participants with order, firmness, and suppression of the threatening new political force. That this is often the basis for military rule in Latin America is well evidenced by the enthusiasm and relief felt by established political groups when an Odría in Peru, or a Rojas Pinilla in Colombia, comes to power to end a "crisis" of enmity and conflict between those elites which dominate the political system, and in which a threatening political force is bidding to come to power in the vacuum thus created. Yet, like that of other contenders, the rule of the military dictator is tentative, contingent on his ability to maintain the coalition of agreements and imputed objectives that brought him to power. Should he fail to maintain his power capability, or to obey the rules of the game that existing contenders are to be permitted to act politically according to the rules of negotiation and coalition, should he, in short, violate the implicit "understandings" that led to his acceptance, he too may be turned out. The fate of Idígoras Fuentes in Guatemala, of Perón in Argentina (particularly in his relations to the Church, the economic elites, and the military), and for that matter, of Odría and Rojas Pinilla, is illustrative.

It is inappropriate to view this classic political system of Latin America as entirely static. Often, we suggest that the normal course of Latin American politics is designed to reinforce the power of the oligarchy against the forces of change at work in the society. This is not entirely the case, and put this way, is somewhat deceptive. The rule of the system is of course that established elites will be permitted to continue to operate and to maintain many of their political and socioeconomic perquisites intact. But the rule of the system is also that new contenders, new holders of significant power capabilities, will be able to partake in negotiation for a share of the resources and powers of the state if they do not jeopardize the right of established elites to similarly act. Hence, although the landowners, the Church, the military, continue as prominent political economic forces, the terms of their share in the perquisites which political involvement can offer have been adjusted by the accommodations of a burgeoning middle class, new types of interest groups and political parties, a working class elite of skilled, organized, industrial laborers, into political life. It is true that these "new" forces have not achieved as great a share of the political economic resources of the society as have their counterparts in the advanced nations because of the requirements of the system that a substantial part of available resources must be allocated to the "older" contenders, the landowners, the military, and the like. However, it is, in almost all Latin American nations, quite untrue to suggest that these new contenders have been denied any share in political economic rewards at all, for the system has accommodated new power contenders, the system has changed. The conflict and crisis of contemporary Latin America is then more accurately described as one in which newer contenders feel that too large a share of social rewards are allocated to established contenders in fulfillment of the terms of the classic political system, rather than that the political system is one of complete rigidity and suppression, in which the emerging forces of change are unable to participate and derive benefit from political economic life at all. The peculiar character of Latin American political economic change then, would seem to be best analyzed, not in terms of our conventional and oversimplified categories of "class warfare" and "resistance to change," but as product of the distinctive political system of the region, one that permits new power contenders to be added to the system but is so designed that older political factors are not eliminated, one that is—if one can accept a most surprising use of the term—more "tolerant" as to the types of power capabilities that are relevant for political participation than are the political systems of the advanced, Western nations.

Ironically then, Latin American politics are not characterized by "revolution" as we conventionally assume, but by the total absence of any historic revolution that could eliminate some power contenders from the political system, and legitimate certain types of power capabilities as exclusively appropriate in the mobilization of political power. The significance of the great democratic revolutions of the eighteenth century in Western Europe and North America, then, is seen as that of rejecting as legitimate power capabilities those based on the feudal control of groups of serfs and land, or sheer military power, or the divine right of monarchy in which Church and state mutually reinforced the other's claims to legitimacy. The significance of the great democratic revolutions was that they effectively eliminated all power contenders who could not, at some point, base their claim to power on the aggregation and mobilization of consent, electorally tested. Latin America never experienced this democratic revolution. Latin America never went through the process by which those whose skills and resources were appropriate to the mobilization and organization of consent (the middle class) became dominant in the society, and could deny political participation to all those who could not base their claim to power on a type of power capability which was, in fact, only one of many possible in organizing power, and which did, in fact, refer to the political resources available to only one part of the population. Latin America did not legitimate democracy, that is to say, it did not restrict political power to only those who could mobilize consent. In fact, Latin America, as a region, has not undergone a revolution that could legitimate any particular type of power capability. Hence, the power systems of divine right monarchy, military authority, feudal power, and constitutional democracy all exist side by side, none legitimate, none definitive, and the political system that has emerged is one in which all of the political techniques that have been experienced by Western man continue as part of the system, and the system prescribes the rules for their interaction, and for the persistence of the system itself, by prescribing that none of these historic power capabilities may be eliminated entirely.

In saying this, we have implied a definition of revolution, which might be stated as follows: revolution occurs when some power contenders or some types of power capabilities are successfully eliminated from political participation. By this definition, some revolutions have occurred in Latin America, some political forces have chosen not to play according to the rules of the classic system just described, and have been successful in their endeavor.

Most students of Latin American politics agree that three regimes exist in modern Latin America that could properly be described as "revolutionary" in nature. These revolutions occurred in Mexico in 1910, Bolivia in 1952, and Cuba in 1959. Some note Guatemala from 1945-1954 as a revolutionary situation, and we will define it as a revolution that failed, or is temporarily in abeyance, perhaps going through a Thermidorian phase.[4] [Nicaragua should be added—Ed.]

All three of these situations essentially fit our definition of revolution. In each, a large part of the thrust of revolutionary agitation was against foreign control of natural resources or economic institutions. It is to be noted that here the intent was to eliminate certain power contenders (the foreign owners) rather than the power capability (control of economic factors as a political resource). In two of the revolutionary situations, Cuba and Bolivia (the latter in relation to at least mineral resources), the objective was to add the power capability of economic control to other political resources of the revolutionary regime through the device of expropriation and nationalization. In Mexico, the economic power capability previously in the hands of foreign power contenders was eventually allocated both to the revolutionary regime (nationalization of some basic industries such as petroleum) and to a new private, but national, group of entrepreneurs (Mexicanization). In all three cases, a prime component of revolutionary ideology was "anti-imperialism," which we would define as the intent to eliminate external power contenders from participation in the political system, to "nationalize" the political process.

Agrarian reform in all three revolutions was designed to eliminate both the power contenders and the power capability represented by the semi-feudal control of land and labor through the institution of the *hacienda*. All three revolutions were to some extent successful in thus "modernizing" the political system (e.g., in eliminating an archaic power capability), but in all three, residual traces remained, and in each, there is some evidence that the power capability of traditional agrarian authority was in some areas merely transferred to the new administrator of the collective or state farm (Cuba) or the agrarian or *ejido* bank (Mexico).

All three revolutions more or less successfully eliminated the traditional military as a prominent power contender. (However, only Costa Rica, which constitutionally abolished its army, can be said to have abolished the power capability of semi-legitimate control of armed force.) In Cuba, this power capability has been incorporated into the other political attributes of the regime through the device of the militia. In Mexico, the military remains as a power contender, though its capacity to use its power capability has been substantially, though always tentatively, reduced by the increasing legitimacy of other types of political resources.

In Mexico particularly, and to some extent in the other two nations, efforts were made, none completely successful, to eliminate the power capabilities of the Catholic Church. In these situations, as throughout Latin America, it is primarily the secular attributes of the Church (the *hacienda* power capability) that have successfully been reduced, while other power capabilities (ideology, capacity to aggregate consent) have remained more intractable.

The revolutionary mystique in Latin America insists that the classic system of politics can be transformed by the elimination of specific power contenders and power capabilities. The revolutionary experience in Latin America suggests that in some instances the characteristics of the older system reemerge, though often in greatly revised form. Revolution may make a great difference in the course of Latin American political life, though generally not all the difference expected by its perpetrators. Thus, the anti-imperialist strain in Cuban revolutionary thought culminated not in the elimination of the foreign power contender, but in the replacement of one set of foreign contenders (the United States interests, public and private) with an alternative set (the Soviet bloc). Similarly, the Bolivian revolution has been kept alive by giant infusions of United States aid, aid that has implied a prominent role for the U.S. in the decision-making processes of that nation. In Mexico, it is to be noted that foreign investors were eventually readmitted to the political economic system, though on terms that radically reduced their ability to use economic resources as a political capability.

The present political regime in Mexico, which Mexicans like to refer to as the "institutionalized revolution" is remarkably suggestive of the tenacity of the classic system of Latin American politics. Although the revolution of 1910 eliminated some power contenders, the eventual outcome of the revolutionary experience was the formation of a new set of elites, each recognizing, on the basis of demonstrated power capabilities, the right of the other to negotiate in the allocation of the resources available through the system. The interaction of the various sectors of the official party in Mexico—the campesino, popular, and labor sectors of the Party of the Institutionalized Revolution, or PRI—can only be described as manipulation and negotiation between mutually recognizing power contenders. The eventual inclusion of the new industrial and commercial elite of Mexico into the political system, though not into the official party, from which they are pointedly excluded, and the reconciliation of the revolutionary regime with the Church, in contradiction to a basic theme of revolutionary ideology, reflects the capacity of the informal system to survive and reshape the formal structure of the Mexican revolutionary regime, just as the informal system survives and describes patterns of political interaction not anticipated in the formal, constitutional, democratic structures of other Latin American nations.

Change is accounted for in the classic system of Latin American politics, but at a pace that is too slow for some of the newer power contenders. For some, revolution, by eliminating some power contenders and power capabilities, promises to change the pace of change, to make the Latin American political system more compatible with those of advanced Western nations, which themselves eliminated certain archaic power capabilities through revolutionary techniques several centuries ago.

However, some Latin American elites see the possibility of increasing the pace of change without revolution, without the drastic elimination of power contenders from the system. The basic conflict between modern power contenders in Latin America concerns the relative merits of "evolutionary" or "revolutionary" change. For proponents of either course of accelerating the course of change, the conflict is with those who would preserve the "legitimacy" of the classic system of politics in Latin America.

The evolutionary route to accelerated change, embraced by such leaders as Rómulo Betancourt of Venezuela, José Figueres of Costa Rica, Fernando Belaunde Terry of Peru, and many others, may be described as the quest to legitimate "democratic" power capabilities (those that rest ultimately on some form of aggregated consent) through the conversion of non-democratic power capabilities into democratic ones. In other words, those whose power does not rest on consent will have their actions redirected through structural change of the system, their power capability converted and not destroyed. Hence, the military will be "professionalized," not eliminated from the political arena, but directed toward a role more appropriate to democratic states. The old *hacienda* owners will not be destroyed, but required to adopt modern means of production, and modern forms of labor relations. Traditional authority, binding the patron and peon, will gradually disappear to be replaced by bargaining between responsible employers and responsible representatives of organized labor. The effort, in short, is to revise the classic system in terms compatible with the classic system. Existing power contenders are assured that their position within the system will not be jeopardized, in fact, so the ideology of the evolutionary reformer goes, it will actually be enhanced. The power of the *latifundista,* for example, is on the wane, his economic importance diminishing. He can only preserve his power, and enhance it, by adopting more modern techniques of production and social and political interaction. Other evolutionary leaders argue that such change is essential if the system is to remain the same, that the alternative to reformed performances by existing power contenders is their elimination through a revolutionary movement.

The ideological framework of this approach appears under the aegis of many conventional categories of contemporary political thought, yet it is adequately described by none. The heritage of Marxism, continental Second International socialism, Christian democracy, and the "New Deal" may be invoked to define what these leaders are about, as well as such indigenous strains as Peruvian *Aprismo* and the experience of the Mexican Revolution. However, none of these describes what really is at issue for such evolutionist movements.

Their prime appeal is to something that can only be described as a notion of the "national interest," made vivid by the awakening of nationalism as a relevant and meaningful notion of reference and interaction for increasing numbers of publics in Latin America. Their vision and context of action is that of the interrelationship of the various sectors of the nation in development. Hence, labor unions must moderate irresponsible wage demands, for investment essential to national industrial development can only be achieved with moderate labor costs, and industrialization is vital if the goal of productivity, welfare, national greatness, and a higher level of industrial employment is to be achieved. However, industrialists must accept extensive programs of education, public health, and social welfare if a "modern" domestic market and pattern of consumption is to be achieved. Agrarian reform is essential if a level of agricultural productivity is to be achieved that will be sufficient to feed increasing urban populations, aside from local subsistence food production, if scarce foreign exchange earnings are not to be wasted on imported foodstuffs, if export agriculture that will provide the wherewithal for industrial expansion is to be developed.

The educational mission of statecraft implied by this approach has made a certain impact. For the modern sector, in some nations at least, the classes seem less antagonistic, the interests of industrialists and workers less contradictory, than they did some years ago. The prospects of the evolutionary approach may be seen by an examination of Betancourt's Venezuela, Rivera's El Salvador, Lleras Camargo's Colombia. Its limitations are also apparent. The pace of change appears faster than that implied in the classic system, but for many, slower than that implied by revolutionary change, particularly that exemplified by the Cuban revolution. The economic shambles of Goulart's Brazil, the demise in frustration of Frondizi in Argentina, bring questions about the validity of the evolutionary approach in these nations. The collapse of Bosch's Dominican Republic and Villeda Morales' Honduras at the hands of the defenders of the "old order" frames the question clearly. The evolutionary style of reform may be undone either from the right or from the left.

Victor Raúl Haya de la Torre of Peru, the father of *Aprismo*, has said, "Latin America is not easy to govern." As this notion of the "system" of Latin American politics should make clear, the tasks of statecraft in this region are intricate, complex, and frustrating. Even the most skilled democratic political craftsman, a man of the stripe of Lyndon Johnson or Franklin Roosevelt, might pale before the task of "creating agreement" among the diverse contenders and forces at work in the Latin American political milieu. In the classic or evolutionary styles of Latin American statesmanship, politics is supremely the art of the possible, the art of combining heterogeneous and incompatible power contenders and power capabilities together in some type of tentative coalition, one in which the various members feel no obligation to maintain the combination intact for any prescribed term of office. George Blanksten, in his *Peron's Argentina*, likens the task of the Latin American politician to that of the juggler, who must keep a large number of balls simultaneously in the air, and is apt to be hit on the head by the one that he misses.

In view of the complexity and frustration of working within the system, it is no wonder that the apparent simplicity and malleability of revolution has an appeal in Latin America that itself adds to the complexity of government. But the attractions of the revolutionary alternative are often deceptive. Its simplicity is premised on the existence of a revolutionary situation, of a vivid and vital mass desire and capacity to start over again, on new terms, under new conditions, and that situation is exceptional rather than predictable. Certainly, there have been revolutions in Latin America, and there will be more, but there have been more insurgent movements that failed, that captured no following, that could not overcome and replace the going system.

Revolution requires exceptional leadership of a certain style to succeed, and those who have possessed it, the Maderos, Zapatas, Castros, and Bolívars and San Martíns, have entered the ranks of the vivid personal heroes of Latin American history. But there is another style of leadership which is relevant to the conduct of Latin American government, and there is no reason to believe that it is less available in this culture than that represented by the revolutionary politician in arms. The skills at the craft of politics, of working within the system to the end of transcending it, have been exemplified by men like Betancourt, Frondizi, Figueres, Lleras Camargo, López Mateos, and many others. They have their historic predecessors in such figures as Sarmiento and Juárez. Their skills and capabilities are not to be despised. In fact, set within the context of the system in which they have operated, and against the background of man's efforts to govern himself, they often appear as little short of incredible.

Notes

1. Kalman H. Silvert, *The Conflict Society: Reaction and Revolution in Latin America* (Hauser Press, New Orleans, 1961), p. 20.

2. This is the core concept in the analyses of Seymour Martin Lipset, "Some Social Requisites of Democracy: Economic Development and Political Legitimacy," *American Political Science Review,* 52, 1, March, 1959, pp. 69-105; and Martin Needler, "Putting Latin American Politics in Perspective," *Inter-American Economic Affairs,* 16, 2, Autumn, 1962, pp. 41-50.

3. Throughout, we will be distinguishing between power contenders and power capabilities. A power capability will be defined as the property of a group or individual that enables it to be influential in political affairs, in other words, a political resource. Examples of prominent power capabilities in Latin American politics would be:

Semi-legitimate control of armed force (control of the military institutions and equipment of the nation).

Capacity to mobilize, organize, and aggregate consent.

Capacity to create non-institutional violence, terror, or civic disruption.

Traditional authority (control of land and labor force through the pattern of social relations involved in the *latifundia* system).

Control of natural resources, or economic institutions.

Skill at the manipulation and recombination of the abstractions, symbols, and processes involved in complex social organization (bureaucratic expertise).

Various power capabilities may appear, of course, in combination. For example, the power of the Catholic Church in Latin America must be defined as an alloy of traditional authority, ideology, capacity to aggregate consent, and in some instances, economic wealth.

A power contender, then, is one who uses a power capability to attain certain specific objectives through political activity, in other words, a political actor. For example:

A military "clique," service, or unit.

A political party, interest group, or movement.

A group or association identified with a specific economic interest.

A community or region.

A family, class, or clique.

4. The term refers to the reactionary period of the French Revolution, and in this context is derived from Crane Brinton's discussion, in his *The Anatomy of Revolution* (Prentice-Hall: New York, 1938).

Part Five

Conclusion

In this final section the editor briefly reviews the Latin American development process in both its historic and contemporary dimensions. He summarizes the main lines of thought set forth in the book, and offers a preliminary model and framework for understanding Latin American politics and social change. But he also emphasizes the challenge to and crisis of the traditional Latin American development model and analyzes the possibilities for its continued viability or, alternatively, its breakdown and/or replacement by other kinds of systems. Finally, the implications of these trends are examined: for research and study, for Latin America's development prospects, for our understanding of the area, and for policy.

The book concludes with some suggestions for further readings.

Toward a Model of Social Change and Political Development in Latin America: Summary, Implications, Frontiers

Howard J. Wiarda

The Latin American Development Process in Historical Perspectives: Review and Discussion

The pull of the past remains exceedingly strong in Latin America and, if we use a culture-area approach rather than a strictly geographic one, in the mother countries of Spain and Portugal as well. In few areas of the world has the weight of history and past tradition been so powerful, so durable, so all-pervasive. Even in the face of the intense contemporary pressures of modernization and accelerated socio-political change, traditional behavior and institutions have proved remarkably adaptable and capable of survival, bending and accommodating to change rather (except in a handful of cases) than being overwhelmed or swept away by it. Economically, Latin America has grown considerably and has modernized in terms of the growing complexity and differentiation of its social and political institutions, but these changes have been accomplished largely on its own terms and through its own preferred processes rather than as pale imitations of the United States or Northwest European developmental models; much of the area's traditional essence and ways of doing things have been retained.

The essays collected here have stressed that Spain and Portugal, the first modern nation-states, and, by extension, their New World colonies founded circa 1500, were established upon a base that was Catholic, corporate, stratified, elitist, authoritarian, hierarchical, and patrimonialist to its core. Largely untouched until recent times by those great revolutionary currents—economic, political, religious, sociological, intellectual—that Northern Europe and North America associate with the modern era, the Iberian and Latin American nations remained locked in a more traditional pattern of values and institutions. Although there have been countless coups d'etat and barracks revolts in these countries, in the more fundamental sense implying a sharp break with the past, the Iberic-Latin nations have remained—again until recently—

profoundly nonrevolutionary in character. With only two or three exceptions (and even in these the revolutions that occurred often had but limited goals or involved a continuation of top-down, hierarchical, and neo-corporatist or syndicalist rule), the hold of traditional institutions has remained amazingly strong. Even as development began to accelerate throughout Latin America in the twentieth century, it took place largely within the established patterns and through an updating and modernization of the traditional institutions, rather than as a rejection of them. Traditional institutions were modified by the newer currents but not necessarily submerged or replaced by them.

In contrast to the secularism, pragmatism, and materialism which they see as predominant in the United States and Northern Europe, the Iberian and Latin American societies took pride in retaining a certain sense of moral idealism; of religious and philosophical unity; a sense of historic continuity; a notion of an ordered and hierarchical universe; a set of personalistic, family-centered, patron-client relationships that could be termed patrimonialist; and a unified ("monistic," Professor Dealy calls it) organic-corporate conception of state and society. This conception, we have seen, derives from the early Greeks, Roman law, the Church fathers, the traditional legal precepts of medieval Spain, and the charters governing the relations between the emerging central state and society's component corporate groups. The theoretical foundations for the structure of the Iberian and Latin American systems lie in what Professor Morse called the "Thomistic-Aristotelian notion of functional social hierarchy."

Sixteenth-century political philosophers such as Suárez laid the foundation for a modern theory of the Christian, Thomistic state. This conception may be usefully contrasted with the Lockean-liberal tradition of the United States. The Iberian and Latin American conception stemming from Saint Augustine and Thomas Acquinas remained, as Morse and Dealy show, the blending of the ethical and the political in contrast to their separation in the North American polity, the fusion of the ancient "City of God" with the "City of Man." Empirical facts were required to show the credentials of logic, rightness in an ethical and Christian sense, and relation to abstract justice. One must be careful not to exaggerate or romanticize these concepts, for obviously in the history of both Iberia and Latin America there were numerous abuses. Nevertheless the Suárezian conception gave certainty; a firm moral foundation; a set of absolutes; concepts of justice, obligation, and even resistance to unjust tyrants; and a particular philosophy of behavior and a dominant Iberian-Catholic political culture that remains quite different from that of the Anglo-American nations.

The Iberic-Latin nations are still in large measure grounded on the Thomistic-inspired hierarchy of laws, orders, and estates. Their theories of state and society continue to be based on historic Christian and

Roman Catholic assumptions, or on semi-secularized versions of these: an ordered universe, "natural" *inequalities* among men, a social order that is elitist, paternalistic, and aristocratic. The perception of the state and society is an organic one, that government is natural and necessary for conserving peace and social harmony, that it must labor for the "common good," that it is ordained of God and from above, and that it is an extension from the spiritual to the temporal world of a superior plan and authority. There is little conception of popular participation or of individual inalienable rights in the Anglo-American sense; rather in Latin America, power is more aristocratic and authoritarian, based upon the ruler's knowledge of the "general will" (which is the Iberic-Latin conception of popular sovereignty), and grounded on the vested rights of the traditional estates and corporate bodies, themselves also organized authoritarianly, and hierarchical and conservative in character. Group or corporate rights ordinarily take precedence over individual rights.

In comprehending the Iberian and Latin American systems, these essays have stressed, one could think in terms of hierarchically structured societies, organized according to horizontal categories of class and caste and in compartmentalized vertical sectors corresponding to the traditional estates, functional corporations (Church, Army, guilds, universities, organized labor, and the like), and juridically defined *intereses* (recall Professor Newton's discussion of the differences between United States style interest-group pluralism and the segmented *intereses* of Latin America). Each class, caste, and corporate group had its "rights" as well as its obligations defined in elaborate laws and charters. Each had certain expected modes of behavior and a "station in life" which all groups were expected to observe and accept. It was a rigid and yet adaptable scheme, with each of the component parts tied to and deriving legitimacy from the Crown or, more recently, the central state.

A strong central state and an authoritative (if not authoritarian) government was necessary to regulate and exercise tutelage over the various groups and classes. If order and absolutism were not maintained, it was feared, anarchy would result—especially in the "wild" and "uncivilized" domains of Latin America. But although the state needed to be strong, each class as well as each corporate sector had its own status and just place in the system, which was also assumed to correspond to natural law. There could be no questioning of fundamental values and few possibilities for change and mobility. But in a political sense there would always be a dynamic tension between the central state seeking to expand its powers and the various societal units trying to maintain theirs. Indeed this arena of state-society relations—of the relations between the central government and the Church, the Army, or, in modern times, the trade unions (and not so much electoral politics, although that may be one aspect of the larger struggle)—is perhaps the chief arena in which Iberian and Latin American politics takes place.

The Crown and, later, the central state occupied the apex of the socio-political pyramid. Through its quasi-monopoly of military, financial, and political affairs and its authority to grant (or withhold) legal recognition, it sought to control and regulate the class, corporate, and group life that swirled around and beneath it. The central administrative machinery served as the focal point through which these units related to each other, instead of directly across a bargaining table (as in the United States model). The central state was also the source of wealth, jobs, patronage, and contracts, which enabled it to regulate the class structure as much as be shaped by it. The several political elites must in effect petition the state for favors that further their advantage, but that means the state can control their activities. It is not hence so much a laissez-faire or a capitalistic system that exists in Latin America or Iberia. Capitalism may exist but it is dependent on the state, has a political orientation, and may be called "neo-mercantilism" or "state capitalism." The model of political authority and political economy is thus an updated patrimonialist one in which the wealth and power of the nation are considered part and parcel of the state's suzerainty, to be doled out to the "deserving" in return for continued loyalty. In such a system there can be no sharp separation between the private and public domains.

The traditions and institutions of the two metropoles—an authoritarian political structure, a class- and corporately segmented social order, a patrimonialist and neo-mercantilist system of political economy, a hierarchical and absolutist system of laws, a closed and immutable set of religious beliefs and educational methods, a pervasive Catholic political culture shaped in the special Iberian tradition—all formed part of the baggage that Spain and, in a more easygoing fashion, Portugal first established at home and then carried over to the New World. In America these institutions were reinforced both by the prevailing institutions of the existing Indian civilizations to which they were remarkably parallel and which the Iberians simply took over, and by the vast distances, disorganization, and potential for chaos in the New World which implied these institutions had to be established even more strongly (if not in fact, then certainly in aspiration) than they were at home. What would soon be anachronistic and eventually dying institutions in Northwest Europe and the North American colonies remained largely intact in Iberia and Latin America, where they were not only transplanted but took root and thrived.

What is surprising, we have said, is not that this conception of the organization of social, political, economic, and religious-cultural institutions should be strongly established in sixteenth-century Spain, Portugal, and their New World colonies, but that it should endure so long. In the mother countries, with their strongly conservative institutions, it persisted through the period of Hapsburg rule in the sixteenth and seventeenth centuries, through the centralizing Bourbon reforms of the eighteenth century, into (in somewhat altered form) the "republican" period of the nineteenth century, and on into the authoritarian-corporate regimes of Primo de Rivera and Franco in Spain and Salazar-Caetano in Portugal. The post-Franco and post-Caetano regimes, in more liberal and democratic or "mixed" forms, also continue to demonstrate some remarkable continuities with that earlier tradition. In Latin America, this same tradition prospered during three centuries of colonial rule, survived in modified form on into the independence period, and has persisted to the present—albeit again in mixed and altered form—despite the impact of industrialization, accelerated social change, and the challenge of new and conflicting ideologies. Even with these newer pressures, about which we shall have more to say later, one still finds powerful echoes of the earlier hierarchical, authoritarian, patrimonialist, and organic-corporatist institutions in virtually all contemporary regimes in Latin America—whether leftist, centrist, or rightist—and in the political-cultural foundations on which they are based. Classic Iberian political theory and practice emanating from the Roman imperial tradition, the Thomistic conception, and the experiences of Spain and Portugal in forging national unity provided the central state with power and imperial grandeur, enabled it to play a directing and moderating role among the contending interests, and in the process served to help preserve the status quo and the continuance of traditional or neo-traditional institutions.

This emphasis on the persistence of tradition is not to imply that there were no changes at all in the Iberian and Latin American nations. In fact the changes were many and significant. But the point made by all our essays is that change has generally come gradually and incrementally, in a controlled and regulated fashion, and within established parameters so as to adapt these systems to new circumstances but without in the process undermining traditional institutions and values or provoking social revolution. Change has generally been limited and structured, chiefly through the state system, in a way consistent with the historic, traditional institutions and preferences described here and designed as much as possible to preserve the status quo or a slightly altered version of it.

This discussion of the dominant Iberic-Latin political culture and tradition has up to this point emphasized their conservative, system-conforming, and perhaps even reactionary features, the fact they are closed to contrary perspectives and have shut out those conflicting modernizing currents they could not safely absorb. This picture, however, is only partially accurate. For beginning in the mid-to-late nineteenth century and continuing into the twentieth, the Iberian and Latin American nations began to articulate a new developmental conception and ideology of their own, one uniquely attuned to their own history and traditions, positive and modernizing rather than negative and reactionary. This newer conception was offered as a "third way," neither capitalist nor socialist, and serving as the Iberic-Latin counterpart to the modernizing ideologies formulated elsewhere in the West. This tradition of corporatist thought and practice remains almost wholly ignored in our texts on the history of ideas or on social change, but it is crucial for an understanding of development in Iberia and Latin America.

By this time Spain, Portugal, and Latin America had also begun to be affected by industrialization, urbanization, faster social change, new demands for expanded participation, and the newer revolutionary ideologies and movements gaining force. In turn their major thinkers began to grapple with the same fundamental issues that preoccupied Marx, Durkheim, Weber, and other well-known writers in our more familiar schools of politics and sociology. The Iberian and Latin Americans built upon the newer and reformist currents emanating from especially Catholic but also secular writers, and drew as well from their own national and historic traditions. Similar ideas were being put forth elsewhere in Europe, but in Iberia and Latin America the combinations and nuances were quite distinctive. These involved an effort to blend and reconcile the traditional regard for order and hierarchy with the new imperatives of change and modernization.

For example, the system of elite rule was retained but the number and size of the elite groups were expanded. The principle of hierarchy was also kept but new avenues of social mobility were opened. The phenomenon of mass man was dealt with through the creation of new corporate agencies that, it was hoped, would provide for class harmony rather than Marxian class conflict, structured participation rather than rootlessness and alienation. Accelerated economic growth occurred but chiefly under state auspices. Representation of the new social forces was to be allowed, but they would require licensing by the state; and participation would be through officially sanctioned associations, not through United States style liberalism. The central state would oversee, regulate, and "harmonize" the entire process, and an expanded patrimonialist state system would enable virtually the entire middle class to be incorporated within the new patronage networks. In this way social justice could be served, modernization could go forward, and the Iberic-Latin nations could face up to the realities of the contemporary period without sacrificing the valued traditional structures of the past. In this way too, an indigenous alternative could be provided to liberalism and Marxism, which were still deemed unacceptable; that alternative would also be nationalistic, because it represented a rejection of inappropriate and heretofore unsuccessful foreign models and the elevation of a solution proclaimed as "genuinely Latin American."

By the third and fourth decades of the twentieth century these ideas had been diffused widely throughout the Iberic-Latin culture area. In some cases a regime or political movement took over the corporate concepts entirely; in others, the corporate forms and notions were fused with various forms of liberalism, populism, or socialism. The point is that in virtually every country the new ideas gave rise to regimes and movements that sought to bridge the gap between the historic tradition and the newer requisites of the mass-industrial age. One need only look for illustration at Vargas's *Estado Novo* in Brazil, the program and ideology of a variety of Christian-Democratic groups, the regime of Lázaro Cárdenas and the structure of the Party of Revolutionary Institutions (PRI) in Mexico, the ideology and sectoral organization of Bolivia's National Revolutionary Movement (MNR), Perón's *justicialismo*, the more traditional regimes of Trujillo in the Dominican Republic and Stroessner in Paraguay, as well as the would-be syndicalist republics of Allende in Chile and Goulart in Brazil. This list illustrates not only the widespread nature and continued presence of the corporate forms and ideas, but also the considerable variety of regimes that could be subsumed under them. There are left-wing governments and right-wing governments, progressive and reactionary regimes, obviously different along some dimensions but quite similar along others. Not only the regimes themselves but their public policy processes, their unitary and organic character, the central role of the state, their *incorporation* of major societal sectors into the state system, the structured and state-directed labor and industrial relations systems, the patrimonialist conception of social programs and bureaucracy—all showed remarkable parallels.

It is to be emphasized that despite the significant differences that marked these various regimes and movements, their common origins and ingredients were at least equally significant. These included the similarity of their historical antecedents, their common colonial background, relatively similar levels of socio-economic development, a common political cultural background, a number of agreed-upon preconceptions about the way society and politics should be organized, a common proclivity to inherit, reshape, and rearrange the older order rather than destroy it. This implied changing it sufficiently to accommodate the new forces and social pressures but maintaining inviolate its paternalistic, hierarchical, segmented, well-ordered, and organic-corporate essentials. Though the political and ideological labels applied to these regimes and movements were often quite disparate, they also shared some fundamental agreement about the role of the state, the structure of society, and the relations between the two. In this way, in different forms in different countries, much of the historic Iberic-Latin conception continued into the contemporary period.

The thesis presented here obviously needs qualification at this point. Authoritarianism, patrimonialism, corporatism, and organic-statism in Iberia and Latin America clearly have multiple causes and they produced multiple effects. Political culture and the historic political sociology of the area were not the only causes. There were economic as well as manifest political forces pushing toward corporatist solutions in the 1930s. The breakdown of established political and economic institutions as a result of the world market crash of 1929–30 offers another important explanation. There were also class-based motives pushing the elites of these societies toward corporatist-authoritarian solutions. Nor should we make the mistake of elevating any useful but still-partial explanation into a single and all-encompassing one. Hence, although it is useful and important to recognize the shaping influence of the political-culture and institutional factors here described, other factors must also be taken into account. Finally, it should be stressed that the degree to which corporatism, organicism, and patrimonialism persisted in Latin America was by no means uniform, varying from country to country with some maintaining and resurrecting these institutions wholeheartedly, others trying to repudiate them, the majority concocting various blends and mixes.

Nevertheless, the sheer persistence of the historic tradition, now again adapted and updated, is quite remarkable. In various forms and under different rubrics it continued in all the countries of the areas. It was reinforced by the new social and economic pressures then building, but the sheer weight of history, of tradition, of "always doing things that way" was also of crucial importance. The more modern corporatist forms gained widespread acceptance because they fit well onto Iberia's and Latin America's historic past, they were comfortable, they conformed to established and venerated norms and practices. The newer corporatist forms were of course a response to crisis but that begs the question of why corporatism was the response and why it was so widely accepted; they also emerged as a result of economic and class trends, but that again does not explain why corporatist responses were the ones chosen, why virtually all the countries adapted one or another variant of them, why such solutions were both more widespread and lasting in Iberia and Latin America than in any other area of the globe. The answer, or at least a partial answer, lies in the lasting impact of that historical legacy and tradition whose main components are outlined here.

Much more work is required to flesh out the Iberic-Latin model in detail, to examine its national variations, to explore where it fits well and where less so. At this point what needs stress is both the importance and lasting impact of this tradition and the diversity of the regimes and movements incorporating features from it. These were not all "fascistic" regimes (with which corporatism is sometimes confused), or reactionary and backward looking. Some were conservative (though probably not fascistic), others middle-of-the-road, still others progressive and "syndicalist." What they had in common was a nationalistic effort to evolve a uniquely Iberian and Latin American ideology and program of action, to build upon indigenous institutions rather than imported ones, to recognize and deal realistically with modern-day problems and social forces while also preserving those hallowed institutions considered valuable in their own heritage. It is this current of thought and sociology—which our courses in theory and development have often lost sight of—that is critical if we are to comprehend the distinct features of the Iberic-Latin development process.

As set forth in this volume, there is a distinctly Iberic-Latin tradition and model of development, whose complex and particular dimensions fail to accord with our more familiar models, and whose functioning these other models are by themselves incapable of fully explaining. The Marxian model, dependency analysis, and the older "developmentalist" approach all offer useful and necessary explanations but not sufficient ones. They provide valid starting points but not final or complete answers. They must be used in conjunction with the explanations offered here. Our approach must thus be open and eclectic rather than closed and narrow.

What also requires emphasis is that the Latin American model and tradition may well contain features that make us uncomfortable. Although from the perspective of the United States or Northwest European democracies the Iberic-Latin tradition may at times seem undemocratic and authoritarian, we may also have to recognize that United States style democracy may not necessarily be the first preference of Iberia and Latin America, that they have evolved a developmental mode and framework of their own which may or may not correspond to our preferred solutions, and that this Iberic-Latin model has proved far more durable and functional than we had thought. All this helps explain why we on the outside have too long ignored, misinterpreted, and been insensitive and vaguely hostile toward the Iberic-Latin tradition. We maintain this ignorance and hold such prejudices, however, at the cost of continuing to misunderstand the experience and realities of the Iberian and Latin American nations.

The Change Process

Up to this point we have been considering the broad background and historic political culture within which development in Iberia and Latin America takes place, but we have not so far dealt explicitly with the change process. We turn to that aspect now.

In keeping with the historic Catholic-corporate conception, the state and society in Iberia and Latin America are thought of as an organic whole with a higher-order purpose. Attempts are thus made, often through family and personal ties, to erect various patron-client linkages, to engender a sense of belonging, preserve unity, and give all groups a place in the system. Branches, associations, and official agencies now exist for nearly everyone: the elites, middle sectors, workers, peasants, women, students. The national system itself is often conceived as a "family" implying strong but benevolent leadership, assigned and accepted obligations and privileges, unity, a purpose greater than merely the sum of its pluralistic parts.

It is now the central state that serves as the major instrument of national integration. The state incorporates diverse societal groups and functions as the agency through which these groups act and by which new social and political forces attain legitimacy and recognition within the system. Power is centered in the executive, whether civilian or military, and in the large bureaucratic apparatus of the patrimonialist state machinery. The president is the symbol of unity; he is looked to as the personification of the nation who directly identifies with and has knowledge of the "general will" or "common good" of his people. In personalistic fashion he hands out goods, services, jobs, contracts, and patronage in return for loyalty and support. Replacing the Crown or the local notables of the past, but retaining the practices of the traditional patron-client system, it is now the modern state that plays the role of great national patron. The old paternalism and patrimonialism persist, dressed up in more modern forms but retaining much of their earlier characteristics.

The same elitist and authoritarian structures that dominated so much of the past histories of Latin America are often still present today, modified by twentieth-century changes but not destroyed by them. The system remains segmented horizontally in terms of still-rigid class-caste layers, and organized vertically in terms of compartmentalized social or corporate groups. The "effective nation" has by now been expanded to include what Professor Anderson called the newer "power contenders," but it still tends to be authoritarianly controlled from the top and joined together at the highest pinnacles of these pyramidal systems. These structures tend to make the establishment of democracy difficult if not impossible, for just as de Tocqueville recognized in the United States the close relations of egalitarianism and democracy, so in Latin America we can recognize the close relations of a system grounded on rank, hierarchy, and compartmentalization, *and* the often nondemocratic character of the area's politics.

The term "corporatism" as used here and in several of the readings merits some special attention, because it is fundamental to the way many Latin American political regimes, left or right, are organized and function. Employed in its historic and cultural sense, corporatism refers to a system based on a belief in or acceptance of a natural hierarchy of social or functional groups, each with its place in the social order and with its own rights and obligations; more specifically, corporate systems are organized on a sectoral basis with restrictions usually placed on their autonomy and horizontal relations with other groups. Corporatism in this traditional sense, based in the religious concepts of medieval Christianity, closely reflected the hierarchical, authoritarian, and organic view of man and civil society. In the corporative system it is the central state that usually licenses, directs, and controls these corporate-societal units, holding the power to grant or withhold official recognition (without which the group cannot function legitimately) but also controlling access to official funds and favors, without which the group is unlikely to succeed or even survive. Corporatism implies not just the manifestly "corporate" or "fascist" regimes of the 1920s and 1930s but more fundamentally refers to an older, historic form of socio-political organization in Iberia and Latin America that persists even today in varied forms.

Group rights or *fueros* thus often take precedence over individual rights; similarly it is the "general will" or "common good," and hence the state that usually defines these vague abstractions and that ordinarily prevails over narrower private interests. In such a corporative system the government dominates and regulates much of the national group life and seeks to tie those interests who have earned their place in the system into a collaborative effort for "integral" national development. This kind of system works best where the number of interests is small and within a context of shared values, as in a "sleepier" nineteenth-century Latin America; but it is not necessarily incompatible with a growing diversity of ideologies and political groups.

In this context issues tend to be dealt with bureaucratically through a process of co-optation rather than from the point of view (more common in the United States) of problem-solving and program implementation. The emerging social forces, once their legitimacy has been recognized, are granted access to some of the spoils and patronage of the system and are hence "bought off." They may be given jobs, favors, even whole government agencies in return for continuing to support "the system." In this way problems are "managed" rather than "solved" as in the United States ethic.

The various groups tend to be represented functionally (as well as, occasionally, electorally—this varying from country to country), with order and administration usually predominating over "politics" and political parties. The government's role is to balance and co-ordinate these competing forces, assimilate them into the state's bureaucratic structure, and thus ameliorate social and political conflict. In this way the personnel of government may fluctuate; new ideas, pressures, and social groups may be absorbed; and the several elites may rotate in power (thus giving the *appearance* of change, but often little of its substance). The *system* itself, however, remains inviolate. Those challenging it will likely be suppressed until they too have made their compromises and come to accept their rightful place. The greatest need is social and political solidarity; opposition challenges to the system, even autonomous political organizations, can hence only be tolerated with difficulty and often not at all. Only when a group has sufficiently demonstrated both a "power capability" (Anderson), that is, the capacity to challenge the system *and* a willingness to accept the system's rules, can it be accepted into the prevailing structure.

Considerable change can and does take place within such a system, but it is usually from the top down and not necessarily as a result of grass-roots pressure from below. The system is elitist and paternalist. It can also exist in several forms: military or civilian, in authoritarian or republican garb, or in varying combinations of these. A type of democracy may be established—as in Colombia, Costa Rica, the Dominican Republic, or Venezuela—but it usually takes the form of guided or tutelary democracy, elite directed, managed from above. Through example and education an attempt is made to transfer the elitist values to the rising newer groups. In this way the socio-political order is founded on a basis of officially institutionalized popular movements. First, as we have seen, the business-commercial elements were "civilized" and domesticated in this way, then the middle classes, now the lower or popular classes. These groups are offered benefits and at least a partial stake in the system as a means of defusing discontent, but at the price of their accepting the paternalistic guidance of the state. That helps explain why in Iberia and Latin America we so often find officially supported and directed trade unions, political parties, and other groups. By assimilating the rising social forces, the system has generally avoided being overwhelmed by them, except in Mexico in the early part of this century, Bolivia for a time, Cuba, and Nicaragua.

In this fashion, which is the prevailing one in Iberia and Latin America, the unfolding of the development process has been administered and channeled in preferred directions that allow for circumscribed and limited change, but not change that can get out of hand. By being flexible and adaptable, indeed, the traditional order has avoided being overwhelmed or discarded as development has gone forward and has profited instead, proving to be remarkably durable and even strengthening itself in the process. Those systems that are not adaptable—for example, Nicaragua or El Salvador—tend to be overthrown, but even this has its pattern and regularities. These features are what help make the Iberic-Latin development process distinctive.

It is the duty of the state and its leader to organize popular opinion and maintain equilibrium in society through the careful balance of these domestic interests and, increasingly in recent decades, outside pressures. Decisions are ordinarily made by a small coterie of leaders representing the society's sectoral organizations—the archbishop, the heads of the armed forces, the rector of the national university, the heads of business, industrial, and agricultural associations, sometimes professional and labor leaders. These leaders are usually linked by formal and informal ties to the highest pinnacles of the administrative state's hierarchy and are usually centered around a single individual, the strong president, who "knows" the general will and is the best and most qualified leader. Reflecting the immense United States influence in these countries, sometimes the ambassador and the heads of the various missions would also be included in this decision-making coterie.

Patronage, status, and access to the channels of influence and wealth, more than program benefits, have traditionally served as the chief media of political currency. Now however, with mass pressures growing, at least lip service (and sometimes more than that) must be paid to program implementation. Patronage, benefits, entire programs may be doled out by the state in return for the backing or acquiescence of those who might otherwise seek to overthrow the system. Hence the public service and its myriad agencies, who may employ 40 percent or more of the labor force, act as a vast reservoir of sinecure jobs, a kind of national social-security agency to give everyone a handout, a haven for actual and potential oppositionists of both left and right and also for a variety of party stalwarts or regime supporters, to say nothing of the friends, relatives, and cronies of those in power. The government sinecure serves as a means by which a large part of the middle class and now increasingly labor and peasant leaders too are "bought off" by being brought into the prevailing system and being given a stake in it. As virtually the only employer of educated people, the state has often been able also to co-opt the otherwise more radical university generations, whose revolutionary plans are frequently moderated by the students' being put on the public payroll. Effective program implementation is thus difficult for bureaucracies for which this function has historically been secondary to these other status and patronage activities.

The historic Iberic-Latin socio-political framework, by aspiration if not always in actual practice, thus helps to keep inviolate the traditional structures and practices of the area, while at the same time providing for limited change by absorbing new social and political units into the system. Corporative, centralized, authoritarian institutions, reinforced by a political culture strongly grounded on hierarchy, status considerations, paternalism, and patronage, are what enable the prevailing systems to hang on so tenaciously. Of course in Latin America—with its vast distances, unassimilated indigenous peoples, and the absence of very many strong national institutions—such central control mechanisms have often been only weakly organized and the political process is hence often more chaotic and less successful than the "ideal type" implies. But there is no doubt this ancient and venerated model, which helps fill the organizational void that Latin Americans have often feared, which promises a measure of order in a continent always threatened by over-whelming chaos, remains the one preferred by political elites of virtually all ideological hues. Such a system helps preserve the status quo but also provides for graduatist, assimilationist accommodation to newer currents. It helps keep the pressures for change from getting entirely out of hand by minimizing the possibilities for full-scale breakdown. The Iberic-Latin nations may thus respond to modernization by adopting those aspects of it that are useful and manageable; but in seeking at the same time to preserve traditional ways of doing things, they may reject or modify extensively the social and political concomitants that, based on the Northwest European and United States experiences, are often assumed to accompany the modernization process. This tradition of derivation, adaptation, assimilation, and reorganization—but not neces-sarily of innovation or revolutionary transformation, unless under exceptional circumstances—is deeply rooted in the Iberic-Latin past.

The Iberian and Latin American development process implies the importation and adaptation of more modern social and political forms and ideas, and their appendage to or superimposition on top of an already established order, not the replacement of the latter by the former. Following the discussion in the pathbreaking essay by Professor Anderson, new social groups and political forces may be added to the system in a kind of continuous fusion process but, owing to the absence of any genuine social revolution in all but two or three of the nations of the area, old ones are seldom discarded. Hence traditional institutions and practices remain strong, and even in the revolutionary regimes cor-portist, authoritarian, and organicist features often persist. One is reminded again of Anderson's "living museum" concept as applied to Latin America, where virtually every form of social and political arrangement from feudalism and mercantilism to the most modern arrangements continue to coexist.

The way Spain, Portugal, and Latin America have typically dealt with change, therefore, is to erect a variety of new corporate and institu-tional pillars (official trade unions, official political parties, official peasant associations) alongside the traditional corporate pillars (Church, Army, wealthy elites) of the *ancien régime*. Each of these pillars or societal sectors remains strictly compartmentalized by function and hierarchically organized by class and status, with recruitment into the upper levels of these pyramidally organized systems still largely a func-tion of social position. As the late Professor Kalman Silvert, one of our leading Latin Americanists, pointed out in a note outlining what he termed this "syndicalist" approach, the major purpose of such a system is to try to subsume the new ideologies and classes spawned by moderni-zation to hierarchy and discipline, preserving the traditional basis of society and leadership, retaining the privileges and power of the old while at the same time adapting selectively to modernity.

Change in the Iberic-Latin context, as Professor Morse noted, has therefore not been so much a matter of "fundamental" change in the European and North American sense (that is, with an implication of the substitution of one historical class or epoch for another) as it has been the mediating and gradual accommodating of the rallying cries and institutional paraphernalia of Western industrial civilization to an order of life that remained Ibero-Catholic, creole-feudal, traditional and patrimonialist. A string of adjustments have been made, but the basic pattern of power and authority has been retained, the fundamental two-class structure of society perpetuated, the values and behavioral norms of the past often preserved, the system of *fueros* and special privileges expanded but slowly, and the essential socio-political structure of elites, hierarchy, and authority maintained. Some new pillars have been added to the old structure, but generally under the tutelage of the traditional elites and system. These latter have also been the chief beneficiaries of the development that has taken place. Latin America's traditional structure, therefore, far from having been entirely rigid and impenetrable, has had sufficient flexibility for a good many of its *parts* to be modernized, without undergoing a swift and radical process of wholesale and society-wide "modernization."

As a result of the singular tenacity of many of these traditional social and political institutions, there has been comparatively little "development" in the Iberic-Latin nations in the sense that we ordinarily use that term. The Latin American change process has not implied the transcendence of one social order by another (feudal, capitalist, socialist) but the combination of diverse elements pertaining to distinct historical epochs in a tentative working arrangement. The question is less that of "development" than it is, following Professor Morse, of reconciling the static vegetative features of the older patrimonialist-corporate order with the necessities of a more modern, urban, and industrial one. Far from being rigid and unyielding, the traditional order has generally proved capable of absorbing many features of modernity without in the process destroying its traditional essence.

There has been an increase in the number of participants and the pyramid has been broadened somewhat as the newer elites and social forces have been absorbed into the dominant system, but the system itself still stands. Hence throughout the Latin American nations one finds a series of layers of quite different social and political forms, superimposed upon one another and continuing to coexist, with new elements being added periodically to the system at one end but without the older tradition being eliminated at the other or even undergoing very many fundamental transformations. These distinct but now overlapping layers originate in distinct historical epochs, but in Iberia and Latin America they have often been combined. Indeed it is the genius and continuing challenge of politics and politicians in Latin America that they have been able to function and accomplish anything at all of a developmental sort, given the heterogeneous and frequently crazy-quilt political systems in which they must operate. This genius for improvisation, for combining and reconciling such diverse elements, forces us to rethink the simplistic notion we have of Latin America politics involving a constant struggle between dictatorship and democracy. That struggle does go on, but even more important on an everyday basis are the constant political negotiations and compromises between Latin America's authoritarian and its democratic tendencies, both strongly present within the region and in perpetual tension within all the nations and their institutions.

The Crisis of the Traditional System

What we have been calling the organic-corporate framework for the analysis of socio-political change in Iberia and Latin America has exhibited remarkable staying power. It survived three centuries of colonial rule, independence, the often chaotic and quarrelsome politics of the nineteenth century, and even in many respects the acceleration of change in the twentieth. Yet at present this traditional system and structure are being challenged as never before and a series of crises of major proportions are building up which may well sweep away the regime of hierarchy, elites, and special privileges, at least in their old form, once and for all.

Even in coming to grips with the contemporary crisis of the Iberian and Latin American nations, however, our earlier discussion helps provide a useful framework for analysis. The fabric of law and political society of the historic past, on which so many institutions in the area are still grounded, could only remain unshaken in a homogeneous and fairly static system where the number of interests to be consulted and satisfied was small and limited to the elite groups, where there were no major cleavages on moral and ideological principles, and little disturbing contact with the outside world. Clearly these conditions no longer apply in the Iberic-Latin nations. They are no longer so homogeneous or so static as they once were, the number of interests to be satisfied has not only multiplied but is no longer confined to the elites, major cleavages have emerged as to the proper way of ordering society and politics, and contact with the outside world, as well as deep foreign involvement in these nations' internal affairs, have broken down traditional isolation and parochialism and made Latin America heavily dependent on the United States. Since the 1930s particularly, the pace of change has increased, new social forces have emerged to challenge the traditional order, the older bases of order and legitimacy has been increasingly undermined, and the foundations upon which the ancient structures rested have been eroded.

The older power bases in Spain, Portugal, and the nations of Latin America—and the religious, social, behavioral, economic, and political foundations on which they rested—seem to be in decline. These include the *hacienda,* the village community, the Church, caudilloism, the older landed oligarchy and its system of rule, the ancient system of estates and orders. At the same time new power bases are emerging, including the educated *técnicos* and professionals, organizations of workers and peasants, new mass-based political parties, a larger middle class, more professionalized and development-oriented militaries, progressive churchmen, the business-industrial-entrepreneurial class. The situation is complicated by the presence of various external agencies (principally the United States but also now including a myriad of international agencies, development banks, and private multinationals) in the domestic politics of these countries, and by complex networks of dependency and interdependency. The fact that new interests, both foreign and domestic, have come to prominence organized around principles not heretofore considered acceptable or legitimate, that the older system of interests is itself undergoing transformation, that new values and organizing principles are competing for men's minds, that government is being called upon to provide services never provided before, that foreign pressures have multiplied—all these changes, coupled with accelerated social change and spiraling economic crises, have added a complex and increasingly conflicted dimension to the Latin American change processes that was not present before.

Politics in Iberia and Latin America have become progressively more class-, issue-, and interest-oriented, instead of revolving around personalities and rival elite factions as in the past. As a result of the newer challenges, the traditional mechanisms for accommodating and adjusting to change have also begun to break down. The application of a little grease here and a little cement there, an accommodation here and a patronage reward there, to hold the system together while easing it along from crisis to crisis may no longer be adequate in nations where wholesale overhauls are required. In many countries the pace of change has become so rapid, the conflicts so intense, and the demands to be satisfied so insistent that the traditional techniques of adjustment and co-optation are proving insufficient.

The demand for participation and a better living standard in a number of Latin American countries has by now reached revolutionary proportions. The level of new demands and expectations has simply outstripped the capacity of their tradition-dominated political institutions to cope with them. The older corporate, authoritarian and gradualist ways of handling change are proving incapable of managing the increasing pressures being thrust upon them. As a result the political situation has tended to become profoundly fragmented, precarious, and unstable, marked by the absence of any single consensus on which the rival groups can agree, by the desperate and tenacious efforts of the traditional elements to hang on to their wealth and power, by rising revolutionary pressures from below, and by the weakness, divisions, and ineffectiveness of those who might occupy a middle way. What we are witnessing is a gradual and long-term erosion and at least partial eclipse of the old order, but without the emergence of a sufficiently strong, institutionalized, or legitimated newer one to take its place.

It is difficult, for instance, to maintain the ideal of the nation as an organic, unified "family'" when the common basis of understanding on which the older system of solidarity was grounded no longer exists. The older notion of the "harmonization" of classes under a paternalistic state is also being replaced by notions of class struggle and conflict. Further, the number of interests to be satisfied has multiplied beyond the capacity of traditional regime politics either to maintain a "well-ordered universe" or to keep them content with things as they are. Similarly the momentum of mass mobilization as contrasted with the earlier system of revolving elites, the new educational and ideological formulas that have replaced the paternalism and accepted truths of the past, and the divisiveness and polarization that have set in as societal modernization has gone forward, have shaken these societies to their foundations.

Increasingly a philosophy of change and movement has replaced the older framework of order and stability. Economic pressures stimulated by world-market forces and inflation fueled by rising oil, food, and other prices have triggered further impatience and discontent. There is a growing sense of how traditional corporate institutions arising out of Iberia's and Latin America's past and culture may be manipulated for the partisan or class advantages of those in power, and how the "natural" and societal corporatism of history is now being supplanted by a newer corporatism of the state with its even stronger socio-economic control mechanisms. New ideologies, interests, movements, and pressures emerging internally, coupled with changed influences from the outside, have combined to provoke a challenge of unprecedented proportions to established ways and institutions.

The type of society and *system* described here—corporatist, patrimonialist, and organic-statist, providing for gradual accommodation to change, absorbing new groups while also retaining the historic ones, more-or-less peaceful, consensual, and stable—was more appropriate for an older time than it is at present. That is, the strategy of co-optation through a corporatist-patrimonialist system worked fairly well in Latin America and Iberia as a means of absorbing the rising business class, the middle sectors, and in the early stages of unionization. In other words, this system was functional until, approximately and varying somewhat from country to country, the 1930s. Then rising expectations, new mass demands, greater class conflict, economic stringencies, accelerated social change and other factors combined to make the system less viable. Now this ancient and venerated system can only be maintained or resurrected through even greater authoritarianism, which helps explain the brutality of a number of recent Latin American regimes. It may well be, therefore, that the alternative model of Latin American development outlined in these pages has been superseded or is in the process of being superseded, and that a more violent, nasty, repressive, and conflict-prone system and society is taking (and in some countries already has taken) its place.

Yet even with all these changes the traditional organic-corporate-elitist-patrimonialist order in Iberia and Latin America remains remarkably strong and omnipresent. With the exception of the two or three genuinely revolutionary regimes and the handful of liberal-democratic ones (and even in these, we have seen, the organic-corporate top-down system is often retained, albeit in altered or often "mixed" forms), it remains the dominant structural system throughout the Iberic-Latin culture area. Its major pillars have been shaken somewhat and the ground beneath them is being furrowed, and in some instances the older pillars have crumbled or been torn down to be replaced by new ones; but the point is that ancient and venerated pyramidal and "pillared" system still generally remains the dominant and the preferred system of national socio-political organization—not a more "liberal," "democratic," or "participatory" regime based on the United States or other external models.

The historic and traditional structures, hence, still provide the frame of reference and organizational mold within which the political society almost instinctively operates. This applies whether we are speaking of regimes of the left, right, or center, whether they are traditional oligarchic regimes, syndicalist republics, or otherwise diversely modernizing ones—the roots of these alternative regimes are sunk deep in a common historic tradition and their basic organizational forms and mode of operations are not altogether different either. That of course is not to say that particular regime types, the class base of the ruling groups, or their ideologies and the directions of public policy make no difference; they obviously do. But it is to point to the continuity of the historic tradition and the common political-organizational forms that exist, as well as the differences. For as Morse concludes, however heavily the Western industrial world—or for that matter the Communist one—may impinge on Iberia and Latin America, quickening the pace of life, engendering new hopes and wants, and introducing new programs and technologies, it seems certain that the changes wrought will ultimately have to be reconciled with the more enduring premises and structures that still underlie the political life of the Iberic and Latin American nations.

Even under the present circumstances of challenge and crises, moreover, the capacity of the traditional structures in many countries to weather the storm, as they have repeatedly weathered others in the past, should not be underestimated. The evidence is considerable that points to the continued capacity of the dominant elites to mobilize workers and peasants into officially sanctioned syndicates that both regulate their activities and provide certain benefits, to provide for structured participation rather than genuinely autonomous mass associations, to give limited economic and social benefits to workers as a way of both defusing their discontent and maintaining the elites' own power intact, to incorporate new and challenging groups into the system without destroying the system per se, to manage the pressures from the United States and the international environment chiefly to their own advantage, to mouth new developmental ideologies and erect new institutional arrangements which provide more the appearance than the substance of change, to continue to control and direct the essentials of the entire change and modernization process. One need only look at the persistence of the *hacienda* system and mentality (land, power, status) of personalism and caudilloism; of patron-client relationships; of traditional beliefs and attitudes; of hallowed institutions and organizations; of a pervasive sense of order, authority, hierarchy, status, place, position, and estate or corporate group; indeed, of a whole way of life and of the structures erected and norms evolved that go with it to recognize how durable—and flexible—the traditional system is. Though as committed reformers and "developmentalists" we may prefer other forms of change and though our analyses, exhibiting often more wishful than realistic political sociology, may focus on those groups and forces seeming to offer better hopes for rapid modernization and democratization, it is the older and still venerated tradition that remains paramount, whose manner and methods of adaptation have not at all been adequately studied, but which we ignore or underestimate at the risk of continuing fundamentally to misunderstand the Iberic-Latin development tradition.

Implications and Frontiers

Using the framework outlined here enables us to understand—in their terms and not ours—the special nature of the institutions and practices that late-medieval Spain and Portugal transferred to the New World, their incredible durability and persistence, and the ways they have adapted to the powerful modernizing currents of the contemporary world. This framework helps us comprehend better the all-pervasive influence of status, rank, order, and authority in Iberia and Latin America, and the almost inherently organic, corporatist, vertically segmented, and pyramidal socio-political structures so strongly present throughout the area. It seems obvious that such a traditional regime as Paraguay's may be understood in terms of this historic model; but what is less clearly comprehended is its perseverance, albeit in updated, modified, rearranged, and sometimes restructured forms of the same or similar structures, in such diverse political systems as Brazil, Peru, Spain, Portugal, Mexico, Colombia, and revolutionary Cuba and Nicaragua.

In terms of the accommodation of traditional norms to modern requirements, of the preferences for hierarchically organized and vertically segmented political societies, of the persistence of monist-authoritarian and organic-corporatist political forms, of the way the several sectors of society still relate directly to and revolve around the central and state authority, of the continuing impact of bureaucratic authority and systems of patron-client relations, of neo-mercantilism and etatism in the economic sphere, indeed of the vitality and longevity of all the major features here outlined as being intrisically a part of the Iberic-Latin tradition and culture, there are striking parallels among these diverse countries regardless of their current ideology or political regimes. The parallels and common features make it imperative that in seeking to comprehend the Iberian and Latin American nations we understand and come to grips with their history, culture, and continuing traditions, behavioral norms, and institutional preferences. The distinct nature of these traditions and institutions also makes it imperative that we treat Iberia and Latin America in their own context and categories, rather than interpreting them in the light of some foreign and ill-suited intellectual framework that has only partial relevance for Iberian-Latin American realities.

The framework here proposed implies that students of Iberia and Latin America study continuities as well as changes, the forces maintaining the status quo as well as those undermining it, the adaptability of historic institutions as well as challenging new ones, "neo-traditionalism" as well as "modernization." We have failed to do so because our biases are usually in favor of that which is new and offers the promise of change, but given the powerful pull of the past in Iberia and Latin America, such a biased emphasis is bound to be both misleading and frustrating. To come to grips with the Iberic-Latin tradition we must turn our attention to such crucially important (but often neglected) subjects as comparative jurisprudence and law; Roman, medieval, and Christian political theory; the historic and evolving contractual relations between the state and its component societal groups; the political economy of mercantilism and/or state capitalism; theories of bureaucracy and administrative-statism; patrimonialism and patron-client relations; personalism and interfamily and interelite relations; and the theory and organization of organic-corporate political society. These are a few of the subject areas that now receive only scant attention in our academic disciplines but that must be studied for a proper understanding of Latin America. A volume of cannon law, the writings of Seneca or Thomas Aquinas, medieval legal codes, the encyclicals of a long-forgotten pope—these tell us more about the nature and functioning of the Iberic-Latin nations than the bulk of the books on modern sociology and political science.

These comments should not be interpreted as suggesting a complete absence of change and modernization in the history of Iberia and Latin America. The emphasis on the traditional and historic patterns is justified by the wholesale neglect of these aspects in the bulk of our research and writing, but to emphasize the older norms and structures to the exclusion of the new would be an equal disservice. In fact, what provides some of the most interesting and exciting frontiers for study and research is the way these traditional forms have been fused with the newer patterns, the complex blends and overlaps that exist in all the Iberic-Latin societies, the mix of old and new in a hodgepodge and frequently conflict-prone kaleidoscope. There are numerous illustrations, but let us look again at the example of the Brazilian labor movement.

In the early stages of union organization in Brazil, as in the other countries of the area, the workers were in large measure mobilized by the ruling elites and under the control of the state in order to inhibit their potentially disruptive influence. The lower classes were made dependent on the government and the employer-*patrão,* with the result that no strong labor organization or sense of class consciousness could emerge. The system of official syndicates was in fact used by the state, in the classic fashion, to prevent such consciousness from growing and to rule out genuinely free and independent labor organizations that might eventually constitute a threat to the system.

By the early 1960s, however, continued industrialization, social mobilization, and overall modernization had produced a change in labor's strength and position. It now wanted genuine participation and a greater share of economic benefits. The older clientelistic structure, which had been based on patronage and paternalistic favors to "deserving" unions, began to give way to one based on independence, class struggle, and strong bargaining power. But even here labor remained in many ways dependent on the government and sought to use its newly acquired control of the Labor Ministry and the traditional patronage powers that flowed from it in order to achieve its goals. Had the process not gotten out of hand, had the traditional ruling groups not felt so threatened by then-President Goulart, and had the chaos and disruption that occurred been avoided, it is possible that Brazilian labor, in the classic fashion, would have been accepted and assimilated into the prevailing system. The older corporate system would have been preserved but another important pillar would have been appended and the military-conservative "counterrevolution" of 1964 would probably not have occurred. In any case, what this illustration shows is both the mutual dependence and the mutual antagonism that have come to characterize labor's relations with the state and its still semi-official trade-union structure. On the one hand the corporate system in Brazil makes labor dependent on the state in the traditional way, while on the other the growth of a genuine mass movement enabled labor to seek greater independence and greater bargaining power—while still working in and through the state. Much the same kinds of tensions between the new and emerging forces and the traditional institutions exist in the other nations of the area as well.

A primary focus of study and research, therefore, should be toward explaining how the older structures of society and polity—the *hacienda,* patron-client networks, top-down rule, corporatism and organicism— continue to adapt to modernization, as well as how such "modern" or "modernizing" agencies as a trade-union organization can adapt to traditional structures and use traditional techniques (for example, the way the Brazilian trade unions used their new-found position within the traditional patron-client network of the Labor Ministry to advance their cause). We must explore the way the Iberian and Latin American systems function regardless of the underdevelopment-related gaps that supposedly exist, how these can be bridged, fudged, glossed over, or ignored altogether, the frequently ingenious patchwork solutions that are devised, the way these nations continue actually to develop and modernize despite their nonconformity with the neat developmental formulas devised by intellectuals. The study and research suggestions made here, therefore, with respect to the need to study the overlaps, fusions, and crazy-quilt patterns of "traditional" and "modern," are not limited just to trade-union movements but may also be applied to our understanding of bureaucratic behavior, the role of the middle classes, the political activities of the Church or Army, and a whole host of other subject areas.

A great deal of research remains to be done before we understand how the political and social systems of Latin America do in fact respond to change, as distinct from the often romantic and wishful notions found in much of the literature. We need new and serious investigations of the blends and coexistence of both traditional and modernizing tendencies within such agencies as the university student movement, peasant associations, religious, military, and governing bodies. We need to know how these agencies *actually* work and function instead of how we imagine them to work. We need to compare these institutions in the several countries to account realistically for the parallels and differences that exist. We require far more case studies of individual groups and interests and their interactions with each other and with the state system. In all these studies we must examine Latin American political behavior in its own terms and context and not through the prisms of Northwest European or North American sociology and political science.

At the same time we need to consider and reconsider the larger theoretical questions raised in this collection of essays. We must examine where the influence of Iberia's and Latin America's cultural heritage is important and where economic constraints and dependency produce more satisfactory explanations. We need to know when corporatism is a product of history and tradition and when it is being used for political and class manipulation. We must examine both the multiple causes of corporatism and authoritarianism in Iberia and Latin America and the diverse forms they may take. We need to be able to define more precisely the real differences and similarities between the nations of Iberia and Latin America and those in other areas, both developed and developing, and to access and interpret these with greater depth and accuracy. We need to sharpen further and clarify our analysis, to distinguish clearly between the key determinants of Latin American socio-political life and those that are merely subsidiary, to determine where the framework for analysis suggested here is useful and how and at what points the insights of the Marxian categories, dependency theory, and other approaches may also be applied. To most scholars these are pragmatic matters rather than ideological ones; they require careful study and empirical evidence, not wishful thinking.

There are many other important subject areas that need to be looked into using the framework and approach suggested here. Once we have thoroughly immersed ourselves in the Iberic-Latin socio-cultural and political-institutional heritage, and its continuing impact, we need also to look at concrete issues of contemporary public policy. We can no more concentrate solely on the historic tradition to the neglect of these newer relations and issues than we can concentrate on contemporary problems without understanding the special historical and political-cultural framework within which they occur. For I am prepared to argue that we cannot understand Iberic-Latin development and such contemporary issues as labor relations, social-security policy, interest-group relations, the position and role of the state, the special place of the Church or the Army, bureaucratic behavior and a great variety of other key issues without first comprehending the pervasiveness of the corporate-organic model presented here. All these issues and policy areas require that we come to grips realistically with Iberia's and Latin America's past and with the particular institutions that have evolved for handling change and for reconciling tradition with modernity.

The continuing importance of such past traditions and influences leads me to suggest that we now require a separate Iberic-Latin model and political sociology of development. The models generally used are so ethnocentric, so closely tied to the Northwest European and United

States experiences, that they have but limited utility for Latin America. It is arrogant and presumptuous, the worst form of cultural imperialism, for European and North American sociologists and political scientists to assume that the categories and processes devised to explain their nations' developmental experiences must also apply to the rest of the world. Of course one must employ the insights of these older analyses where they are useful. But one should think of them as partial and not complete explanations, beginning points of research rather than end points. To fully understand Iberic-Latin development patterns, a separate sociology and political science for that area needs to be devised.

It is not possible here to provide a complete outline of such a distinct Iberic-Latin political sociology of development. The main ingredients have been provided in earlier chapters. Some of the principal components would include a political sociology of corporatism in its various forms, an understanding of organic-statism, patron-client networks now organized on a national scale, the Iberic-Latin patterns of state-society relations. Such a distinct political sociology of Iberic-Latin development would of course have to be combined with dependency analysis, an understanding of class relations, and the relations of center and periphery, both internationally and nationally. There can be no doubt, however, that the formulation of such a distinct Iberic-Latin model of development constitutes the next greater frontier of research and theory.

In looking at all these questions, we have repeatedly said, we must view Latin America on its own terms and in its own cultural context. We must try to put aside the biases and ethnocentrism, the patronizing attitudes of superiority, that so often shape particularly the United States perception of other culture areas. We must resist the temptation to bring the supposed "benefits" of North American political society to a set of countries where the traditions are quite distinct. We must deal with Latin America as a culture and civilization, certainly every bit as humane and perhaps as viable as our own. That perspective need not blind us to the warts and problem areas of Latin America with which we are familiar, nor lead to a romantic nostalgia for and defense of the status quo. But it does call for a greater sensitivity to and appreciation of the values and operational codes of a culture area grounded on different bases than our own, and to a greater sense of cultural relativism than most North Americans in the past have exercised.

In the Introduction we questioned whether, given the malaise and seemingly intractable problems of United States society, it is any longer justified for us to treat Latin America as a "backward" or "underdeveloped" area. Latin America is assuredly less developed according to economic criteria, but morally, socially, or politically we are today less than confident that such terms apply. The many United States assistance programs, all committed to remaking Latin America in our own image, have been notably unsuccessful in achieving this goal; and the disturbing fact is now being brought home to us that Latin America (and other Third World areas) does not wish to be recast in the United States mold. There is a new effort on the part of intellectuals and political leaders throughout Latin America to develop and refashion their societies in terms of their own culture and institutions rather than as some late-blooming imitation of the United States. It seems to me these Latin American efforts at fashioning indigenous models, dealing realistically with their own past and history, and trying to create from that uniquely Latin American political and social institutions—or at least achieving a new and refined balance between the imported and the homegrown—merit our attention and support.

Meanwhile, as the United States becomes more aware of the problems of its own society—not only problems of race and poverty but also of over-centralization, over-bureaucratization, and the rise of administrative-statism—we may begin to approach an understanding of other nations with greater empathy than in the past. The United States cannot solve the problems in its own house, and it is arrogant and presumptuous to think "we know best" for other lands. We need therefore not only to understand Latin America on its own terms in ways we have not done in the past, but we also require a greater degree of modesty regarding our own accomplishments and a sense of how—difficult though that it is for North Americans to accept—we can actually learn from the Latin American experience. The subject matter is beyond the limits of this book, but it is time we stopped thinking what *we* can do *for* Latin America (everything except read about and seek to understand it, *New York Times* columnist James Reston once wrote) and began thinking how we might learn from the Latin American experience. For as centralization, bureaucratization, statism, and corporatism increase in the United States polity, Latin America, which has had long experience with all of these phenomena, offers us abundant lessons that we may profit from studying.

Finally, what of the implications of the distinctive model and framework presented here for the future development of the Iberic-Latin nations themselves?

First, it is not fatuous to remind ourselves that the development process is exceedingly long and difficult and that the journey—if it can be accomplished at all—is full of disappointments, frustrations, setbacks, and wrenching, agonizing dilemmas. Development and modernization will not come overnight regardless of the means or strategies used. Nicaragua is a poor country and will remain so, regardless of what development route it opts for. The slow pace of real change seems especially the case in Latin America where the past lingers on so powerfully and the weight of history and traditions are so omnipresent.

Second, we must bear in mind that development is an exceedingly complex and multifaceted process and that our understanding of it will

355
Howard J.
Wiarda

not be served by resort to antiseptic phrases or pat formulas. We delude
ourselves if we think that pleasant, optimistic phrases like "the revolution of rising expectations," the "stages of growth," or even "power to
the people" accurately mirror the disruptive, contortive, terrible, and
often bloody forces that modernization sets in motion, or the complex
and difficult choices involved. Modernization in fact may initiate forces
that lead more to disruption and chaos than to growth. Nor can we be
certain that even if a people make the sacrifices now and endure the
suffering that any sound development strategy calls for, they or their
children or their society will be any better off in some usually vague and
distant future. Often these countries have neither the resources nor the
institutional base on which to build a more affluent and socially just system. Un-American though it may sound, we must recognize that for
most Latin American countries there may not be any light at the end of
the tunnel, only continued underdevelopment. Abstract arguments,
furthermore, over this or that route to modernity may have little to do
with the realities of life, power, and poverty in countries like Haiti,
Paraguay, and Bolivia. Such arguments are too simple, too remote
from the everyday experiences of people, too divorced from the Latin
American actualities, and they often have little relevance either for popular wants or for the existing developmental possibilities of these
nations.

Third, we must recognize a wide variety of possible developmental
goals and strategies. The alternative liberal-democratic and communist
routes to modernization are by no means the only ones; rather we must
recognize various starting points in Latin America, a variety of alternating and/or overlapping patterns en route, and multiple and often ingen-
iously formulated paths along the journey. The nations of Latin America are exceedingly diverse and becoming more so; there is no one single
formula appropriate for all of them. In Mexico a single-party system
has helped bridge the gaps between tradition and modernity and is not
altogether unacceptable; in Costa Rica and Venezuela a form of liberal
representative democracy has been established; in Argentina, Chile, and
Brazil varying forms of military bureaucratic-authoritarianism have
helped achieve economic development but have also been repressive of
human rights; in Peru, Ecuador, Bolivia, and Panama more reformist
and populist military regimes have come and gone in power; and in
Colombia a form of elite-dominated alternation between the major parties served to help preserve political stability for some three decades.
Various forms of socialism and syndicalism have been attempted with
varying degrees of success; a number of conservative regimes have also
met with mixed results in trying to maintain the ancient structures while
also moving toward change. Regimes that combine features from two
or more of these formulae, or countries that alternate between them, are
by no means unusual. What is most clear is that we cannot prescribe

any one single strategy for all the nations of the area or foreclose on their options, for not only are these nations more and more dissimilar but the developmental options open to them have greatly widened as well.

Fourth, it seems imperative that whatever development occurs in Iberia and Latin America will be carried out by the Latin Americans themselves and on their own terms, not ours. Latin America will of course be affected by what occurs in the advanced industrial nations, but it is unlikely the Latin American nations will blindly follow the same path as the already developed countries. There is continued and resurgent pride in Iberia and Latin America in their own institutions, and they have become more adept at borrowing and adapting from Europe and the United States without necessarily emulating them. The imposition of inappropriate foreign models onto societies where they fail to "take" or prove dysfunctional simply will not do anymore. Surely one of the great lessons of the aborted Alliance for Progress is that United States style solutions not only won't work in a different cultural context but may also be damaging to the nations that attempted them. Further, as the United States comes to recognize that it is no longer the model which other nations seek to emulate, and that these other nations are at the same time stronger, more nationalistic, and more assertive, the fact must be faced that Latin America cannot and will not imitate our ways.

The Iberic-Latin nations have devised and will continue to devise their own developmental strategies uniquely attuned to their own wants and needs. One of the most striking features of Latin America in the present context is the efforts of its leaders to find indigenous solutions and institutions appropriate for dealing with their own problems in their own way. Concurrently, Latin American scholars, intellectuals, and university students are embarked on a strenuous search to find a politics and sociology of development spoken of earlier that will be appropriate to their own nations' and culture-area's needs. It bears repeating in this context that the theoretical models with which students in the Northern Hemisphere countries are more familiar are of only limited utility when applied to Latin America.

Fifth and following from this is the reminder of the special nature of the Iberic-Latin development process. That implies a recognition of the historic—and continuing—preference for organic-corporatist solutions especially in times of crises, for systems of patron-client relations, for statism and monism in the political sphere and state-capitalism or neo-mercantilism in the economic. Even where the change process has been accelerated dramatically as in Cuba, Peru, or Mexico for a time, it has generally remained elite controlled and directed, paternalistic and tute-lary rather than egalitarian and democratic. The fact is that Iberia and Latin America find it rather easy to throw off the regime of the moment; what is far more difficult is to erase more than five hundred years of history. Even political violence, hence, may often be looked at as a means not necessarily for toppling the system but for securing a place in it for the group seeking to demonstrate its power capability.

Change in the Iberic-Latin context, we have stressed, has ordinarily gone forward gradually and incrementally—at times almost imperceptibly—through adaptation and assimilation, within a framework that seeks to combine and reconcile traditional and modern rather than implying the final triumph and transcendence of the one over the other or of one class or historical epoch over another. In the past most change has come sporadically and unevenly, not usually as the result of some great and glorious revolution or even through much purposeful action. Although the pace of change seems to have accelerated in recent years, many of the old ground rules still apply. Despite the growth of a more modern system of state capitalism in Brazil, for example, the old adage that "Brazil develops at night while the government sleeps" still applies. *Jeito* or "grease" still oils the machinery of the government at all levels. Paternalism, patrimonialism, and an updated structure of organicism and corporatism still reign—not only in Brazil but throughout the Iberic-Latin culture area.

Change has generally come by fits and starts and through the repeated crises and alterations of government that Iberia and Latin America are popularly known for. Thus seen, the frequent barracks revolts, cabinet shuffles, and comings and going of various regimes are not really the stuff of "comic opera," as the media frequently treats them, but usually represent some subtle shifts in the constellation of the ruling groups. They often signal a change in public policy or in the balance among contending forces, a signal most in the United States are not informed enough to pick up. Such changes may be just as functional in the Iberian and Latin American contexts, just as representative of public opinion, as elections are in the United States. In this as in other respects, bias and ethnocentrism frequently blind us to the realities of Iberic-Latin politics and the change process.

Change has ordinarily occurred piecemeal and bit-by-bit, through constantly evolving coalitions, the frequent accommodation and absorption of the rising social forces into the prevailing system, and the gradual remodeling and remolding of the political order. Shifts in the balance among the rival elites and power contenders that also necessitate new institutional arrangements and ad hoc rebuilding are what help give the Iberic-Latin systems flexibility and the capacity to respond to change. Violence may at times be an integral part of the process by which a new social group gains recognition and legitimacy, but it is usually violence of a highly structured and purposeful kind that falls short of full-scale revolution or the possibility of society-wide breakdowns. Such complete breakdowns do of course occur from time to time, and this may open the door to profounder structural change. But even those who go outside "the system" and employ revolutionary tactics usually conform to some established regularities (the "right to rebellion against unjust tyrants") which also have their basis in long Iberic-Latin traditions. The revolutionary regimes established as a consequence have also generally conformed to the organic and corporatist premises of the society, albeit obviously in quiet altered form.

Students of Iberia and Latin America must deal with these processes and their regularities realistically, not from the point of view of automatic, knee-jerk condemnation. Proceeding from some quite different societal assumptions, philosophical orientations, and institutional bases, the Iberic-Latin nations have devised a system of governance that is *different* from that of the United States but probably not inferior, a way of managing and coping with development that is probably just as rational and maybe as humane as those *systems* operating in the northern countries. Theirs may not always be a very soul-satisfying way to achieve development and it seldom conforms to our usual theoretical and ideological models of change. But it is development nonetheless, cumulative and hence often of a profound or structural kind; and it does correspond closely with the realities of both power and society in these nations as well as being in accord with the special nature of the Iberic-Latin development tradition. It is time that both North American students of the area, and the Latin Americans themselves, came to grips with these realities.

One final consideration merits mention and that involves the outcome of the process we have described. Based on the analysis presented, one might at this stage come away from a reading of this study with a hopeful and perhaps even optimistic prognosis for the future development of the Iberian and Latin American nations. Up to a point such optimism would seem to be justified, but only up to a point. For as the development process proceeds in the context described here, as new social groups and power contenders are constantly added on, without the old and anachronistic ones being sloughed off, there may come a time when saturation and *immobilisme* set in; when the number of groups is so great and their interests so divergent that paralysis results; when, in the absence of any common consensus or of one single dominant group, the national fabric begins to unravel and the entire system breaks down into conflict and praetorianism. There may not be any happy liberal pluralism at the end of the development tunnel in Iberia and Latin America, only divided, fragmented, chaotic exhaustion.

The future of Iberia and Latin America, therefore, may not lie in Cuba or Bolivia or the United States or Europe, either west or east. More likely it lies in Chile, Uruguay, or Argentina (to use some Latin American examples), or in Italy to use a European one. These are among the most "modern" of the Latin American and Southern European nations by almost any standard; but it is precisely because they are so modern, so highly differentiated, with so many groups competing so intensely for the spoils of power, but with so little attachment to any central nucleus, that they have progressed farthest toward a state of chronic, almost perpetual conflict. Crises in these nations have become a constant and virtually everyday fact of life; violence and civil strife lie just beneath the surface and boil over with regularity; politics has become almost a Hobbesian state of war of all against all. It may well be, therefore, that the future of Iberia and Latin America will not be the harmonious and well-ordered society that some of our authors suggest but more a "mosaic of discord," a system of endemic conflict occasioned by the gradual decline of an older society but lacking any fundamental agreement concerning what the new society should look like.

Suggested Readings

The readings listed here include some of the best interpretive overviews of Latin American history, culture, sociology, and politics. Unless they have more general applicability, specific country and topical studies have been omitted; readers interested in examining these issues in the several countries are urged to consult the analyses and bibliographies contained in Howard J. Wiarda and Harvey F. Kline, Latin American Politics and Development *(Boston: Houghton-Mifflin, 1979). The present listing seeks to offer suggestions for reading on Latin America's historical background, its patterns and processes of development, and the distinctiveness of Latin American culture, political society, and civilization.*

Adams, R. N. *The Second Sowing: Power and Secondary Development in Latin America.* San Francisco: Chandler, 1967.

———— et al. *Social Change in Latin America Today.* New York: Vintage, 1960.

Adie, R. F., and Poitras, G. E. *Latin America: The Politics of Immobility.* Englewood Cliffs: Prentice-Hall, 1974.

Alba, V. *The Latin Americans.* New York: Praeger, 1969.

Anderson, C. W. *Politics and Economic Change in Latin America.* Princeton: Van Nostrand, 1967.

Arciniegas, G. *Latin America: A Cultural History.* New York: Knopf, 1967.

Arguedas, A. *Pueblo Infermo.* Barcelona: Tasso, 1910.

Bagú, S. *Estructura social de la colonia.* Buenos Aires, 1952.

Beezley, W. H. "Caudillismo: An Interpretive Note," *Journal of Inter-American Studies* 11 (July 1969).

Bishko, C. J. "The Iberian Background of Latin American History." *Hispanic American Historical Review* 36 (Feburary 1956): 50–80.

Buckland, W. W., and McNair, A. D. *Roman Law and Common Law: A Comparison.* Cambridge: Cambridge University Press, 1965.

Cardoso, F. H., and Faletto, E. *Dependency and Development in Latin America.* Berkeley: University of California Press, 1978.

Castro, A. *The Spaniards: An Introduction to Their History.* Berkeley: University of California Press, 1971.

Cespedes, G. *Latin America.* New York: Knopf, 1974.

Chalmers, D. A. "Crisis and Change in Latin America." *Journal of International Affairs* 23 (1969): 76–88.

————. "Parties and Society in Latin America." *Studies in Comparative International Development* 7 (Summer 1972): 102–30.

"Colonial Institutions and Contemporary Latin America." *Hispanic American Historical Review* 43 (August 1963).

Cortes Conde, R. *The First Stages of Modernization in Spanish America*. New York: Harper and Row, 1974.

Crawford, W. R. *A Century of Latin American Thought*. New York: Praeger, 1966.

Dealy, G. *The Public Man: An Interpretation of Latin American and Other Catholic Countries*. Amherst: University of Massachusetts Press, 1977.

Duncan, W. R. *Latin American Politics: A Developmental Approach*. New York: Praeger, 1976.

Economic Commission for Latin America. *Economic Survey of Latin America*. New York: United Nations, 1969.

Economic Commission for Latin America. *Social Development of Latin America in the Post-War Period*. New York: United Nations, 1964.

Einaudi, L., ed. *Beyond Cuba: Latin America Takes Charge of Its Future*. New York: Crane, Russak, 1974.

Erickson, K. P. *The Brazilian Corporative State and Working Class Politics*. Berkeley: University of California, 1977.

Fals Borda, O. "Marginality and Revolution in Latin America, 1809–1969." *Studies in Comparative International Development* 6 (1970–71): 63–89.

Faoro, R. *Os Donos do Poder: Formacão do Patronato Politico Brasileiro*. Pôrto Alegre: Globo, 1976.

Fitch, J. S. *The Military Coup as a Political Process*. Baltimore: Johns Hopkins University Press, 1977.

Fitzgibbon, R. H., and Fernandez, J. A. *Latin America: Political Culture and Development*. Englewood Cliffs: Prentice-Hall, 1981.

Foster, G. M. *Culture and Conquest: America's Spanish Heritage*. Chicago: Quadrangle, 1960.

Gaspar, E. *The United States and Latin America: A Special Relationship?* Washington: AEI-Hoover, 1978.

Germani, G. "Stages of Modernization." *International Journal* 24 (Summer 1969): 463–85.

———, and Silvert, K. "Politics, Social Structure, and Military Intervention in Latin America." *European Journal of Sociology*, no. 2 (1961), pp. 62–81.

Gibson, C. *Spain in America*. New York: Harper, 1966.

———, ed. *The Black Legend: Anti-Spanish Attitudes in the Old World and the New*. New York: Knopf, 1971.

Glade, W. *The Latin American Economies*. New York: American, 1969.

Glassman, R. *Political History of Latin America*. New York: Funk and Wagnalls, 1969.

Góngora, M. *El estado en el derecho indiano*. Santiago, 1951.

Graham, L. S. *Civil Service Reform in Brazil: Principles versus Practice*. Austin: University of Texas, 1968.

Green, O. H. *Spain and the Western Tradition*. Madison and Milwaukee, 1963–66.

Hale, C. A. *Mexican Liberalism in the Age of Mora, 1821–1853*. New Haven: Yale University Press, 1968.

Halpern-Donghi, T. *The Aftermath of Revolution in Latin America*. New York: Harper and Row, 1973.

Hamill, H. M., ed. *Dictatorship in Spanish America*. New York: Knopf, 1965.

Hamilton, B. *Political Thought in Sixteenth-Century Spain*. Oxford: Oxford University Press, 1963.

Hanke, L. *The First Social Experiments in America*. Cambridge: Harvard University Press, 1935.

Haring, C. H. *The Spanish Empire in America*. New York: Harcourt, Brace and World, 1963.

Harris, L. K., and Alba, V. *The Political Culture and Behavior of Latin America*. Kent: Kent State University Press, 1974.

Hartz, L. *The Liberal Tradition in America*. New York: Harcourt, Brace and World, 1955.

———— et al. *The Founding of New Societies*. New York: Harcourt, Brace and World, 1964.

Herring, H. *A History of Latin America*. New York: Knopf, 1968.

Hillgarth, J. N. *The Spanish Kingdoms, 1250–1516*. Oxford: Clarendon, 1976.

Hirschman, A. O. *Journeys Toward Progress: Studies of Economic Policy-Making in Latin America*. New York: Anchor, 1965.

Hyman, E. "Soldiers in Politics." *Political Science Quarterly* 87 (September 1972): 401–18.

Jaguaribe, H. *Political Development: A General Theory and a Latin American Case Study*. New York: Harper and Row, 1978.

Jane, C. *Liberty and Despotism in Latin America*. Oxford: Clarendon, 1929.

Johnson, H. B., Jr., ed. *From Reconquest to Empire: The Iberian Background to Latin American History*. New York: Knopf, 1970.

Johnson, J. J. *The Military and Society in Latin America*. Stanford: Stanford University Press, 1964.

————. *Political Change in Latin America*. Stanford: Stanford University Press, 1958.

————, ed. *Continuity and Change in Latin America*. Stanford: Stanford University Press, 1964.

Johnson, K. F. *Argentina's Mosaic of Discord, 1966–1968*. Washington: Institute for the Comparative Study of Political Systems, 1969.

————. "Causal Factors in Latin American Instability." *Western Political Quarterly* 17 (September 1964).

Kadt, E. de. "Paternalism and Populism: Catholicism in Latin America." *Journal of Contemporary History* 2 (October 1967): 89–106.

Karst, K., and Rosenn, K. S. *Law and Development in Latin America.* Berkeley: University of California Press, 1975.

Kling, M. "Toward a Theory of Power and Political Instability in Latin America." *Western Political Quarterly* 9 (March 1956): 21–35.

———. "Violence and Politics in Latin America." *Sociological Review* 2 (1967): 119–32.

Lafaye, J. "The Spanish Diaspora: The Enduring Unity of Hispanic Culture." Washington: Wilson Center, Latin American Program, 1977.

Landsberger, H. A., ed. *The Church and Social Change in Latin America.* Notre Dame: University of Notre Dame Press, 1970.

———. "The Labor Elite: Is It Revolutionary?" in *Elites in Latin America,* edited by S. M. Lipset and A. Solari. New York: Oxford University Press, 1967.

Lanning, J. T. *Academic Culture in the Spanish Colonies.* London: Oxford University Press, 1940.

Lewy, G. *Constitutionalism and Statecraft During the Golden Age of Spain.* Geneva: Droz, 1960.

Lieuwen, E. *Arms and Politics in Latin America.* New York: Praeger, 1960.

Lipset, S. M., and Solari, A., eds. *Elites in Latin America.* New York: Oxford University Press, 1967.

McAlister, L. N. "Changing Concepts of the Role of the Military in Latin America." *Annals,* no. 360 (July 1965): 85–98.

———. "Civil-Military Relations in Latin America." *Journal of Inter-American Studies* 3 (July 1961): 341–50.

———. *The "Fuero Militar" in New Spain, 1746–1800.* Gainesville: University of Florida Press, 1957.

———. "Social Structure and Social Change in New Spain." *Hispanic American Historical Review* 43 (August 1963): 349–70.

MacKay, A. *Spain in the Middle Ages.* London: Macmillan, 1977.

Madden, M. R. *Political Theory and Law in Medieval Spain.* New York: Fordham University Press, 1930.

Maier, J., and Weatherhead, R. W., eds. *Politics of Change in Latin America.* New York: Praeger, 1954.

Malloy, J., ed. *Authoritarianism and Corporatism in Latin America.* Pittsburgh: University of Pittsburgh Press, 1977.

Mander, J. *The Unrevolutionary Society: The Power of Latin American Conservatism in a Changing World.* New York: Knopf, 1969.

Marsal, J. *Cambio Social en America Latina: Critica de Algunas Interpretaciones Dominantes en las Ciencias Sociales.* Buenos Aires: Solar/Hachette, 1967.

Martz, J. "The Place of Latin America in the Study of Comparative Politics." *Journal of Politics* 28 (February 1966): 57–80.

———, and Jorrin M. *Latin American Political Thought and Ideology.*

Chapel Hill: University of North Carolina Press, 1970.

Mecham, J. L. *Church and State in Latin America.* Chapel Hill: University of North Carolina Press, 1966.

Mercier Vega, L. *Roads to Power in Latin America.* New York: Praeger, 1969.

Merryman, J. H. *The Civil Law Tradition.* Stanford: Stanford University Press, 1969.

Middlebrook, K. J., and Palmer, D. S. *Military Government and Corporativist Political Development.* Beverly Hills: Sage, 1975.

Moreno, F. J. "The Spanish Colonial System: A Functional Approach." *Western Political Quarterly* 20 (June 1967): 308–30.

Morse, R. M. "Recent Research on Latin American Urbanization." *Latin American Research Review* 1 (Fall 1965).

———. "The Strange Career of Latin American Studies." *Annals,* no. 356 (November 1964).

Needler, M. *Political Development in Latin America.* New York: Random, 1968.

O'Callaghan, J. F. *A History of Medieval Spain.* Ithaca: Cornell University Press, 1975.

O'Donnell, G. *Modernization and Bureaucratic Authoritarianism: Studies in South American Politics.* Berkeley: University of California, Institute of International Studies, 1973.

Ortega y Gasset, J. *Invertebrate Spain.* New York: Norton, 1937.

Packenham, R. A. *Liberal America and the Third World: Political Development Ideas in Foreign Aid and Social Sciences.* Princeton: Princeton University Press, 1973.

Palmer, D. S. *"Revolution from Above": Military Government and Popular Participation in Peru.* Ithaca: Cornell University, Latin American Studies Program Dissertation Studies, 1973.

Parry, J. H. *The Spanish Theory of Empire in the Sixteenth Centrury.* Cambridge: Cambridge University Press, 1940.

Payne, J. L. *Labor and Politics in Peru: The System of Political Bargaining.* New Haven: Yale University Press, 1965.

———. "The Politics of Structured Violence." *Journal of Politics* 27 (May 1965): 362–74.

Paz, O. *The Labyrinth of Solitude: Life and Thought in Mexico.* New York: Grove, 1961.

Petras, J. *Politics and Social Structure in Latin America.* New York: Monthly Review, 1970.

Phelan, J. L. "Authority and Flexibility in the Spanish Imperial Bureaucracy." *Administrative Science Quarterly* 5 (June 1960): 47–64.

Picon-Salas, M. *Cultural History of Spanish America.* Berkeley: University of California Press, 1968.

Pike, F. "Corporatism and Latin American-United States Relations."

Review of Politics 36 (January 1974): 132–70.

————. *Hispanismo.* Notre Dame: University of Notre Dame Press, 1971.

————. *The United States and the Andean Republics.* Cambridge: Harvard University Press, 1977.

————, ed. *The Conflict Between Church and State in Latin America.* New York: Knopf, 1964.

————, and Stritch, T., eds. *The New Corporatism: Social and Political Structures in the Iberian World.* Notre Dame: University of Notre Dame Press, 1974.

Post, G. "Roman Law and Early Representation in Spain and Italy." *Speculum* 18 (April 1943): 211–32.

————. *Studies in Medieval Legal Thought: Public Law and the State, 1100–1322.* Princeton: Princeton University Press, 1964.

Powell, J. D. "Peasant Society and Clientelist Politics." *American Political Science Review* 66 (June 1970): 411–25.

Rio, A. del. *The Clash and Attraction of Two Cultures: The Hispanic and Anglo-Saxon Worlds in America.* Baton Rouge: Louisiana State University Press, 1965.

Rivera, J. *Latin America: A Sociocultural Interpretation.* New York: Appleton-Century-Crofts, 1971.

Roett, R. *Brazil: Politics in a Patrimonialist Society.* Boston: Allyn and Bacon, 1972.

Sarfatti, M. *Spanish Bureaucratic-Patrimonialism in Latin America.* Berkeley: University of California, Institute of International Studies, 1966.

Schmitter, P. "Military Intervention, Political Competitiveness, and Public Policy in Latin America: 1950–1967," in *Armies and Politics in Latin America,* edited by A. Lowenthal, pp. 113–64. New York: Holmes and Meier, 1976.

————. "Paths to Political Development in Latin America," in *Changing Latin America,* edited by Douglas Chalmers. New York: Academy of Political Science, Columbia University Press, 1972.

Schurz, W. L. *Latin America.* New York: Dutton, 1963.

Scott, R. E. "The Government Bureaucrats and Political Change in Latin America." *Journal of International Affairs* 20 (1966): 289–308.

Silvert, K. H. *The Conflict Society: Reaction and Revolution in Latin America.* New York: American Universities Field Staff, 1966.

————. *Essays in Understanding Latin America.* Philadelphia: ISHI, 1977.

————. "National Values, Development, and Leaders and Followers." *International Social Science Journal* 15 (1964): 560–70.

————. *The Politics of Social and Economic Change in Latin America.* Sociological Review Monographs. University of Keele, 1967.

_____, ed. *Expectant Peoples: Nationalism and Development*. New York: Vintage, 1967.

Soares, G. A. D. "Latin American Studies in the United States." *Latin American Research Review* 11 (1976).

Stein, S. J., and Stein, B. H. *The Colonial Heritage of Latin America*. New York: Oxford University Press, 1970.

Stepan, A. "Political Development: The Latin American Tradition." *Journal of International Affairs* 20 (1966): 223–34.

_____. *State and Society: Peru in Comparative Perspective*. Princeton: Princeton University Press, 1978.

Stoetzer, C. *The Scholastic Roots of the Spanish American Revolution*. New York: Fordham University Press, 1979.

Véliz, C. *The Centralist Tradition in Latin America*. Princeton: Princeton University Press, 1980.

_____, ed. *Obstacles to Change in Latin America*. London: Oxford University Press, 1965.

_____, ed. *The Politics of Conformity in Latin America*. London: Oxford University Press, 1967.

Vicens Vives, J. *Approaches to the History of Spain*. Berkeley: University of California Press, 1970.

Wagley, C. *The Latin American Tradition*. New York: Columbia University Press, 1968.

_____, ed. *Social Science Research on Latin America*. New York: Columbia University Press, 1964.

Weinstein, M. *Uruguay: The Politics of Failure*. Westport, Conn.: Greenwood, 1975.

Whitaker, A. "The Argentine Paradox." *Annals*, no. 334 (March 1961).

Wiarda, H. J. *The Continuing Struggle for Democracy in Latin America*. Boulder: Westview Press, 1980.

_____. *Corporatism and National Development in Latin America*. Boulder: Westview Press, 1981.

_____. *Critical Elections and Critical Coups: State, Society and the Military in the Processes of Latin American Development*. Athens: Ohio University, Center for International Studies, 1979.

_____. "The Ethnocentrism of the Social Sciences: Implications for Research and Policy." *Review of Politics* 43 (April 1981): 163–97.

_____. "The Latin Americanization of the United States." *New Scholar* 7 (1978): 51–85.

_____. "Toward a Framework for the Study of Political Change in the Iberic-Latin Tradition: The Corporative Model." *World Politics* 25 (January 1973): 206–35.

_____. *Transcending Corporatism? The Portuguese Corporative System and the Revolution of 1974*. Columbia: University of South Carolina, Institute of International Studies, 1976.

_____, and Kline, H. F., eds. *Latin American Politics and Develop-*

ment. Boston: Houghton Mifflin, 1979.

Wilenius, R. *The Social and Political Theory of Francisco Suárez.* Helsinki: Societas Philosophica Fennica, 1963.

Willems, E. *Latin American Culture.* New York: Harper and Row, 1975.

Williams, E. J., and Wright, F. J. *Latin American Politics: A Developmental Approach.* Palto Alto, Calif.: Mayfield, 1975.

Wolf, E. R., and Hansen, E. C. "Caudillo Politics: A Structural Analysis." *Comparative Studies in Society and History* 9 (January 1967): 168–79.

Worcester, D. C. "The Spanish American Past: Enemy of Change." *Journal of Inter-American Studies* 9 (January 1969): 66–75.

————, and Schaeffer, W. *The Growth and Culture of Latin America.* New York: Oxford University Press, 1970.

Zea, L. *The Latin American Mind.* Norman: University of Oklahoma Press, 1963.